SHORTCUT KEYS

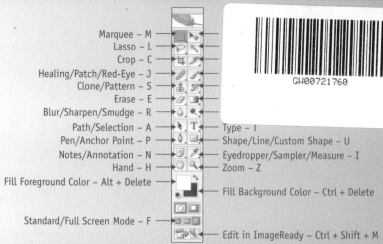

Marquee – M
Lasso – L
Crop – C
Healing/Patch/Red-Eye – J
Clone/Pattern – S
Erase – E
Blur/Sharpen/Smudge – R
Path/Selection – A
Pen/Anchor Point – P
Notes/Annotation – N
Hand – H
Fill Foreground Color – Alt + Delete

Type – T
Shape/Line/Custom Shape – U
Eyedropper/Sampler/Measure – I
Zoom – Z

Fill Background Color – Ctrl + Delete

Standard/Full Screen Mode – F

Edit in ImageReady – Ctrl + Shift + M

GW00721760

SHORTCUT KEYS

File Menu

New	Ctrl+N
Open	Ctrl+O
Browse	Ctrl+Alt+O
Edit in ImageReady	Ctrl+Shift+M
Close	Ctrl+W
Revert	F12
Save	Ctrl+S
Save As	Ctrl+Shift+S
Save Optimized As	Ctrl+Alt+Shift+S
Print	Ctrl+P
Print with Preview	Ctrl+Alt+P

Edit Menu

Undo/Redo	Ctrl+Z
Step Forward	Ctrl+Shift+Z
Step Backward	Ctrl+Alt+Z
Fade	Ctrl+Shift+F
Cut	Ctrl+X
Copy	Ctrl+C
Copy Merged	Ctrl+Shift+C
Paste	Ctrl+V
Paste Into	Ctrl+Shift+V
Free Transform	Ctrl+T
Color Settings	Ctrl+Shift+K

SHORTCUT KEYS

Frequently Used Menu Items

Levels	Ctrl+L
Auto Levels	Ctrl+Shift+L
Image Size	Ctrl+Alt+I
Canvas Size	Ctrl+Alt+C
Select All	Ctrl+A
Deselect	Ctrl+D
Inverse	Ctrl+Shift+I
Feather	Ctrl+Alt+D
Last Filter	Ctrl+F
Extract	Ctrl+Alt+X
Vanishing Point	Ctrl+Alt+V

Zoom In	Ctrl++
Zoom Out	Ctrl+-
Extras	Ctrl+H
Target Path	Ctrl+Shift+H
Grid	Ctrl+'
Guides	Ctrl+;
Rulers	Ctrl+R
New Layer	Ctrl+Shift+N
Create Clipping Mask	Ctrl+Alt+G
Group Layers	Ctrl+G
Ungroup Layers	Ctrl+Shift+G

SHORTCUT KEYS

Marquee – M — Move – V
Lasso – L — Magic Wand – W
Crop – C — Slice/Slice Select – K
Healing/Patch/Red-Eye – J — Brush/Pencil/Color Replacement – B
Clone/Pattern – S — History Brush/Art History Brush – Y
Erase – E — Gradient/Paint Bucket – G
Blur/Sharpen/Smudge – R — Dodge/Burn/Sponge – O
Path/Selection – A — Type – T
Pen/Anchor Point – P — Shape/Line/Custom Shape – U
Notes/Annotation – N — Eyedropper/Sampler/Measure – I
Hand – H — Zoom – Z
Fill Foreground Color – Opt + Delete —
— Fill Background Color – ⌘ + delete
Standard/Full Screen Mode – F —
— Edit in ImageReady – ⌘ + Shift + M

SHORTCUT KEYS

File Menu

New	⌘+N
Open	⌘+O
Browse	⌘+Opt+O
Edit in ImageReady	⌘+Shift+M
Close	⌘+W
Revert	F12
Save	⌘+S
Save As	⌘+Shift+S
Save Optimized As	⌘+Opt+Shift+S
Print	⌘+P
Print with Preview	⌘+Opt+P

Edit Menu

Undo/Redo	⌘+Z
Step Forward	⌘+Shift+Z
Step Backward	⌘+Opt+Z
Fade	⌘+Shift+F
Cut	⌘+X
Copy	⌘+C
Copy Merged	⌘+Shift+C
Paste	⌘+V
Paste Into	⌘+Shift+V
Free Transform	⌘+T
Color Settings	⌘+Shift+K

SHORTCUT KEYS

Frequently Used Menu Items

Levels	⌘+L
Auto Levels	⌘+Shift+L
Curves	⌘+M
Image Size	⌘+Opt+I
Canvas Size	⌘+Opt+C
Select All	⌘+A
Deselect	⌘+D
Inverse	⌘+Shift+I
Feather	⌘+Opt+D
Last Filter	⌘+F
Extract	⌘+Opt+X

Vanishing Point	⌘+Opt+V
Zoom In	⌘++
Zoom Out	⌘+-
Extras	⌘+H
Grid	⌘+'
Guides	⌘+;
Rulers	⌘+R
New Layer	⌘+Shift+N
Create Clipping Mask	⌘+Opt+G
Group Layers	⌘+G
Ungroup Layers	⌘+Shift+G

the Unofficial Guide® to Photoshop® CS2

Alanna Spence

WILEY

Wiley Publishing, Inc.

This book is dedicated to Tom. I count my lucky stars each and every day that I get to share this wacky, wonderful life with you.

Acknowledgements

I would first like to thank Lynn Kyle for recommending me for this project and for being a terrific virtual colleague. Special thanks to the following: Jade Williams, Scott Tullis, Dennis Short, Jody Lefevere, and Lynn Haller for their hard work on this project. Cole Valley Café for keeping me caffeinated. LeeAnn Heringer, Hunter Hubby, and Lisa Hilgers for use of photos. Flickerbox Inc. for offering a spare desk. My friends at Computer Generation for getting me started in graphic design at the tender age of 18. Diane at Dinc Type for all the fantastic fonts. My dad for passing along the technical writer gene. The iTunes development team at Apple, the Rosebuds, Old 97's, 20 Minute Loop, Nada Surf, Neko Case, the NPs, the Shins, the Glands, Pinback, Broken Social Scene, and the Decemberists for keep my ears happy. A very special thanks to Tom for making sure I slept, ate, and stayed relatively sane.

Credits

Acquisitions Editor
Jody Lefevere

Project Editor
Jade L. Williams

Technical Editor
Dennis Short

Copy Editor
Scott Tullis

Editorial Manager
Robyn Siesky

**Vice President & Group
Executive Publisher**
Richard Swadley

Vice President & Publisher
Berry Pruett

Project Coordinators
Maridee Ennis
Adrienne Martinez

Graphics & Production Specialists
Beth Brooks
Carrie Foster
Joyce Haughey
Lynsey Osborn
Amanda Spagnuolo
Ron Terry

Quality Control Technicians
Robert Springer
Brian H. Walls

Proofreading
Vickie Broyles

Indexing
Anne Leach

About the Author

Alanna Spence is paid on a daily basis to use Photoshop in the real world. She doesn't belong to any organizations; she uses Photoshop every day, just like you! Her career has been intertwined with Photoshop since the first Adobe release. She also has experience in design for Web and print, and amateur photography.

Contents

Introduction xix

I Mastering Your Workspace 1

1 Digging into the Photoshop Workspace......................3

Exploring the Welcome Screen 4

Maneuvering around your workspace...........................5
  Creating and editing your first file 5
  Open, rotate, crop, and save a JPEG photo.................11
  How the menu items are organized.........................14
  Resizing from the Document window.......................17

Managing image files with Bridge..............................18

Creating files to suit the job 21
  Creating document dimensions from the
    Presets menu 22
  Making big Photoshop files 22
  Selecting a color mode for your project....................23
  Choosing the right resolution for the job.................24
  Adding a background color layer............................25

Saving to different file formats 26

Just the facts..28

2 Getting to Know the Tools 29

Getting around in the Toolbox 29
  Using Toolbox flyout menus..................................31
  Mousing over tools for information 34
  Exploring tool options 35

Exploring palettes..36
  Customizing your palette arrangements 37
  Tidying up with the palette well.............................38
  Viewing palettes with function keys........................39
  Saving your custom workspace settings....................40
  Photoshop's preinstalled workspaces 41

Organizing with grids, guides, and rulers....................42
  Using rulers for precision placement.......................42
  Adding your own guides for organization 43
  Modifying grid settings...45

Toggling between Full Screen and Standard Screen Modes..............46

Editing in Quick Mask Mode 47

Zooming in and out of images...51
   Using the Zoom tool...*51*
   Speedy zooming with key commands *52*

Moving around large files 53
   Moving around with the Navigator *53*
   Getting around with the Hand tool..............................*54*

Jumping to ImageReady..54

Just the facts 55

3   Working with Colors, Swatches, and Styles............57

Interpreting color modes...57
   When to use RGB and CMYK *58*
   About Lab color...*60*
   Indexed Color mode when you need tiny files...................*62*
   A bit about bit depth *63*
   Choosing a color setting......................................*64*

Choosing with the Color Picker and Eyedropper 65
   Pick a color for a thought bubble with the Eyedropper tool..........*65*
   Coloring text with the Eyedropper tool *67*
   Sharing colors among files....................................*68*
   Exploring the Color Picker window.............................*68*
   Picking foreground and background colors *70*

Saving custom swatches and styles....................................72

Creating and sharing custom swatch sets 73

Adding shadows and emboss effects to layers 74

Adding to the Styles menu..76
   Quickly saving styles to the Styles palette...................*76*
   Replacing and appending style sets............................*77*
   Resetting to Photoshop's default styles.......................*77*

Just the facts 78

II Putting the Graphics Tools to Work............79

4   Embracing Layers 81

Working with multiple layers...82

Create duplicates of your layers 84

Making layer groups..85

Linking and aligning layers..87

Spicing up layers with bevels and shadows............................90
   Adding bevels, overlays, and shadows..........................*90*
   Creating your own layer styles................................*92*

Changing a layer's visibility 95
Dragging and dropping layers between files 97
Nondestructive color correction with adjustment layers 98
Just the facts 100

5   Drawing with Vector Tools 101
Drawing circles, squares, and lines 102
Creating pill-shaped buttons with rounded rectangles 102
Creating instant arrowheads 105
Exploring the custom shape libraries 106
Creating and modifying shapes with Pen tools 107
Drawing straight lines with the Pen tool 108
Converting straight lines into curves 108
Creating Bézier curves with the Pen tool 110
Easy curves with the Freeform Pen 112
Creating designs using shapes 114
Create a retro '50s sign 114
Working with paths 117
Modifying paths with the Direct Selection tool 117
Reshape your photo with a vector mask 119
Just the facts 121

6   Painting with the Brush Tools 123
Controlling brush size and flow 124
Blending modes 125
Changing sizes with the brush options 126
Letting it flow with the Airbrush setting 126
Getting more control with the Brushes palette 128
Using brush presets 130
Working with photos and paint tools 133
Edit out extras with the Clone Stamp tool 133
Add texture with the Pattern Stamp tool 134
Alter the focus of an image with the Sharpen and Blur tools 137
Designing custom brushes 139
Create a textured brush from a photo 140
Create a custom stamp for quickly adding logos to images 141
Erasing with precision 142
Erasing large areas of color 143
Adding custom brush preset libraries 144
Keep your favorite custom brushes handy 144
Add third-party custom brush sets 144
Just the facts 146

7 Selecting and Extracting Images **147**

Selecting geometric shapes 148
   Adding, subtracting, and dissecting your selections 148
   Select a single row of pixels 150
   Create a circular vignette around your photos 151
   Create close-up thumbnails of your photos 154

Precision selecting odd shapes with the Lasso tool 155
   Tricky lassoing with advanced techniques 156
   Outlining with the Magnetic Select tool 156

Selecting and changing areas of color 159

Removing backgrounds with the Eraser tools 162

Just the facts 166

8 Masking and Blending Images **167**

One click masking with layer masks 167

Extracting images from their backgrounds 168
   Getting quick results with the Extract tool 169
   Painting masks in Quick Mask Mode 171
   Back up your mask selections as alpha channels 174

Masking photos into odd shapes 177
   Mask your photo using custom shapes 177
   Create a mask shape from another photo 178

Performing subtle fadeouts using gradients 181

Combining your masking skills 183

Just the facts 188

9 Creating Elements in Type **189**

Adding headlines and paragraphs 190
   Creating paragraph type 192
   Which anti-alias method should I choose? 195
   Picking the right font family 195
   Adding fun third-party fonts 197

Masking type with photos 199
   Adding depth to text with photo masking 199
   Creating a distressed type look with masking 201

Typing on a curve or shape 204

Wrapping text around an object 205
   Warp text around a cup 205
   Rasterize text for more warping power 207

Adding special effects to your text 208
   Creating stylistic text 208
   Create a 3-D reflection on a shiny surface 210

Just the facts 212

10 Undoing and Redoing with History and Actions......................**213**

Memorizing key commands for undoing 214

Time-traveling with the History palette....................................214

Leave mistakes in the past with one click *215*

Saving a longer history list *215*

Selective undoing with nonlinear history *216*

Dragging and dropping history between files *217*

Saving History Snapshots...217

The History Brush...219

The Art History Brush...220

Saving and applying your own actions 222

Create your own action sets *222*

Record an action for performing Auto Levels and Smart Sharpen ...*223*

Create a droplet for drag and drop editing of multiple files *224*

Using preinstalled action sets to enhance photos and text...........226

Applying text effects to type using action sets......................*227*

Running actions with dialog boxes *229*

Running action sets on photos..*231*

Instant photo borders with the Frames action set......................*232*

Just the facts 234

III Enhancing Digital Photos...**235**

11 Perfecting Your Photo's Color...**237**

Tips for happy color correcting 237

Keep copies of your originals.....................................*238*

Edit in 8-bit of 16-bit color...*238*

Translating histograms *239*

Auto adjusting color and contrast 240

Brightening lights and darkening shadows with Levels 241

Mastering color adjustments with Curves...............................242

Changing tint and color cast 244

Correcting color cast *244*

Give your photo an old sepia tone look *247*

Correcting exposure problems in photos 248

Lightening dark photos with exposure adjustments....................*249*

Make adjustments to isolated areas of your photo.....................*250*

Colorizing photos for effect...252

Intensify a color photo with colorizing effects *253*

Add spots of color to a black-and-white photo *254*

Just the facts 256

12 Exploring Adobe Bridge and the Camera Raw Plug-In **257**

Organizing your files in Adobe Bridge 258
Rotate several photos with the click of a button 259
Switching to a more compact view 261
View your photos as a slideshow 262
Rename several files at once 263

Adding metadata and keywords..265
Adding fine details with metadata.....................................265
Categorizing photos with keywords 267
Finding your photos...268

Editing your Camera Raw files..269

Perfecting your image with image settings 272
Adjusting exposure, contrast, and saturation.......................273
Maximizing color and contrast adjustments in the Curves panel ...273
Calibrating color in Camera Raw......................................275
Sharpening and removing noise with Detail.........................276
Fixing halo color with the Lens panel................................276

Applying changes to several Camera Raw files 278
Applying adjustment settings to a photo set 278
Saving your settings for the future 279

Just the facts 281

13 Resizing and Retouching Photos **283**

Cropping photos with the Crop tool.....................................284
Crop your photos nondestructively....................................285
Crop to a specific width and height 286

Resizing your image and canvas size....................................290
Adjusting your canvas size...292
Create a quick border by increasing your canvas size................293
Creating rescalable photos as Smart Objects 295
Editing Smart Objects 297

Performing cosmetic surgery without a doctor.........................298
Remove skin blemishes with the Healing Brush 298
Tackle large problem areas with the Patch tool 299
Performing plastic surgery with the Liquify tool 300

Exorcise demons by removing red eye 302

Removing the green glow from your pet's eyes 304

Just the facts 306

14 Fixing Fuzz, Tilt, and Perspective **307**

Rotating and fixing distortion 308
Straightening tilted photos 309
Fixing barrel distortion...310
Rotating by degrees...312
Creating reflections in water..313

Sharpening blurry and noisy photos......................................315
   Smart sharpening for the shaky hands syndrome......................*316*
   Reducing digital noise in low-light situations *319*
   Use the Dust & Scratches filter to finish the job......................*321*
Keeping things in perspective 322
   Widen piano keys with the Vanishing Point tool......................*323*
   Copy and paste in perspective......................*326*
   Changing a photo's perspective......................*328*
Just the facts 330

IV Exploring Your Inner Artist 331

15 Getting Creative with Filters......................333
Getting in touch with your inner artist 334
   Create an instant watercolor *334*
   Make your photos look like screen prints......................*336*
   Creating tritone drawings with the Sketch filters *337*
   Turn your photo into a charcoal sketch......................*339*
   Get black-and-white images with Photocopy......................*340*
   Create nice textures with Water Paper *342*
   Create abstract art from a photo *343*
Applying multiple filters......................345
Creating seamless tiles and patterns......................346
Create a background pattern for your Web site 349
Creating mosaic patterns with Textures 351
   Create a stained glass window......................*351*
   Convert your image to square tiles with Patchwork......................*352*
   Fading and blending filters for special effects......................*355*
Just the facts 356

16 Adding Lighting, Blur, and Distortion Special Effects......................357
Adding light with the Render filters......................357
   Add highlights with the Lens Flare filter *358*
   Adding a light source with Lighting Effects *359*
Blurring to accentuate an action shot......................362
   Add motion with the Wind filter......................*362*
   Adding Motion Blur to speedy subjects *363*
   Soften photos with the Surface Blur filter......................*364*
   Blurring out the background with Lens Blur......................*366*
Distorting, diffusing, and rippling......................368
   Quickly fixing lens distortion *368*
   Turn a flat surface into a globe......................*371*
   Create a funhouse mirror with the Shear filter *373*
   Generate a countdown clock with Polar Coordinates......................*374*
   More fun with Distortion filters......................*378*

Rendering clouds and fiber texture 379
   Add puffy clouds to clear skies 379
   Creating wood grain with the Fibers filter 381
The Stylize filters 383
   Diffusing light to add subtle texture 383
   Embossing your image 384
   Create 3-D squares that extrude from your image 384
   Accentuate your image edges with Trace Contour 385
Just the facts 387

17 Combining Images and Creating Collages **389**
Creating a photo collage 389
   Create a large document canvas for your collage 390
   Combine several images into one document 391
   Convert your images to Smart Objects 393
   Create a circular mask around an image 394
   Create type on a curve 394
   Add outlines to your photos using Blending Options 395
Adding eyeballs to vegetables 396
Creating your own mythical creatures 399
   Create a mask from a modified channel 401
   Create consistent colors across multiple layers 404
   Blend images together using the Clone Stamp tool 405
Design a personal greeting card 407
Stitch several photos together 411
Just the facts 414

18 Designing Stunning Graphics **415**
Creating a business card with custom brushes 416
Combining photos and text into a brochure design 421
Combining filters and adjustment layers 427
Creating resizable graphics from low-resolution images 432
Just the facts 438

V Preparing for Print or Web **439**

19 Printing Your Work **441**
Understanding megapixels and printing 442
Finding the right printer 443
   Purchasing a home printer 443
   Don't skimp on paper 445
   Use the right printer driver 446

Choosing a printing option *447*
   Scaling your artwork to fit your printed page.....................448
   Getting good color from your inkjet printer 450

Printing in CMYK color mode *452*
   Converting to CMYK 452
   Installing a color profile for a CMYK laser printer......................453
   Soft-proofing colors 455

Finding a printer and preparing files........................... *456*
   Choosing a printer type 457
   Getting a quote 457
   Can I use color text?..459
   Bleed and trim 459
   Preparing final artwork — saving to EPS or TIFF......................459
   Using rich blacks for text 459

Ordering prints online *460*
   Order personal postage stamps 462
   Print a postcard or greeting card.................................463

Just the facts *464*

20 Preparing Images for the Web.................................445 *465*

Choosing a file type for the Web *466*

Optimizing photos in JPEG format............................... *466*
   No-fuss resizing and optimization photos 466
   Additional JPEG settings and what they mean 468
   Comparing multiple optimization settings for the best option......468

Optimizing graphics in GIF format............................... *469*
   Saving a simple GIF...469
   The Options panel in the Optimize palette 472
   Avoiding halos and fringe with transparent GIFs 473

Optimize to file size.. *474*

What is happening with PNG?....................................... *475*

Slicing layouts for Web sites.. *476*
   Create a simple Web page with the Make Web page action 477
   Customize the Make Web page template 478
   Add images and text to your Web page design 479
   Add links and customize optimization settings..............481
   Generate HTML and image slices for your Web page 484

Optimizing single images from Photoshop *486*

Just the facts *487*

21 Creating Animated GIFs...489

Building a multi-framed animation *490*
   Create a multi-framed animation 490
   Add a link to your animation......................................493

Change the number of times an animation plays........................495
Add several links to one image with image maps......................495
Exporting animations to Flash SWF files 498
Tweening between frames 498
Fading elements in and out with tweening.............................498
Reversing frame order 501
Creating an animated button...502
Creating an animation with a transparent background 504
Just the facts 506

VI Going Beyond the Basics **507**

22 Exploring Advanced Color Calibration and Correction **509**
Calibrating your monitor..510
Calibrating monitors on a Mac..510
Calibrating monitors on a Windows machine...........................514
Picking out a hardware monitor calibrator 516
Removing out-of-gamut colors..518
Changing the default Auto Color settings 521
Creating healthy skin and sparkling whites 523
Adjusting skin tones 524
Whitening and brightening teeth..525
Making eyes sparkle...528
Advanced shadows and highlights 530
Just the facts 533

23 Creating and Using Automation Scripts.................................**535**
Creating print and Web designs using automation tools 536
Creating a Web photo gallery...536
Generating contact sheets of your photos 539
Create a grid design using contact sheets 542
Printing out a picture package..542
Create a PDF presentation of your photos 546
Running actions in batches for speed editing..............................548
Adding copyright text to photos...548
Batch processing and renaming 550
Add frames to several photos at once with droplets 551
Getting the most out of ImageReady actions...............................553
Creating instant Web page templates 554
Adding flaming or freezing text..555
Creating slide frames for thumbnails......................................556
Creating conditional actions in ImageReady............................556
Just the facts 559

24 Managing Your Designs **561**

Saving layer comps 562
   Save your layer comps to separate files *566*
   Create an instant Web Photo Gallery from layer comps *568*

Exploring the Bridge Center.......................................570
   Saving file groups in the Bridge Center...............................*572*
   Adobe content and RSS feeds *574*
   Exploring Adobe stock photos *575*

Tracking changes in Version Cue.............................578
   Adding a new project...*578*
   Add a Photoshop file to your Version Cue project *579*
   The Version Manager...*579*
   Administering your project *580*

Just the facts 582

25 Adding Plug-ins and Hardware Devices **583**

Using graphics tablets...583
   Choosing the right graphics tablet..*585*
   Adjusting your tablet settings...*586*
   Controlling brush flow with tablet brush settings.....................*588*
   Tracing from paper sources with graphics tablets.......................*590*

Picking out a scanner...591
   Finding flatbed scanners...*592*
   Scanners with slide or film scanning features *595*

Using scanner software with Photoshop 596
   Scanning directly into Photoshop *596*
   Changing scale and resize settings...*596*
   Scanning text into Photoshop..*598*
   Straighten and crop crooked scans...*598*

Using digital camera software features...................601
   Uploading from your digital camera into Bridge *601*
   Camera Raw plug-ins for your digital camera *603*

Installing third-party plug-in filters 604

Just the facts 608

26 Expanding Your Photoshop Knowledge **609**

Getting around the Adobe Help Center 610
   Explore the Help topics through the Contents and Index tabs *610*
   Bookmark your favorite Help topics *610*
   Quickly find answers with the search feature *612*
   Print out Help content for easy access....................................*614*

Subscribing to Expert Support 615

Adding contacts and Web sites in More Resources...................616

Get up and running with How To................................617

Training resources on the Adobe Web site......................................618
    Adobe-authorized training centers...619
    Exploring tutorials on Adobe Studio..620
    Find answers on Adobe forums..622
Finding classes at local colleges 622
Just the facts 623

Appendix A: Troubleshooting and Tips **625**

Appendix B: Third-Party Filters, Brushes, and Actions **635**

Appendix C: Stock Photos, Clip Art, and Fonts **641**

Appendix D: Recommended Reading **649**

Glossary...**653**

Index...**663**

First, I just want to say thank you for choosing my book. I know there are dozens of Photoshop books you could have chosen, and I am honored you picked my humble little book. When I told people I was writing this book, the one overwhelming request I got was to make a reader-friendly guide that real people can understand, without wasting time with a lot of techno-babble. It has been my intention throughout the writing of this book to treat each subject as if I were sitting next to you, talking you through each project step by step. Whether you are a beginner who wants to hit the ground running or an intermediate Photoshop user looking to advance your skills, this book will take you beyond the standard fare of Photoshop books.

What makes this book special

Most Photoshop books cover only specific subjects or merely skim over the basics. This book was written to give you an in-depth understanding of the many aspects of Photoshop by giving you real-world projects. By the time you've picked through this book, you'll be retouching photos like a pro and correcting the color and exposure of JPEG and Camera Raw photo files. I'll give you some techniques for creating designs that combine images and text elements into multilayered compositions. You'll learn several different techniques for masking and extracting images from their backgrounds, and you'll be able to discern which technique works best in any given situation. I'll show you how to create your own illustrations using Photoshop's vector graphics tools. Most importantly, you'll have a strong grasp on uses for the various color modes, file formats, resolution, and how to get great-looking prints or Web graphics.

I've written this book with the intention of getting you up and running fast on all of the various aspects and real-world applications of Photoshop. I've organized the book into fun, creative projects that will teach you how to use Photoshop's many tools while exploring your artistic side. You can read through from cover to cover, but feel free to jump around. If you are familiar with Photoshop, you have my full permission to thumb through to whichever subject tickles your fancy at a given moment. I've included many insider tips throughout the book, and each chapter should offer a little bit of something for everyone, even if you consider yourself a Photoshop pro. If you are new to Photoshop, the first four chapters will give you a strong base to expand on with coverage on the workspace, toolbox, colors, and layers. I've worked hard to offer consistently clear, concise steps in each and every chapter, so you don't need to read one chapter to understand another.

Learn through experience

In the 15 plus years of my professional career, I've worn many hats. As a self-taught graphic designer, software tester, Web developer, artist, and amateur photographer, I've explored and conquered many sides of Photoshop. In the pages that follow, I'll share with you my knowledge of photo editing, illustration, print design, and Web graphics. I strongly believe in learning through hands-on experience. The chapters in this book are designed to give you a solid foundation by showing you step-by-step techniques for creating and editing your own work in Photoshop.

This book will teach you:

- **Adobe Bridge:** Organize, find, and manage image files with scalable preview thumbnails. Create instant slideshows, add metadata, and edit Camera Raw files.

- **New CS2 features:** Learn how to get the most out of the new features of Photoshop CS2 like the Vanishing Point tool, Smart Objects, one-click red-eye correction, and the new Image Warp tool.

- **Masking and extracting:** Learn the best methods for extracting subjects from their backgrounds using the Extract tool, layer masks, and alpha channels.

- **Printing tips:** Get the most out of your home inkjet printer. Prepare designs for professional four-color printing presses.

- **Editing and designing:** Create complex images with multiple layers by taking advantage of layer groups, styles, and opacity settings.
- **Text effects:** Advanced type features like type on a curve, masked type, and text warping.

You'll learn these techniques and more by using your own images to create compelling and unique designs.

What's new in CS2

If you aren't new to Photoshop and are looking for a book that will show you how to take full advantage of the latest features in CS2, you've come to the right place. The new features are interwoven into the book and used in conjunction with the rest of Photoshop, just as you'll be using them in the real world. I've wound up spending copious amount of time with CS2 in the writing of this book, and I've rekindled my love for this program. Throughout this project, many friends have asked me if I was getting sick of Photoshop. On the contrary, I feel more excited about it now than I was when I got my hands on the very first Adobe release of Photoshop. I have found myself soapbox preaching on the vast improvements and exciting new tools of CS2, much to the chagrin of innocent bystanders. Here are just a few of my favorite new things.

Organize your images with Adobe Bridge

This powerful file organizing and previewing application is a much more fleshed-out version of the File Browser that was introduced with Photoshop CS. I'll cover advanced features of Bridge in Chapter 12, like editing multiple Camera Raw files, viewing instant slideshows, changing your preview thumbnail sizes, and customizing your views.

Rescalable images with Smart Objects

In Chapter 18, I'll show you how to create rescalable photos by converting them to Smart Objects. This new feature enables nondestructive editing by storing original image information. By converting your images to Smart Objects, you can shrink and enlarge images without losing image quality.

Fix photo problems like red eye and blemishes

There are a couple of new and exciting tools for quickly fixing common photo problems. With one click, the Red-Eye tool removes the red caused by flash photography. The Spot Healing Brush blends away blemishes and wrinkles by sampling the pixels around the brush stroke. The Smart Sharpen tool lets you brush the areas you want to sharpen without having to perform a sharpen filter on the entire image. I'll cover these cool new tools in Chapter 13.

Warping and perspective tools

The Lens Correction and Image Warp tools let you fix common lens distortion issues caused by wide-angle lenses. You can use the Image Warp tool to simulate the illusion of objects wrapping around cylindrical objects. Play with the perspective of an object by warping the edges to make an angled photo of a building become a straight-on photo. You can now paint in perspective with the New Vanishing Point filter. In Chapter 14, I'll show you how to add a window to a building or paint in additional keys on a keyboard while staying in perspective.

Customizable workspace

Save your favorite tool settings and workspace arrangement using new improvements to customizable workspace features. In Chapter 2, I'll show you how to save your own custom workspace settings and how to return to the default settings when you need to.

Advanced layer management

The Layers palette has been improved to offer a higher level of management capabilities with layer groups, layer comps, and adjustment layers. 4 shows you pro tips for organizing layers. Layer comps are a designer's dream. In Chapter 24, we'll create different design versions to share with clients by saving layer configurations into layer comps.

Preview fonts in the menu

Thank you Adobe! Photoshop has added a preview to the Fonts menu so you can see a sample of the font. You used to have to try out a font on a type layer to see what the font looked like. You can now choose fonts by appearance, without having to memorize which font looks like what. This should free up valuable storage space in your brain for more important things, like how far the earth is from the sun (93 million miles on a good day).

Conventions used in this book

This book is for both Mac and Windows users. The Mac and Windows versions of Photoshop CS2 are nearly identical in every aspect except the cosmetic look of the user interface. Most of this book was written using Photoshop CS2 on an Apple Macintosh computer. I also own and use a Windows machine and worked on both computers in tandem, checking for differences. Important differences are noted throughout the book. Specifically, I note the Mac key command first followed by the corresponding Windows key command in parentheses.

Right-clicking is the same as Ctrl-clicking. I've been using a two-button mouse on a Mac for so long, I often forget this is not a common scenario for the rest of the Mac world. If you are using a single-button mouse, you can substitute right-click with Ctrl-click.

A brief history of Photoshop

In the late '80s, an avid photographer and software developer created his own photo-editing application. After a few years of development and a growing audience, he decided to take it to the next level. Strangely, it took him a while to find anyone interested in it.

Photoshop started out as a raster image-editing program with minimal support for type. It is now a fully featured raster image-editing program as well as a powerful type layout program, Web graphics editor, vector drawing program, and pre-press manager. Today, this application is truly a multi-disciplinary tool. Its development since the early 90s has reflected all of its users' wants and needs. Adobe has a fantastic reputation of supporting its users, and in turn, the program's user base is full of helpful, creative individuals that love to share their knowledge. This is good news for you. The amount of support available on the Internet and in books is quite phenomenal. This book should serve as a solid guide, but I encourage you to seek out video-based tutorials on the Web or look for books that cater to advanced techniques of a particular subject.

Digital photography is all the rage right now, and if this is your main interest, you are in luck. The appendices in the back of this book, list just a few of the many advanced digital photography books there are available.

Tips for happy Photoshopping

Now that you've decided to take the Photoshop plunge, I'd like to share some words of wisdom to help make your Photoshop experience a pleasant and rewarding one.

Keep back-up copies. Photoshop is truly a creative application. Sometimes creative genius is born out of happy mistakes. You won't become really comfortable with Photoshop until you set aside your fears. With computers, mistakes don't have to be painful. The key to becoming an expert is in back-up files. Keep copies of your work. Keep copies of your original photos. Working from a copy releases you from any fear of destroying something precious to you. If you mess up, just throw it away and start on a fresh copy.

Learn key commands and save your arms. Trying to maneuver around Photoshop using a mouse can get your fingers twisted up in knots faster than I can say repetitive stress injury. If you haven't yet done so, stop what you are doing, tear out the handy little tear card included in this book, fold it into a handy triangle, and find a prominent place on your desk for it. Getting around with key commands will save you time and pain.

Keep your eyes open to new ideas. Now that you are on your way to becoming an expert digital photographer or designer, you'll be seeing the world in a completely new light. Inspiration is all around you. The key to becoming a great designer is to absorb the visual beauties around you like a sponge and allow them to influence your work. Poke around at the design or photography books at your local bookstore. Surf the Web for cool design ideas.

Finally, have fun! This is a creative program after all. The more fun you have, the faster you'll learn. Take some time to goof off. You never know what you are capable of until you try. Check out this book's Web site at www.unofficialguidetophotoshopcs2.com.

Mastering Your Workspace

GET THE SCOOP ON...
Creating your first Photoshop document ▪ Cropping,
resizing, and saving a digital photo for e-mail or Web ▪
Previewing and organizing images in Adobe Bridge ▪
Choosing the right color mode and resolution ▪ File
formats and their proper uses

PART I

Digging into the Photoshop Workspace

Congratulations on taking the Photoshop plunge. Photoshop is a powerful, multipurpose tool, not just for editing photos, but also for creating designs for print or the Web. Projects can range from simple fliers to large billboard signs. Throughout the book, we'll be trying out techniques for editing photos, creating designs for print or Web, and preparing files for professional printing. This chapter serves as a strong base for introducing you to the world of Photoshop. Even if you have some Photoshop experience under your belt, I encourage you to thumb through this chapter. I've covered some features, such as the Adobe Bridge file manager, that are new to Photoshop CS2.

Photoshop is a complex tool with a lot of moving parts with which you will become familiar. To handle all this different content, Photoshop allows you to create, open, and import all sorts of formats. You can export files in just as many formats to be used in other programs. The workspace of Photoshop is arranged much like what you'd find on a designer's or photographer's desk. This chapter gives you some easy assignments for getting acquainted with the Toolbox and menu items, and then introduces you to the rest of the objects in the Photoshop workspace. File formats are discussed, as well as the appropriate uses for them. You'll also be introduced to Adobe Bridge, a new file

3

browser application that comes with Photoshop. It's one of my favorite tools in Photoshop and is a lifesaver for digital photographers.

Exploring the Welcome Screen

The first time you launch Photoshop, the Welcome Screen appears, as shown in Figure 1.1, offering you a few options for introductions. The What's New section opens two PDF files with information on the latest features. The See it in Action link takes you to the Adobe Web site and a page with some great video clips demonstrating some of the most exciting new features. The movies are a great visual aid in introducing you to the newest tools and will help you get up to speed much faster.

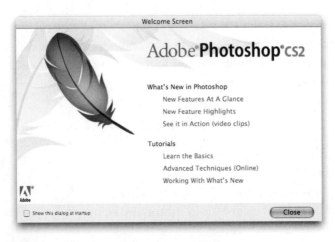

Figure 1.1. The Photoshop CS2 Welcome Screen.

The Tutorials section has some basic-to-advanced tutorials. This chapter covers the basic tools for getting up to speed, but I recommend reading through the tutorials when you have some free time. They will strengthen your understanding of the tools and make your Photoshop experience that much more enjoyable.

By default, the Welcome Screen appears every time you launch Photoshop. You can disable the Welcome Screen by unchecking the Show this dialog at startup check box at the bottom of the screen. Don't worry; you can access it any time you want from inside Photoshop by choosing Help ⇨ Welcome Screen.

Maneuvering around your workspace

Time to remove the training wheels and get you up and running. I think the best way to learn is by doing. In this section, I'll step you through some exercises for trying out tools and menu items in Photoshop. I hope this accelerated approach doesn't frazzle your nerves. If at any point you are feeling a little edgy, put the hammer down, take a walk around the block, and start over. Photoshop has a lot of buttons, knobs, and switches; it might take you a little time to get used to them. Stick with it and you'll be a pro in no time.

Creating and editing your first file

Let's create a new file and try out some of Photoshop's tools. If your Welcome Screen is still visible, click the Close button and get started with the fun stuff! You need not worry if you don't understand everything you see; I'll explain things in more detail later on in the chapter.

To create a new file:

1. Launch Photoshop CS2 if it is not currently open.

2. Choose File ⇨ New or use the key command ⌘+N (Ctrl+N). The New window appears, as shown in Figure 1.2.

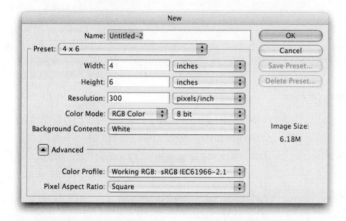

Figure 1.2. The New window with the 4 x 6 preset selected.

3. Choose Letter from the Preset drop-down list.

4. Make sure your resolution is set to 300 dpi, your Color Mode is RGB, and your Background Contents are white. Don't worry about the Advanced settings for now. The default settings are fine.

5. After you've defined the size, resolution, and color mode for your file, click OK. Your newly created file will appear in your Photoshop workspace.

Now that you have a file to work with, let's take a tour of your workspace. After you've created your new file, your workspace looks something like Figure 1.3. Photoshop has many more floating palettes and toolboxes than you are probably used to. Don't panic! The three big pieces you should focus on for now are the Toolbox on the far left, the Document window where you'll be creating your artwork, and the Layers palette in the lower right side of the screen. These are your core tools, and you'll spend the majority of your time in them.

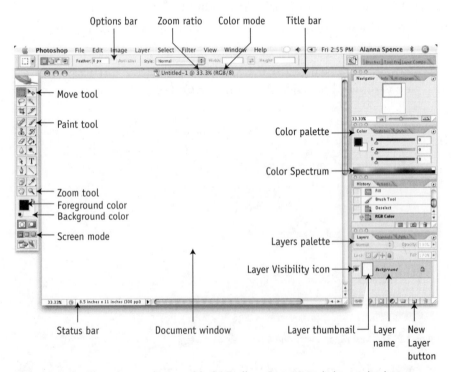

Figure 1.3. The Photoshop workspace with the Toolbox, Document window, and palettes.

The Toolbox on the left side of your screen acts like a real-world tool-box. It stores all the various drawing, selecting, and editing tools that you'll use to edit and paint images. The tools are semi-organized into sets of similar functions. Chapter 2 goes into more detail about what each tool does. For now, I just want you to get used to selecting and using tools. First, try painting something with the Brush tool. Don't worry about creating a masterpiece; just focus on learning about the options and controls.

You can try out the Brush tool by following these steps:

1. Create a new file if you don't currently have one open.

2. Click the Brush tool icon in the Toolbox on the left-hand side of your screen. It looks like a paintbrush and is in the second column, fourth tool down. A tool fly-out menu appears when you click it. Choose the Brush tool from the top of the list. Figure 1.4 shows the toolbox with the Brush tool highlighted.

3. Draw in your Document window by clicking and dragging your mouse around.

4. Click the Brush drop-down list in the Options bar. Each time you choose a new tool, the content in the Options bar changes to the options that pertain to the current tool.

5. Choose a new brush diameter by adjusting the slider or clicking another brush tip from the thumbnail list that you see in Figure 1.5. The numbers underneath each brush tip and in the Master Diameter value slider represent the pixel width of the brush.

Figure 1.4. The Brush tool highlighted in the Toolbox.

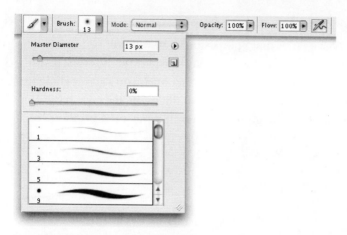

Figure 1.5. The Brush fly-out menu in the Options bar.

6. Choose a new foreground color by clicking anywhere in the Color Spectrum bar in the Color palette on the right-hand side of your workspace. The Color Spectrum is the rainbow-colored bar on the bottom of the Color palette.

7. Try out your new brush size and color by clicking and dragging your mouse around the screen.

8. Choose Edit ⇨ Undo to undo your last brush stroke. You can also use the key command ⌘+Z (Ctrl+Z).

9. Step back through multiple edits by choosing Edit ⇨ Step Backwards a few times. You can also use the key command ⌘+Shift+Z (Ctrl+Shift+Z).

Congratulations, you've just made your first marks. You are on your way to becoming a master. Save your file so I can introduce you to many of the file options in Photoshop.

Inside Scoop

Hover your mouse over tools to see their tool tips. Most tools have hot keys assigned to them. Press the letter B to select the Brush tool.

To save your new file, follow these steps:

1. Choose File ⇨ Save As. A dialog box similar to the one you see in Figure 1.6 appears. Your dialog box may look a little different if you are on a Windows machine. If you are on a Mac, you can try clicking the Use Adobe Dialog button. These two dialog boxes have few differences, and this early in the game, it's merely a personal preference.

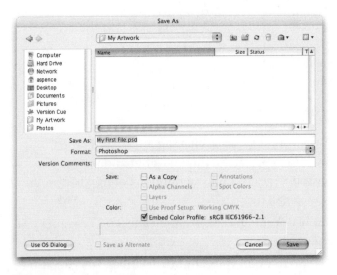

Figure 1.6. The Save As dialog box.

2. Make sure you choose Photoshop from the top of the Format drop-down menu. Don't get confused with the other Photoshop options like Photoshop PDF or Photoshop 2.0. You want the top option. Choosing the Photoshop format ensures that any Photoshop-only features such as layers, masks, and adjustment layers are saved along with your image. If you want to share your image with friends and want to save your image as a JPEG or PDF, always save a Photoshop (.psd) version first. Otherwise, you won't be able to edit most of your hard work.

3. Don't worry about the Color options just yet. The default probably has the Embed Color Profile check box checked. That's fine.

4. Find a nice place for your new file, give the file a name, and click Save just as you would in any other application.

From here on out, any changes you make to your file can be saved the old-fashioned way, by choosing File ⇨ Save or using the key command ⌘+S (Ctrl+S).

Inside Scoop

The first time you save a file, you'll automatically be taken to the Save As dialog box, even if you choose File ⇨ Save.

Open, rotate, crop, and save a JPEG photo

I thought it would be a useful exercise to try out some of the menu items in Photoshop on a digital photo. I assume 99.9 percent of you will be working with JPEG photos from a digital camera at some point in your Photoshop explorations. In this next exercise you'll open a JPEG, rotate it to correct its orientation, resize and crop it, and then save a copy of it. Don't worry if you feel rushed. Chapter 13 is dedicated to the art of rotating, resizing, and cropping.

To Edit a digital photo for use on a Web site, follow these steps:

1. Open a JPEG file. If you can't find one on your machine, you can always download one from the Internet by right-clicking an image and saving it to your desktop.

2. Choose Image ⇨ Rotate Canvas ⇨ Rotate 90° CW. The CW stands for clockwise. CCW stands for counterclockwise. To enter your own rotation amount in degrees, choose Image ⇨ Rotate Canvas ⇨ Arbitrary and enter a value in the Angle field.

3. Select the Crop tool from the Toolbox. It is the third tool down on the left side and is shown highlighted in Figure 1.7.

How to Save an Image from a Web Site to Your Computer

Right-click an image on a Web page; a drop-down list of options appears. Each browser will have slightly different options. Choose either Save Image As, Save Image to Desktop, or Save Target As. Choose a place on your computer to download the image and click Save.

Respect people's copyright notices. Most people post copyright notices on the bottom of their Web sites, and you are sure to lose karma points by ignoring them. Just because you can download an image doesn't mean you have the right to use it as your own.

Figure 1.7. The Crop tool highlighted in the Toolbox.

4. Click and drag across your image to select an area to crop. The area outside the crop selection will appear slightly grayed out.

5. Adjust your crop area by clicking and dragging the little boxes on the sides of the crop selection.

6. Click the big check button on the top right of the Options bar to accept your selection and perform your crop. If you'd like to cancel the crop and start over, click the Cancel button, located to the right of the Accept button. It looks like a circle with a slash through it.

7. Choose Image ⇨ Image Size. The Image Size dialog box appears, as shown in Figure 1.8.

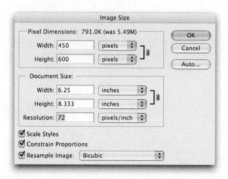

Figure 1.8. The Image Size dialog box.

8. Change the Resolution to 72 pixels per inch. It's important that you do this step first. When you change the resolution, Photoshop automatically updates the pixel dimensions of your image. If you tried to change them first, you'd have to change them again anyway once you changed the resolution.

9. Change your width value. As long as you have the Constrain Proportions check box checked, the height value automatically updates. I think an image size of around 600 × 450 or 450 × 600 is a nice size for e-mailing photos to friends or as a largish image on a Web site. I'll leave it up to you.

10. Click OK to accept your settings and resize your image.

11. Choose File ⇨ Save As to open the Save As dialog box.

12. Give your newly resized image a name.

13. Choose JPEG from the Format drop-down list.

Inside Scoop

Are you confused about the differences between resizing and cropping? When you resize an image, you are changing the scale of your image. When you crop an image, you are trimming your image down by removing pixels from the outside edges of your image.

14. Click Save. The JPEG Options dialog box appears, as shown in Figure 1.9.

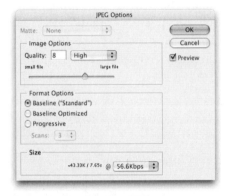

Figure 1.9. The JPEG Options dialog box.

15. Choose High from the Quality drop-down list. Find out more about JPEG quality settings in Chapter 20.

16. Click OK to save your image as a JPEG file.

Phew! You did it! I know that seemed like a lot of steps, but as you read through the book and become more familiar with Photoshop, you'll learn shortcuts and tricks for cutting down on the number of steps.

How the menu items are organized

As you get more and more familiar with Photoshop, you'll discover that there always seem to be multiple ways of doing things. Many of the tasks that can be done from the palettes are actually just shortcuts for tasks that can be done from the menu items. Some things, like rotating, resizing, and scaling, can be done only from the menu items. Following is a basic outline of where different tasks live within the menu items. Go ahead and try some of them out. As you work your way through the book, most of them will be covered in various exercises. This list serves as a way of outlining all of the tasks that you can perform in Photoshop.

Here is a list of Photoshop menu items and the options associated with them:

- **File:** Menu items for opening; file browsing using Adobe Bridge; saving and printing; importing and exporting from files, scanners, or other hardware devices; automation tools; and reverting to last saved file version.

- **Edit:** Standard edit menu items such as edit, cut, copy, and paste; transform options for rotating, warping, and scaling selections; and menu items for editing workspace settings such as color management, tool presets, key commands, and menus.

- **Image:** Menu items for color modes, color correction options (see Figure 1.10), and resizing options; and menu items for image rotation, cropping, and trimming.

- **Layer:** Menu items for creating, duplicating, deleting, grouping, and aligning layers.

- **Select:** Options for selecting items, inverting selections, and feathering selections to soften edges. You can also load and save selections to the Paths palette.

- **Filter:** Lists all of the image filters, separated by category.

- **View:** Document view options including zoom, fit on screen, and actual print size; options to toggle layout controls such as rulers, grids, guides, and slices; and soft-proof options and gamut warnings (see Chapters 19 and 22).

Bright Idea!

If you lose your handy tear-out card of key commands, you can always find the key commands by looking at the menu items. Photoshop lists all of them to the right of the menu items.

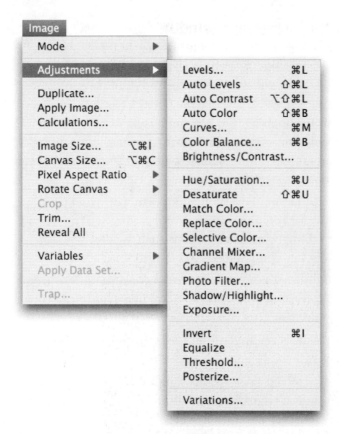

Figure 1.10. The Adjustments options for color correction under the Image menu item.

- **Window:** Options for rearranging your workspace. The Window menu item lists all of the palettes available in Photoshop. Visible palettes have check marks next to them. To revert to the default workspace settings, choose Window ⇨ Workspace ⇨ Default Workspace. Lists all open documents. When you have multiple documents open, you can switch between documents by selecting a different document from the list.

- **Help:** Lists the menu items for viewing Help topics in the Adobe Help Center; gives you access to the Welcome Screen; and offers a list of How Tos, which take you to tutorials in the Help Center.

Resizing from the Document window

You can tell a few things about your file just by looking around the Document window. In Figure 1.11, I can tell the name of my file ReverieCat.jpg by looking at the title bar on the top of the document window. Next to the file name, you can see that the file is currently being viewed at 33.3% of its total size and it is in RGB 8-bit color mode. On the bottom of the Document window is a percentage field where you can enter a specific amount instead of using the Zoom tool. This field gives you more control; the Zoom tool can zoom only in 25-percent increments.

Figure 1.11 shows a Document window.

Figure 1.11. The Document window with the options pop-up list visible.

Hack

If you have one, you can use your mouse's scroll wheel to change the viewing percentage. You can click the percentage field on the bottom of the document window to highlight it; then just spin your scroll wheel up or down to change the value.

The black arrow on the bottom of your Document window opens a drop-down menu with the option to show different document information. Photoshop defaults this setting to Document Sizes, but Document Dimensions, the option currently selected in Figure 1.11, displays your document's dimensions in your preferred unit of measure. I think this comes in handy much more than knowing your file size. To find out which color profile you are using, switch to Document Profile.

Managing image files with Bridge

If you are a digital photographer, you will most likely be handling JPEG, DNG, or other common digital camera files. You are going to love Adobe Bridge. This side application comes installed with Photoshop and is a fantastic file-browsing program. Inside Bridge, you can preview image file contents from a number of formats and record metadata with your images so you can quickly find the photos you need. They've done a great job of creating a useful interface, so you should be able to start using it right away with few hiccups.

Bridge is an image file browser application similar to applications like iPhoto or Picasa. It shows you a preview of your images as you see in Figure 1.12, and offers some cool tools for rating and labeling your images. The Metadata panel in Bridge lets you add information such as descriptions, names, dates, places, and times to your file so you can find images quickly. If your images came from a digital camera, the metadata also shows you information about the camera and settings that were used when the photo was taken.

When it comes to talking about all the cool things about Bridge, I tend to yammer on. I cover Bridge extensively in Chapter 12. For now, here is a list of ten cool features worth mentioning about Bridge.

- Adjustable thumbnail size for images. Adjust the thumbnail size slider on the bottom of the screen.

- One-click image rotation. Rotate multiple images at once by Shift-clicking them.

- Keyword, rating, and labeling features for categorizing and tagging photos.

- Extensive metadata features for keeping detailed notes with your images. Makes searching for a particular image quick and painless.

Preview panel

Favorites and Folders panels

Back/Forward buttons   Look In menu   Ratings and Label filters   New Folder   Delete

Compact/Full mode

Rotate buttons

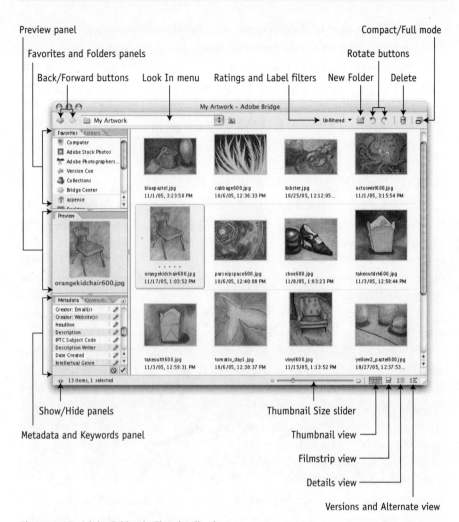

Show/Hide panels

Metadata and Keywords panel

Thumbnail Size slider

Thumbnail view

Filmstrip view

Details view

Versions and Alternate view

Figure 1.12. Adobe Bridge in Thumbnails view.

▪ Quick access to the Camera Raw plug-in for adjusting Digital Negatives with .dng or .nef file extensions. See Chapter 12 for more details on Camera Raw.

▪ Open multiple files at once by Shift-clicking file thumbnails and choosing File ⇨ Open.

▪ Save your previous searches as collections. To revisit them later, click the Collections icon in the Favorites panel.

- Drag and drop files or folders from one place to another. Pressing and holding the Option (Alt) key while dragging and dropping creates new copies.

- You can use Bridge with or without Photoshop as a file manager. Create a Bridge shortcut on Windows machines or add Bridge to your Dashboard. You'll find the application in your Applications folder on a Mac or your Program Files on Windows in a folder called Adobe Bridge CS2.

- Instant slideshows. Browse to the folder you'd like to show. Select all of the images in the folder and choose View ⇨ Slide Show. To review the list of commands, press H on the keyboard. A menu appears, similar to Figure 1.13.

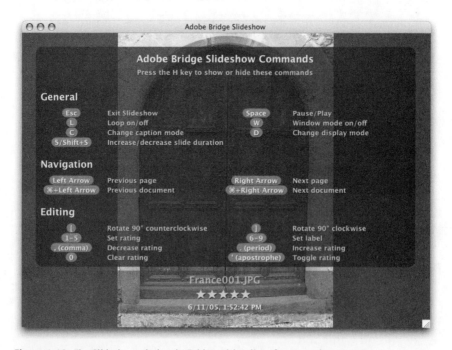

Figure 1.13. The Slideshow window in Bridge with a list of commands.

Watch Out!

Bridge takes a long time to launch. Save time by leaving it open once it's launched. Use the minimize buttons to hide it when you aren't using it.

Creating files to suit the job

Photoshop can create files from the very tiny to the very, very large. The New window, shown in Figure 1.14, has a complex array of options. The Presets menu gives you a list of commonly used file sizes, but it doesn't cover all bases. You can create your own custom file sizes, and if you know you'll be using that file size often, you can save your own custom presets to the list of standard ones.

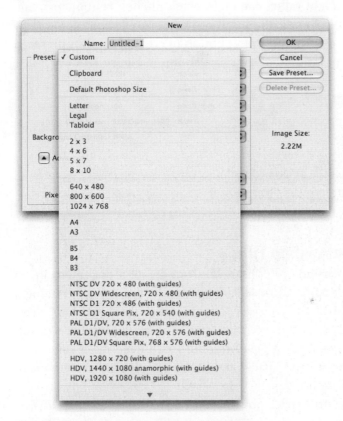

Figure 1.14. The New window and its array of options.

Unlike other programs, you have many decisions to make when creating a new file. You'll need to know not only the dimensions you want for your file, but also what color mode and resolution you want. You'll also need to decide if you want to start out with a solid background or a transparent document. There are also advanced color profiles to consider. This section covers these options and more.

Creating document dimensions from the Presets menu

The presets menu has a long list of common document sizes from which you can choose. Many include standard photo sizes; letter, legal, and tabloid-size paper; A3 and A4 international paper sizes; and some standard screen sizes like 640 × 480, 600 × 800, and 1024 × 768 pixels. You can change the units of measure for width and height by selecting a new unit of measure from the drop-down menu on the right of each field. The Width and Height values can be in pixels, inches, centimeters, millimeters, points, picas, and columns. If you know you'll be using the same document size, click the Save Preset button to create your own preset in the New Document Preset dialog box, as shown in Figure 1.15.

Figure 1.15. The New Document Preset dialog box for saving your document size presets.

Making big Photoshop files

Your documents can be quite large. You can create a document up to 1,000 inches (over 83 feet!) or 300,000 pixels. Before you go creating a gigantic piece of artwork, consider the amount of RAM and hard drive space you'd need to make a file that large. The maximum file size you can create in Photoshop is 4 gigabytes, but you'll need many times that amount in free hard drive space, and at the very least that amount in RAM to get any work done.

    Photoshop uses free space on your hard drive, called a *scratch disk,* as virtual memory when working with large files. The New window tells you how large your file size will be depending on what settings you choose. If you try to create a document that is bigger than your available free space, it'll give you an error message telling you that your scratch disk is full. Photoshop won't let you create files too big for your RAM and hard drive to handle. If you need to go even bigger, you can use the new file format PSB for files larger than 2 GB.

Inside Scoop

Configure your scratch disk for multiple hard drives by choosing Photoshop ⇨ Preferences ⇨ Plug-ins & Scratch Disks.

Selecting a color mode for your project

The Color Mode drop-down menu in the New dialog box offers you five options. Choose RGB for images you plan to use for viewing on a computer screen, digital video, inkjet printing, or CD/DVD ROMs. If you are planning on printing to a high-end color printer or laser printer, or you plan to use your image in a page layout program such as Adobe InDesign, you'll want to use CMYK Color.

After you select a color mode, you'll want to avoid converting back and forth between color modes. Each time you do, you could lose color information. If you need to convert an RGB file to a CMYK file, Photoshop recommends that you do all your editing in RGB mode and then convert to CMYK as one of your last steps before printing. I go into detail about color modes in Chapter 3. Table 1.1 is a basic list of color modes and when to use them.

Table 1.1. Color modes and common uses

Color Mode	Description
Bitmap	Black and white only. Commonly used for line art or clip art.
Grayscale	Gives you 256 shades of gray. Used for scanning black-and-white photos.
RGB Color	Used for images that will be viewed on a computer monitor or printed on most inkjet printers. Web graphics use RGB Color Mode. When in doubt, use RGB color. You can always convert later.
CMYK Color	Used for professional and mid-range printing. Most color laser printers and some high-end inkjet printers use CMYK Color Mode.
Lab Color	The Luminance, or dark and light information, is separated from the color information. This mode is sometimes used for high-end printing and is gaining popularity among digital photographers.

Choosing the right resolution for the job

All Photoshop files are made up of pixels. Each pixel is a tiny square of solid color. Think of Photoshop files as maps of color squares, like a pointillist painting by Seurat. Figure 1.16 shows a photo of an orchid zoomed out at 33% of its actual size, and the same photo zoomed in at 1600%. The zoomed-in view is like a 1,600-percent-magnified view of our flower. What we see as orchids, Photoshop just sees as different colored pixels. The resolution of an image is the amount of dots per inch, or dpi, you assign to your file. The more dots, the more detail.

Figure 1.16. Comparing a zoomed-in image.

The two most used pixel settings are 300 dpi for most printing needs and 72 dpi for Web graphics. One of these two resolutions is probably all that most of you will ever need for digital photography or graphic design. Many inkjet printers now boast the ability to print photo-quality prints from files with 1200 dpi. Some professional printers, such as Linotronic printers, can print a document with up to 2540 dpi.

Determining what your final output will be is an important aspect when creating a new file. If you are planning to send a file to a professional printer, ask them for guidelines. Most printing places are more than happy to help you set up your documents. If they can help you out before you send them files, it saves them enormous amounts of time and saves you from potential heartache and disaster. Some places that offer printing for business cards, postcards, and greeting cards often supply you with Photoshop templates and detailed guidelines.

If you are just creating images for your own use, stick with 72 dpi for Web and 300 dpi for print. If you think you might be using graphics for both print and Web, always go with the higher resolution of 300 dpi; you can always sample it down. Once you create a 72-dpi image, you won't be able to enlarge it without ending up with a terrible-looking image.

Adding a background color layer

This field gives you the option of choosing a white background, creating one using the background color you currently have selected in your background color swatch, or having a transparent background. The first two choices add a background layer to your document. The third creates a file with a regular transparent layer. You can always add a background layer later on to a file. Any layer can be converted to a background layer by choosing Layer ⇨ New ⇨ Background From Layer.

You'll see me constantly requesting that you convert your background layers into regular unlocked layers throughout the book. It's easy to do this. You can double-click the Background layer to open the New Layer dialog box. By simply renaming the Background layer, you convert it to a regular, unlocked layer. Since you'll be doing this throughout the exercises in this book, it's worth taking a minute to try it out.

To convert a locked Background layer to a regular unlocked layer, follow these steps:

1. Open a JPEG file.

2. In the Layers palette, double-click the thumbnail or layer name to open the New Layer dialog box.

Bright Idea!

Kill two birds with one stone. Drag your Background layer onto the Create New Layer icon to make an unlocked copy of your photo and save the Background as a backup.

The Font Smoothing Warning Message on a Mac

If you are using Photoshop on an Apple Macintosh computer, you may run into a warning message when you first launch the application. The warning message reads:

For the Photoshop UI to display correctly, open System Preferences, click Appearance, and turn off text smoothing for font sizes 8 and smaller.

The Mac OS sets its default font size for text smoothing to 12. This gives the User Interface for all of your menu items and file-names a crisp, easy-to-read look. Photoshop, however, relies on font smoothing to preview fonts properly. This dialog box is asking you to change your font smoothing settings from a font size of 12 to a font size of 8. By complying, you'll get a more accurate preview of what your text will look like when it's printed. I recommend that you do change your font smoothing settings, but you don't have to. You can click the Don't Show Again check box in the warning message and Photoshop will never bother you again.

---

3. Rename your layer to whatever you want. Most of the time, I just leave the default name of Layer 0.

4. Click OK.

You'll notice the lock icon has disappeared, your layer name is no longer in italics, and your layer name has changed. That's all there is to it. I know this doesn't make a whole lot of sense. It's just one of those funky things you have to get used to. Maybe Photoshop will come up with a creative solution to this in future releases.

Saving to different file formats

If you snuck a peak at the Format drop-down list in the Save As dialog box, you might feel a little overwhelmed with all of the file format choices presented to you. Along with the Photoshop PSD format, you can choose TIFF, JPEG, EPS, Targa, and a handful of other options. The full list of options is shown in Figure 1.17.

Figure 1.17. The Save As dialog box and format options.

Photoshop allows you to save files in several different types of formats for use in other applications. Formats such as TIFF and EPS are universal formats that can be imported into most image-editing programs such as Illustrator and InDesign. Table 1.2 shows you a list of commonly used file formats. The Photoshop format can handle files of up to 2 GB. PSB, or Large Document Format, is a new file format with Photoshop CS2 that supports files larger than 2 GB.

Table 1.2. Common file formats and their uses

File Type	Full Name	Description
PSD	Photoshop Document	This and PSB are the only formats that save all of Photoshop's features such as layers and styles.
JPEG	Joint Photographic Experts Group	Most commonly used for displaying photographic images on the Web. Compresses data to decrease file size.

continued

Table 1.2. *continued*

File Type	Full Name	Description
TIFF	Tagged Image File Format	A high-quality file format for exchanging images between different applications and operating systems. Most graphics and page layout programs support TIFF. Best with photos with no text.
EPS	Encapsulated PostScript	A multipurpose, high-resolution file format that can be opened by most graphics and page layout programs. Can store vector information and is great with images that combine text and shapes.
PDF	Portable Document Format	A very portable file format that is viewable with Adobe Acrobat Reader, a free document-viewing application that comes standard on most computers and is downloadable from the Web.

Saving your designs as PDF format is a great way to share high-resolution design comps with clients who may not have Photoshop. If you'll be using Photoshop-generated documents in page layout programs like InDesign or other image-editing programs, save photographic images as TIFF and designs with both graphics and text as EPS.

Just the facts

- Access hidden tools by clicking a tool to display its fly-out menu.
- Always save a copy of your file in Photoshop PSD format to retain all of the layers and options for future editing.
- Resize your image by first changing the resolution and then adjusting the width or height values.
- Preview and organize your images using Adobe Bridge through File ⇨ Browse.
- Choose the right color mode and resolution for the job.
- Save Photoshop files as TIFF or EPS files to use in other programs.

Watch Out!

Changing a file's extension doesn't mean you are converting the file to that file type. Don't use the Rename feature to convert file types! Instead, use a batch process, covered in Chapter 23.

GET THE SCOOP ON...
Navigating the tool fly-out menus ▪ Clear your workspace in one click ▪ Customizing your palette layout ▪
Zooming and maneuvering like a pro ▪ Precision
aligning with drafting tools

Getting to Know the Tools

Whether you use Photoshop for digital photography, print design, Web design, or digital art, take
some time to master the tools. You'll be more
comfortable with your workspace and more able to create
your vision without being hindered by learning hurdles.
Like any other tool, Photoshop is most powerful when it
becomes second nature to you. The more comfortable you
are with the Toolbox, palettes, and screen views, the easier
it'll be for you to bring your artistic visions to fruition.

This chapter covers the Photoshop's Toolbox and the
Options bar associated with each tool. I'll give you some tips
on how to use the Toolbox like a pro, as well as how to save
presets for your most commonly used tool settings. We'll look
at the different screen views available to help keep your workspace uncluttered. We'll investigate the various palettes for
managing type, layers, and actions. I'll give you some pointers on managing large files, and show you how to keep your
designs organized using Grids, Guides, and Rulers.

Getting around in the Toolbox

As an image editing application, Photoshop has all the
tools you'd find in a photographer's workshop and artist's
studio. The Toolbox, shown in Figure 2.1, located on the
left-hand side of your Photoshop workspace, is chock full
of creative tools like pens, brushes, erasers, exacto knives,
and tools for adding type. You also get tons of pixel-pushing
tools for smudging and warping pixels.

29

Figure 2.1. The Photoshop CS2 Toolbox.

Photoshop's Toolbox is split into seven categories, more or less. Table 2.1 shows you a list of tool categories and which tools live in each category.

Table 2.1. Tools separated by category

Tool Category	Tools
Selection Tools	Rectangular Marquee, Elliptical Marquee, Single Row Marquee, Single Column Marquee, Patch Tool, Lasso, Polygon Lasso, Magnetic Lasso, Magic Wand, Crop, Path Selection, Direct Selection
Paint Tools	Brush, Pencil, Color Replacement, Spot Healing Brush, Healing Brush, Red Eye, Clone Stamp, Pattern Stamp
Text Tools	Horizontal Type, Vertical Type, Horizontal Type Mask, Vertical Type Mask
Shape and Path Tools	Rectangle, Rounded Rectangle, Ellipse, Polygon, Line, Custom Shape, Pen, Freedom Pen, Anchor Point, Convert Point
Color and Measurement Tools	Eyedropper, Color Sampler, Measure
Maneuvering Tools	Hand, Move, Zoom
Note Tools	Notes, Audio Annotation

The remaining sections in the Toolbox provide swatches for selecting background and foreground color, a mode for masking images, and some screen view modes that allow you to hide your desktop for an uncluttered work area. The last icon in the Toolbox is a quick way to jump to ImageReady, Adobe's sister application for creating professional images and animated gifs for the Web. ImageReady comes free with Photoshop and is a great companion for those of you interested in Website design or creating images for the Web. Once you can find your way around Photoshop, the learning curve for ImageReady is relatively painless. I'll go over ImageReady in more detail in Chapter 20, when I cover creating professional graphics for the Web.

Using Toolbox fly-out menus

Several of Photoshop's tools are stacked on top of each other in the Toolbox. Any time you see the tiny black arrow on the bottom right corner of a tool, there are several more tools hidden underneath it. Clicking once on a tool icon selects the tool and clicking a second time brings up a fly-out menu displaying all the optional tools available. The fly-outs work like any standard hierarchical menu. Move your mouse up and down the list to highlight a tool and click to select it. Figure 2.2 shows an example of the Toolbox with the fly-out menu for the various shape tools displayed.

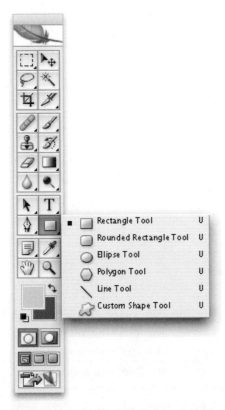

Figure 2.2. The Toolbox with Drawing tool fly-out menu visible.

I'm sure some of you are antsy to know what all of these tools do. As you read this book, I'll cover most of the Photoshop tools in detail. If you are new to Photoshop and would like a general overview of all the tools and what they do, I'd like to introduce you to Adobe's fantastic Photoshop Help system. The Help system, which comes automatically installed with Photoshop, has a great section on all the tools, including screenshots and examples. They've saved me the trouble so that I can focus on teaching you more in-depth features and showing you some tricks of the trade.

Read all about the tools and their purposes by visiting the Photoshop Help topic on the Toolbox:

1. To launch Photoshop Help in a new window, choose Help ⇨ Photoshop Help.

   Alternatively, press ⌘+/(Ctrl+/).

2. With the Content tab highlighted, click the words Work Area in the Help Topics list as shown in Figure 2.3.

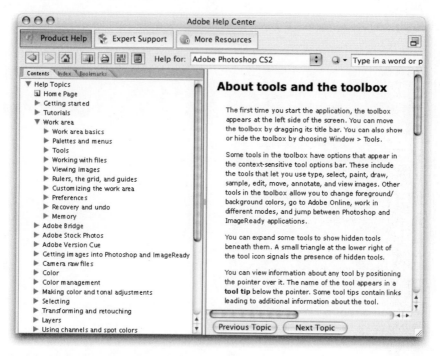

Figure 2.3. The Help Center with expanded Work Area Topic.

3. Choose Tools ⇨ About the Tools.

The content in this Help subtopic and the following subtopics get you acquainted with all the tools in the Toolbox. I hope I've also turned you on to what a great Help system you have at your fingertips. With each release, the Photoshop Help system has gotten better and better. Even a seasoned veteran can learn a great deal by keeping Photoshop's Help system as a faithful and trusty companion.

Mousing over tools for information

Get quick information about a tool by rolling your mouse over a tool and waiting a couple seconds. A little yellow title box appears with the name of the tool and a handy letter command for instantly toggling to it without having to click it with your mouse. Typing the letter command while pressing and holding the Shift key toggles between the tools available underneath the main tool as shown in Figure 2.4.

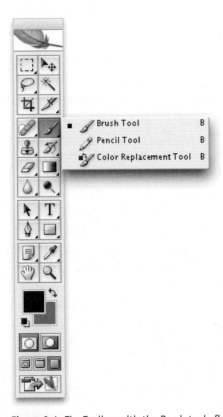

Figure 2.4. The Toolbox with the Brush tools fly-out menu.

Now it's your turn. Give the tool commands a spin by exploring the different options for the Brush tool:

1. Highlight the Brush tool by pressing the letter B.

2. Press Shift+B to switch to the Pencil tool.

3. Press Shift+B again to switch to the Color Replacement tool.

4. Press Shift+B again to return to the Brush tool.

You just switched to three different tools without touching your mouse. Getting used to the letter commands for commonly used tools can save your wrists a lot of unnecessary work. After you become familiar with using the letter commands, switching tools will become second nature.

Exploring tool options

Each tool has a separate set of options associated with it and can be modified via the Options bar at the top of the screen, just below the menu bar. Tool options include things like brush size, selection size and feathering size, alignment options, blending modes, and opacity settings. This is where you'll fine-tune your tools.

The drop-down menu on the top left of the Options bar allows you to save your own tool presets. You can save Brush tool options for commonly used brush sizes and opacity settings, type settings like font size and color, and save custom vector shapes that you know you'll be using often.

One immediately useful way to work with tool presets is by adding presets for making fixed-size selections. Figure 2.5 shows the Marquee tool presets drop-down list. In the next set of steps, you'll create a fixed-size rectangular marquee selection to save time in creating a banner photo for a Weblog. I've based this off a common banner size, but you can create a selection for anything you like. You could instead save a preferred size for cropping your photos.

To create a Rectangular Marquee tool preset for a fixed size:

1. Select the Rectangular Marquee tool from the Toolbox by pressing the letter M.

2. In the Options bar, select Fixed Size from the Style menu.

3. Add values for width and height. For this example, I used 760 px for the width and 120 px for the height.

4. On the far left of the Options bar, click the tool preset drop-down menu and click the Create New Tool Preset button on the right. It's the little icon just below the arrow on the right-hand side of the drop-down menu.

5. Give your new preset a descriptive name. I've named mine Rectangular Marquee 760px × 120px so that I can find it easily in the tool preset menu.

Inside Scoop

To use inches instead of pixels as your unit of measure in the Marquee tool height and width fields, type **in** after the numeric value.

Figure 2.5. The Options bar for the Marquee tool with a newly added preset.

After you've saved your selection preset, you can click anywhere in a photo to create a fixed-size selection area, and then either copy and paste it into a new file, or choose Image ⇨ Crop to crop it to your selection size. You can reselect your saved preset at any time by selecting it from the tool presets list; refer to Figure 2.5.

Exploring palettes

Photoshop gives you additional control over tools and other features with floating palettes. Palettes help you manage layers, navigate large files, and give you greater control over some of the tools in the Toolbox. Among other things, there are palettes that help you fine-tune type, keep a history of your edits, provide an interface for recording actions, and give you more control over brush settings.

Photoshop arranges the palettes in a default group arrangement that you can rearrange however you like. For example, if you know you will be working with type regularly, you'll probably want to add the Paragraph and Character palettes to your workspace. The palettes can be grouped together in stacks or pulled out into their own independent palettes.

Customizing your palette arrangements

The menu item entitled Window gives you a list of all the different palettes available to you. Figure 2.6 shows the palettes that appear in Photoshop's default workspace. You can view the remaining palettes, such as the Paragraph and Character palettes, by choosing them from the Window menu item.

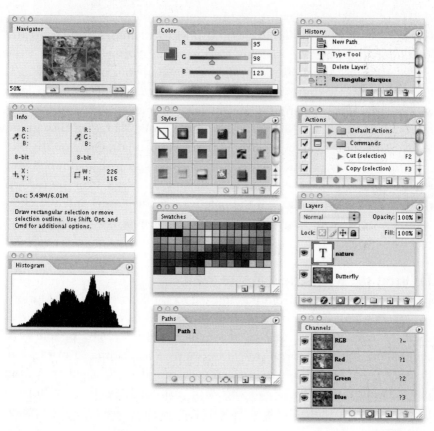

Figure 2.6. Photoshop's many palettes.

Hack

You can double-click the title bar of any palette to collapse the palette down to the size of the title bar. This is a convenient way to keep your palettes at the ready.

Photoshop by default has grouped the palettes into different sets:

- Navigator, Info, and Histogram
- Color, Swatches, and Styles
- History and Actions
- Layers, Channels, and Paths
- Paragraph and Character

These sets work logically together. For example, Navigator, Info, and History palettes all deal with general document information, and the Paragraph and Character palettes have type formatting options.

Palettes work much like any other window on your operating system. You can rearrange your palettes by dragging them by their tabs or palette window bars. Each palette has a close and minimize button on the top. Most palettes, with the exception of the Paragraph, Character, Histogram, and Color palettes, can be expanded by clicking and dragging on the bottom right corner of the palette. Each palette has a drop-down list of palette options that you can access by clicking the black arrow on the top right of each palette. Many of the palettes, such as Layers and Swatches, let you choose from larger-sized thumbnails or allow you to display the palette items in a list.

Tidying up with the palette well

Photoshop CS2 has added a palette well to the far right of the Options bar. The well allows you to add as many palettes as you want and access them by clicking their tabs as shown in Figure 2.7. For people with smaller monitors, or for anyone who wants a less-cluttered workspace, this is a great way to keep your screen clean. To add a palette to the palette well, drag it by its tab and drop it into the well. To remove a palette from the well, click and drag it by its tab and place it anywhere on your screen.

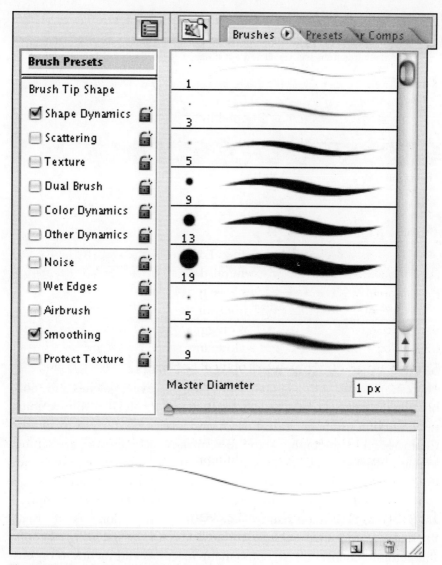

Figure 2.7. The Palette well with Brushes palette visible.

Viewing palettes with function keys

Some of the more popular palettes can be shown and hidden via the function keys that appear at the top of your computer keyboard. Table 2.2 shows function keys available for quickly accessing some of the most-used palettes.

Watch Out!

Mac portables such as the PowerBook and iBook use the function keys to control monitor and sound settings. They need an additional key to work as a regular function key would. This key is on the bottom left of your keyboard, below the Shift key, and is labeled fn. Hold it down while pressing the various function keys.

Table 2.2. Function keys for displaying palettes

Function Key	Palette
F5	Brushes
F6	Color
F7	Layers
F8	Info
Alt F9 (Option F9 on Mac)	Actions

Saving your custom workspace settings

Photoshop comes with a default setting for displaying palettes and tools, but don't feel like you have keep things that way. If you know you are going to be working with a great deal of text, it makes sense for you to add the Character and Paragraph palettes to your own custom workspace setting, so that whenever you launch Photoshop, you don't have to rearrange your workspace. Your workspace can also include any special keyboard shortcuts you've created and any menu settings you've modified. For example, I always like to have rulers handy (View ⇨ Rulers) and I don't like the Snap to Guides feature (View ⇨ Snap To ⇨ Guides). In the following example, I'm going to choose to save both palette locations and menus to my custom workspace. I don't have any custom keyboard shortcuts, so I'll leave that one unchecked.

After you've gotten your workspace arranged how you like it, you can save your custom workspace by adding it to the custom workspace list.

To save your custom workspace list:

1. Choose Window ⇨ Workspace ⇨ Save Workspace.

2. In the Save Workspace dialog box, type a name for your workspace, as shown in Figure 2.8.

3. Check the Palette Locations check box, and if you have any custom menu settings, or keyboard shortcuts, select those boxes as well.

4. Name your workspace and click the Save button to add your custom workspace to a list of available workspaces.

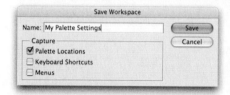

Figure 2.8. The Save Workspace dialog box.

The next time you launch Photoshop, it uses your new custom workspace. You can switch workspaces any time by choosing Window ⇨ Workspace and choosing from the list. Your newly created one will appear at the bottom of the list.

Photoshop's preinstalled workspaces

You might have noticed the workspace list has several custom workspaces automatically installed with Photoshop CS2. These workspaces help you identify menu items that are commonly used for different disciplines that use Photoshop. There is a workspace for Color Correction, Painting and Retouching, Proofing and Printing, Web Design, What's New in CS2, and Working with Type. Commonly used menu items, including recommended palettes, appear in colored highlight from the various dropdown menus inside Photoshop. Choosing these workspaces won't change your palette layout; they just highlight the most commonly used tasks in your menu items. Figure 2.9 shows the Filter menu items added in CS2 highlighted in blue using the What's New in CS2 workspace preset.

Inside Scoop

To revert to Photoshop's default workspace, choose Window ⇨ Workspace ⇨ Default Workspace.

Figure 2.9. New Filter menu items highlighted via the What's New in CS2 workspace preset.

Organizing with grids, guides, and rulers

With grids, guides, and rulers, you have some powerful drafting tools to help design for print and Web with precision alignment. All three of these tools are on-screen only so you can use as many as you want; they won't come out in your prints or final Web graphics files. Rulers give us some perspective of the actual size of our documents. Guides are non-printable horizontal and vertical lines that you can place anywhere in your document to help you align and place images. Grids come in handy for traditional artists who are working on enlarged paintings or drawings from photo sources.

Using rulers for precision placement

Photoshop Rulers help you place, crop, and organize images by showing you the height and width of your document. It's easy to lose a sense of scale, especially when working on documents with resolutions of 300 pixels and more. By default, rulers are not visible. To show the rulers, you can either choose View ⇨ Rulers or type the command key ⌘+R (Ctrl+R). Right-click anywhere in the ruler to change the units of measure quickly. Figure 2.10 shows a drop-down list where you can choose from pixels, inches, centimeters, millimeters, points, picas, or percent as your unit of measure.

Figure 2.10. Changing your ruler's unit of measure.

Adding your own guides for organization

Now that you have turned on the rulers feature, you have access to Photoshop's guides feature. Guides are a fantastic way to organize your designs, especially when adding text elements to a photo or designing a Web site with elements that need to line up perfectly. You have the option of manually dragging guides into place or creating a guide at a specific horizontal or vertical position. Figure 2.11 shows a Web site design with rulers visible and a few grids to aid with placement of text and graphics. As

I mentioned before, guides won't show up on your prints, so you can add as many as you want without affecting your final output.

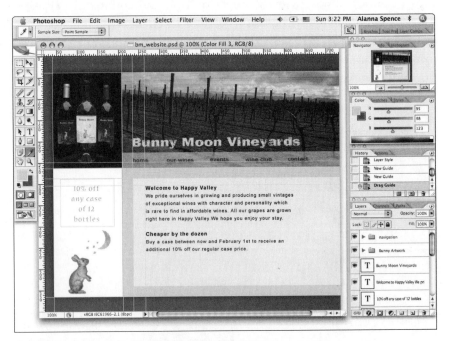

Figure 2.11. Rulers and guides in a Web site design.

Try adding rulers and guides to your own document:

1. To make the rulers visible, choose View ⇨ Rulers.

    Alternatively, you can press ⌘+R.

2. To change the units of measure, right-click inside either ruler and select your preference from the drop-down list.

3. Create a horizontal guide by clicking and dragging from the top horizontal ruler, and place the guide anywhere in your document by releasing your mouse button.

4. Create a vertical guide by clicking and dragging from the left vertical ruler, and place the guide anywhere in your document by releasing your mouse button.

5. Reposition either guide by pressing the ⌘ key (Ctrl) and then clicking and dragging the guide.

6. To create a guide at a particular spot, choose View ⇨ New Guide.

Inside Scoop

Temporarily hide your guides at any time by typing ⌘+H (Ctrl+H). To get them back, type ⌘+H again.

7. Select either vertical or horizontal orientation, and enter a value followed by *px* for pixels or by *in* for inches.

   In Figure 2.11, I used this feature to create a 20-pixel margin around my Web site design.

8. To make sure your elements snap into place, choose View ⇨ Snap To ⇨ Guides.

Now that your guides are in place, positioning your design elements is a snap. If you ever want to create new guides from scratch, you can clear out all of your existing guides by choosing View ⇨ Clear Guides.

Modifying grid settings

Using Photoshop as an aid for creating nondigital art has become increasingly popular as traditional artists and illustrators begin to use computers in their work. Using grids is a handy way of preparing a photo to be enlarged into a painting or drawing. Grids can come in handy when you need help organizing layouts designed for print or Web. Digital artists interested in creating or editing their artwork on a grid have a great deal of control over the spacing and size of their grid. Figure 2.12 shows the Preferences window for Guides, Grid & Slices.

You can change your grid options through Photoshop's Preferences window by following these steps:

1. Choose Photoshop ⇨ Preferences ⇨ Guides, Grid & Slices

2. Under the Grid section, change your color and style of your grid.

3. Change your Gridline in increments of pixels, inches, centimeters, millimeters, points, picas, or percent.

   For example, I find percentage particularly handy, and I like to set mine to increments of 25 percent.

4. Change the number of subdividing lines between main grid lines to get a better organization.

After you've gotten your grid preferences set, you can view them by choosing View ⇨ Show ⇨ Grid.

Bright Idea!

Select View ⇨ Snap ⇨ Snap to Grid to have Photoshop automatically snap to a grid when you are dragging and placing images.

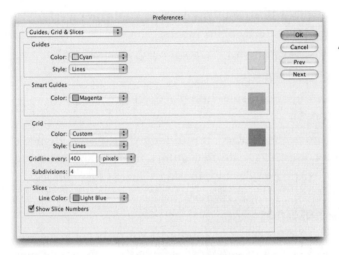

Figure 2.12. Guides, Grid & Slices Preferences window.

Toggling between Full Screen and Standard Screen Modes

If you are like me, the desk in your office is cluttered with all sorts of junk. Unopened mail, candy wrappers, music CDs, and pictures have completely taken over my work area. Sometimes it's hard to find my computer through all the junk. Its not surprising my computer's desktop is just as messy. I know many of us keep shortcuts and frequently used files on our desktops for easy access. On Windows machines, it's impossible to avoid. It's distracting to design when your background is cluttered with random files and hard drive icons.

Clicking Full Screen Mode hides all the junk. It's like having a magic button that clears all the junk off your desk and puts it into a magic drawer. The best part is, with the click of the Standard Screen button, you can get all of your prized junk right back where you are used to seeing it. Figure 2.13 shows Photoshop in Full Screen Mode. Photoshop also gives you a choice of showing the menu bar or viewing your artwork on an

Inside Scoop

If you just want to hide the palettes temporarily and keep the Toolbox handy, Shift+Tab does the trick.

unfettered black background. If you want to get clean, pressing the Tab key on your keyboard hides everything—and I mean everything—but your artwork. Don't panic! Pressing Tab again brings it all back for you.

Figure 2.13. Photoshop in Full Screen Mode.

If you don't like the gray or black color of the Full Screen Mode, you can change it by choosing the color you want in the foreground color swatch, and then selecting the Paint Bucket tool, located in the Gradient tool's fly-out menu, and Shift+clicking inside the gray or white background.

Editing in Quick Mask Mode

Quick Mask Mode is essentially a view that allows you to select complex areas of your image by painting out the negative space. When you return to Standard Mode, you'll see a marching ant selection around the areas you've painted. If you click the new layer mask icon on the bottom of the Layers palette, a mask is created, using the painting or selections you created in Quick Mask Mode. I spend a great deal of time on masks in Chapter 8. In this chapter, I'll give you a simple exercise in using the Quick Mask Mode to get you started. The example in Figure 2.14 shows my favorite dog in an organically shaped, feathered mask. I'm going to add a solid color background to make him look like he's floating in a sea of color.

Figure 2.14. Editing a photo in Quick Mask Mode.

Let's create an image mask by editing in Quick Mask Mode with the Brush tool:

1. Open an image you'd like to mask. If it consists of one Background layer, double click the layer's icon to rename and unlock it.

2. Click the Quick Mask icon in the Toolbox. It's just below the color swatches and is shown highlighted in Figure 2.14. Don't worry, you won't notice any change at this point other than the Quick Mask icon's being highlighted.

3. Select the Brush tool by pressing the letter T.

4. Increase your Brush size by selecting a new size in the Brush Options bar or by typing the] key a few times. You'll want a big enough brush to cover quite a bit of area with a few quick strokes.

5. Increase your brush Hardness to 100% in the Brush Options bar so you get a nice solid brush. The keyboard shortcut for adjusting brush hardness is Shift+[for less hardness and Shift+] for more.

6. Begin to paint around your object, leaving a little bit of space between your brush strokes and the object. Your brush should be creating a translucent red brush stroke.

7. After you have filled up everything but your masked image with red, soften your brush a bit by pressing Shift+[a few times. You'll see the brush stroke preview in the Options bar get fuzzy around the edges as shown in Figure 2.15.

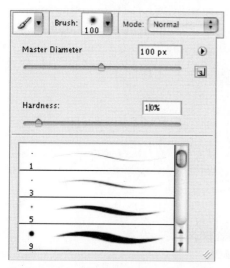

Figure 2.15. Brush diameter with fuzzy edges created by adjusting the Brush Hardness setting.

8. Now, paint a fuzzy edge around your object to create a nice, soft vignette effect.

You should now have a document with everything except your subject covered in red. The next step is to switch out of Quick Mask Mode and create the actual Mask layer. To do so, follow these steps:

1. Click the Standard Mode icon next to Quick Mask to switch back. You should now see a line of marching ants circling your subject. The ants indicate the selection area that you'll use for your mask.

2. Click the Layer Mask icon on the bottom of the palette. It looks like a gray box with a white circle in the middle of it. You should now see your subject masked from its background.

3. To add a solid colored background, choose Layer ⇨ New ⇨ Layer.

4. In the Layers palette, click and drag your newly created layer below your masked layer so that it doesn't cover up your image.

5. Click inside the color spectrum on the bottom of the Color palette to pick a new foreground color quickly.

6. Press Option+Delete (Alt+Delete) to fill your new layer with the foreground color.

You should now see your subject floating on a color background similar to the photo in Figure 2.16. There are many ways of fine-tuning masks. Quick Mask Mode works best when used in conjunction with other tools. Chapter 8 covers the fine art of masking in much more detail.

Figure 2.16. Vignetted photo created in Quick Mask Mode.

Inside Scoop

Change the color and opacity of the Quick Mask color by double-clicking the Quick Mask icon in the Toolbox.

Zooming in and out of images

Image editing requires a lot of zooming. In some instances, you'll want to magnify a portion of your image and get in close for precision editing. For other editing instances, like color correction or cropping, you'll probably want to zoom out to see your image in its entirety. The Zoom tool lets you zoom in up to 1600% of your document size and out as far as 0.17%. It has options for fitting your image to your screen or for viewing it at actual size. Photoshop has some very handy key commands to make zooming in and out an effortless task.

Using the Zoom tool

You may find that, after getting used to using the spacebar for all of your zooming in and out, clicking the actual tool in the Toolbox is unnecessary. There is one terrific setting in the Zoom tool's Options bar that can be worth the extra effort of choosing the Zoom tool from the Toolbox. Among the options in the Options bar that you see in Figure 2.17 is a check box entitled Resize Window to Fit. When you have several document windows floating around your desktop, some sticking halfway off the screen, some resized to odd shapes, this option resizes your document window to fit snuggly around your tools and palettes. If you are Shift-Tab happy with toggling your palette windows and would rather have your document take up as much space as it can, there's an additional option to ignore your palettes and fit your window flush right with your screen.

Figure 2.17. Options bar with Zoom tool options.

Inside Scoop

Use Full Screen mode and click the Fill Screen button in the Zoom tool Options bar to make better use of screen real estate.

Speedy zooming with key commands

It's time to combine some of the skills you've learned in this chapter and start maneuvering like a pro. Adobe has placed many of the key commands for zooming and moving right next to each other on the keyboard so that you can get around effortlessly.

Let's try navigating around a file by using a combination of keyboard commands and using the mouse:

1. Open a Photoshop file. Any file will do, but in this case, bigger is better.

2. If you have just one locked background layer in your file, double-click it to rename and unlock it.

3. With one hand, press and hold ⌘+spacebar (Ctrl+spacebar) to zoom in.

4. Option+click (Alt+click) and drag to select an area of your image.

5. ⌘+click (Ctrl+click) to temporarily change to the Move tool and drag your selection to a new position in your document.

6. Option+Shift+click (Alt+Shift+Chick) to deselect your rectangular selection area.

7. Making sure you are zoomed in enough to see scrollbars, press and hold the spacebar to temporarily change to the Hand tool while clicking and dragging up or down, left or right, to move to a new area of your image.

8. Press and hold ⌘+Option+spacebar (Ctrl+Alt+spacebar) and then click to zoom out.

9. If you'd like to undo the cutout in your image, press ⌘+Z (Ctrl+Z) to undo your last action, or ⌘+Option+Z (Ctrl+Alt+Z) to undo several steps.

Congratulations! You are now an official two-handed Photoshop gunslinger. You'll soon find that using key combinations of ⌘, Option, Shift, and the spacebar will become as second nature as using your mouse. You may even find yourself trying to use the same commands in other programs.

Moving around large files

When you get down to editing fine details on a large photo, getting around your document can feel like navigating around a large map. These tips will help you sail around your document window with the ease and grace of a modern-day Magellan.

Moving around with the Navigator

The Navigator palette on the top right of your list of palettes serves as a virtual "you are here" marker. The red box shows you what section of your big document you can currently see in your Document window. It gives you the 30-thousand-foot view of your document. In Figure 2.18, I've zoomed into my photo at 128%. The Navigator palette shows you the entire document in a small thumbnail and places a red square around the area you are currently viewing. You can easily move to a new area of your document by clicking and/or dragging the red box around your Navigator palette. The move happens in real time so you can precisely place yourself right where you want to go.

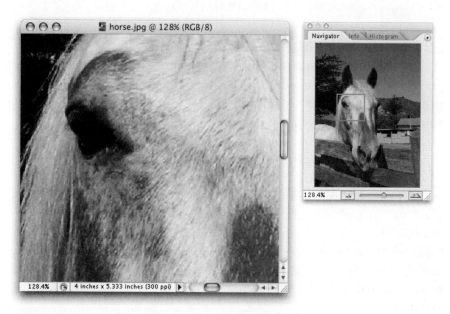

Figure 2.18. The Navigator palette serves as a "you are here" map.

Inside Scoop

Change the color of your navigator box to another color by clicking the black arrow at the top of the Navigator palette and choosing Palette Options. Click the color swatch to select a custom color, or select a new one from the drop-down menu.

You can also use the Navigator palette as a zoom tool. The slider bar on the bottom of the palette zooms you in and out of your document.

Getting around with the Hand tool

You can select the Hand tool three easy ways. The first one is to select it from the Toolbox. To save yourself some mousing energy, typing H highlights it for you. My favorite way to switch to the Hand tool, and I think the handiest, is to simply press and hold the spacebar. As long as the spacebar is depressed, you can move around your file by clicking and dragging in your Document window. Remember, the Hand tool works only for images larger than your Document window, so if you don't see scroll bars, it means there's nowhere else to move.

Jumping to ImageReady

When you bought Adobe Photoshop CS2, you also got a powerful Web graphics application called ImageReady. This application was designed to help Web designers create professional graphics. With ImageReady you can create image slices and have Photoshop generate HTML code for your Web site so that you don't have to mess with learning HTML. ImageReady also includes tools for creating animated gifs.

Many of ImageReady's features are available to a certain extent inside Photoshop, but because ImageReady was created as a professional Web graphics aid, its tools offer more features than you'd get when using Photoshop's equivalent tool. The good news is that all the features work together. If you create slices in Photoshop, you can jump to ImageReady and continue to edit and add to those slices. What Photoshop can't do when it comes to slicing and dicing for the Web, ImageReady picks up the slack.

I'll be going over ImageReady in more detail in Chapter 20, but I'd like to give you a sneak peak at ImageReady's interface. In Figure 2.19, I've created some slices and image maps in my Web site design. The palettes that you see are very similar to Photoshop's, with the exception of the Optimize, Slice, Table, and Image Map palettes. If you've used Photoshop's Save As Web feature, some of these options should look familiar to you.

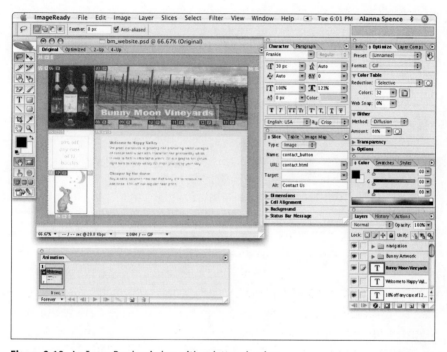

Figure 2.19. An ImageReady window with palettes showing.

Just the facts

- Rearrange your palettes and save your custom workspace for the future.
- Get the name and key command for most tools and icons in Photoshop by hovering over them with your mouse.
- Align and arrange your designs with guides, grids, and rulers.
- Create your first mask selection in Quick Mask Mode.
- Learn the key commands for moving, selecting, and zooming to navigate your files effortlessly.
- Jump between ImageReady and Photoshop and retain your image slices.

GET THE SCOOP ON...
Choosing the right color mode ▪ Fixing Brightness and
Contrast in Lab Color mode ▪ Adding color and pattern
overlays to text ▪ Sharing color palettes ▪ Creating
glassy buttons with style sets

Working with Colors, Swatches, and Styles

Chapter 3

When you start dealing with creating artwork for print versus digital media, color modes and all their eccentricities can quickly become nightmarishly complicated. Why do we need more than one type of color mode? Why is that when you print, you have to use CMYK, but when you design for the Web or other digital medias, you use RGB? What are Lab and Index Color modes used for?

Computers are tools for humans. Not surprisingly, their color systems are based off the human eye and how it perceives color and light. Once you understand how the human eye works, the computer world and all its many different color modes start to make more sense. I'm going to attempt to explain this very complicated world in a few short paragraphs, so bear with me.

Interpreting color modes

Your eye perceives light and color through little receptors in your eyes called rods and cones. The human eye has about 120 million rods and somewhere between 6 and 7 million cones. Rods sense light or radiance; cones sense color hue and saturation. Cones are split into three different color sensors:

- **Red:** Makes up a little over 65 percent of the total amount of cones.

57

- **Green:** Makes up around 30 percent of the total amount of cones.

- **Blue:** Accounts for less than 5 percent of the total amount of cones.

When stimulated, your cones fire off impulses to the brain. Depending on how much each type of cone is stimulated, your brain receives different color information.

Rods receive light information. They are in charge of perceiving luminosity and they help us see in the dark. They are so sensitive they can pick up tiny reflections of light in very dark environments. Cones don't work as well in the dark, which is why colors are more difficult to pick up in low light situations. Rods are what give your eyes the dreaded red eye from camera flashes. In animals with great night vision, rods are what make their eyes glow in the dark.

When to use RGB and CMYK

RGB (red, green, and blue) color mode is used for displaying images on computer monitors. It works like the cones in your eyes, more or less. The higher the red value, the brighter, or more saturated the red. The higher the green, the brighter the green, and so on. If you add the maximum values of red, green, and blue, you get pure white. RGB mode is called additive color because when adding all three colors at 100% their value, you get white. When all the values are set to 0%, you get pitch black.

RGB is used for Web designs, on-screen presentations, CD ROMs, and digital video. Most inkjet printers also work in RGB, even some that have CMYK cartridges. Figure 3.1 shows a photo and its separate RGB color channels in the Channels palette.

Use RGB color mode for the following:

- On-screen presentations

- Web sites and e-mail attachments

- CD-ROM and DVD-ROM artwork

- Most inkjet printers and digital video

Inside Scoop
Some inkjet printers have special printer drivers that convert from RGB images to CMYK cartridges. Check your printer's manual to make sure you are using the best color mode for your model.

Figure 3.1. An RGB photo and the Channels palette.

CMYK (cyan, magenta, yellow, and black) is a little trickier. CMYK is used mainly in color printers and is called subtractive color because the absence of all four colors is white. With CMYK you are using pigments to simulate natural colors by printing them onto a white surface — in most cases, paper. Not all whites are made equal. If you took a sampling of every piece of white paper available at the office supply store, you'd find they are all varying degrees of white. Additionally, black is a very difficult color to produce by blending man-made pigments. If it were a perfect world, we could probably get by with just cyan, magenta, and yellow. However, it's not perfect, so we get a little help from black. Getting your colors to print exactly how you want them can be tricky. I'll cover more color printing tips and techniques in Chapter 19.

CMYK is made up of four channels. You can look at them in the Channels palette shown in Figure 3.2. I've colored each one of the bubbles at 100% their value for Cyan, Magenta, Yellow, and Black and overlapped them a bit. The overlapping areas show up as a lighter shade of gray in the Channels palette because the colors are blended together.

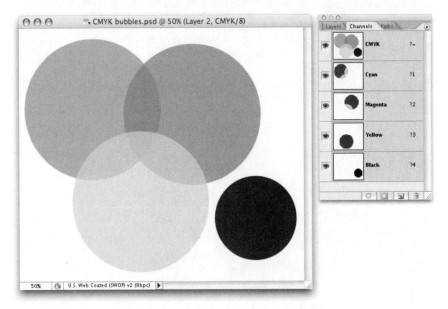

Figure 3.2. The Channels palette for an image in CMYK color mode.

Use CMYK color mode for the following:

▪ Color laser printers

▪ Professional printing

▪ Page layout programs

About Lab color

Lab color consists of three values: Lightness, a, and b. It works more like your eyes than any other color mode. A represents the spectrum of red to green and b represents the spectrum of yellow to blue. The benefits in using Lab color are that, if you look at Lab color split into its different channels, you are able to separate color data from detail. By adjusting the L channel of an image, you can adjust its brightness and contrast without touching any color data, and are able to yield much better results. Figure 3.3 shows adjustments to the Lightness channel of a photo with the Brightness/Contrast dialog box.

Figure 3.3. Adjusting Brightness and Contrast on the L channel.

To see Lab color at work, let's convert a photo and try changing its brightness and contrast in Lab Color mode:

1. Open a photo that has an RGB color mode.

2. In the History palette, right-click the thumbnail of your document and select New Document to create a new document with a duplicate of your photo.

3. In the new file, choose Image ⇨ Mode ⇨ Lab color.

4. At the top of your Layers palette, click the Channels tab to open the Lab Channels.

5. To hide the visibility of the a and b channels, click the Visibility icon (an eye) next to each. You've now isolated the blacks and whites, or shadows and highlights, from the color data in your photo.

6. Choose Image ⇨ Adjustments ⇨ Brightness/Contrast.

7. Modify your Brightness and Contrast settings until you've found something you like.

   In Figure 3.3, I set my Brightness level to –5 and my Contrast to 15. Click OK when you are done.

8. Click in the Visibility box to the left of the first composite channel to make all four channels visible again.

As you can see, you get much greater control over your lights and darks when the lightness data is separated from your color data when editing in Lab Color mode. I encourage you to compare adjusting Brightness/Contrast settings on an RGB file to compare the experience.

With increasing popularity in the Camera Raw or DNG format, Lab color could very well become the color mode of choice for professional digital photographers. As it stands, the more conventional RGB or CMYK color modes are more commonly used for general-purpose photo editing. Lab color, however, can come in handy when editing photos with tricky color or brightness and contrast issues. It is worth exploring if you are an avid digital photographer. Because it is a device-independent color mode, you have a much wider range of colors to choose from when editing.

Indexed Color mode when you need tiny files

The Indexed Color mode converts your document to a single-channel 8-bit image. It creates a custom color palette of up to 256 colors, called a CLUT, using dithering when colors don't match up perfectly. Files converted to Indexed Color mode are significantly smaller than RGB images that have 3 color channels. Due to its limited palette, you'll lose a lot of image quality when converting to Indexed Color mode, so it should be used only when you really need to squeeze your file size down. Indexed Color works best with Web graphics or on-screen presentations. It's best to do all of your editing in RGB first and convert to Indexed Color as a last step.

When you are ready to convert to Indexed Color, make a copy of your file and then change your color mode. Most editing tools won't work in Indexed Color mode. In addition, you'll get better results by working bigger and then sampling down. The window in Figure 3.4 shows you the options associated with Indexed Color mode.

You can covert your RGB image to Indexed Color by following these steps:

1. To change color modes, choose Image ⇨ Indexed Color to open the dialog box.

   If the Preview check box is checked, you can see how your image will look with the various settings.

   If you are planning to use the image for a Web site, I'd recommend using either Web or Local (Selective) for your Palette settings and change the Forced drop-down menu to Web.

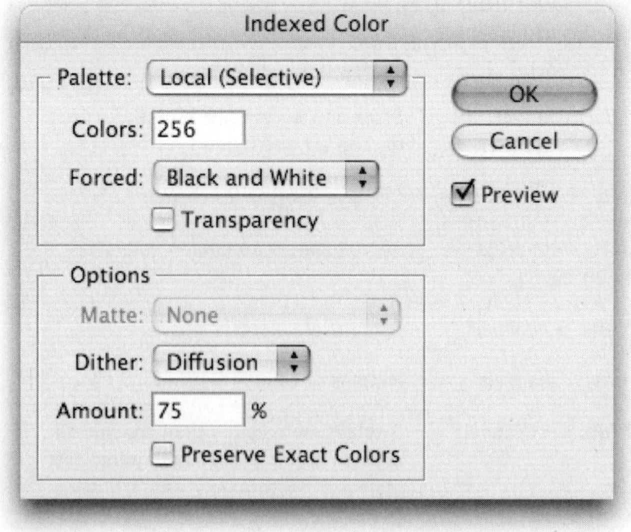

Figure 3.4. Dialog box for Indexed Color mode settings.

2. Try out different diffusion settings.

I find that diffusion dither works best for photos. The lower the percentage, the less blending occurs. This setting really depends on your image, so try several settings to get the best results.

Again, Indexed Color is a very limited palette, so your images are going to look choppy. Use this color mode only when you have to. In Chapter 20, I go into much more detail about optimizing your files for the Web to achieve the smallest files while retaining the best image quality.

A bit about bit depth

The bit depth of your images defines how much color or grayscale information you can store. The most commonly used bit depth in Photoshop is 8 bits per channel. In RGB color mode, you have 3 channels, so you are working in 24-bit color mode. CMYK has 4 channels, so it's 32-bit color. When you create a new file in Photoshop and you select 8 bits from the bit depth drop-down list, you are telling Photoshop you want to store 8 bits of data per color channel. Table 3.1 shows a list of color modes, bit depths, and the amount of colors that can be displayed per color mode.

Table 3.1. Color modes and bit depths

Color Mode	Bit Depth	Amount of Colors
Black and White	1 bit, 1 channel	Black and white only, no gray — used for clip art and line art
Grayscale	8 bits, 1 channel	Displays 256 shades of gray
8-bit RGB	8 bits, 3 channels (24-bit color)	Approximately 16 million colors
16-bit RGB	16 bits, 3 channels	Trillions of colors
CMYK	8 bits, 4 channels	Millions of colors
HDR (High Dynamic Range)	32 bits per channel	Displays more colors than the human eye can see — used mostly in movies, high-end photography, and 3-D work

Choosing a color setting

Photoshop uses color working spaces to determine how to display the colors in your documents. For most users, the default RGB working space is sRGB, which works well for creating Web graphics or working with consumer-grade digital cameras.

Here is a guide to the best working color spaces to use for color images:

- **sRGB:** Images for use on the Web and consumer-grade digital cameras, on-screen presentations, interactive CD-ROMs, and DVDs.

- **Adobe RGB:** Use this when creating images for printing or professional-grade digital cameras.

- **CMYK:** The working spaces for CMYK are device-dependant, so check with your printer. U.S. Sheetfed Coated is a safe bet if you aren't sure.

To change your color setting, select Edit ➾ Color Settings. You can edit the default working spaces for all color modes, or choose from a list of recommended color settings for the creation of different content types. You'll also get a chance to change your working space when creating a new file. If you click the More Options button, you'll see a more complete Settings drop-down list for selecting a Color Profile. Figure 3.5 shows the Color Settings dialog box with More Options visible.

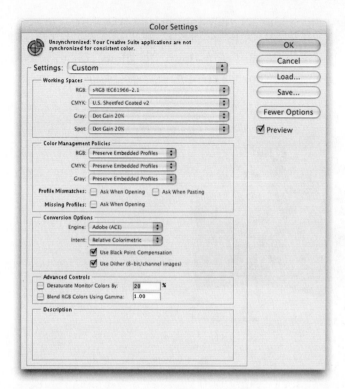

Figure 3.5. The Color Settings dialog box.

Choosing with the Color Picker and Eyedropper

Any time you choose colors in Photoshop, unless you are picking directly from the Swatches palette, you'll be using the Adobe Color Picker. The Color Picker is a dialog box that appears whenever you click the background or foreground swatch in the Toolbox, the Color palette, the Gradient tool, or the Text tools. The three main components of the dialog box are the color field, color slider, and color values. In the next section, you'll select colors using a few different techniques and tools.

Pick a color for a thought bubble with the Eyedropper tool

The Eyedropper tool is a quick way to pick colors, and when working with photos, it can be a great way to choose a complementary color to use for text or other added graphics. The Eyedropper tool in the Toolbox changes the foreground color each time you click an area in your image. In Figure 3.6, I selected a color with the Eyedropper tool to use for my thought bubble. The Sample Size drop-down list allows you to select color from a single point, or average a color based on 3 pixels or 5 pixels.

Figure 3.6. A photo with the Eyedropper tool selected and Sample Size.

After you have selected your foreground color, it will automatically be used in any tool that uses the foreground color swatch in the Toolbox. Using the Eyedropper tool also automatically changes the foreground in the Colors palette. I created the thought bubble in Figure 3.5 by selecting a color and then painting a thought bubble with the Brush tool. Now it's your turn to try the Eyedropper tool.

Pick a color to use as a thought bubble:

1. Open a photo.

2. Select the Eyedropper tool in the Toolbox or type the letter I.

3. Click a light spot in your photo to pick a light shade for your bubble. You should see the foreground color change in the Toolbox.

4. If you're not quite happy, keep clicking around until you have a color you like. Try increasing your sampling size to get a better result.

5. Choose Layer ⇨ New ⇨ Layer to create a separate layer for your thought bubble.

6. Switch to the Brush tool by clicking it in the Toolbox or pressing the letter B.

7. In the Options bar on the top of the screen, change your diameter to something bubble-like and change your hardness setting to 100%.

8. Click your brush around in a circle or ellipse, slightly overlapping your last brush stroke. Fill in any empty spots in the middle of your bubble.

9. In Figure 3.6, I used a slightly smaller brush diameter to create the bubbles connecting the thought bubble to my subject. Add yours however you like.

Now you have a cool thought bubble in a complementary color to your photo.

Coloring text with the Eyedropper tool

You can use the Eyedropper tool every time you use the Color Picker window. With the Color Picker open, your cursor automatically changes to the Eyedropper tool when you mouse over your image. In Figure 3.7, I've selected a color for my text element using the Color Picker window and the Eyedropper tool.

Figure 3.7. The Color Picker window launched from the Text tool color swatch.

Now create some colored text using a complementary color from a photo:

1. Open a photo you would like to add text to.

2. Select the Horizontal Type tool and enter some text.

3. Click and drag with your mouse across your text to highlight it.

4. Choose a font and make the font size nice and big. In Figure 3.7 I've set mine to 48-pt Myriad Bold.

5. In the Type tool Options bar at the top of the screen, click the color thumbnail to open a Color Picker window and arrange it so you can see most of your photo behind it.

6. Move your mouse over your photo. You should see your cursor turn to an Eyedropper tool.

7. Choose a color for your text. If your text is over a dark area, select a light part of your photo to complement it, or vice versa.

By picking a color from within your photo, you'll achieve a more natural look and the sampled color will blend in much better with the image than if you were to choose an arbitrary color.

Sharing colors among files

The foreground and background colors in your Toolbox are available to all Photoshop documents, not just your currently open one. This makes sharing colors between files a piece of cake. Choosing a color from another file using the Eyedropper tool changes the foreground color swatch, and that color can be used in any Photoshop document until it's replaced with a new color.

Exploring the Color Picker window

Adobe's Color Picker window will probably be one of your most-used pieces of Photoshop, so it's worth spending a few minutes to go over its features. You've already gotten a sneak peak by using the Eyedropper tool to select an existing color. Now look at the Color Picker and all of its details in Figure 3.8.

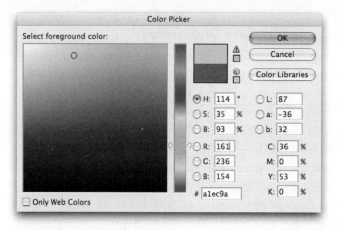

Figure 3.8. The Color Picker window.

Try selecting colors using the Color Picker window:

1. Keep the Hue radio button selected.

   To pick a color hue, click inside the color slider in the middle of the Color Picker window. This changes the display in the Color field box on the left side of the Color Picker.

2. In the Color field box, click to select a hue and saturation setting. You'll see the values under S and B change as you click around.

   If you check the Web Safe Colors Only check box, you'll be able to choose only from a Web-safe palette of 216 colors.

3. Click around in the Color field box until you see an icon with an exclamation point in a triangle. This warning icon means that if you convert your image to CMYK mode, there isn't an equivalent color in the CMYK color space to match it. If you plan to convert your image to CMYK, click the icon to have the Color Picker select the closest available color that converts well to CMYK.

Choosing a color based on hue is just one of many ways you can choose colors in the Color Picker window. Clicking the radio buttons for the other values changes the Color Picker display so that you can choose your colors from a wide variety of ways.

Is Web-Safe Color Dead?

The Web-safe palette was created in the late 1990s when many computer monitors could display only a very limited range of 256 colors. Some of the more delicate colors, especially very light ones, would wind up looking pretty wacky on less sophisticated monitors, so the palette was shrunk to 216 extensively tested colors. Choosing colors from a Web-safe palette meant you were assured your Web design would look good on any computer. Since then, most computers can now display millions of colors. Even PDAs and other portable wireless devices can display 16,000 colors or more. The Web-safe color palette and its 216 monitor-friendly colors have become a bit of a dinosaur. When I last checked, the average number of computers connected to the Internet using 256 colors was 0 percent, give or take a few fractions of a percent. Some people argue that there are still benefits to using a Web-safe palette. When dealing with non-Web-safe colors, monitors displaying at 16 bit display slightly different colors that on a 24-bit monitor. Some say that using Web-safe colors give you the most consistent colors across all monitors. I say, realize it's not a perfect world and use whatever colors you want. Matching color from monitor to monitor is a difficult if not impossible task. Your best bet is to test out your color choices on a few different monitors and operating systems.

Picking foreground and background colors

Photoshop has two different color swatches available in the Toolbox. The top one is for foreground color, and the bottom one is for, you guessed it, background color. The foreground color is what Photoshop uses for any coloring activities such as using brushes for adding text. The background color can be used to create a fill, add a stroke, or fill your screen with a background color.

The little black and white images to the bottom left of the swatches are for setting the colors back to Photoshop's default black and white. The arrows on the top right of the swatches allow you to switch the foreground and background colors.

Try using key commands to fill your screen or a selection with either the foreground or the background color:

1. Create a new document in RGB color.

2. Create a new background color by clicking the background swatch in the Toolbox and choosing a new color from the Color Picker.

3. Create a new foreground color by clicking the foreground swatch in the Toolbox and choosing a new color from the Color Picker.

4. Try using the key command ⌘+Delete (Ctrl+Delete) to fill the current layer with the background color.

5. Create a new layer by choosing Layer ⇨ New ⇨ Layer.

6. Switch to the Marquee tool and drag it inside your document to create a rectangular selection.

7. To fill your selection automatically with the foreground color, press Option+Delete (Alt+Delete).

The Color palette also has swatches for foreground and background color. Figure 3.9 shows the Color palette with the options drop-down list visible. You can modify your foreground or background color in the Color palette by clicking the foreground or background swatch to select it and adjusting or clicking in the sliders for each color channel.

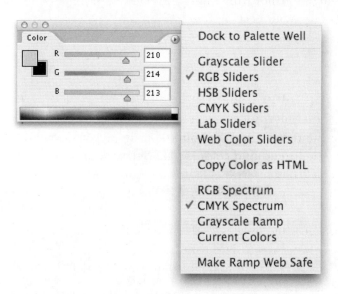

Figure 3.9. The Color palette and options drop-down list.

Saving custom swatches and styles

Once you start getting into designing with lots of colors, you'll quickly discover that having just background and foreground colors is not enough. You'll probably want to save several custom colors and have them at the ready. The Swatches palette does just this, as well as offering you an assortment of color menus to choose from. By adding new color swatches, you can save as many custom colors as you like.

To add and rename a few custom colors, perform the following steps:

1. Choose a new foreground color by clicking the foreground color thumbnail in the Toolbox and selecting from the Color Picker.

2. Click the New Swatch icon on the bottom right of the Swatches palette.

3. To rename it, right-click your new swatch and select Rename Swatch from the drop-down menu seen in Figure 3.10.

Now that you've added your swatch, you can click it to make it the current foreground or text color.

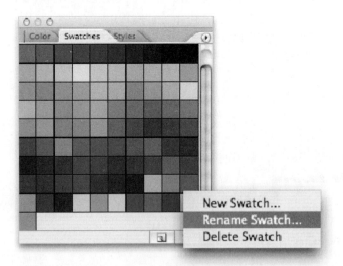

Figure 3.10. The Swatches palette with Swatch Options drop-down list.

Inside Scoop

Change your swatch view to include the swatch's name by clicking the top right arrow in the Swatches palette and selecting Small List from the top of the drop-down menu.

Creating and sharing custom swatch sets

You can create and save a custom swatch set for safe keeping. Photoshop stores the information about your swatch set in a special file format. These files will work for anyone using Photoshop CS2. This means that, just by copying the file to another computer running CS2, you can share and load custom palettes with friends and co-workers. This can come in very handy in a large company that uses standard colors and has several designers creating artwork for Web, video, or print.

Here's how to save your color swatch sets:

1. From the Swatches palette, click the little arrow on the top right and select Save Swatches.

2. You can name and save your swatch file anywhere, but if you save it in the Adobe Photoshop CS2/Presets/Swatches folder inside your Applications folder (Program Files folder), it automatically loads into the swatches list the next time you launch Photoshop. Figure 3.11 shows the Save Swatches dialog box.

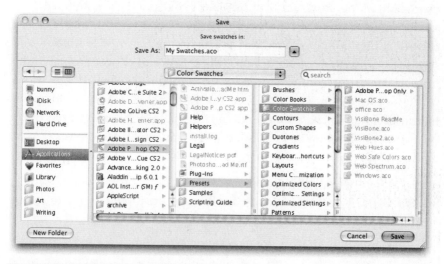

Figure 3.11. Save Swatches dialog box.

Bright Idea!

You can share swatch sets within any other CS2 Creative Suite product by selecting Save Swatches for Exchange from the drop-down list accessed through the little arrow on the top right of the Swatches palette.

After you've saved your swatch set file, you can share your file with other Photoshop users:

1. Locate your saved swatch set file on your hard drive.

2. Add it as an attachment to an e-mail to a friend or coworker, or copy your swatch set file to your coworker's computer.

If they would like the swatch to load automatically whenever Photoshop launches, instruct them to place the file in the Presets/Color Swatches folder inside your Photoshop CS2 Applications folder.

A simpler way of loading swatch sets is by selecting Load Swatches from the swatch options menu, available by clicking the arrow at the top right of the Swatches palette. Be aware that you have to load the swatches explicitly each time you launch Photoshop if they are not located in the Presets/Color Swatches folder in your Photoshop Applications folder.

Adding shadows and emboss effects to layers

You can add blending options to layers to spice up an image's text with drop shadows, beveling, gradient overlays, strokes, and glow. Right-clicking a layer's name brings up the layer options drop-down list, in which you can select Blending Options. This brings up the Layer Style window and shows you a list of blending options, where you can choose from a multitude of effects for adding dimension to your images. Figure 3.12 shows you examples of some of the effects you can achieve. You could spend half a lifetime playing with blending options. The next example introduces you to blending options by adding a Pattern Overlay to text.

To add a Pattern Overlay to a text element:

1. Create a new file in RGB color mode.

2. Select the Type tool from the Toolbox, or press the letter T to select it using the key command.

3. Click anywhere in your document and type your favorite word.

4. Drag your mouse over your newly typed word and make your font nice and big: Choose 72 pt from the drop-down list in the Options bar at the top of the page. Change your font weight to bold.

5. Press Enter to accept your new text addition.

Figure 3.12. Examples of blending options.

6. Right-click your text layer in the Layers palette and select Blending Options from the drop-down list. The Layer Style window appears with a list of blending modes.

7. Click the check box in front of Pattern Overlay to select it.

8. Click the words Pattern Overlay to open the options for it. Figure 3.13 shows the Pattern Overlay options.

9. Click the Pattern drop-down list and select a pattern.

10. Click OK to save your new blending option.

These patterns are just the small list of default patterns that come with Photoshop. If you click the little black arrow in the Pattern submenu, you'll see a list of additional patterns to choose from. There are tons of free patterns available for download from the Internet. See the resources section in the back of this book for some Web sites where you can find free patterns. Figure 3.13 shows the Blending Modes dialog box with Pattern Overlay options displayed.

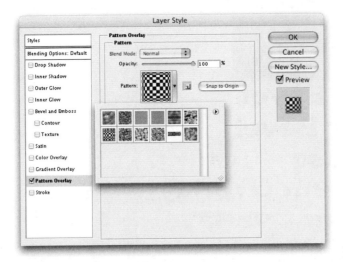

Figure 3.13. Pattern Overlay blending options.

Adding to the Styles menu

Styles are groups of blending options that combine several options like drop shadow, inner glow, and color overlay. Styles can be a combination of several styles, or just one style. Photoshop comes with tons of styles to choose from, or you can create and save your own custom styles. They offer quick and easy ways of adding drop shadows, outlines, and texture to text or objects.

Quickly saving styles to the Styles palette

Any time you create a blending option that you'd like to save for future use, you can add it to the Styles palette by clicking the New Style button on the bottom of the styles palette, as shown in Figure 3.14. A new style will be added to the bottom of the menu and can be applied to any new layer by clicking the new style.

Figure 3.14. Styles palette with hovering text below New Style button.

Replacing and appending style sets

By clicking the black arrow on the top right of the Styles palette, you can replace or add styles. Try adding a few sets in the next exercise.

To add style sets to your Styles palette:

1. Click the black arrow on the top right of the Styles palette to view the Styles palette options, as shown in Figure 3.15.

2. Select Glass Buttons from the list of styles.

3. A dialog box appears with the message "Replace current styles with the styles from Glass Buttons.afl?" Click the Append button to add them to your currently available styles.

Glass Buttons is one of my favorites for creating candy-like buttons for Web sites. To try it out, select the Rounded Rectangle tool from the Toolbox, create a button, and click the various Glass Button styles.

Figure 3.15 Shows the Styles palette and palette options drop-down list.

Resetting to Photoshop's default styles

Don't worry, if you get the Styles menu all jumbled up by trying out different style sets and want to start fresh, you can just select Reset Styles from the little black arrow in the Styles palette. A dialog box appears that offers you the option to save or ignore your current styles and either append your current style set with the default one, or completely replace your current style set with the default style set.

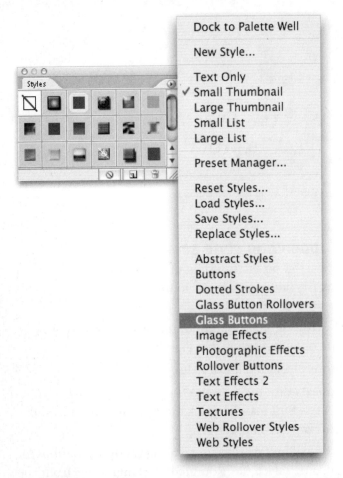

Figure 3.15. The Styles palette with the style options drop-down list visible.

Just the facts

- Choose RGB for Web graphics, CD-ROM or DVD artwork, and inkjet printing.

- CMYK color mode is best for color laser printing, professional printing, and page layout programs.

- Save a custom color palette and share it with others.

- Add drop shadows and embossing effects with Blending Options.

- Select the right color mode for your content.

Putting the Graphics Tools to Work

PART II

GET THE SCOOP ON...
Layering transparent elements ▪ Adding style to
buttons and text ▪ Aligning multiple layers ▪ Sharing
elements between files ▪ Adjusting color without
destroying your art

Embracing Layers

T o get an idea of just how revolutionary Photoshop layers are, let's go back in time to a darker period in Photoshop's history. Photoshop was first developed in the late 1980s as a pixel-based paint program. It consisted of a single layer of pixels. If you opened a digital photo in Photoshop and added some paint strokes or text, it would overwrite the pixels underneath, destroying parts of your original photo: After you painted some brush strokes, they were there for good. If you later tried to move the paint strokes, you'd be left with a white patch, the shape of your selection. In addition, you couldn't scale objects independently, or change the opacity of an object. It was very much like painting on a canvas: What you put down covers up what's underneath permanently.

In 1996, Photoshop 3.0 introduced a very new way of creating imagery. With the introduction of layers, you could now keep your type separate from your photo, and you could stack your elements on several transparent layers, much like overlaying acetate sheets. If one of those sheets isn't cutting the mustard, you just simply remove it from the stack. If you want to rearrange the order of your layers, you just move them up and down your list of layers.

I'm telling you all of this not because I want you to feel sorry for those who came before you, but because I see many new Photoshop users avoiding layers. At first glance, layers can seem confusing and cumbersome. They may take a little time to get used to, but learning to use them right from the start is going to save you a lot of heartache down the road.

This chapter introduces you to working with layers and teaches you some nice tricks for creating exciting layered compositions. You'll also learn how to move and align multiple layers at once by linking them. Photoshop CS2 introduced a huge leap forward in layer management; you'll find out some cool new ways of organizing your layers into layer groups.

Working with multiple layers

Working with layers is much like arranging sheets of acetate, but with much more flexibility. You can scale them, duplicate them, add effects, change their opacity, or modify their color. You can group them together into folders or link them so that you can move them together as one layer. You can perform nondestructive adjustments to color, brightness, and contrast on adjustment layers so you can keep your original artwork edit free.

To get a better idea of how layers work, look at an example with a few simple layers. Figure 4.1 contains three layers. The layers are listed in the Layers palette on the right of the screen. The top layer, named Bunny Moon, is a text layer that includes a Bevel and Emboss effect. The second layer, named Clouds, is a photo of clouds that I used to add a little texture. If you click it, then look at the opacity setting on the top right of the palette, you'll see it's set to 30% opacity. This allows the dark blue background to show through. The third layer is a solid-colored fill layer.

Figure 4.1. Three simple layers.

To create a few layers from a photo, follow these steps:

1. Open a photo or JPEG file on your computer to use as your base. Any file from a digital camera will do.

2. Your file probably has just one locked Background layer. Double-click its thumbnail in the Layers palette to rename it and unlock it.

3. Click the Horizontal Type tool in the Toolbox. You can also high-light it by pressing the letter T.

4. Click inside your document and type something. You'll notice that a new text layer was automatically created when you started typing.

5. Choose Edit ➪ Select All to select your text, and then change the text size to something nice and big like 48 or 72 points. Press Enter when you are done formatting your text to accept the changes.

6. Click the Create New Fill or Adjustment Layer button on the bottom of the Layers palette. It looks like a half white, half black circle. Choose Solid Color from the top of the drop-down list.

7. A Color Picker window appears (see Figure 4.2). Choose a color and click OK.

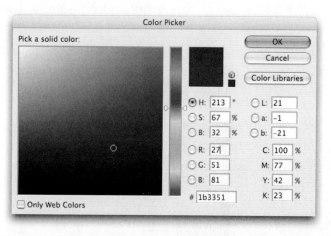

Figure 4.2. Color Picker window for choosing a solid color for a fill layer.

Watch Out!

The key command for selecting the layer directly under your cursor has changed in CS2. Instead of ⌘+clicking the layer, you now need to use ⌘+Option+Ctrl+click (Ctrl+Alt+right-click). To select from a list of layers, use ⌘+Ctrl+click (Ctrl+right-click).

8. At this point, your solid color layer may be on top of your photo image. To have it appear below your photo, click the solid color layer and drag it underneath your photo layer in the Layers palette to change its position in the stack.

9. Change the opacity of your photo layer by clicking it in the Layers palette to select it and then moving the Opacity slider to the right until it gets to about 30%.

Your photo is now semitransparent so you can see the solid color background behind it. The text should be the top layer in the list, so it should appear on top of all three layers.

Create duplicates of your layers

Keeping backups of your images is always a good plan. You might run into a situation where you want to try several different effects on the same image. By duplicating a layer several times, you'll have several copies to compare.

There are two ways to duplicate a layer. Open a digital photo or JPEG file and then complete one of the following steps:

■ Click and drag the layer you want to copy onto the New Layer icon on the bottom of the Layers palette, shown highlighted in Figure 4.3

■ Choose Layer ⇨ Duplicate Layer to create and name a copy of your highlighted layer.

Inside Scoop

Use Layer ⇨ Duplicate Layer and select a new file or other open Photoshop file as your destination.

Figure 4.3. Duplicating layers via the Create New Layer icon.

Making layer groups

Now that you've embraced the power of layers, you've probably noticed how quickly they can add up. Lucky for you, Photoshop CS2 has added some great new improvements to its layer organization capabilities. Previously called "layer sets," CS2's new Layer Groups are a giant improvement. With layer sets, you used to have only one level of folders. Now, with Layer Groups, you can nest multiple folders inside one another. This is a great feature when you are dealing with tons of layers, and it especially comes in handy when designing a multi-page Web site.

There are a couple of ways to create Groups. Here is the easiest way:

1. Click the folder icon on the bottom of the Layers palette to create a new Layer Group.

2. Drag your layers into your newly created Layer Group.

A quicker and easier way automatically creates a group with your selected layers inside:

1. Select all the layers you'd like to add to a group by ⌘+clicking to select them.

2. Press ⌘+G to create a new group. The layers will automatically be added.

Just like regular layers, you can move groups up and down the layer list by dragging them. The arrow to the right of your group's icon expands and collapses the contents inside. To remove a layer from within a group, just drag it outside the folder, back to the main layer list, or into another group. To nest a group inside another group, simply drag it inside another group.

I've added two different groups in Figure 4.4. You can quickly turn entire groups on and off to see different designs. Now it's your turn to create a few layers and group them together.

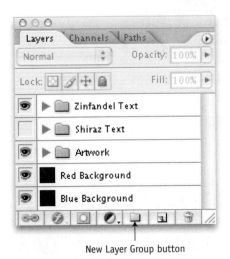

New Layer Group button

Figure 4.4. Layers palette with two different Layer Groups.

To create four layers and add them to new groups:

1. Create two different text layers with different content.

2. Click the Create New Fill or Adjustment Layer button on the bottom of the Layers palette and choose Solid Color.

3. Create another solid color fill layer, but use a different color.

4. Drag the text layers above the solid color layers so that you can see the text.

5. Click the first text layer to select it, and then ⌘+click (Ctrl+click) on the first solid color layer to add it to the selection.

6. Press ⌘+G (Ctrl+G) to group the first text and solid color layers together.

Inside Scoop

Copy an entire group to a new file by choosing Duplicate Group and selecting New from the document drop-down list.

Repeat these steps with the second text and solid color layers.

You've now created your first Groups. Now try viewing and organizing them by following these steps:

1. Double-click the Group names to rename them.

2. Toggle the Visibility icon in first group to hide it. The Visibility icon looks like an eyeball. You'll be able to see the contents of the second group.

3. Turn the visibility back on for the first group. Click the Group folder icon and change its opacity to 30% using the opacity slider on the top of the Layer palette. Your first group becomes semitransparent.

4. Click and drag the second group above the first. Be careful not to drop it inside the first group.

This is just a taste of what you can do with Groups. You can have multiple groups inside a group. If you right-click a group icon, you can open the Group Properties window to add a colored label to your group, so that you can easily find it in the list (see Figure 4.5). You can also control the visibility of the color channels in your document. This great feature comes in handy when you need to create color separations for professional printing.

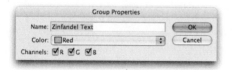

Figure 4.5. The Group Properties window.

Linking and aligning layers

In the last exercise, you created two text layers and placed them in two different groups. What if you wanted to make changes across several layers of text? Even though the text layers live in different groups, you want to make sure that if you reposition the first text layer, the second text layer follows suit. The best way to do this is by linking the layers. Even if one of the linked layers isn't visible, it moves right along with the visible one.

Try it. Using the Layer Groups example, try linking the two text layers you created by following these steps:

1. Click the first text layer.

2. ⌘+click the second text layer. Both layers should now be highlighted.

3. On the bottom of the Layers palette is a link icon that looks like a piece of chain. Click this icon to link your layers together.

   You should see a link icon appear next to the each layer's name (see Figure 4.6).

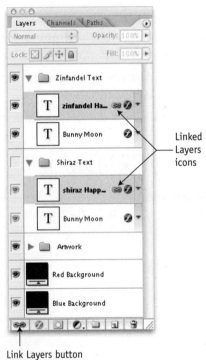

Link Layers button

Figure 4.6. Linked text in the Layers palette.

4. Click the first text layer to select it.

5. Press the letter V to switch to the Move tool, or select it from the top right of the Toolbox.

Hack

Temporarily switch to the Move tool at any time by pressing and holding the ⌘ key (Ctrl key). As long as ⌘ key (Ctrl key) is pressed, you can drag the currently highlighted layer around.

6. Click and drag the first text in your document window to a new location on the screen.

7. Hide the first text group by clicking the group's Visibility icon.

8. Show the second text group. The Shiraz text has also moved to the new location.

While you are using the Move tool, make sure that the two text layers you just linked are aligned. The Options bar for the Move tool has six options for aligning objects and six options for evenly distributing objects. The first three alignment buttons control vertical alignment, the last three alignment buttons control the horizontal alignment. The distribution buttons will only be activated when three or more layers are selected. See Table 4.1 for a list of alignment and distribution options. Hold your cursor over any button to see its title. Make both the first and second text layers visible so you can check their alignment.

Table 4.1. Align and distribute buttons in the Move tool Options bar

Button	Alignment/Distribution Option
	Align top edges
	Align vertical centers
	Align bottom edges
	Align left edges
	Align horizontal centers
	Align right edges

continued

Table 4.1. *continued*

Button	Alignment/Distribution Option
	Distribute top edges
	Distribute vertical centers
	Distribute bottom edges
	Distribute left edges
	Distribute horizontal centers
	Distribute right edges

To align your linked text layers, follow these steps:

1. Making sure one of the linked layers is highlighted, click the first horizontal align button to align top edges.

2. Click the second vertical align button to align horizontal centers.

As you might have noticed, there is an abundance of alignment buttons in the Move tool's Options bar. Try the other.

Spicing up layers with bevels and shadows

Add some dimension to your designs by taking advantage of Photoshop's layer styles and blending options. Photoshop CS2 comes equipped with easy tools for adding drop shadows, bevels, color overlays, and textures. You can create your own or choose from a large assortment of preset styles. You can also save your own styles for use in other layers or files.

Adding bevels, overlays, and shadows

There are gobs of blending options available with Photoshop CS2, and the best way to be acquainted with them is to play around. Create a new file and try some of them out.

1. Choose File ⇨ New or press ⌘+N to open the New File dialog box.

2. Create a file that is 500 x 300 pixels.

3. Press the letter T to select the Type tool, or click it in the Toolbox.

4. Click anywhere in the file and type your favorite word; mine is "sandwich."

5. Make sure the type is nice and big by selecting it and increasing the font size from the Font Size drop-down list just below the menu bar.

6. Right-click your new text layer in the Layers palette and choose Blending Options.

Welcome to Photoshop CS2's Layer Style dialog box (as shown in Figure 4.7). Clicking any of the check boxes next to each blending option turns the option on and off. Go ahead; click some check boxes to try them out. You can have many options turned on at the same time, or just one.

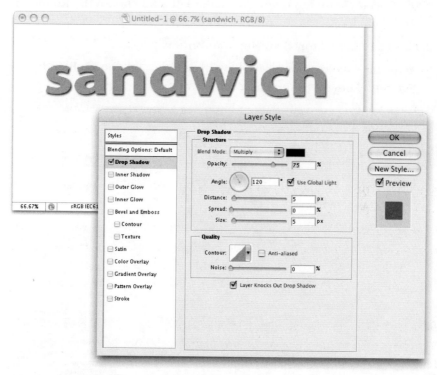

Figure 4.7. The Photoshop CS2 Drop Shadow blending option.

Click Drop Shadow to edit its options. Play around with opacity, angle, distance, and size until you get something you like. As long as the Preview box is checked on the right side of the Layer Style window, you'll be able to see your changes take affect. Each blending option has several settings and I'd put you to sleep trying to explain them all. If you are curious about a certain option, mousing over its name opens a short description of what it does.

Creating your own layer styles

A layer style is a saved combination of blending options and effects. Photoshop CS2 comes with some preset layer styles that are great for making quick buttons or adding a little zing to text. First, have a little fun and create some buttons using Photoshop's preset layer styles.

1. After creating a fresh, new file to play around in, click and hold on the Rectangle tool to open its flyout menu and choose the Rounded Rectangle icon.

2. Create a nice button shape for your button.

3. Right-click the name of your new shape layer and choose Blending Options. This opens the Layer Style window (see Figure 4.8).

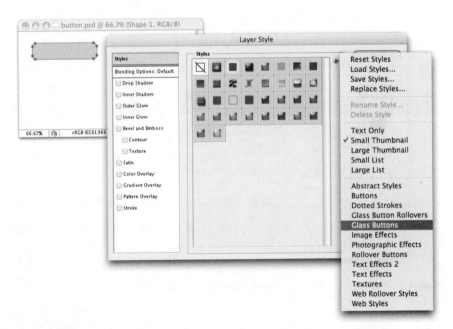

Figure 4.8. Layer Style dialog box with style presets list visible.

4. On the left side of the screen you'll see styles and blending options. Click Styles to display the preset layer groups.

5. Click the little arrow to the right of the style thumbnails to open the Style Options drop-down list.

6. Choose Buttons from the list and click OK to replace the current set.

This gives you a few fun options to play with. Mousing over the style thumbnails displays the name of each style. I like the third from the left, the Bevel Normal style.

7. Click the Bevel Normal style and you should see your button take on a nice bevel effect.

If you hadn't noticed, each time you click a preset style, the check boxes under blending options turn on and off depending on the style. You can fine-tune your style from here by going into each blending option. First, soften the bevel a little.

1. Click Bevel and Emboss to make some modifications to your bevel style.

2. Change the Size to 6 pixels and set the Soften controls to 5 pixels. This results in a softer look (see Figure 4.9).

Figure 4.9. Button with modified Bevel Normal style.

3. Save this style for use in future layers. Click the New Style button and name your new style My Soft Button.

Make sure you select the check boxes for Include Layer Effects and Include Layer Blending Options.

Inside Scoop

Press the letter U to select the Rectangle tool from the Toolbox. Pressing Shift+U cycles through the different tools under the Rectangle tool flyout menu.

You've now added your own Layer Style that can be used any time by clicking it either in the Layer Styles dialog box or the Styles palette. Your new style always appears at the bottom of the list.

You can save your own file full of your custom style presets and load them into other Photoshop files or share them with others. After you've gathered up all the styles you'd like to keep, choose Save Styles from the Layer Style options drop-down list. Name your file something meaningful like My Button Styles.asl and save this file inside the folder Photoshop CS2 ⇨ Presets ⇨ Styles (Program Files\Adobe\Adobe Photoshop CS2\Presets\Styles). Photoshop looks for styles in this folder, so it is important you save your ASL files to the right place. If you are having trouble finding the folder, try searching your hard drive for files with an .asl file extension. To see your full file browser on a Mac, click the arrow next to the name field in the Save Styles dialog box (see Figure 4.10). To load this style set later, choose Load Styles from the Layer Style options drop-down list and find your saved styles file.

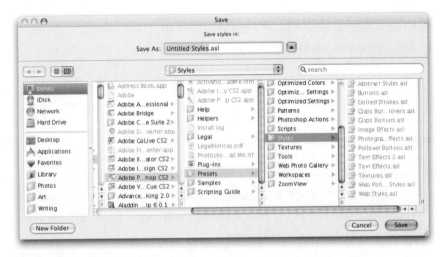

Figure 4.10. The Save Styles dialog box.

Photoshop CS2 comes with some nice layer styles for creating buttons. I encourage you to load up as many styles as you want. To see several sets at once, just click the Append button to add them to the current list of styles. You can always tidy up later by choosing Reset Styles from the Style Options drop-down list.

Changing a layer's visibility

You have some options when it comes to how much of a layer you want to show. The Visibility icon (shown in Figure 4.11) to the left of each layer means the layer is currently visible. Clicking it turns off a layer's visibility so you can keep it around without having to see it. This is great when you want to try out some options on a layer. By duplicating a layer several times and then applying different blending options to each copy, you can toggle each layer's visibility on and off to see the results of your experiments. Toggling visibility also comes in handy when you are designing a Web site: You can design all the pages at once and only have the elements from one page visible. ⌘+clicking (Ctrl+clicking) the Visibility icon brings up a few more options for showing and hiding layers, including the ability to hide all but the selected layer. This is great for quickly isolating a layer for precision editing.

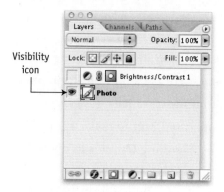

Visibility icon

Figure 4.11. The Visibility icon in the Layers palette.

You can control the amount of opacity on a layer by using the opacity slider on the top of the layers palette:

1. Select the layer you'd like to change.

2. Click the opacity percentage field; a little slider appears.

3. Type a specific amount into the percentage field, move the slider with your mouse, or use your keyboard's up and down arrows to change the percentage in tiny increments.

4. Place your semitransparent layer on top of a solid one and the layer underneath shows through.

The fill control is similar to opacity, but changing this setting affects only the object or text layer and leaves the layer effects as they are. This comes in handy when you want to separate a layer's effects completely from the actual artwork. I've used this when I want to play with the positioning of a text layer's drop shadow. You can also create a cool ghost text effect (shown in Figure 4.12) by adding blending options to text and then changing the fill to 0%. This works especially great when layering text over photos.

Figure 4.12. Ghost text effect with a Fill setting of 100% and a drop shadow applied.

Try creating some text with 0% fill and a drop shadow ghosting effect.

1. Press the letter T to select the Type tool, or click it in the Toolbox.

2. Create a text layer and make your font nice and big.

3. Right-click the layer and choose Duplicate Layer to make a copy.

4. Right-click the copy layer and choose Blending Options to open the Layer Styles window.

5. Create a nice drop shadow. After you have completed your masterpiece, click OK.

6. Set this layer's fill to 0% and move the layer away from its master a little bit so you can differentiate the two.

What you should see is a drop shadow with invisible "ghost" text. Now you can either offset it or use it all by itself. One great way to use this effect is layered on a photo. Because it creates a less-intrusive text effect, your image won't be overpowered with text.

Inside Scoop

To hide all but one layer, Option+click the layer's Visibility (eyeball) icon; to show them all again, Option+click the layer's Visibility icon again.

Dragging and dropping layers between files

When you really start cooking on a design, you can wind up creating several different files full of your design experiments. Sometimes you'll want to use an image from one file or a layer style from another. Lucky for you, with Photoshop CS2 it's easy to drag and drop layers from one file to another.

1. To drag from one file to another, position your documents so you can see a little of both.

2. Click a layer's thumbnail to select it and drag it onto your other file window.

3. If you'd like it to drop into the same position, press and hold the Shift key while dragging.

Adding a group from another file is just as easy: Click the group's name to select it and drag it over to the other file. You'll have a copy of the group and all of its contents.

You can copy layer styles or blending options such as drop shadows or color overlays from one file to another by following these steps:

1. In the layer you'd like to copy, right-click the layer name to open the Layer Options drop-down list and choose Copy Layer Style.

2. Open the file you'd like to copy it to, right-click the layer, and choose Paste Layer Style.

3. If you accidentally drop it into the wrong layer, just click and drag it into the correct one.

You don't have to limit yourself to dragging between files. Copy Layer Styles within the same document by simply pasting your copied style to a different layer. You can also create copies of a layer within the same file by pressing and holding the Option key (Alt key) while dragging a layer up and down the list.

Watch Out!

Make sure your files are close in dimension and resolution. If you drag from a 72-dpi file to a 300-dpi file, your copied layer is going to look like it was scaled way down.

Nondestructive color correction with adjustment layers

You no longer have to modify your original artwork with Color Overlays or Brightness/Contrast adjustments. By adding an adjustment layer, you can add a transparent layer that corrects brightness, contrast, and color problems without touching your original work. You can create several different adjustment layers and control their opacity separately, giving you much more control.

Try adding a separate adjustment layer to a photo:

1. Open a photo or JPEG file.

2. Click the Create New Fill or Adjustment Layer button on the bottom of the Layers palette.

3. In the drop-down list, choose Brightness/Contrast. This creates a new layer and opens a Brightness/Contrast adjustment screen (see Figure 4.13).

Figure 4.13. The Brightness/Contrast adjustment layer.

4. Punch up the contrast to about 40 and click OK. Because the layer is still at 100% opacity, this might look a little harsh.

5. If you click the new adjustment layer in the Layers palette and change its opacity to something lighter, like 40%, you'll get a more subtle contrast adjustment.

The great part is that later on, if you decide you want a lower-contrast photo, or if you want an entirely different look, you can just discard the adjustment layer and you are left with your original, unfettered artwork.

Photoshop comes with some great photo filters for quick photo adjusting. Try them out by creating a new adjustment layer and choosing Photo Filter from the drop-down list. You'll see a dialog box with a list of filters to choose from (see Figure 4.14). You can customize the color even further by clicking the Color radio button, clicking the Color thumbnail, and choosing from the Color Picker. Adjust the color density with the slider and keep your highlights bright by selecting the Preserve Luminosity check box.

Figure 4.14. Photo Filter dialog box with list of available filters.

Here are a couple more tips for your adjustment layer tricks bag. If you have a photo that has too much contrast, you can create an invert adjustment layer and turn down the opacity to between 10% and 20%. Here's one of my favorite adjustment layer effects:

1. Create a threshold adjustment layer. You'll see a black-and-white rendered version of your photo in the threshold preview window.

2. Click OK and change the threshold layer to between 30% and 40%.

Now it's your turn. I encourage you to play around with adding adjustment layers of your own and modifying their opacity levels.

Just the facts

- Linking layers makes moving several layers at once easy.

- Grouping layers is a quick way to see several design variations with just a couple of mouse clicks.

- Reuse your favorite styles by copying and pasting them between files.

- Share artwork from other files by dragging and dropping it between files.

- Correct color without editing your original artwork by using adjustment layers.

GET THE SCOOP ON...
Creating buttons for Web designs ▪ Adding arrowheads
to lines ▪ Creating graphic illustrations from photos ▪
Designing retro '50s signs with vector shapes and styles

Drawing with Vector Tools

Photoshop's vector drawing tools are resolution independent and allow you to create rescalable shapes that retain crisp edges no matter how many times you reshape them. They are great for creating buttons or for drawing shapes to use as type guides, as covered later in Chapter 9. Just like any other layer, you can add blending options and styles to drawn shapes to create professional graphic elements for your designs.

I should warn you that although you can create simple illustrations with the vector tools, Photoshop is not meant to be a drawing program. Creating complex illustrations in Photoshop is not an easy or enjoyable task. For that purpose, Adobe Illustrator is king of the mountain. If you have Adobe Creative Suite and are interested in graphic illustration, I recommend learning Illustrator for more complicated vector drawing. It is just as powerful in the vector drawing arena as Photoshop is in the raster graphics world. That said, there is still an awful lot you can accomplish with Photoshop's drawing tools.

This chapter introduces you to the shape and line drawing tools available in Photoshop CS2. You'll create some button graphics for use on a Web site and design a retro '50s diner sign. You'll see how to trace a photo using the Freeform Pen tool to create a graphic illustration. Using the Custom Shapes library, you'll mask a photo into a fun shape.

Chapter 5

101

Buckle up and put on your patience cap: The drawing tools can be a load of fun but can also be frustrating to be accustomed to.

Drawing circles, squares, and lines

The shape tools include a Rectangle, Rounded Rectangle, Ellipse, Polygon, Line, and Custom Shape tool. You can create solid colored shapes or outlined shapes. By using the add or subtract to shape option, you can combine different shape tools to create more complex illustrations. When you are creating shapes, you have three different drawing options. Table 5.1 lists the different drawing options, their descriptions, and their uses.

Table 5.1. Drawing options and descriptions for use

Icon	Drawing Option	Description	Use
	Shape Layers	Creates a shape on a layer that can be edited with the Shape or Pen tools	Create rescalable graphics for Web or print; use blending options for adding styles and strokes
	Paths	Creates outlines that can be transformed into selections or filled and stroked with color	Create vector shapes for masking; manage paths in the Paths palette
	Fill Pixels	Paints pixel-based shapes that can't be edited after they are created	Use this as you would use the paint tools

Figure 5.1 shows the Shape tools flyout menu in the Toolbox.

The Line tool can create straight and diagonal lines. Press and hold the Shift key to constrain the tool to creating horizontal, vertical, and 45-degree lines. You can change the thickness of a line in the Options bar in the Weight field. Weight can be specified as inches (in), pixels (px), points (pt), centimeters (cm), or millimeters (mm).

Creating pill-shaped buttons with rounded rectangles

The Rounded Rectangle tool allows you to adjust the radius of your corners to control the size of the curve. If you are creating buttons for a Web design, increasing the radius gives you more rounded, pill-like buttons. The default radius is 10 pixels. To increase or decrease the amount of curve, select the Rounded Rectangle tool and increase the radius

Watch Out!

You can create a radius only as big as half of your rectangle. This gives you a circular side to your rectangle. If you draw a rectangle that is 80 pixels high, each corner can't have a radius larger than 40 pixels.

amount in the Radius field in the Options bar. I've created four rounded rectangles in Figure 5.2 of varying corner radiuses.

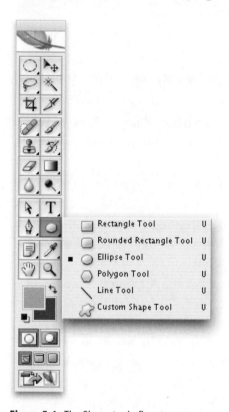

Figure 5.1. The Shape tools flyout menu.

Figure 5.2. Rounded rectangles with different corner radiuses.

Using the Rounded Rectangle tool and the button styles, create some buttons for a Web site design by following these steps:

1. Create a new Photoshop document in RGB color mode with a resolution of 72 dpi.

2. Select the Rounded Rectangle tool from the Toolbox. You can toggle to it by pressing Shift+U a couple times.

3. On the far left side of the Options bar, make sure the Shape Layers button is selected as the current Drawing Option.

4. Click the down arrow just left of the Radius text box to open the options for the Rounded Rectangle tool.

5. Choose Fixed size and enter 100 px for width and 20 px for height.

6. Change the radius value to 10. This results in rounded sides.

7. Click anywhere in your document to create a button. Because you selected Fixed size, you don't need to click and drag to create your button.

Now that you've gotten your button set up, load some of the button Style libraries by following these steps:

1. In the Options bar for the Rounded Rectangle tool, click the Styles drop-down list and click the black arrow on the top left of the drop-down list to show a list of style options.

2. Select Glass Buttons from the list. Click the Append button to add them to your current list of styles, or click Add to replace all your styles with the Glass Buttons Style library.

3. Try out a style. Click your button shape layer to highlight it. Now ⌘+click (Ctrl+click) the shape thumbnail in your Layer palette to select the shape.

4. Choose one of the styles from the Styles menu by clicking it.

5. Add text for your button with the Horizontal Type tool.

Watch Out!

If you try to add a text layer while your button layer is highlighted, your Type tool icon changes to the button text icon, with a circle around the insertion point. The button text option won't give you much control over text placement and I recommend against using it. Create your text separately, and then move it on top of your button.

In Figure 5.3, I've created several buttons by duplicating the first one. You can duplicate your button by dragging and dropping its layer thumbnail on top of the Create New Layer icon.

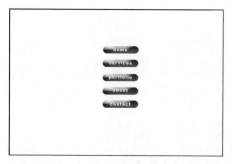

Figure 5.3. Buttons created with the Rounded Rectangle tool.

Creating instant arrowheads

The Line tool has a few options for creating arrowheads of different shapes and sizes. If you select the Line tool and then click the Shape Options drop-down list to the right of the Custom Shape icon in the Options bar, you'll see options for creating start and/or end arrowheads (see Figure 5.4). You can control the width, length, and concavity of your arrowheads.

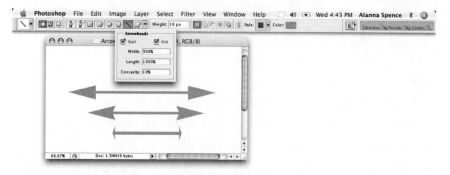

Figure 5.4. The Line tool with Arrowhead drop-down list.

Inside Scoop

Shrink, stretch, and rotate your arrow after you create it by choosing Edit ➪ Free Transform Path. Press Enter to accept your changes.

Exploring the custom shape libraries

Photoshop comes with tons of fun shapes that you can use as clip art for Web and print designs or digital collage. There are 13 shape libraries in all, which include things like animals, flowers, ornaments, picture frames, and common signs and symbols. Each one can be modified to suit your needs. You can load all of them into your list of custom shapes, as I've done in Figure 5.5, so that you can sample from all 13 sets.

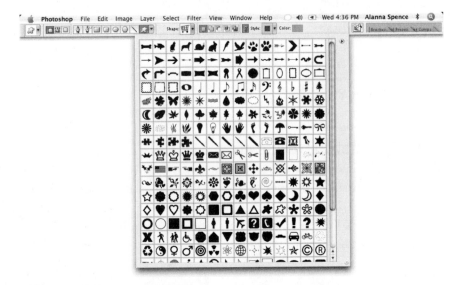

Figure 5.5. The Shapes drop-down list.

Load all of the available Custom Shapes into the Custom Shape tool:

1. Choose the Custom Shape tool from the drawing tools flyout menu. You can toggle to it by pressing Shift+Tab a few times. The Custom Shape tool icon looks like a wobbly, rounded star shape.

2. Click the Shape menu to view its contents.

3. Click the little arrow on the top right of the Shape drop-down list to show the options drop-down list and choose All from the list.

4. You'll see a dialog box asking you if you want to replace all the shapes. Click OK to replace your current list with a full list of all shapes.

All the shapes are now loaded. Try a few out. To draw an object from the center out, press and hold the Option key (Alt). Pressing and holding the Shift key constrains proportions. Click the drop-down menu next to

Bright Idea!

Enlarge your shape thumbnails by selecting Large Thumbnail from the Shape Options drop-down list.

the Custom Shape icon in the Options bar. This menu has an additional options menu for creating specific sizes and controlling proportion.

Creating and modifying shapes with Pen tools

The Pen tools in Photoshop give you the freedom to create vector shapes from scratch, or add, subtract, and modify points in a pre-existing shape. You can use them to create and edit both straight and curved shapes. Table 5.2 lists the Pen and Path tools and a brief description of what they do.

Figure 5.6 shows a line drawing and the Toolbox with the Pen tool fly-out menu visible.

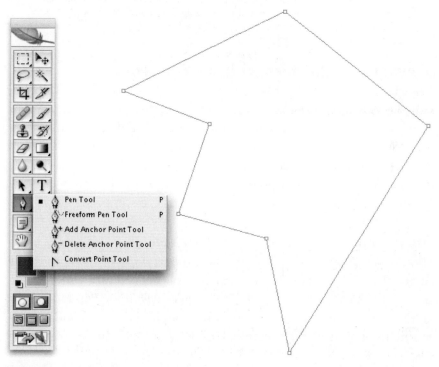

Figure 5.6. Toolbox with Pen tool flyout menu.

Table 5.2. Pen and Path tools

Icon	Tool	Description
	Pen	Creates straight or curved lines by clicking point to point for lines or clicking and dragging to create curves
	Freeform Pen	Click and drag to create curved lines — the tool automatically creates anchor points for you
	Add Anchor Point	Clicking a path line adds an anchor point
	Delete Anchor Point	Clicking a anchor point removes it
	Convert Anchor Point	Click a curved anchor point to convert it to a straight anchor point; click and drag a straight anchor point to convert it to a curved one
	Path Selection	Selects the entire path for moving, stretching, or shrinking
	Direct Selection	Selects a specific point to be moved separately from the entire path; Shift-select multiple points at once

Drawing straight lines with the Pen tool

By clicking point to point, you can create straight-edged lines and shapes with the Pen tool, just like connecting dots. After you've created your shape or line, you can move each point by pressing and holding the ⌘ key (Ctrl). When your cursor moves over a point, it temporarily changes to the Direct Selection tool. Move several points at once by ⌘+Shift+clicking (Ctrl+Shift+clicking) each point to add them to the currently selected points.

Converting straight lines into curves

The Convert Anchor Point tool can take the pain out of trying to create curved shapes from scratch with the Pen tool. You can turn a square into an oval much easier than you can create an oval with the Pen tool on the first try. In Figure 5.7, I've started with a simple star shape, and by converting the points of the star to curves, I've created a funky '60s flower shape.

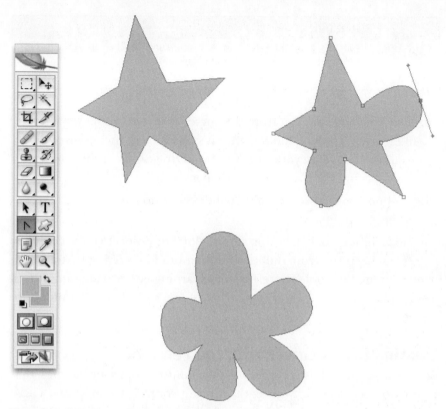

Figure 5.7. Shapes created with the Pen tool.

To create a star and turn it into a flower:

1. Open a new Photoshop document.

2. Select the Pen tool from the Toolbox or press the letter P to high-light it. Make sure the Shape Layers Drawing Option is highlighted in the Options bar.

3. Click to create a star shape. Be sure to close your shape by clicking the starting point. Your cursor will change to a Pen icon with a little circle next to it when you are hovering over your starting point.

4. Choose the Convert Anchor Point tool from the Pen tool flyout menu.

5. Click and drag one of the star points until you create a rounded petal for your flower.

Watch Out!

If you drag away from the point and your curve bunches up like a figure eight, drag in the other direction to untangle it.

6. The arms that stick out from the curve, as shown on the second star in Figure 5.7, will be hidden after it's unselected; they control the amount of curve in your line. Click and drag some of them to try out adjusting the curve of your shapes.

7. Continue converting straight anchor points to curves with the rest of the star points.

The technique of converting straight anchor points to curved anchor points can keep you from pulling your hair out when trying to draw free-hand with the Pen tool. There is a steep learning curve to creating curves from scratch, and this is a nice alternative method when you don't have time to mess around.

Creating Bézier curves with the Pen tool

Bézier curves are adjusted by moving the control points, or handles, that belong to each point in your path. You can control the angle and curve of your line by stretching, shrinking, and changing the angle of your control points. Even straight lines have control points, but in their case, they are hiding under the corner points for perfectly straight lines. To get them to appear when drawing a curved shape, you'll need to click and drag when creating a point. Figure 5.8 shows a typical Bezier curve with control points.

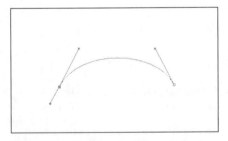

Figure 5.8. A Bezier curve with control points.

Creating curved lines with the Bezier curve can be a bit tough to do. The number one tip to creating objects with the Pen tools is to keep your thumb close to the ⌘ key (Ctrl) so that you can temporarily switch to the Direct Selection tool and adjust your curves as you go. The easiest way to explain Bezier curves and the Pen tool is by having you create some curves of your own.

To create a curved line with the Pen tool:

1. Create a new Photoshop Document. Double-click the Background layer to rename and unlock it.

2. Select the Pen tool from the Toolbox or press the letter P to high-light it.

3. Make sure the Paths Drawing Option is selected in the Options bar. It is the second one and looks like a Pen icon in a rectangle.

4. Switch to your Paths palette. If it's not visible, choose Window ⇨ Paths.

5. Click and drag your mouse up to create control points for your line.

6. Choose a place for the second point in your curve. Click and drag your mouse down to create a curved line.

7. To adjust your curve, press and hold the ⌘ key (Ctrl) and drag a control point in any direction to change the angle or length of your curve.

You've just created your first Bézier curve from scratch. That wasn't so bad, was it? I encourage you to play around; this tool takes time to get used to. Try out the Add Anchor Point and Delete Anchor Point tools by selecting them from the Pen tool flyout menu. Try adding an anchor point to the top of your curve and see what happens when you twist its control points around. Then, using the Delete Anchor Point, click it to remove it.

Bright Idea!

Preview your line before clicking to add anchor points. Select the Rubber Band check box in the Pen Options drop-down menu in the Pen tool's Options bar. Access the Pen Options by clicking the black arrow to the left of the Auto Add/Delete check box.

Easy curves with the Freeform Pen

No patience for creating your own point-to-point Bezier curves? The Freeform Pen does all the hard labor for you. This pen works like a real pen. Simply click and drag to create a curved line. Photoshop automatically creates the points in your line for you. After you've gotten roughly the line you want, you can modify it just as you did with the other curves by clicking points and either moving the points, or adjusting the arc of your curves with the control points. The tool tends to add extra anchor points that you don't need, so you can go in later with the Delete Anchor Point tool to streamline your drawing.

The Freeform Pen also gives you a Magnetic option where you can trace the shapes of other images just as you did with the Magnetic Lasso tool. This is a great way to create illustrated renditions of photos. Create outlined drawings of a photo and add stroke and fill. In Figure 5.9, I took a photo of a piece of cake and created separate shapes for the chocolate cake parts, the frosting areas, the strawberry, and the plate. I added highlight and shadow shapes to give it some depth. With this many shapes, organizing layers in the Layers palette was important to managing the shapes. Highlights and shadows are towards the top of my list of layers; background and base colors are underneath. This is a challenging exercise and if you haven't done so, I recommend reading Chapter 4 to get a strong grasp on Layer management.

Figure 5.9. An illustration created with the Freeform Pen tool.

To create an illustration from a photo:

1. Open a Photo to use as your design.

2. Select the Freeform Pen tool from the Pen tool's flyout menu, or press Shift+P to highlight it. It looks like the Pen tool with a curvy line coming out of the tip. Make sure the Shape Layers Drawing Option is selected in the Options bar.

3. Click a point in your photo and begin tracing around the image. Click to add a few points along the way. Be sure to close your shape by clicking the start point. Your cursor will have a circle icon next to it when you hover over the start point, indicating that if you click it, you will close the shape.

4. Don't worry if it's not a perfect trace. You can go in later and clean it up using the Direct Selection and Delete Anchor Point tools.

5. Double-click the Color thumbnail in the Layers palette and choose a new color for your shape.

6. Continue tracing the various shapes in your drawing.

7. You might need to hide larger layers in order to add shadow or highlight areas. To hide a layer, click the Visibility icon in the Layers palette. It looks like an eyeball.

8. Click and drag your different layers up and down the list in the Layers palette to arrange them correctly: background layers on the bottom of the list, foreground layers on the top.

9. Adjust any funky spots by ⌘+clicking (Ctrl+clicking) on parts and tweaking control points.

How did your design turn out? Don't worry if the first one doesn't turn out perfect. Getting the results you want might take a little practice, but it creates a nice effect and is a great way to design graphics for print, t-shirts, or the Web.

Bright Idea!

Limit your color palette for a more professional-looking design. Choose darker or lighter colors by clicking existing ones with the Eyedropper tool and lightening or darkening them slightly in the Color Picker.

Creating designs using shapes

This section looks at tweaking vector shapes created with any of Photoshop's drawing tools. You can modify any vector shape by using the Direct Selection tool on vector art created with any of the shape tools. For this section, you'll be stretching squares into oddly shaped rectangles to create a retro '50s sign.

Create a retro '50s sign

Combine what you've learned and make a cool sign using a combination of shapes and blending options. The sign in Figure 5.10 uses the Rectangle tool, the Line tool, the Direct Selection tool, the Custom Shape tool, and the Ellipse tool. It might look complicated, but it's mostly just a lot of copying and pasting. This is an advanced tutorial and works under the assumption you are familiar with the Blending Options dialog box. For more about blending options, see Chapter 3.

Figure 5.10. A retro sign created with Shape tools.

Create a few oddly shaped rectangles for our retro sign:

1. Select the Rectangle tool. Draw a rectangle that is slightly longer than it is wide.

2. Switch to the Direct Selection tool by pressing Shift+A once or twice until your cursor changes to a white cursor.

3. Click one of the top corners of your rectangle. Stretch it up and out just a bit to create a slightly angled corner. Repeat for the other top corner.

4. Right-click the layer's color thumbnail and select Blending Options.

5. Add a Drop Shadow. Increase the Distance and Size; decrease the Opacity to about 50%.

6. Add an Inner Shadow. To get the double-ringed effect like you see in Figure 5.10, choose Ring-Double from the Contour drop-down list. Increase the Choke to 10% and the Size to 8 pixels. Decrease the Opacity to about 25%.

7. Add a 1-pixel black stroke.

8. Drag and drop your rectangle shape layer onto the Create New Layer icon in your Layers palette to make a copy.

9. Click the newly copied layer and select Edit ⇨ Transform ⇨ Rotate 180°.

10. Move the newly copied layer to the right of the first rectangle. Press and hold the ⌘ key (Ctrl) to temporarily change to the Move tool, and then click and drag your copied rectangle.

11. Make additional copies of each shape layer and arrange them as you like.

12. Change the color of each rectangle. Double-click the color thumbnail for each shape layer and click the color swatch in the Options bar.

Now that you have your basic sign, you can add some type. Don't limit yourself to Bowl-O-Rama: What about making a sign for a scrapbook or photo album? What about Steve's Scrap-O-Rama?

To add type to your sign:

1. Select the Horizontal Type tool. Click inside your document and type a letter for your sign. Move it over your rectangle.

2. Right-click your new type layer and choose Blending Options.

Inside Scoop

Copy layer styles by right-clicking a layer and choosing Copy Layer Styles. Right-click the target layer and choose Paste Layer Styles.

3. Add an Inner Glow. Select Ring-Double from the Contour drop-down list (see Figure 5.11).

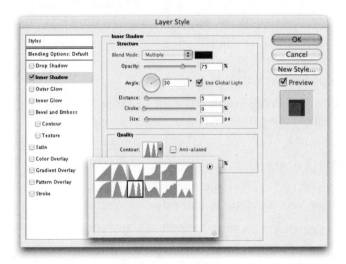

Figure 5.11. The Ring-Double Inner Shadow style in the Blending Options dialog box.

4. Copy your text layer by dragging and dropping it onto the Create New Layer button on the bottom of the Layers palette.

5. Move your newly copied type layer by pressing and holding the ⌘ key (Ctrl) to temporarily change to the Move tool and drag the layer over the next rectangle.

6. Repeat the last two steps until you've created all the letters you need.

7. Double-click each type layer thumbnail to select them and change the letters for your sign.

The rest of the sign was created by adding a simple oval with the Ellipse tool and adding a text layer to it. The starbursts were created with the starburst shape included in the Symbols shapes libraries. I used the same set of blending options for the type elements and another for the sign elements. The frame for the sign was created with the Line tool set at 40 pixels thick. I added a stroke of 1 pixel for each shape using the Blending Options. The background was created by adding a new Gradient Fill layer.

Working with paths

The one palette associated with the drawing tools is the Path palette (see Figure 5.12). It is grouped with the Layers and Channels palette. The Paths palette helps you manage your shapes. Several buttons along the bottom of the palette allow you to add stroke and fill to your shapes. Just like layers, you can create separate paths to organize your drawing.

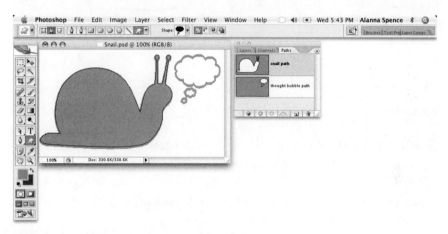

Figure 5.12. The Paths palette with two paths listed.

Modifying paths with the Direct Selection tool

You can take an existing shape and modify it using the Direct Selection tool. By selecting different areas of the dog custom shape on the left side of Figure 5.13, I was able to transform it from a Rottweiler to a Dachshund. I selected the points around his nose and elongated it, then selected the points in his legs and made him stubby. After a little bit of shrinking and stretching, I was able to turn my tall, beefy dog into a short, stubby one.

To modify a Custom Shape:

1. Create a new file.

2. Select the Custom Shape tool from the Toolbox.

3. In the Options bar, select the Paths setting. It is the second icon from the left and looks like a rectangle with a pen icon in it.

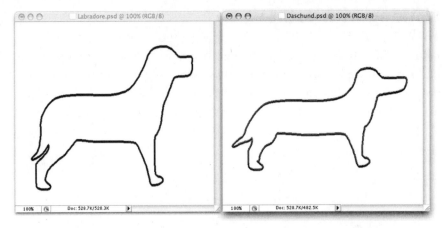

Figure 5.13. A reshaped path using the Direct Select tool.

4. Choose the dog from the Shape drop-down list. If you don't see a dog, you'll need to add the Animal Custom Shape library to your list. In the Shape drop-down list, click the arrow on the top right and choose Animals from the list. Click Append to add them to your current list of custom shapes.

5. Click and drag to draw a dog.

6. Select the Direct Selection tool from the Toolbox or press Shift+A to toggle to it. It is under the Path Selection tool and looks like a white cursor.

7. Click and drag around the dog's muzzle. The points that were in your selection area turn black, and the other points in the dog stay white. To add or remove points from your selection, Shift+click them.

8. Using your right arrow key, stretch out your dog's muzzle.

9. Select the foot and ankles of the two legs and use the up arrow key to shrink the legs.

10. Select the upper half of the dog and shrink it using the down arrow keys.

11. Continue selecting and moving points until you're happy with your newly formed dog.

12. To add a stroke or fill to your dog shape, choose a color in your foreground color swatch, click the Paths tab in the Layers palette group, and click either the Fill Path or Stroke Path buttons on the bottom of the palette.

Figure 5.14 shows a dog Custom Shape with nose points selected with the Direct Selection tool.

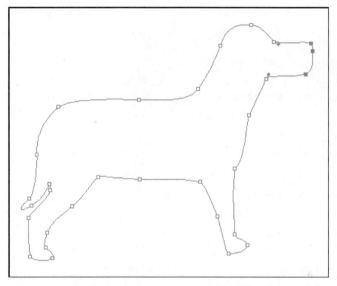

Figure 5.14. A path with selected points using the Direct Selection tool.

Reshape your photo with a vector mask

In this section you'll create a vector mask using one of the fun shapes that come with Photoshop CS2. You can use this cropped image later to create a photo collage in Chapter 16. In Figure 5.15 I used the Snowflake Custom Shape tool to create a vector mask of a ski resort photo. I added a solid color fill layer as a background color for my design.

Figure 5.15. A shape vector mask over a photo.

To create a vector mask using one of the Custom Shape tools:

1. Open a photo to mask. If the file has just one background layer, double-click it in the Layers palette to rename and unlock it.

2. Select the Custom Shape tool from the Toolbox.

3. Click the Paths button in the Options bar. It is the second rectangular icon. There is a pen graphic in the middle of the icon.

4. Click and drag to create your shape. After you create the initial shape, you can reposition it by clicking and dragging it into position.

5. To resize your shape, choose Edit ⇨ Free Transform Path and then drag the corners to resize it. When you are done, press Enter to accept your transformation.

6. Create a vector mask by selecting Image ⇨ Vector Mask ⇨ Current Path.

Just the facts

- Draw straight lines with the Pen tool and convert them to curves with the Convert Anchor Point tool.

- Trace photos with the Freeform tool to create graphic illustrations.

- Reshape paths using the Direct Selection tool.

- Create vector masks of your photos by using custom shapes.

- Create pill-shaped buttons by increasing the radius size in the Rounded Rectangle tool options.

GET THE SCOOP ON...
Creating texture with scatter brush settings ▪ Create
artist brushes with advanced brush settings ▪ Softening
shadows with the Dodge tool ▪ Adding textured
vignettes to photos

Painting with the Brush Tools

Whether you are touching up photos or creating digital artwork, the brush tools get a lot of heavy use. Painting in color is just one of numerous ways you'll be using the brush tool options. Many of the photo editing tools in Photoshop are brush based and work very much like the regular Brush tool. If you are interested in creating your own digital artwork from scratch, you have some great options for creating custom brush strokes with the improvements Photoshop has added to the Brushes palette.

Several of Photoshop's most heavily used tools are based on the Photoshop brush tool technology. The following tools also use brush settings such as brush size, hardness, and blending mode.

Tools that work like brushes:

▪ Healing Brush, Spot Healing Brush

▪ Erase, Background Eraser

▪ Brush, Pencil, Color Replacement

▪ Clone Stamp, Pattern Stamp

▪ Blur, Sharpen, Smudge

▪ Dodge, Burn, Sponge

This chapter covers the basics of the many varieties of brush tools in Photoshop and shows you how to create your

123

own custom brushes. The online Photoshop community has a vast number of beautiful custom brushes available as free downloads. You'll learn how to paint parts of an image onto another using the stamp tools, and how to play with sharpening one area of a photo and blurring out another to clarify the focal point of an image.

Controlling brush size and flow

Brush options for most of the paint tools are broken down into Master Diameter, Hardness setting, Blending Mode, Opacity, and Flow. Some of the tools offer strength or exposure settings in the place of opacity settings.

Look at the brush options:

1. Select the Brush tool from the Toolbox by pressing the letter B.

2. In the Options bar at the top of the screen, click the Brush dropdown menu.

    Figure 6.1 shows the drop-down list in the Options bar for the Brushes tool.

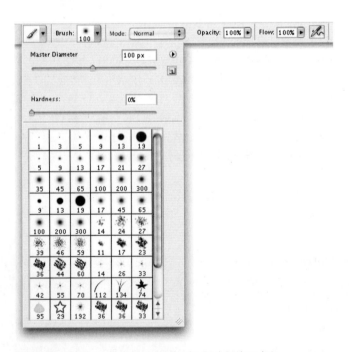

Figure 6.1. Brushes drop-down list in the Tool Options bar.

Inside Scoop

Paint a straight line by pressing and holding the Shift key while using any of the paint tools.

A submenu of brush options appears as seen in Figure 6.1 that displays settings for brush diameter, hardness, and brush shape. Master Diameter refers to the diameter of your brush, and Hardness refers to how much feathering or anti-aliasing you want on your brush. If your hardness is set to 0%, you'll have a soft brush similar to what you'd get using an airbrush. At 100% hardness, you'll get a solid pencil-type stroke. Incidentally, that's the only difference between the Brush and Pencil tool. The Pencil tool is always set at 100% hardness. The hardness controls are there, but if you try to adjust Hardness, you'll find the Pencil always behaves like it's set to 100% hardness.

Blending modes

Both layers and brushes in Photoshop have a long list of possible blending modes determining how they blend together with other colors. You'll be working with many of them throughout this book, so don't feel like you need to understand them all from the get-go. If you are ever curious about all of the various blending modes and how they work, I recommend visiting the Photoshop Help system and reading up on blending modes.

You can get a complete list of brush blending modes and a description of how they work from Photoshop's Help system by following these steps:

1. Choose Help ➪ Photoshop Help.

2. In the search box at the top, type **list of blending modes**.

3. Click the Search button.

Bright Idea!

Use the Color blending mode when colorizing black-and-white photos. It colorizes pixels without losing shadow and highlight details.

You'll see a list of all the available blending modes. If for any reason the list doesn't appear, you can also get to it by clicking the small house icon to return to the main help screen and then clicking Painting, then clicking Blending modes, and then clicking List of blending modes.

Changing sizes with the brush options

There are three ways to increase the size of your brush. One is to click the brush size drop-down arrow in your Brush Options bar. Another is through the Brush Tip Shape panel in the Brushes palette. The quickest way is to use the keyboard shortcuts. Pressing the] key increases the size, and pressing [decreases the size. Additionally, you can control the softness/hardness of the brush by pressing and holding the Shift key while pressing] or [.

Letting it flow with the Airbrush setting

The Airbrush setting, which works best when you have your hardness set to something below 50%, acts much like a real airbrush. As long as your mouse button is pressed, the paint continuously flows out of the brush, much like a real airbrush would do. The brush area continues to bleed out over several pixels until you let go of the mouse button. Figure 6.2 shows dots painted by clicking and holding the mouse button down for 0, 1, 3, and 5 seconds.

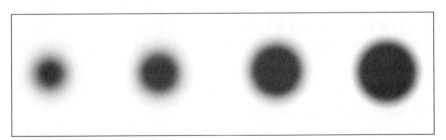

Figure 6.2. Painted dots with the Airbrush setting enabled.

You'll probably get more use out of the Airbrush setting if you are using a graphics tablet. The Airbrush setting works well with slow deliberate brush strokes that can be tricky to do with a mouse, unless you are a world champion mouser. If you don't have a graphics tablet, the Airbrush setting can come in handy for simple edits or touch ups. It is a good tool to use when creating fuzzy stars of varying sizes. Click and hold your mouse for different amounts of time to make fuzzy stars of different sizes.

You can create a night sky with the Airbrush setting enabled by following these steps:

1. Create a new file in RGB color mode.

2. Click the background color swatch in the Toolbox and select from the Color Picker a dark navy for your sky.

3. Click the foreground color swatch in the Toolbox and select from the Color Picker a bright yellow for your star color.

4. Fill your background with navy by pressing ⌘+Delete (Ctrl+Delete).

5. Click the Create New Layer icon in the Layers palette to create a new layer for your stars.

6. Select the Brush tool in the Toolbox by pressing the letter B.

7. Click the Brush drop-down list in the Options bar and select one of the star brushes. Hover your mouse over a brush thumbnail to see its name appear in a ToolTip.

8. Click the Enable Airbrush button in the Options bar (see Figure 6.3).

Enable Airbrush button

Figure 6.3. The Enable Airbrush button in the Brush Options bar.

9. Click around your document to create stars. Press and hold your mouse button for different periods of time to create big bright stars and duller small stars.

10. Press] or [to increase or decrease your brush size to add variation.

Keep adding until you get a result you like. You can add large, dark smears of color to add some dimension like I did in Figure 6.4. Decrease your brush's opacity to around 30% to give it some transparency so that it blends well.

Inside Scoop

Toggle the Airbrush option on and off by pressing Shift+Option+P (Shift+Alt+P).

Figure 6.4. Stars created with the Airbrush option enabled.

Getting more control with the Brushes palette

The Options bar displays only a subset of all the brush options available to you. There is also a more complex Brushes palette where you can modify your brush to your heart's content. The Brushes palette, as shown in Figure 6.5, by default lives in the palette dock on the top right of your screen. Click it to expand it to full size. It is a large palette, so keeping it in the palette dock is probably the best use of space on most monitors. If you have the luxury of a very large screen, or two screens, and you know you'll be using it quite a bit, you can pull it out and use it as a floating palette.

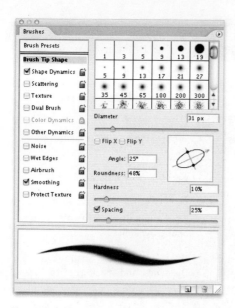

Figure 6.5. The Brushes palette with the Brush Tip Shape options panel.

To pull out the Brushes palette to use as a floating palette:

1. Click the Brushes palette tab in the palette dock and drag it into position inside your workspace.

2. To put the Brushes palette back in the palette dock and out of the way, simply click the Brushes palette tab and drag it back into the palette dock.

The Brush Tip options panel lets you control the shape and angle of your brush to get a more calligraphic shape. The Brush tool works by painting many dots in a row; by default, it paints many, many dots close to each other to give the illusion of a continuous stroke. You can control the frequency by adjusting the spacing setting. Increasing the spacing gives you a dotted brushstroke. Below the Brush Tip Shape in the list of brush options are tons of adjustments you can apply to your brushes to customize them even further. Table 6.1 describes a few of my favorites.

Table 6.1. Description of adjustment settings in the Brushes palette

Adjustment	Description	Tips for Use
Shape Dynamics	Randomizes the size of each paint dot	Set spacing to 100% or more
Scattering	Scatters your paint dots around	Set spacing to 50% or more
Texture	Select a pattern to use as texture for your brushstroke	Works best with hardness set to 0%
Dual Brush	Lets you paint with two brushes at once	Great when used with Scatter and Shape Dynamics
Color Dynamics	Changes hue, saturation, brightness, or purity with each paint dot	Use it with Scatter, Shape Dynamics, and spacing set to 50% or more
Other Dynamics	Changes opacity with each paint dot	Increase the jitter setting to increase variety of opacity
Noise	Adds a crunchy texture around your paint stroke	Best when hardness is set to 25% or less

Using brush presets

Photoshop comes loaded with some great brushes with textures and symbols. There are brushes shaped as leaves, grass, fabric texture, paper texture, and graphics symbols. If you enlarge some of them and play with their opacity, they can add interesting texture to images. All of the brush presets installed with Photoshop can be further modified with adjustments like Scattering and Noise. You can combine them with other custom brushes by using the Dual Brush adjustment to get some creative imagery. Figure 6.6 shows the Brushes palette with the Scattered Leaves brush selected in the Brush Presets panel.

Hack

Create a new brush by copying an existing one. Click the brush you'd like to copy and click the Create New Brush icon on the bottom of the Brushes palette.

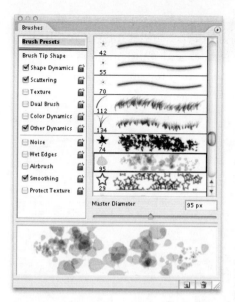

Figure 6.6. The Brushes palette with Scattered Leaves brush selected.

Photoshop automatically loads a set of stylized brushes like the star brushes you used to create your night sky in the last section, or the Autumn Leaf brush I used for Figure 6.7. If you look at the list of available brush presets in the Brush palette options drop-down list, you'll see

Varying Brush Pressure with Graphics Tablets

You may have noticed in the Brush Presets panel of the Brushes palette, and also in the Options bar, the brushes are displayed with variable thickness from tip to tail; but when you try to use the brush, you just get one thickness from your brush. This thick-to-thin graphic is representing what a line might look like if you were using a graphics tablet that uses a pen with a variable-pressure tip. If you are interested in the digital paint aspect of Photoshop, graphics tablets are a powerful way of really taking advantage of Photoshop's variable-pressure brush tools. With a graphics tablet you can control the thickness and flow of your brush by applying more or less pressure on your pen stylus. Chapter 25 covers more about graphics tablets, so be sure to read it if I've piqued your interest.

you have quite a few sets to play with. We could spend the rest of the book playing with all of these cool brushes, but instead let me tell you how to load them. I'll give you a few of my favorites and some pointers on getting good results out of them, and leave the rest up to your imagination.

Figure 6.7. Photo using the Autumn Leaf brush preset.

To try out some more brush presets, follow these steps:

1. Click the Brushes palette arrow to open the brush options drop-down list.

2. Select one of the Brush presets from the bottom half of the list.

3. In the Replace Brushes dialog box that appears, click Append to add the brushes to your current list or OK to replace it.

Inside Scoop

Restore your brush presets to their defaults by selecting Reset Brushes from the options drop-down list in the Brushes palette.

If you've appended your list, the newly added brushes will appear on the bottom of the list. Some of my favorites are the Nagel brushes, which give you excellent fabric textures, and the Wet Media brushes that imitate fine-art media like watercolor and ink wash. Be sure to check out the resources section in the back of the book for Web sites that offer artistic brush sets for free download.

Working with photos and paint tools

Much of your photo editing and enhancing can be done using paint tools that let you pinpoint areas of your photo to manipulate. Photoshop has tools for blurring and sharpening so that you can blur out sections of a photo and sharpen others. The Clone Stamp tool lets you sample parts of your image and stamp them onto different areas. Adding transparent textures using the Pattern Stamp tool can give your photo a subtle artistic edge.

Edit out extras with the Clone Stamp tool

The Clone Stamp tool is one of my favorite painting tools in Photoshop. With this tool, you can edit out unwanted objects in your photos by taking a sample of one part of your photo and painting a clone of it over other parts of your photo. It's also a great tool for creating photomontages because it allows you to paint areas of one Photoshop document into another one. You can control opacity and flow so you can clone transparent images on top of one another giving a layered look. By using the Clone Stamp tool as an editing tool, you can stamp out unwanted parts of a photo by covering them up with samples from other parts of your photo. Figure 6.8 takes advantage of this feature by painting over the gravel using the same sample area.

Try editing out parts of your photo with the Clone Stamp tool:

1. Open a photo to edit.

2. Select the Clone Stamp tool from the Toolbox. You can also select it by pressing the letter S.

3. Press and hold the option key (Alt) to select a sampling area.

4. Adjust the Clone Stamp brush diameter, opacity, and flow in the Options bar.

5. Click and drag to paint a clone of your sample area.

> **Hack**
> Keep one hand on the [and] keys to increase and decrease your brush size while painting with your mouse in the other.

Figure 6.8. A photo edited with the Clone Stamp tool.

6. Try turning the Aligned check box off to paint from the same sample area with each brush stroke.

7. Adjust the hardness setting in the Brushes palette under the Brush Tip Shape section to control your brush's fuzz factor.

Isn't this a fun tool? Here are a couple more tips to get great results. In Figure 6.8, I selected the cat and chair using the Magic Wand tool, and then chose Select ⇨ Inverse to make sure I didn't paint over the cat. It's okay if you accidentally paint over an area you want to keep. Keep your cloned areas on a separate layer. Create a new layer and click the Sample all layers check box in the Clone Stamp Options bar.

Add texture with the Pattern Stamp tool

The Pattern Stamp tool lives under the Clone Stamp tool and is a fun way to add some texture to your photos. Photoshop comes with some interesting patterns, but you can also make your own or find tons of free pattern downloads on the Internet. I've listed some great Web sites in the resources section of this book to help you find them. Using the Pattern Stamp tool on a new layer and then playing with the opacity of the layer can give you some great effects. Figure 6.9 shows a water pattern painted around my central image of a record player.

Figure 6.9. A photo with Pattern Stamp tool effects.

Try adding a pattern to a photo:

1. Open a photo to edit.

2. Select the Pattern Stamp tool from the Clone Stamp tool flyout menu. You can also press Shift+S to toggle through the list of Stamp tools. The Pattern Stamp tool has a small checker icon in the top left corner as shown in Figure 6.10.

3. Click the pattern flyout menu in the Options bar for the Pattern tool. If you click the little black arrow, a drop-down list with pattern options appears. Select Large Thumbnail so you can see the patterns a little better.

Figure 6.10. The Pattern Stamp tool highlighted in the Toolbox.

4. Select a pattern you like from the flyout menu. I chose Satin, which looks like the reflections on a swimming pool.

5. Click the Add New Layer icon on the bottom of your Layers palette to keep your pattern separate from your photo.

6. Adjust your brush size and hardness and paint around the subject in your photo.

7. Adjust your opacity setting for your new layer in the Layers palette.

Adding a little bit of texture can add a little creative flare to your photos. You can add color overlays to adjust the pattern colors. Right-click the layer and select Blending Options from the top of the list to explore more ways of personalizing the pattern.

The satin pattern I used in the last section is one of the default patterns that automatically load into Photoshop when you launch it. To load them, click the black arrow in the patterns flyout menu and select one

Inside Scoop

Lower the opacity of your Pattern Stamp tool to blend areas of pattern into your photo.

Watch Out!

Loading patterns eats up memory. Reset your pattern menu to save on RAM. Select Reset Patterns from the drop-down list in the patterns flyout menu. Click OK to go back to the default set.

from the list. You'll be asked if you'd like to append or replace the current selection. To create a nice big menu to choose from, like I've created in Figure 6.11, click the Append button.

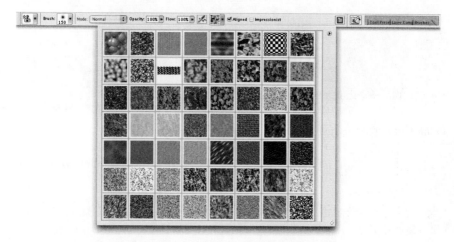

Figure 6.11. The pattern drop-down list in the Pattern tool's Options bar.

Alter the focus of an image with the Sharpen and Blur tools

Sometimes you have a great photo but the subject gets lost in the busy background behind it. By targeting specific areas of your photo to blur and sharpen, you can adjust the focal point of a photo and get a stronger image. In Figure 6.12 the leprechaun was fighting for importance over the strong contrasting horizontals and verticals of the brick wall. By using the Dodge tool, Blur tool, and Sharpen tool, I was able to adjust the focus on to the leprechaun and add a softer focus to the bricks.

Figure 6.12. A photo edited with Blur, Sharpen, and Dodge tools.

For the first set, let's soften some of the contrast in the background of your image:

1. Open a photo with a high contrast background.

2. Next, lighten up some shadows. Select the Dodge tool from the Toolbox. It looks like a black licorice lollipop. You can also select it by pressing the letter O.

3. In the Options bar, change the Range to Shadows. This allows you to dodge, or wash out, some of the shadows and soften up their contrasts.

4. Adjust your brush size and change the Exposure setting to between 15% and 20%.

5. Paint around the dark areas of your background to lighten up their contrast. Because the tool is set to target just the shadows, the light areas won't be affected.

Next, blur out the background and sharpen up the foreground by following these steps:

1. Select the Blur tool from the Toolbox. The flyout menu for the Blur, Smudge, and Sharpen tools is visible in Figure 6.13. You can press the letter R to select it and save your wrists some unnecessary work.

> **Bright Idea!**
> Zoom in close when sharpening and blurring to get good control over your brush strokes.

Figure 6.13. The Blur, Smudge, and Sharpen tools fly-out menu.

2. Adjust your brush size and change the brush strength to somewhere between 80% and 100%.

3. Paint in the background to blur it slightly.

4. Select the Sharpen tool from the Blur tool's flyout menu. It looks like a triangle.

5. Adjust your brush size and change the brush strength to between 60% and 80%.

6. Paint around areas like facial features and folds in fabric to sharpen their focus.

Designing custom brushes

The possibilities of brush tips in Photoshop are endless. You can take any of the existing brush presets in the multitude of libraries that come with Photoshop and modify them to your liking. You can also create your very own brushes from scratch.

Create a textured brush from a photo

I love adding texture to images by creating custom brushes from photos. The patterns you get are much more interesting than creating a traditional brush. Finding the right photo might take a little practice. Generally, photos with a lot of contrast work well.

First create a textured brush and save it as a brush preset by following these steps:

1. Find a photo with a lot of texture.

2. Choose Edit ⇨ Adjust Threshold. You'll see a preview of your photo as a black-and-white image like you see in Figure 6.14. Adjust the slider until you create texture in an area of your image that you like.

Figure 6.14. A photo with Threshold adjustment.

3. Select the Circular Marquee tool by pressing the letter M and then pressing Shift+M until the Circular Marquee tool is highlighted.

4. Pressing and holding the Shift and Option keys, drag a circular selection around the texture. Choose Edit ⇨ Define Brush Preset. Give your brush a name.

5. Select the brush tool by pressing the letter B and selecting your new preset from the bottom of the list.

Try your new brush. I tend to get the best textures when combining them with the spacing, Shape Dynamics, and Scatter adjustments in the Brushes palette.

Create a custom stamp for quickly adding logos to images

Adding your logo as a custom brush preset is a great way to have a quick stamp. Keep in mind that the brushes can only use one color at a time and you won't be able to have drop shadows or other layer styles. The logo stamps still come in very handy when you are creating graphics for your business and just want to add a quick stamp.

I've created the logo you see in Figure 6.15 using a piece of clip art and adding some text. You can open and place any artwork you like. The brush automatically creates a bitmap out of your artwork.

Figure 6.15. A logo saved as a custom brush.

Bright Idea!

Add a drop shadow to your logo stamps by putting them on their own layer. Right click the layer and select Blending Options from the drop-down list.

It's a good idea to create a logo from a piece of high resolution artwork so that it will still look good at various sizes.

To create a quick logo stamp by adding a graphic to your brush presets, follow these steps:

1. Create a new document by choosing File ⇨ New. Set the document size to 4 × 6 inches, the dpi to 300, and the color mode to RGB.

2. Open a high resolution file of your logo. Copy and paste the logo into your new file.

3. Select the type tool and add your company's name.

4. Select the Rectangular Marquee tool by pressing the letter M.

5. Create a rectangular selection box around your logo.

6. Choose Edit ⇨ Define Brush Preset. Give your brush preset a name.

You've just saved your logo stamp as a custom brush. Now try it out:

1. Create a new file or layer to try your stamp on.

2. Select the Brush tool by pressing the letter B.

3. From the Brush Options menu at the top of the screen, select your logo from the bottom of the brush presets list.

4. If you'd like, change your brush size and choose a new foreground color.

5. Click anywhere in your document to create a stamp of your logo.

You now have a one-click logo that can be used at any size and with any color.

Erasing with precision

The regular Eraser tool has been with Photoshop since its inception. It's a simple tool but has a few idiosyncrasies and features you should know about to get the most out of it. It works the same as the other brush tools with the exception of removing color instead of adding it. You can control opacity, flow, hardness, and diameter. You can use all your custom

Inside Scoop

The Eraser tool icon tends to get in the way when you are trying to get at hard-to-reach spots. Change it and all other tools to a precision cross hair by engaging your Caps Lock key.

brush presets with the Eraser tool and get some interesting effects by removing parts of one layer and allowing others to show through.

Here are a few of the idiosyncrasies I was telling you about. Some of them might work to your advantage once you get used to them. If your background layer is locked, the Eraser tool acts more like paint tool and fills what you erase with the background color instead of erasing to transparency. If you are editing JPEG files from a digital camera or other source, chances are your image is locked on a single background layer. To unlock it, just double click the layer's thumbnail and rename it. This is the quickest way to unlock a background layer. The Eraser tool has three different modes to choose from: Brush, Pencil, and Block. Pencil has a hardness of 100%, which is the only difference between it and the brush mode. Block mode gives you a square block that can't be resized, and the brush options can't be used with it. The only semi-useful thing I can think of for it would be to use it while pressing and holding the Shift key to erase vertical and horizontal stripes down and across your images.

Erasing large areas of color

The Magic Eraser tool works like a big color-sensitive vacuum. Click an area of solid color and the whole chunk disappears. Erase areas of nearly the same color by increasing the tool's tolerance settings in the Options bar. A higher tolerance is less fussy about slight color differences. The tolerance value can range from 0 to 255. The results vary widely between photos, and resolution can play a part. The higher the resolution, the more pixels you are dealing with. I find tolerance settings between 30 and 80 work well for large areas of color, and settings of 0 to 16 work well for tighter spots.

Watch Out!

Sometimes the Eraser tool gets rid of more than you intended. To undo several steps, press ⌘+Option+Z (Ctrl+Alt+Z) until you are back where you wanted.

Adding custom brush preset libraries

So many brushes! It's hard to keep track of them all. Once you create a few custom brushes, save them in their own library for safe keeping. There are also tons of free downloadable brush libraries available on the Internet that you can load into Photoshop. This section covers how to create your own brush preset library as well as install one from the Internet.

Keep your favorite custom brushes handy

Once you get a few brushes saved, you'll want to save them in a brush preset library for safe keeping. Libraries are saved as ABR files and can be shared among other Photoshop users.

Follow these steps to save your custom brushes in a brush preset library:

1. With the Brush Tool highlighted, click the Brushes drop-down menu in the Options bar and click the arrow on the top to display the Brush options drop-down menu.

2. Select Save Brushes. A save dialog box appears.

3. Name your file and save it in Adobe Photoshop CS2/resets/Brushes. If you are on a PC, the Adobe Photoshop folder is in your Program Files folder. If you are on a Macintosh, it is in Applications.

The next time you launch Photoshop, your brushes library will be available from the Brush Options menu in the Options bar of the Brushes tool.

Add third-party custom brush sets

The Photoshop online community is huge. It's not surprising that there are numerous free downloads of custom brushes available on the Web. The resources guide in the back of the book points you to some of the most popular Photoshop tutorial sites where you can download free

---

Inside Scoop

You can save your brushes library file anywhere you like, but it will only show up in the Brush library list if it is saved in your Presets/Brushes folder.

brushes, filters, and other plug-ins. These brushes are usually created by avid Photoshop users and are available free of charge. Most brushes are available in downloadable zip files. Once expanded or unzipped, you'll find a file with a file extension of .abr. You won't be able to open this file in Photoshop. You'll need to place your ABR file in the Brushes folder as shown in Figure 6.16 for Photoshop to find it.

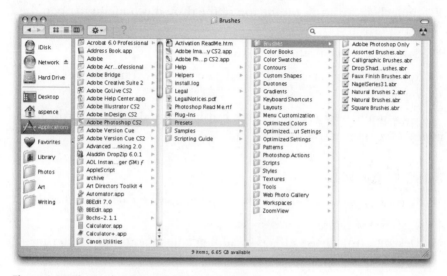

Figure 6.16. The Brushes Presets folder on a Macintosh.

To download and install a custom brush from the Internet, follow these steps:

1. Follow the Web site instructions for downloading the file. You will either click or right-click a link and save it to your computer.

2. If the downloaded file has an extension of .zip, you'll need to run an unzip program on it such as WinZip or StuffIt.

3. Find the ABR files that have been unzipped and place them in Adobe Photoshop CS2/Presets/Brushes. Your Photoshop folder resides in the Applications folder on a Mac, and the Program Files folder on a PC.

4. Relaunch Photoshop so that it loads your new brush into the preset menu.

5. Select the Brush tool by pressing the letter B.

Watch Out!

Always run a virus scanner on files downloaded from unknown sources.

6. In the Brush Options bar, click the Brush drop-down menu and then click the arrow on the top of the drop-down menu to open the list of brushes.

7. Select the name of the brush you just installed.

8. You can choose to either append your list of current brushes or replace it.

You should now see your new brush set in the Brush drop-down menu. Give them a try!

Just the facts

- Clarify a photo's focal point by blurring out the background and sharpening the foreground.
- Design artistic brush effects by adding adjustments like Scattering and Color Dynamics.
- Create a custom brush of your logo to use as a quick stamp.
- Save your custom brushes in a library.
- Add third-party brush libraries and expand your creative ability.

GET THE SCOOP ON...
Selecting oddly shaped objects ▪ Changing the
color of someone's shirt ▪ Removing backgrounds ▪
Creating a soft-focus vignette

Selecting and Extracting Images

W hether you want to isolate an area of pixels to perform a color correction on, or select parts of your image to use in a collage of images, Photoshop has tons of tools for selecting geometric shapes, odd shapes, and areas of similar color. In Chapter 1 I talk about how Photoshop organizes images in a grid of dots. There are a few exceptions, such as objects created with the vector tools, but for the most part, Photoshop documents represent a map of pixels. This makes selecting objects in a photo a little tricky. You aren't able to select a flower out of a photo. In Photoshop, you need to select the pixels that represent the flower. Because the pixels on the outside of the flower blend in with the background, you'll have to do a little modifying when you place a flower from a red background onto a green background.

This chapter introduces you to all of Photoshop's powerful selecting tools such as the Marquee, Lasso, and Magic Wand. You'll learn how to select an area of color and change its hue. You'll see how to create a circular vignette around a photo, and you'll be introduced to the world of masking and see some ways of getting rid of unwanted fringes of color around your selected images.

Chapter 7

Selecting geometric shapes

The marquee tools, in the first square of the Toolbox, offer ways of selecting rectangular or circular shapes. You can add to the shapes, create donut cutouts inside them, or create selection shapes based on the intersection of two selections. The last two marquee tools are handy for trimming off one row or column at a time.

Adding, subtracting, and dissecting your selections

The Rectangular and Circular Marquee tools each have four selection options available in the Options bar. There are two additional features in the Options bar for feathering or anti-aliasing your selections. You can find them in Table 7.1 and then see how they work in Figure 7.1. The add and subtract options can be used while the regular selection option is highlighted. To add to a selection, you can press and hold the Shift key. To subtract from a selection, you can press and hold the Option or Alt key.

Table 7.1. Marquee tool options in the Options bar

Options	Description	Fig 7.1
Regular	Creates a single selection	A
Add	The second selection adds to the first selection	C
Subtract	The second selection subtracts from the first selection	B
Intersect	Creates a selection from the intersection of two selections	D, H
Anti-alias	Creates smooth pixel transition on curves — not available for Rectangular Marquee tool	F
Feather	Adds feathering to the outside of an image	G

To try the Marquee tools, create a rectangular marquee selection with a circular cutout in the center:

1. Create a new document.

2. Select the Rectangular Marquee tool from the Toolbox, or press the letter M to highlight it.

3. Click and drag to create a rectangular selection.

4. Select the Circular Marquee tool from the Marquee tool flyout menu, or press Shift+M to switch to it using the key command.

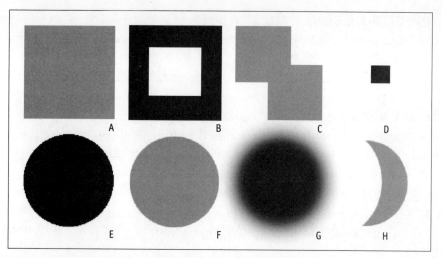

Figure 7.1. Rectangular and circular selections made by the Marquee tools.

5. Press and hold the Shift key and then click and drag to deselect a circular area inside your rectangle.

You can undo a selection by pressing ⌘+Z (Ctrl+Z).

6. Fill in your selection with the foreground color by pressing Option+Delete (Alt+Delete).

You should have something like you see in Figure 7.2. When selecting things like chairs or tables, objects that have negative space within the borders of the object, you'll really put adding and subtracting to selection areas to the test.

Figure 7.2. A rectangular selection with circular cutout.

Inside Scoop

Create a perfect circle or square by pressing and holding the Shift key after you start making your selection.

Select a single row of pixels

The last two tools in the Marquee tool flyout menu allow you to select a single row of pixels. This comes in handy after you've cropped an image but have missed just a tiny bit of the image that you want to get rid of.

To crop out a single row of pixels:

1. Select the single-row or single-column Marquee tool from the Marquee tool's flyout menu (see Figure 7.3).

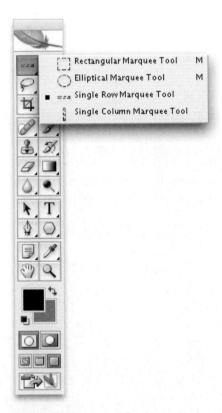

Figure 7.3. Marquee tool fly-out menu.

2. Zoom in to your image so you can see what you are doing, and select the unwanted row or column.

3. Choose Select ⇨ Inverse or use the key command ⌘-Shift+I (Ctrl+Shift+I).

4. Choose Image ⇨ Crop to crop out the pixels.

Surprisingly, I find that I use this technique more often than you'd think. It comes in handy when creating images for the Web where every pixel counts.

Create a circular vignette around your photos

By using the Circular Marquee tool and adding a layer mask to your photo, you can create instant soft-edged vignettes around any photo or image. In Figure 7.4, I've added a soft vignette around a family photo and added a warm brown solid background color. By pressing and holding the Option key (Alt key) while selecting my circle, I'm able to select an area from the center out as opposed to the tool's standard mode, where you select from side to side.

Figure 7.4. A photo selected with a Circular Marquee tool and feathering set to 20 pixels.

The following steps show you how to create a vignette in just a couple of minutes:

1. Open a photo or other image to use for your vignette.

2. To create a copy of your photo for backup automatically, click and drag your photo layer on top of the New Layer icon on the bottom of the layers palette.

3. Hide the original or background layer by clicking the Visibility icon to the left of the thumbnail in the Layers palette.

4. Click the layer you would like to mask to make it the active layer.

5. Select the Circular Marquee tool from the Marquee tool flyout menu by pressing Shift+M until it is highlighted.

6. To get that soft-edged look, change your feather amount in the Marquee tool options menu at the top of the screen. The amount will vary depending on what resolution your document is set to. I am creating my image for the Web, so my resolution is set to 72 dpi. I've found that a feather of 20 pixels suits me fine.

7. Place your cursor roughly in the center of where you'd like your circle and press and hold the Option key (Alt) while making your selection from the inside out.

8. If you aren't happy with your selection, you can move it in small increments by using your keyboard's arrow keys; or you can click and drag it to a better location.

9. Once you have a selection you like, click the gray-and-white Layer Mask icon on the bottom of the Layers palette.

You should now have a circular cutout of your photo with a nice feathered edge (see Figure 7.5). If you don't like how your mask turned out, you can delete it by right-clicking the layer mask icon next to your photo and selecting Delete Layer Mask.

Inside Scoop

Create a perfect circle by pressing and holding the Shift key while making your selection.

Figure 7.5. Masked circular photo with a feathered edge.

Now add a solid background color behind your mask:

1. Create a new solid color layer by clicking the New Fill or Adjustment Layer icon on the bottom of the Layers palette. From the drop-down menu, select Solid Color from the top of the list. It's probably going to cover up your entire photo; that's okay for now.

2. Select a color you would like to use for your background color and click OK.

3. Click and Drag your new color layer below your marked layer so that you can see your photo.

You now have a great-looking soft-photo vignette. If you ever want to modify the color of your background, you can double-click the layer's color thumbnail and a color picker window will appear.

Create close-up thumbnails of your photos

You can use the selection tools as a Crop tool. Using the Rectangular Marquee tool, you can select a rectangle and then choose Image ⇨ Crop. There are some disadvantages to using the Marquee tool for cropping. For example, you can't adjust your selection once you've created it without creating a new selection. I still use this method regularly. It takes fewer steps than the Crop tool, and using the Rectangular Marquee tool allows me to add a colored stroke around an image while cropping it, as I've done in Figure 7.6.

Figure 7.6. A cropped selection with a solid stroke.

Try cropping an image with the Marquee tool by following these steps:

1. Open a photo you'd like to crop.

2. Select the Rectangular Marquee tool from the Toolbox.

3. Click and drag inside your image to create a rectangular selection.

4. To add a stroke to your image, choose Edit ⇨ Stroke to open the stroke dialog box.

Bright Idea!

Instead of cropping, copy your selection and create a new document for it. Photoshop defaults to the size of your current selection when creating a new file.

5. Change your stroke width and click the color swatch to select a new color from the Color Picker. Be sure to select the Inside radio button under Location because you'll be cropping anything outside the selection.

6. Click OK when you are done.

7. Choose Image ⇨ Crop to crop your image.

If you ever have an oddly shaped selection, using the crop feature crops your image to a rectangle using the selection as a guide.

Precision selecting odd shapes with the Lasso tool

The Lasso tools, just below the Marquee tool in the Toolbox, allow you to create your own selection shapes. They lasso pixels so that you can copy and paste them into other files, create oddly shaped masks, or isolate areas to perform edits on them. In the next section, you'll create some interesting shapes by combining the features of the three Lasso tools listed in Table 7.2.

Table 7.2. Lasso tools and their features

Icon	Tool	Description
	Lasso tool	Lets you create a freehand selection by dragging your mouse around an area. Great if you are using a graphics tablet, but hard to control with large selections. Pressing and holding the Alt key on PC or Option key on Mac changes it temporarily to the Polygon Lasso tool.
	Polygon Lasso tool	You can create point-to-point selections. To have the tool snap to 45-degree increments, press and hold the Shift key while clicking.
	Magnetic Lasso tool	This tool snaps the edges of things by recognizing sharp changes in pixel color.

Tricky lassoing with advanced techniques

The most common way to select an object is by using the regular Lasso tool, but pressing and holding the Option key to change to a point-to-point selection as you would with the Polygon tool. You have the most amount of control when using these two tools in conjunction, and in most scenarios this will probably be your selection tool of choice.

With Photoshop, you can change selection tools at any time and add or subtract from your selection by pressing and holding the Shift key to add to a selection, and the Alt or Option key to subtract from it. Your cursor displays a plus (+) or minus (–) symbol on the top right of the icon.

If you are selecting large, complicated areas, using the Magnetic Lasso tool for your first pass, then perfecting your selection by adding and subtracting to it with the regular Lasso tool is usually the easiest way to get good selections.

Preview your selection by clicking the Quick Mask Mode icon in your Toolbox. Wherever you have not selected will be in red.

On complicated selections, it's a good idea to start with a copied layer of your image. If the pizza delivery person shows up with your pizza, and you are only halfway done with your selection, click the Add Layer Mask icon on the bottom of the Layers palette. This creates a layer mask of your selection. To reselect your selection, ⌘+click (Ctrl+click) on the Layer Mask icon in your layer and you'll get the marching ants back. Then highlight the copy of your photo and continue to add to or subtract from your image. When you are ready to create your mask, click the Layer Mask icon again.

Outlining with the Magnetic Select tool

The Magnetic Select tool guesses where the outline of an image is by deciphering differences in pixel color. It does a great job of roughly selecting an object very quickly. You can then go in and adjust your selection by adding to and subtracting from it using the Lasso and Polygon Lasso

---

Watch Out!

Make sure you set your Feather value before beginning a selection. Once you have created a selection, you can't change its Feather value.

tools. Figure 7.7 shows a before and after of an image that I extracted using a combination of the Magnetic Lasso and Polygon Lasso tool. Once I extracted it, I added the selection as a Layer Mask and put it on a nice cloud background.

Figure 7.7 shows an extraction of a photo by roughly selecting the image with the Magnetic Lasso tool, then perfecting the selection with the Polygon Lasso tool.

Figure 7.7. An image extracted using the Magnetic Lasso and Polygon Lasso tool.

For even the most complicated images, you should be able to get a good extraction in less than an hour. The more you practice, the better you'll get. The photo of the chicken I used had very similar colors in the background and foreground; the Lasso tools still did a great job of quickly selecting most of the chicken.

Now try selecting an image with the Magnetic Lasso tool:

1. Open an image you'd like to extract.

2. Make a backup of your image by dragging its layer onto the New Layer Icon and then turning off the visibility of your original layer so it doesn't get in the way.

Hack

If you lose track of where you started but you know you are close, double-click your mouse to close the selection automatically. There's no way to undo an incomplete selection, so only use this as a last resort.

3. Select the Magnetic Lasso tool from the Lasso tool flyout menu. You can press Shift+L a couple of times to toggle to it.

4. Click the edge of your subject and begin moving your cursor around your image, hugging the side and clicking every 20 or 50 pixels to anchor the selection.

5. Continue your way around your subject until the entire thing is roughly selected. When you reach your starting point, your cursor changes to include an "O"; click that point to close the loop on your selection. Don't worry about parts where the tool went astray; you're going to perfect your selection in a minute.

You should have a good selection now. If you zoom in to a few areas, you'll probably notice the tool missed spots or included parts of the background. You can perfect your selection with the Polygon Lasso tool by following these steps:

1. Select the Polygon Lasso tool in the Lasso tool flyout menu. You can also press Shift+L a couple times until it's highlighted.

2. Find an area where the Magnetic Lasso tool selected too much. Press and hold the Option or Alt key while clicking to select the area you want to remove. You'll have to complete the selection by clicking the beginning anchor, so don't forget where you started!

3. Find an area where the Magnetic Lasso tool missed a spot and press and hold the Shift key to add to it.

4. Keep this up until you've gotten a satisfactory selection.

5. Click the Add Layer Mask button on the bottom of the Layers palette to make your selection a mask.

6. Choose Layer ⇨ New Fill Layer ⇨ Solid Color and create a colored background. You may need to move this layer below your masked layer to see your masked image.

You might have a little fringe around your image where the pixels surrounding your image don't blend well with your solid color background. Chapter 8 covers a great deal more about Masks. For now I'll give you a quick tip.

Add a blending mode to your masked layer to blend out a little bit of the fringe by following these steps:

1. Right-click the thumbnail of your masked image (not the mask itself) and select Blending Options.

2. Check the Inner Glow check box and click its name to see the options.

3. Click the color swatch and change it to the color of your solid color layer.

4. Leave the Blend mode as normal. Depending on your image, you might want to change the amount of pixels in the size field. I usually prefer 3 pixels over the default 5 pixels.

That should be enough to tide you over until the next chapter. The next section covers making selections from areas of color.

Selecting and changing areas of color

Using the Magic Wand tool, you can select areas of the same or similar color value and add to them by Shift+clicking other areas. After you isolate sections of your images, you can edit them without affecting other areas. By taking advantage of the invert command, you can select a simple solid background and then invert your selection to select a more complicated subject. The next selection shows you how to select an area of color and change its color and saturation.

My little friend in Figure 7.8 used to be a big fan of pink. She's recently grown tired of pink and wishes to explore new color options. Her shirt is a solid color except for some shadow areas. Doing a color replace on her shirt should be relatively pain free.

Watch Out!

Selecting solid areas with the Magic Wand can be tricky if there is any texture. Try adjusting the tolerance to get the best results.

Figure 7.8. The Color Replacement dialog box.

To select an area of color to modify, follow these steps:

1. Select the Magic Wand tool by pressing the letter W.

2. In the tool options on the top of the screen, change the tolerance to 80. This setting changes how tolerant the Magic Wand tool is with minor color variations from pixel to pixel.

3. Click inside a large area of your subject's shirt to select it.

4. If most of the shirt if selected, you are ready to start doing some fine-tuning on your selection area. If not, Shift+click other large areas.

5. If you accidentally select some of the background or some of your subject's face, undo your last selection by pressing ⌘+Z (Ctrl+Z).

6. Change the tolerance to 10 and Shift+click inside areas of your shirt that weren't originally captured. Shadow areas can be tricky and you might need to click around quite a bit.

7. To get at areas with many tiny little unselected spots, switch to the Lasso tool by pressing the letter L.

8. Press and hold the Shift key while drawing a lasso around an area of unselected pixels to add them to the selection.

Inside Scoop

Press and hold the Option or Alt key to switch to the Polygon Lasso tool and click instead of dragging to create a selection.

You should have your shirt pretty well selected by now. For best results, make sure you get all the little bits along the bottom and the collar that tend to be in deep shadow. Little girls can be fickle, so we want to give her several different color choices. You can make several copies of your shirt selection to try out every color in the rainbow.

To make some extra copies of your selected shirt:

1. Copy your selection by pressing ⌘+C.

2. Click the New Layer button on the bottom of your Layer palette and paste your shirt into the layer by pressing ⌘+P. You should now have two layers.

3. To make a couple more copies of your new layer, click and drag your shirt layer on top of the New Layer icon on the bottom of the Layers palette.

4. Repeat the last step until you have three or four shirts to play with.

5. Turn off all but one of the shirt layers by clicking the Visibility (eyeball) icon next to each layer's thumbnail.

6. Click a visible shirt layer to highlight it, and from the Images menu item choose Adjustments ⇨ Replace Color.

7. You should see the Replace Color window that's shown in Figure 7.8.

8. With the Eyedropper tool selected inside the Replace Color window, click anywhere inside your subject's shirt.

9. Making sure the Selection radio button is selected, move the Hue slider over to a new color. Your shirt should look funky. So far you've only selected one shade from the t-shirt, so all the shadow areas need to be added to the selection. Click the second Eyedropper tool, the one with a plus sign. Click inside other areas of your shirt to add to your color replacement.

10. Once you've gotten all the color variations selected and your new shirt color looks solid, click OK to apply your changes.

Bright Idea!

While adding colors in the Replace Color window, you can click inside your actual image window and zoom into tough areas by pressing and holding ⌘+space and then clicking your image.

Figure 7.9 shows the same blouse before and after color replacement.

Figure 7.9. Before and after color replacement.

This technique works for just about anything from shirt color to eyes to sky to your couch and curtains. I've used this method to create sets of product photos for Web and print. You can create very consistent images using the same photo and adjusting the colors for each color available for the product.

Removing backgrounds with the Eraser tools

The Background Erase and Magic Eraser tools make a strong team in quickly erasing the background or negative space around an image. With the Background Eraser tool, you hug your image and erase around it, making sure the tool's center sample pixel doesn't touch pixels inside the subject. Once you've isolated your image, you can quickly click around large areas of color with the Magic Eraser tool, and then finish off with the regular Eraser tool on any areas you might have missed. All three are based off Photoshop's Brush engine so you can control the brush size and opacity. For the Magic Erase and Background Eraser tools, you can control the tools' tolerance similar to the Magic Wand tool.

The more simple your background, the better results you'll get out of using the background tools. You might find that your image has colors that are too similar and you'll have to resort to the lasso tools. When you are able to use the Eraser tools, it can save you tons of time. Figure 7.10 shows a photo of a chair on a simple background that is easy to isolate using the Eraser tools.

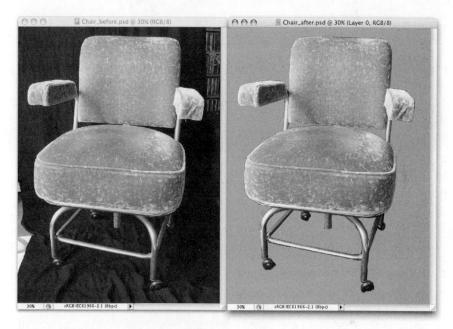

Figure 7.10. Removing backgrounds with the Eraser tools.

Now try removing an image from its background using the Eraser tools:

1. Open a digital photo with a semi-solid colored background.

2. Select the Background Eraser tool from the Eraser tools' fly-out menu. Press Shift+E to toggle between Eraser tools.

3. Increase your brush size to something nice and big. You'll want to be able to see the cross hairs in the middle of the brush so you can avoid painting them over your image. Use the] key to increase the brush size; the [key decreases it.

4. Change the tolerance of the Background Eraser tool in the Options bar to something between 20% and 30%. This is going to vary greatly from image to image.

5. Zoom in and begin to drag your Background Eraser tool around your image. Be careful to keep the cross hairs outside your subject.

6. Erase all the way around your image. On some areas you may find that you need to adjust the tolerance setting. The legs of my chair in Figure 7.10 are very similar in color to the background, so I had to adjust my tolerance when erasing around them. You should have something like I have in Figure 7.11.

Figure 7.11. The subject isolated with the Background Eraser tool.

To erase a subject with the Magic Eraser tool and then clean up with the Eraser tool, follow these steps:

1. Switch to the Magic Eraser tool. You can toggle to it by pressing Shift+E.

2. Adjust the tolerance settings. For my image, I used a tolerance of 30 for most areas and then changed to a tolerance of 10 or 5 for tough areas around the chair feet.

3. Change to the Eraser tool for a final cleanup. Increase your brush size and then set your opacity and fill to 100%. Clean up around your image.

4. Choose Layer ⇨ New Fill Layer ⇨ Solid Color and select a color for your background. You might have to drag your new layer below your image's layer in the Layers palette.

If there are any areas you missed, they'll be more apparent when you add the solid colored background and you can clean up even further.

Using the Background Eraser tool on its own can lead to frustration if used on the wrong image. Unless you have an image with vastly different colors in the foreground and background and with little texture, it's very difficult to erase the background of your image effectively.

What the Background Eraser tool essentially does is sample a pixel in the center of your brush and erase anywhere inside your brush that matches that sample. The sampling hot spot is represented by cross hairs in the center of your brush. Theoretically, if you run your brush around the outside of an object, being careful not to get the sampling cross hairs inside your foreground image, you can isolate your foreground image quickly. I have yet to find an image that this works well on. What I've found is that no matter what tolerance setting I give the tool, I always end up with leftover texture or even worse: I wipe out important parts of my foreground.

One giant benefit you get from the Background Eraser tool is that the tool is good at extracting background colors from the pixels around the edge of your image, thus eradicating the dreaded fringe effect that is common when extracting images from their backgrounds using other methods.

There are, however, some more creative uses for this tool. I've found I can get great background textures when using this on images with rough or patterned backgrounds like walls or bushes. Figure 7.12 shows an example of a photo that I manipulated using the Background Eraser tool. By erasing some parts of your image and placing a solid color background behind them, you can achieve some nice textural effects.

Bright Idea!

Use the Polygon Lasso tool to clean up large areas quickly around the outside of images. Once you select your area, click the Delete button to erase its contents.

Figure 7.12. Creating texture with the Background Eraser tool.

Just the facts

- Add and subtract to a selection by pressing the Shift and Option or Alt keys.
- Add feathering to a selection to give a soft-focused vignette effect.
- Use the Lasso tools to select oddly shaped subjects.
- Select areas of similar color with the Magic Wand tool.
- Remove backgrounds and create texture using the Background Eraser tool.

GET THE SCOOP ON...

Extracting images from their backgrounds ▪ Masking with the paint tools ▪ Saving mask selections for future use ▪ Creating custom shape cutouts of photos

Masking and Blending Images

Chapter 8

Think of a layer mask as a layer with a bunch of masking tape on it. There is a portal or cutout of the tape where your image shows through. When you mask an element of your image in Photoshop, you are deselecting everything around it so that only the element shows through. Whether editing in Quick Mask Mode or editing your selection as a saved alpha channel, Photoshop lets you take advantage of all its various tools for selecting and painting.

This chapter covers all the various ways to make masks, and you'll do some fun projects involving shape masks. I'll show you how to blend images into one using gradient masks. You'll save a selection as an alpha channel for future use. Finally, you'll put everything you've learned to use by creating an image with several masks.

One click masking with layer masks

Masked layers have two parts, the original layer and a layer mask. The layer mask clips the image based on a selection. In Figure 8.1, I've created a basic layer mask from an elliptical selection. To get you warmed up for the rest of the chapter, you'll make a simple mask using a layer mask.

167

Inside Scoop

Right-click the Layer Mask icon in the Layers palette and select Disable or Delete to remove the layer mask temporarily or permanently.

Figure 8.1. A photo with a circular layer mask.

To create a circular layer mask:

1. Open a photo to mask. If there is one locked Background layer, double click it to rename and unlock it.

2. Select the Elliptical Marquee tool from the Toolbox and draw a circle around the subject of your photo.

3. Click the Create New Layer Mask icon on the bottom of the Layers palette. It looks like a gray box with a white circle in it.

Your image will be masked by the circular selection like you see in Figure 8.1. By default, if you click the layer and move the image around, both pieces move as one. By ⌘+clicking either of the thumbnails in the Layers palette, you can select them individually and then move them using the Move tool.

Extracting images from their backgrounds

Photoshop offers several different options for extracting images from their backgrounds. The newest one, the Extract tool, which is accessed in the filters menu, lets you quickly draw a highlighter line around your image and remove anything outside that line. It is quick and does a good job of vacuuming up unwanted color or the fringe pixels that encircle your image. The bad news is that it's a lossy process, meaning once you create your extraction, you can't edit it. When you create a mask, you are creating a selection, and in some cases a permanent alpha channel that can be edited, duplicated, scaled, and dragged into other files. The mask stays separate from the image, giving you a heck of a lot more options. Both methods have their place in the world and are worth looking at. How you choose to use masks is going to help determine which method you use.

Getting quick results with the Extract tool

The Extract tool is a mini application that runs from within Photoshop. The Smart Highlight options work much like the Background Eraser tool covered in Chapter 7. The brush guesses where the edge of your image is. It might not do a perfect job in all places, but it's usually much faster to start with this option and then go back and delete or add to your highlight.

The highlight brush paints a temporary green glow around your subject to help you see what you are doing (see Figure 8.2). I recommend using a large brush diameter for most of your work. It doesn't matter how much green is outside your subject, but you want to keep your subject as green-free as you can. When you are ready to fine-tune, you can switch to a smaller brush diameter for both the Highlight tool and the Eraser tool to get into tight areas. Using the key commands for zooming in and out really comes in handy with this tool. In tight areas, it's so much easier to zoom in really close. Once you finish selecting your subject, you'll select the Paint Bucket tool and click the area you want to save. This turns the area you want to keep blue. That and the green outer glow go away once you click the OK button to accept your Extraction.

To isolate a subject with the Extract tool:

1. Open a photo with a subject to extract.

2. Choose Filter ➪ Extract to launch the Extract tool in a separate window.

3. Select the Edge Highlighter tool from the left. Select the check box for Smart Highlighting on the right.

Figure 8.2. The Extract tool with highlight.

4. Adjust your brush size by pressing the] key several times to enlarge it or the [key to shrink it.

5. Hugging the outside of your subject, draw around your subject. Paint in small segments; if you mess up, it's better to have to undo a small piece than the whole thing.

6. If you mess up, press ⌘+U (Ctrl+U) to undo. To zoom in and out for better control, press and hold ⌘+spacebar (Ctrl+spacebar) and click your mouse. To zoom out, press and hold ⌘+option+spacebar (Ctrl+Alt+spacebar) and click your mouse.

7. Clean up any extra green inside your subject with the Eraser tool. You can adjust its brush size just like the Highlight tool.

8. Click the Preview button to see how you are doing. You might find that you have some extra bits. I sometimes leave these and clean them up later with the Lasso tool, but for major stuff, you can just click the Highlight tool and start editing out. You'll need to use the Paint Bucket tool again before clicking OK or the Preview button.

9. When you are done, click OK to accept your extraction.

In Figure 8.3 I added a patterned background to my finished extraction. You can always undo it if you aren't happy with the results. Use your Lasso to clean up any extra bits.

Watch Out!

The Paint Bucket tool is selectable only when you've managed to isolate your subject in an enclosed highlight area. If the tool isn't selectable, make sure your highlight goes all the way around your image.

Figure 8.3. A photo of a dog extracted using the Extract tool.

Painting masks in Quick Mask Mode

Photoshop has an alternative screen mode for creating masks. It's called Quick Mask Mode, and you can switch to it by clicking on the circular icon below your background color swatch in the Toolbox. The area that will be masked is tinted red, and you punch out areas of the red that you don't want masked. Figure 8.4 is an example of a photo being masked in Quick Mask Mode. Quick Mask Mode is an opposite approach to the other methods and can be used in conjunction with them to tighten up selections.

You can switch back and forth from Quick Mask Mode to Standard Mode at any time to edit your selection area, and then when you are done, you create a new layer mask just as you did in the first two examples. The benefits of working in Quick Mask Mode are that you get to take advantage of the paint and Eraser tools to create your mask. Just remember that you are working in reverse here. You want to erase the areas you don't want masked and paint the areas you want to block out.

Figure 8.4. Quick Mask Mode.

To create a mask in Quick Mask Mode:

1. Open a photo to mask. Make sure you unlock your layer if it's a Background layer by double-clicking the layer thumbnail and renaming it.

2. Get a head start on your mask selection by selecting the Magic Wand tool or pressing the letter W. The Magic Wand tool is located directly to the right of the Lasso tool in the Toolbox.

3. Click an area to select it. Shift+click another area to add it to the selection. If the tool selected more of the image than you wanted, try lowering the tolerance setting in the Options bar. If the Magic Wand tool selected too little, raise the tolerance setting in the Options bar. A tolerance level of between 8 and 16 is usually a good moderate level to start with.

4. Click the Quick Mask Mode button in the Toolbox. It is just below the background color swatch. Your image should turn translucent red except for where you selected areas with the Magic Wand tool.

5. Add to your mask selection. Switch to the Eraser tool by pressing the letter E. Increase or decrease your Brush size by using the [and] keys. You'll also want to adjust the Brush Hardness setting in the Options bar to 100%. The key command for increasing Brush Hardness is Shift+].

6. You can use the Lasso tool to select an area, and then press the Delete key to get rid of the red and add it to the mask selection.

7. You can switch back and forth between modes to check your progress.

8. Once you've gotten your image masked, go back to Standard Mode by clicking on the icon below the foreground color swatch in the Toolbox.

9. Click the Create New Layer Mask button to mask your image.

The benefits of using a variety of tools to create your mask can come in handy for objects that have complex shapes and need fine detailing. Figure 8.5 shows an image that has been masked using Quick Mask Mode. A patterned background has been added.

Figure 8.5. An image that has been masked in Quick Mask Mode.

Inside Scoop

Make slight adjustments to your selection area by choosing Select ⇨ Modify and choosing from Smooth, Expand, or Contract.

Back up your mask selections as alpha channels

All masks are temporary or permanent grayscale channels just like the other color channels and can be edited with any of Photoshop's editing tools. Any time you edit in Quick Mask Mode, Photoshop creates a temporary alpha channel in the Channels palette. You can create a more permanent mask by saving your selection as an alpha channel. In fact, any selection can be saved as an alpha channel. You can edit it or load it as a selection any time you need to use it. It can be heartbreaking to spend a long time on a selection, only for something happen to it and have to start over. Keeping a copy handy in the Channels folder can be a lifesaver. It's also handy for using on other folders. You can drag and drop your channels from one file to another just like you can with layers.

While I'm showing you how to save a selection as an alpha channel, I'd like to introduce you to one more way of creating a mask: by using the Selective Color feature (see Figure 8.6). This works only on images that have background colors vastly different than the foreground colors. Even under good conditions, you may need to go in with the Lasso tool and unselect areas of shadow or highlight. Still, it can be a quick and effective method under the right conditions.

To save a selection as an alpha channel:

1. Open a photo to mask. Create a copy of your image layer by dragging its thumbnail onto the Create New Layer button on the bottom of the Layers palette.

2. Choose Select ⇨ Color Range (see Figure 8.7). Make sure the Image radio button is selected.

3. On the bottom of the Color Range window, choose Quick Mask from the Selection Preview drop-down list. Your image will have a transparent red cast over it.

Figure 8.6. A mask created from an alpha channel.

4. Click the subject you'd like to mask. Press and hold the Shift key and drag your cursor over your image; you'll see areas of your image being revealed through the red. If you are seeing large areas of the background coming through, try deselecting them by Option+clicking (Alt+clicking) them. You might not get a perfect selection, but try to get a good start so that finishing up with the Lasso tool or in Quick Mask Mode will be easier.

5. Once you have a good start on a selection, click OK to create a selection based on your selections in the Color Range dialog box.

6. Switch to Quick Mask Mode and clean up your selection. Press and hold the Option key (Alt) to remove areas from the selection using the Marquee or Lasso tools. Use the Eraser tool to clean up areas inside your selected object.

7. When you have a good selection, open the Channels palette. If it's not on your screen, choose Window ⇨ Channels.

8. Click the Create Channel from Selection button on the bottom of the Channels palette. It looks just like the Layer Mask icon in the Layers palette.

Figure 8.7. The Color Range dialog box.

Now that you have created a channel like the one you see in Figure 8.8, you can load it as a selection by either ⌘+clicking (Ctrl+clicking) its thumbnail or clicking the Load Channel as Selection button on the bottom of the Channels palette. It looks like a selection circle on white.

Figure 8.8. A new alpha channel created from a selection.

Hack

You can create a channel without going to the Channels palette by choosing Select ⇨ Save Selection and choosing channel as the destination.

Masking photos into odd shapes

Because masks are created from selections, and the possibilities for creating selection shapes are endless, you can create cutouts of your images in any number of ways. By creating selections from existing shapes like the ones in the Custom Shapes library, or by developing your own by using photographs, you can create some unique and artistic shapes to use as collage pieces, or simply frame your photos in interesting ways.

Mask your photo using custom shapes

Chapter 5 discussed the Custom Shape tool and the many libraries that come installed with Photoshop. By choosing one of the shapes that come with Photoshop, there are many possibilities for creating fun photo shapes for use as an element in a design or photomontage.

1. Open a photo to mask. Be sure to unlock and rename your background layer by double-clicking it in the Layers palette.

2. Select the Custom Shape tool from the drawing tools fly-out menu and choose a custom shape to use as your mask from the Options bar.

3. Using the Paths Drawing option, draw a shape over your image. The Paths Drawing option is the second button in the Options bar, and shows a Pen icon in the middle of a rectangle.

4. Go to the Paths palette. It should be underneath your Layers palette. If it's not visible, choose Window ⇨ Paths.

5. Right-click the path you just created and select Make Selection.

6. To soften the edge just a bit, change the Feather to 2 pixels (see Figure 8.9). If you'd like to play with vignette effect, increase the Feather.

7. Click OK to accept your selection settings.

8. Go back to the Layers palette and click the Create New Layer Mask icon.

Figure 8.9. A photo being masked by a Custom Shape.

You've now added a layer mask to your photo layer. You can always disable or remove the layer mask by right-clicking on the layer mask thumbnail in the Layers palette and choosing Disable Layer Mask or Delete Layer Mask from the drop-down list.

Create a mask shape from another photo

By using high contrast pictures, you can create masks by adding a Threshold adjustment; and then using the Magic Wand to select an area for your mask shape, you can paste it into another photo to use as a layer mask. The flower in Figure 8.10 was a perfect specimen for this exercise. The flower is almost all lights and middle values, and the background is all darks. By adding a Threshold adjustment, I just pushed the pixels to either white or black. I needed only to erase little bits here and there to get a clean flower shape. To get help adjusting your photo's darks and lights, look at Chapter 11, which covers color correction.

Watch Out!

For this exercise, make sure you adjust the Threshold on a copy of your photo layer by choosing Image ⇨ Adjustments ⇨ Threshold. If you try to do this on a separate adjustment layer, you won't be able to edit it.

Figure 8.10. A shape created by adjusting the Threshold of a photo.

To create a masking shape from a photo:

1. Open a photo to use as your masking shape.

2. If you need to, make some color adjustments so that the foreground or shape you want is either very dark or very light, and the background or negative space is the opposite.

3. Drag the photo layer onto the Create New Layer icon to make a copy of it.

4. Click the top layer to select it and choose Image ⇨ Adjustments ⇨ Threshold.

5. Adjust the Threshold slider until most of your foreground is either all white or all black. You might have some areas that you'll need to edit.

6. Using the Brush tool, Eraser tool, or Lasso tool, clean up any areas that you don't want in your mask.

You should now have a nice black-and-white shape to use as your mask. It doesn't matter if the foreground is white or black; you're just going to use the shape to select, so it can be either. The most important thing is that you have a shape that's easily selectable with the Magic Wand tool. Next you'll copy your shape to the photo you want to mask.

To create a mask from a black-and-white shape:

1. Click the black-and-white layer to select it.

2. Select the Magic Wand tool from the Toolbox or press the letter W. Click the shape you'd like to use as your mask.

3. Choose Edit ⇨ Copy or press ⌘+C (Ctrl+C).

4. Open a photo to mask. Be sure to unlock your background layer by double-clicking on it.

5. Choose Edit ⇨ Paste or ⌘+P (Ctrl+P) to paste your selection in.

6. If you need to rescale your selection to fit your photo better, choose Edit ⇨ Free Transform or press ⌘+T (Ctrl+T) and then resize your image by stretching it by the corner points. Press Enter to accept your changes.

7. ⌘+click your black or white shape to create a selection area around it.

8. Click your photo layer to select it and click the Create New Layer Mask icon on the bottom of the Layers palette. Figure 8.11 shows a photo that was masked using a shape from another photo.

Now that you've gotten your mask, you can delete or hide the layer you pasted in. Add a Pattern Fill or Solid Color layer to your document and add some blending options to your mask like Stroke or Outer Glow.

Figure 8.11. A layer mask created using a selection from a photo.

Bright Idea!
Drag and drop a mask saved as an alpha channel to use as your cropping shape.

Performing subtle fadeouts using gradients

You can create masks using the Gradient tool to blend images together. By choosing a Radial Gradient, you can blend faces or other circular subjects with more delicacy than you can get with feathering selections. Using Linear Gradients, you can blend things along a horizontal or vertical plane. In Figure 8.12 I blended a baby's face into clouds using a mask created with a Radial Gradient.

Figure 8.12. A layer mask created with the Gradient tool.

To blend two images together using the Gradient tool:

1. Find two photos to use as your source. The first photo you'll work on is the blended photo, like the baby face in Figure 8.12.

2. Create a selection of the area you'd like to blend. You can use the Marquee tool, Magic Wand tool, or Quick Mask Mode to create your selection.

3. Copy your selection to the second file by choosing Edit ⇨ Copy or pressing ⌘+C (Ctrl+C).

4. ⌘+click (Ctrl+click) the thumbnail of your newly copied image to create a selection area around it.

5. Select the Gradient tool from the Toolbox.

6. Make a couple of changes in the Options bar. If it's not selected, choose the Gradient called Black, White — it's in the default Gradient set that comes automatically loaded with Photoshop.

7. Click the Radial Gradient button from the Gradient options. It's the second Gradient button.

8. Check the Reverse check box.

9. Starting from the center of your selected area, click and drag your mouse to slightly outside your selection area. Figure 8.13 shows a photo in Quick Mask Mode with a Gradient applied to the selection of the baby's face.

Figure 8.13. A Radial Gradient in Quick Mask Mode.

10. Go back to Standard Mode by clicking the button just below the foreground color swatch in the Toolbox.

11. Click the Create New Layer Mask icon, located at the bottom of the Layers palette.

You can play around with the opacity of your Gradient mask to achieve more subtle effects. If your gradient faded out too much or not enough of your image was covered, you'll need to redo your gradient. Press ⌘+option+Z (Ctrl+Alt+Z) a few times to undo several steps. Go back into Quick Mask Mode and try again. Once you get used to how the

Hack

You can avoid hard edges by initially creating a feathered selection of your first photo with the Lasso tool. The feather options are in the Options bar.

Gradient tool works, this will get easier to gauge. If your gradient is almost perfect, but you still see some hard edges, you can soften them up with the Eraser tool set at a low Opacity setting like 10% or 20%.

Combining your masking skills

It's time to take what you've learned and combine imagery to create a composite poster of several masks and type elements. Because your designs will be vastly different from mine, I think it makes more sense to talk through how I created Figure 8.14 so that you can use the examples to create your own images. The poster in Figure 8.14 was created with four different photos that I've taken over the years. The two ducks in the foreground were extracted separately and then pasted in and scaled using Free Transform.

Figure 8.14. Combining masked images.

It doesn't matter which method you choose to extract your images. I wanted to stick with a quick and dirty copy-and-paste method so I chose to use the Extract tool for most of mine. The following exercises assume that you are comfortable working with layers, blending modes, and the Lasso tool, as well as the different masking methods.

To try out the following methods, find a few elements in photos you'd like to piece together. Find a nice photo to use as your background image. When choosing your images, make sure you think about document dimensions. It's better to use elements that are larger in dimension than your background image so that if you need to do any scaling, you are scaling down instead of enlarging. You want to avoid enlarging images beyond their original size because you'll get pixilated or chunky-looking images.

To paste your elements into a background photo:

1. In each document containing an element, create masks or extractions of the images.

2. Paste each element into your background image.

3. To adjust an element's scale, click the layer to highlight it. Choose Edit ⇨ Free Transform. Press and hold the Shift key to constrain proportions and drag the corner points to scale your element.

4. For areas in your background image that you want to appear in the foreground, like the streetlight in Figure 8.15, temporarily lower the opacity of the extracted image layer so that you can see the background photo through it. The opacity adjustment slider is on the top right of the Layers palette.

5. Select the Lasso tool and select an area in your masked area to delete, thereby revealing parts of the background image. Then change your opacity level back to 100%.

Watch Out!

Consider lighting when looking for images to combine. If one of your elements has strong light coming from the left, and another has strong light coming from the right, the image won't be as believable.

Figure 8.15. A cutout of a layer created by using the Lasso tool.

If your image doesn't quite blend into the background, try adding an inner glow, but instead of using a light color, use a dark one.

To blend your extracted image into the background:

1. Right-click the thumbnail of the element's layer and select Blending Options. Click the Inner Glow check box to select it and view its options.

2. Click the light yellow color swatch, and using the Eyedropper tool, select a dark area in your background photo to use as a blending color.

3. Choose Darken as the Blending Mode. Increase the Opacity, Size, and Choke settings until you get the desired effect.

4. Click OK to save and apply your blending options.

To create a fake shadow for my mother duck, I've made a copy of the mother duck layer, flipped it vertically, and lowered the color saturation to make it look like a shadow. Using the Skew feature in Photoshop, I could change the direction of the shadow to match other shadows in the photo.

To create a shadow for an extracted image:

1. Drag and drop the thumbnail of your extracted image on the Create New Layer button in the Layers palette.

2. Choose Edit ⇨ Transform ⇨ Flip Vertical to create an image for your cast shadow. Move it by ⌘+dragging (Ctrl+dragging) it into place.

3. To match the angle of other shadows in your image, choose Edit ⇨ Transform ⇨ Skew. Stretch and skew your image to match the angle of the other shadows (see Figure 8.16).

Figure 8.16. The image angle being changed with the Skew tool.

4. Choose Image ⇨ Adjustments ⇨ Hue/Saturation and change the saturation level to –100.

5. Change the Opacity of your shadow layer to match other shadows in your photo.

This method works great for casting shadows on solid surfaces. If you are working with an object on water, check out my lesson on creating realistic water reflections in Chapter 14. If your shadow overlaps areas of your foreground, as mine did in Figure 8.17, create a cutout of your shadow by selecting the shadow area that overlaps your foreground with the Lasso tool and delete it. If your shadow image still doesn't quite match the other shadows in the photo, try adding a Color Overlay and using the Eyedropper tool to select the color of another shadow in your image. Choose Layer ⇨ Layer Style ⇨ Color Overlay. Be sure to lower the opacity of your color overlay to match over shadows.

Figure 8.17. An area of shadow deleted with the Lasso tool.

Just the facts

- Add a layer mask by selecting an area of a layer and clicking the Create New Layer Mask button in the Layers palette.
- Create a mask using Brush and Eraser tools by painting in Quick Mask Mode.
- Create alpha channels of your mask selections for safe keeping and future use.
- Crop photos into odd shapes by creating selections with custom shapes or selection areas created from other photos.
- Blend images together by creating gradient masks in Quick Mask Mode with the Gradient tool.

GET THE SCOOP ON...
Formatting paragraph type ■ Masking photos
with type ■ Warping text around a ball ■
Creating a reflective shadow

Creating Elements in Type

J ohannes Gutenberg first invented movable type some time around 1450. His printing method, which involved organizing individual letters together like a jigsaw puzzle, revolutionized printing and publishing. Before then, all books were either copied by hand or carved out one page at a time on wood blocks. Moveable type not only made printing words faster, cheaper, and easier, it also opened up a new world of word typefaces. Since its invention, people have been creating and designing typefaces for every conceivable application. With the development of PostScript in the 1980s, the technology for creating digital typefaces became more and more accessible. Since then, most of the traditional typefaces and a million new ones have been created in digital format.

Photoshop has been taking advantage of the Postscript font technology and the subsequent TrueType font technology since their inception. Combining the right typeface with the power and flexibility of Photoshop's type tools, you can become a master digital typesetter. The type tools create vector-based type objects that can be resized without losing quality, much like the vector drawing tools discussed in Chapter 5. Using the options in the Character and Paragraph palettes, you can control font family, font size, weight, and formatting.

In the previous chapters, I've introduced you to adding some simple text elements to your designs and photos. This chapter delves even deeper and explores Photoshop's powerful type tools. It shows you how to create paragraph text in a bounding box so that you can add and format blocks of text like you would in a page layout program. This chapter also takes a look at the type masking tools to create text from photographs, and shows you a couple of different ways to wrap text around a cylindrical object and create a realistic reflection of text on a shiny surface.

Adding headlines and paragraphs

You can add text using two methods. The most commonly used one, and one I've used in the previous chapters, is point type. This is used for things like headlines, single lines of type, buttons, and basically any short snippet of text. For this, you just select the Horizontal or Vertical Type tool, click where you'd like your text to appear, and start typing.

Paragraph type lets you define a rectangle that you'd like your text to flow in. When using this method, you have more control over text wrapping and hyphenation. Photoshop's type in a box behaves similarly to how page layout programs handle text. The bounding box that the text resides in can be stretched and shrunk. Figure 9.1 has a combination of point and paragraph type. I created the small copy in a paragraph type box so that I could try out different shapes and sizes without having to redo line breaks with every change.

The Options bar for the type tools lets you change the most commonly used features of text like font family, style, and size. From the Options bar you can also control anti-aliasing (which is similar to feathering), text alignment, color, and text warping.

The palettes associated with type tools give you much more control over type attributes such as leading, kerning, tracking, subscript, and superscript. Character and Paragraph palettes are the two palettes associated with editing text (see Figure 9.2). These palettes handle things like font families, font sizes, colors, leading, kerning, text alignment, and justification.

Figure 9.1. Examples of point type and paragraph type.

By default, these two palettes don't appear in your workspace, but they can be viewed at any time in a couple of ways. The first is through the type tools. Whenever you have a type tool highlighted, you'll see an icon in the Options bar to view the Character and Paragraph palettes. The icon is located two buttons over from the color swatch and looks like a folder with a bulleted list. Clicking that icon toggles the Character and Paragraph palettes on and off. You can also show the palettes by choosing Window ➪ Character. They are grouped together, so both will appear. If you know you'll be using text quite a bit in your work, I'd recommend adding them to your default workspace. I talk a little bit about customizing and saving your workspace in Chapter 2.

Inside Scoop

Automatically select all the text in a layer by double-clicking the layer's thumbnail icon.

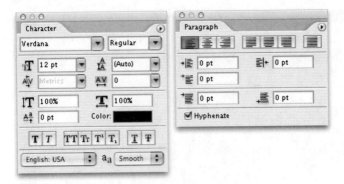

Figure 9.2. The Character and Paragraph palettes.

Photoshop gives you the ability to change different pieces of text in the same layer independently. Whenever you are changing font family, style, size, or color, you need to make sure the text you want to change is highlighted. If you'd like a different font color for each word in a paragraph or each letter in a word, just select each element one at a time and change them individually. The Paragraph palette options work on entire blocks of text, so you only need to highlight the layer you'd like to change.

Creating paragraph type

As I mentioned earlier, paragraph type is type that you create inside a bounding box. With point type, you have to add a hard return if you want a new line of text. Paragraph type takes care of that for you, no matter how you resize your text area. If your text doesn't quit fit inside the box, you'll see a little plus symbol on the bottom right of the box, letting you know that there's overflow text (see Figure 9.3). With paragraph type, you are able to control the text justification so that you could force each line of text to take up the same line width.

To add a text layer using paragraph type:

1. Create a new Photoshop document, big enough for a paragraph or two.

2. Click the Horizontal Type tool in the Toolbox or press the letter T.

3. Click and drag to create a bounding box for your paragraph text.

4. Type until your box is filled and you can no longer see the text you are typing. A little plus sign appears in the bottom right corner of the bounding box, letting you know there is text that cannot be displayed in the box's current size.

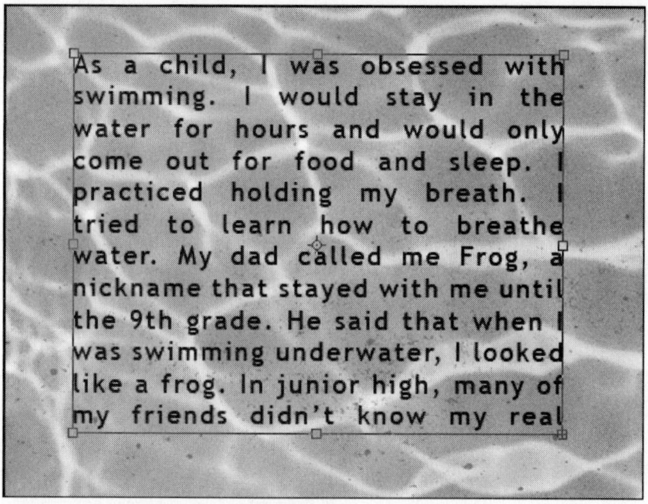

As a child, I was obsessed with swimming. I would stay in the water for hours and would only come out for food and sleep. I practiced holding my breath. I tried to learn how to breathe water. My dad called me Frog, a nickname that stayed with me until the 9th grade. He said that when I was swimming underwater, I looked like a frog. In junior high, many of my friends didn't know my real

Figure 9.3. Paragraph text with overflow.

5. To resize your text, position your mouse pointer over the corner boxes until they change into two-way arrows.

6. You can change your font size and font family by selecting your text and changing it in the Character palette.

7. Change the font color by clicking the color swatch in the Character palette. A Color Picker appears and you can select your new text color.

These are the basics of creating paragraph type in a resizable bounding box. The Paragraph palette gives you additional options for aligning, justifying, and indenting your text. The Character palette has additional options for changing your text to all caps, superscript, subscript, underline, or strikethrough.

Next, take a look at all the type options available in the Paragraph and Character palettes. Table 9.1 gives you a list of options in the Characters palette and their description. Like all of Photoshop's tools, you can find out each one's name by moving your mouse over an icon and waiting a few seconds. A yellow title box will appear with the name of the option.

Hack

Rotate your paragraph text while using a Type tool. Move your cursor to about a half inch away from one of the corners of your bounding box. You'll see your cursor icon change to a rotation icon. Click and drag to rotate.

Table 9.1. Options in the Character palette	
Type Option	**Description**
Kerning	Creates space between two letters. Click between the letters you'd like to add space to and adjust the kerning value. Use only when you need fine-tuning between specific letters.
Leading	The spacing between lines. Auto is the default, which gives you a leading that is approximately 2 points larger than your font size.
Tracking	Controls the space between letters. Use this over kerning to space out a block of text.
Horizontally Scale	Stretches each letter horizontally.
Vertically Scale	Stretches each letter vertically.
Anti-aliasing method	Controls how crisp or smooth your letters appear.

I've given some examples of these options in Figure 9.4. The other type options in the Paragraph palette let you control things like alignment, justification, and indentation.

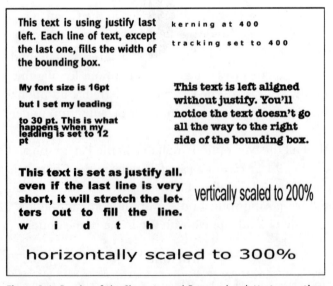

Figure 9.4. Results of the Character and Paragraph palette type options.

Which anti-alias method should I choose?

The anti-aliasing feature in the Character palette and Type Options bar allows you to control how your font blends into the background. Anti-aliasing adds fuzzy pixels around your characters so that they appear smooth. The drop-down list has four options that range from aliased (or non-anti-aliasing) to maximum anti-aliasing. As a general rule of thumb, use less anti-aliasing on smaller font sizes, 12 points or smaller. Anti-aliasing on smaller text tends to lessen its readability. Larger font sizes look better with more anti-aliasing. When designing graphics for the Web, try to use aliased text when creating buttons or navigation links for maximum readability. The amount of anti-aliasing you use really comes down to personal choice. Figure 9.5 shows aliased type and smooth anti-aliased type enlarged to 400%.

Figure 9.5. Comparing aliased and anti-aliased type.

Picking the right font family

Fonts and font families can consist of one or many typefaces. Typefaces can come in different weights like regular, bold, or black. Some fonts include condensed typefaces that have more narrow letters than regular type. With all the fonts available, it's easy to go font crazy. A good rule of thumb when designing with type is to stick to no more than two or three typefaces. If you need to accentuate a part of your text, try using bold or italics instead of going for a third or fourth font. Whenever possible, use the bold typeface that comes with your font family. The Character palette has a faux bold option, but it won't look nearly as good as the font family's bold version. If the font family you are using doesn't have bold, consider using a different font family.

Fonts can come in a variety of typeface styles. The two most familiar ones are serif and sans serif. Serifs are the little embellishments on your text, the little hooks and lines that hang on the ends of letters like little feet. Times, which is shown in Figure 9.6, and Georgia are two common serif fonts. Sans serif in French means "without serif." These fonts are without serifs and have a simpler, streamlined appearance. Arial and Verdana are two common sans serif fonts.

sans serif

serif

script

display

Figure 9.6. Different styles of typefaces.

Symbol fonts are typefaces that are made up of symbols like check-marks or smiley faces. They can be used as decorative bullets in lists or as clip art in your designs. Zapf Dingbats is the most commonly known symbol font. I've seen symbol fonts with pirate icons like ships and parrots, or retro symbols like bowling balls and coffee cups.

Display fonts are more decorative than regular serif or sans serif fonts. They often have a thematic feel, like a holiday or retro style. They should be used sparingly in designs because they can get a little busy if overused.

Adding fun third-party fonts

The font resources available on the Web are endless. Many downloadable fonts are free; others are quite affordable, usually ranging from $5 to $150. Many professional typeface creators, such as LinoType, Émigré, and ITC, allow you to pay and download professional-quality fonts when you need a font in a hurry. I've listed some of my favorite font Web sites in Appendix D in the back of the book, and I've included a few examples of some of my favorite fonts in Figure 9.7. Before you start downloading, there are just a few things you should know about fonts and font technology.

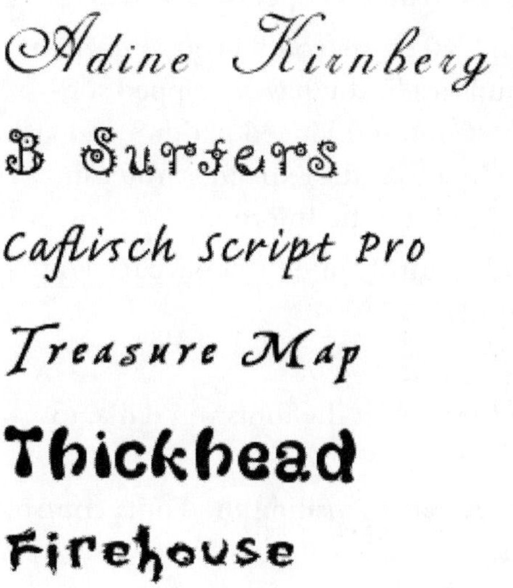

Adine Kirnberg

B Surfers

Caflisch Script Pro

Treasure Map

Thickhead

Firehouse

Figure 9.7. Examples of downloadable fonts.

Fonts are platform-specific. If you are on a Mac, don't try to download Windows fonts. They won't work. If you are on a Mac and you find a Windows font that you must have, there are some free font-converting tools available on the Internet. Problems in converting fonts are common, and often the converted fonts lose some quality in the process. I'd recommend sticking to platform-specific fonts whenever possible.

You'll sometimes see an option for TrueType or PostScript fonts. As font technology improves over the years, the differences between the two are disappearing. The TrueType font technology was created as an alternative to PostScript fonts. People argue that when it comes to fine print, Postscript is king. I tend to agree that when it comes to professional printers outputting high resolution prints, Postscript gives you sharper,

Watch Out!

Be careful what you download. Always run a virus scanner on files down-loaded from the Internet.

better-looking type. For most applications such as home printing or Web design, the difference in quality between the two is minimal. Font technology has advanced to the point that previewing, installing, and using either is a painless process.

To install fonts on a PC running the Windows operating system:

1. If your downloaded file has a .zip extension, you'll need to unzip it. Try double-clicking it. If it expands itself, you have unzipped software installed in your computer. If not, you'll need to download an unzipping program such as WinZip or Stuffit Expander. You can find either of these as free downloads on the Internet.

2. Click Start and then Settings and Control Panel. Double-click Fonts to open the control panel for fonts.

3. Choose File ➪ Install New Font.

4. Navigate to your unzipped font files, select the fonts you'd like to install, and click OK.

You can uninstall fonts in a similar way by visiting the Fonts control panel and using the uninstall feature.

To install fonts on a computer running Macintosh OS X:

1. Unzip your downloaded font package if it has a .zip extension. If you need unzip software, two common Mac applications are ZipIt and Stuffit Expander.

2. Double-click a font file to install it. A font program called Font Book launches and a preview of your font appears (see Figure 9.8). Click the Install Font button.

Bright Idea!

Change your font preview size in the font family drop-down list. Choose Photoshop ➪ Preferences ➪ Type. Check the check box for Font Preview Size and choose Large from the drop-down list.

That's all there is to it. You'll need to restart Photoshop for your font to appear in the font list.

Figure 9.8. The Font Book font installation program on Mac OS X.

Masking type with photos

There are two ways to created masked type. This section introduces you to both. The first method is by using the Type Masking tools. Chapter 8 discusses how you can create masks by converting a selection area into a layer mask. The Horizontal Type Mask and Vertical Type Mask tools work in the same way. The masking tools essentially create selection areas where your type would be. As you enter your text, your screen turns translucent red as you type, just as when you are in Quick Mask Mode. When you press Enter to accept your text, what you are left with is a selection area where text would normally appear. Although this method requires fewer steps than the second method, you won't be able to edit your text after you accept it.

The second method involves creating a clipping mask with the regular Type tools. After the mask is created, you can change your text or font family and font size. Look at both methods by creating some masked text. Once you've mastered creating text masks, I'll show you a technique to give your text a battered, well-worn look.

Adding depth to text with photo masking

Creating text that uses photos or pattern as its background is a great effect that can add a lot of pizzazz to a design. You can use a photo of a flower to create a logo for a florist, or a photo of wood grain for a furniture maker's logo. On designs that need to stay plain, a header graphic with a photo background can add an extra element and give depth to your design. Figure 9.9 shows a text mask over a photo of glittery wallpaper.

Figure 9.9. A text mask over a photo.

To create text out of a photo:

1. Open a photo to use as a background image for your text. If there is just one locked Background layer, double-click it in the Layers palette to rename and unlock it.

2. Select the Horizontal Type Masking tool from the Type tool fly-out menu. You can toggle to it by pressing Shift+T a couple times.

3. Click and type your word or phrase. Your screen turns pinkish, meaning you are in Quick Mask Mode. Your type will be semitransparent.

4. You can change your font family and size by selecting your text and changing it in the Character palette.

5. When you are satisfied with your text, press Enter to accept it. Your text should be surrounded by the marching ants selection lines.

6. Click the Add Layer Mask button on the bottom of the Layers palette. It looks like a white circle in a gray box.

If all went well, you should see something like Figure 9.9. There are some drawbacks to creating a text mask like this, the biggest being that you can't edit your text after you've created it. I'm happy to announce there's a better way that will give you editable text.

To create an editable masked text:

1. Select the regular Horizontal Type tool from the Toolbox. Enter your text. When you like what you have, press Enter to accept it.

2. Drag your photo layer above your text in the Layers palette so that it is completely covering your text. If you have other layers in your file, make sure your photo layer is directly above your text layer.

Hack

Temporarily disable a layer link by Shift+clicking the link icon in the layer's name. A red X appears. To re-enable it, Shift+click the link icon again.

3. With your photo layer still highlighted, choose Layer ⇨ Create Clipping Mask, or use the key command ⌘+Option+G (Ctrl+Alt+G).

You should be looking at your text with the image masked inside it. If you look in your Layers palette, you'll notice a little arrow in the photo layer and an underline in your text layer like you see in Figure 9.10. These are to indicate that the two layers comprise a clipping mask. This method is far superior to the previous one. You can undo the mask at any time by choosing Layer ⇨ Release Clipping Mask. You can move each layer independently from one another like you would any other layer. You can link the two layers together so that you can move them as a unit. The text layer has stayed a text layer, so you can edit it or change font size, font family, or any other text attribute.

Figure 9.10. Masked text using a grouped clipping mask.

Creating a distressed type look with masking

You can get that grungy text look by masking your text over an image that's been modified to a black-and-white image using a Threshold adjustment. This effect takes the right photos for the job. I've found cityscapes usually make the best candidates: something that is very busy, with lots of lines. The noisier the photo, the better. In Figure 9.11, I've created a rock poster using the distressed text method.

Figure 9.11. Distressed text created with a photo.

To create a distressed text look:

1. Find a photo with lots of contrast and texture. Cityscapes seem to work well because they have many lines and tend to be on the busy side. Be sure to make a copy of your photo. You'll be destroying this copy of the photo in the process.

2. If your image has just one locked Background layer, double-click it in the Layers palette to rename and unlock it.

3. Choose Image ⇨ Adjustments ⇨ Threshold to make a Threshold adjustment to your image. Threshold forces all the pixels in your

image to be either black or white. Move the slider around until you get a big area with some nice texture. This is going to take some practice to get the result you are looking for.

4. If your image is mostly white, you'll need to invert it. Choose Image ⇨ Adjust ⇨ Invert, or press the key command ⌘+I (Ctrl+I).

5. Delete the white areas by selecting the Magic Wand tool, clicking an area of white to select it, and then choosing Select ⇨ Similar. Once all the white is selected, press Delete to remove it.

6. Select the Horizontal Type tool from the Toolbox and type a word or phrase. Change the font size and font family through the Character palette. You'll want something nice and big to get the full effect. Make your font color match the background color to get a transparent look. When you are done, click Enter to accept your text.

7. In the Layers palette, drag your photo layer above your text layer. You'll be creating a clipping mask, so it needs to be directly above your text in the layer list.

8. Choose Layer ⇨ Create Clipping Mask to merge the two layers together.

You can move your texture layer separately from your text layer. Once you've found a position you like, select both layers and link them so that they move as one unit. Figure 9.12 is an example of what your image and Layer palette should look like. I added a solid color fill layer so you can see the effect more easily.

Figure 9.12. A grungy text mask from a photo.

Typing on a curve or shape

Photoshop takes advantage of the vector drawing tools to guide text around an object. By drawing a vector line, rectangle, or ellipse to mimic objects in your photos, you can add text that flows along shapes in your photo. This method works only for point type and takes a little getting used to. It can seem awkward at first when you are trying to rotate or reposition your text around an object, but once you get used to its quirks, it's straightforward. If you've used Adobe Illustrator, this feature works very similar to Illustrator's type-on-a-curve feature.

To create type on a curve:

1. Create a new document or open a photo to add text to.

2. Select the Ellipse tool from the vector tools fly-out menu. You can press Shift+U to toggle to it.

3. Click the Path shape option in the Options bar. It is the second from the left and has a pen icon surrounded by a rectangle.

4. Click and drag your mouse to create a circle.

5. Select the Horizontal Type tool from the Toolbox or press the letter T.

6. Move your mouse over the circle until your cursor changes to include a slanted line, and then click to place your text cursor and enter your type.

7. To rotate your text or move it to the inside of the circle, press and hold the ⌘ key (Ctrl) and drag your text around by clicking the small square text anchor. Move your cursor inside the circle to make your text flip over into the center, or keep it outside the circle to have your type wrap around the outside of the circle.

The image in Figure 9.13 was created by creating an ellipse and then adding type on a curve. You can type on any vector shape. Create any type of curved or jagged line you want with the Pen tools or any of the vector drawing tools covered in Chapter 5. Just remember to select the Path shape option in the Options bar of each tool. Your text is editable, and you can add blending options just as you would to a regular text layer.

Watch Out!

The text anchor can sometimes be buried under your text and is hard to find. Your cursor changes into dark, two-way arrows when your mouse is on top of the anchor.

Figure 9.13. Type on a curve.

Wrapping text around an object

Photoshop has a few transform features for skewing, rotating, and scaling images or type. All of the transform features can be accessed by choosing Edit ⇨ Transform and choosing one of the options. When transforming text, keep in mind that you are limited to the types of warping you can do so that your text is still editable. There is always the option of rasterizing your text so that you can do anything you want to it. Once text has been rasterized, you won't be able to edit it, so make sure you keep copies of layers.

This section looks at the Warp feature. Using Photoshop's Warp feature, you can stretch your text to make it appear like it's wrapping around an object such as a cylinder or sphere. Warping text works slightly different than warping an object. You have slightly less control, but the trade-off is that you can edit your text even after you've warped it. This section looks at both options.

Warp text around a cup

Add the illusion of three dimensions by warping text around a coffee cup, beer bottle, or anything else spherical. In Figure 9.14, I've warped a logo around a coffee cup to preview what it would look like. By arching the text, I can give the illusion of perspective and three dimensions. By using the Warp tools on my text layer, I can still go back and edit my text later. The warping effect will automatically be applied, no matter what changes I make to the type.

Figure 9.14 shows text with Arc Upper warping applied and the other warp options available from the Type Options bar.

Figure 9.14. The Arc Upper warp applied to text.

To warp text around an object:

1. Find a photo of a cylindrical object.

2. Select the Horizontal Type tool and add some type. Change your font family and size.

3. Click the Create Warp Text button in the Options bar. It looks like a letter T with a rounded arrow below it. A dialog box appears.

Hack

Warp text through a handy dialog box. Right-click your text layer and select Warp Text from the bottom of the list. Select a style and change warping through percentage sliders.

4. Select an option from the drop-down list. I used Arc Upper on my coffee cup in Figure 9.14.

5. Adjust your Bend and Vertical Distortion until your text looks like it's wrapping around your object. Press Enter when you are done.

This method gets pretty good results in most circumstances while keeping the text editable. Use this method whenever possible. If you have an extreme case where you really need to warp the heck out of your text, the next method gives you much more freedom to do so.

Rasterize text for more warping power

Using the Warp feature on a text layer can usually yield good results with most objects. It does, however, limit you by only allowing you to warp in one style or another. You can't combine an arc warp with a bulge warp. Sometimes the only way to get the results you want is by combining different types of warping. Rasterizing your text layer before using the Warp feature gives you much more control over the realism of your text's perspective. Once rasterized, you can squeeze, arc, and stretch your text to your heart's content.

To warp rasterized text for more control:

1. Choose Layer ⇨ Rasterize ⇨ Type.

2. Choose Edit ⇨ Transform ⇨ Warp to add the warping grid to your selected layer.

From here you can adjust the grid in any number of ways to get the result you are looking for. In Figure 9.15, I shrunk the edges, bulged out the middle, and arched my text so that it looks like it's wrapping around the softball.

Figure 9.15. Warped text with perspective.

Adding special effects to your text

In previous chapters I've used blending options to add drop shadow, embossing, gradients, and stroke to text and layers. This section covers adding styles to text and modifying them to get a unique look, and how to create a reflection of text on a shiny surface.

Creating stylistic text

By adding layer styles to your text, you can create dynamic, stylistic text with very little effort. Modify the preinstalled styles even further to get a truly unique effect. The headline in Figure 9.16 was created by taking advantage of some of Photoshop's styles. I found a style that was close to what I wanted and then modified it just a bit. I adjusted the stroke and emboss blending options associated with the style.

Bright Idea!

Increase the size of your style swatches. Click the arrow on the top right of the Styles palette and choose Large Thumbnail from the drop-down list.

Figure 9.16. Type with a modified layer style.

To load some of Photoshop's additional style sets for special type styles:

1. Add a type layer to a new document.

2. Bring the Styles palette to the front. If it's not visible on your screen, choose Window ⇨ Styles to open it.

3. Click the arrow on the top right of the Styles palette and select Text Effects from the drop-down list. A dialog box asks you if you'd like to replace current styles.

4. Click the Append button to add the Text Effects to your styles list.

5. Repeat the last two steps to add the Text Effects 2 styles set to your Styles palette.

Once you've gotten some styles loaded, click them to apply them to the current text layer. You can modify them even further by right-clicking the layer name and selecting Blending Options. You can modify the options associated with the style you have currently selected or add more Blending Options to the style.

Create a 3-D reflection on a shiny surface

You can create an effect that makes your text look like it is standing up on a shiny surface. By duplicating your text layer, flipping it vertically, stretching it, and adding a little bit of Gaussian blur, you can create a realistic reflection of your text. The text in Figure 9.17 appears to be sitting on the surface of the sand. This effect works great on any shiny surface.

Figure 9.17 shows a reflective layer with skewed, stretched, and blurred text.

Figure 9.17. Reflective text created with skew, scale, and Gaussian blur.

To add a reflective text layer:

1. Find a photo with a shiny reflection. Wood, water, or glass surfaces work well.

2. Select the Horizontal Type tool from the Toolbox or press the letter T.

3. Create your main text. Change your font family, size, and color. Press Enter to accept your text.

4. Copy your text layer by dragging and dropping it on the Create New Layer icon in the Layer's palette.

5. Click the copied layer to select it.

6. Choose Edit ⇨ Transform ⇨ Flip Vertical to create a mirror image of your main text.

7. Temporarily change to the Move tool by pressing and holding the ⌘ key (Ctrl) and move your reflection text just below your main text.

8. Choose Edit ⇨ Transform ⇨ Skew. Drag the corner boxes to stretch and skew your image. Try to create shadows that are as long as other ones in your photo and try to match their angle. Press Enter when you are ready to accept your skew.

Next, add a gradient and blur to your reflection to make it look more realistic. I'd recommend making a backup copy of your reflection text. When you add the Blur, you won't be able to edit the text any more.

To add a gradient and blur:

1. Choose Layer ⇨ Layer Style ⇨ Gradient Overlay. Select the second gradient option in the drop-down list for gradient styles. Adjust your gradient angle so that your shadow fades like other shadows in your photo.

2. Click the gradient thumbnail to open the Gradient Editor as shown in Figure 9.18. Click the dark-color stop on the bottom left of the gradient. Using the Eyedropper tool, change the color to match other shadows in your photo.

3. To add a Gaussian blur to your shadow, choose Filter ⇨ Blur ⇨ Gaussian Blur. You'll be warned that the text needs to be rasterized before proceeding. Click OK. Adjust your blur. I used a Radius of 12 pixels in Figure 9.17.

Bright Idea!

Adjust the opacity stop while in the Gradient Editor to fade out the lightest part of your shadow. The opacity stop is the top left black arrow just above the large gradient adjuster.

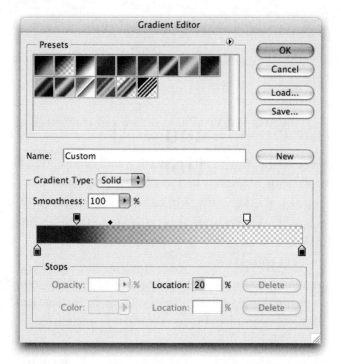

Figure 9.18. The Gradient Editor, accessed from the Blending Options dialog box.

Just the facts

- Add paragraph text and control alignment, justification, and indentation through the Paragraph palette.

- Control type by adjusting Leading, Kerning, Tracking, and Scaling through the Character palette.

- Type on a curve by creating a circle with the Ellipse tool.

- Wrap text around a cylindrical object with the Warp feature.

- Create a text reflection on a shiny surface by copying a layer, flipping it vertically, and modifying the layer to look like a shadow.

GET THE SCOOP ON...
Undoing multiple edits in the History palette ▪ Creating
Snapshots of your work as you go ▪ Selective image
adjustments with the History Brush ▪ Adding stylish
frames around photos

Undoing and Redoing with History and Actions

T he power of the Actions palette in Photoshop is sadly neglected in most Photoshop books and tutorials. Recording repetitive tasks like running your favorite filters or adjustments is a quick way to batch-edit an entire set of photos. If you use the same blending modes over and over again, saving them as an action can keep your work consistent as well as save you time.

The History palette gives you access to a list of changes you've done in your current session. Because Photoshop allows multiple undos, it needs to keep a list of every change you've made to an image so that it can manage those undos. Each time you undo a change, you are essentially going back in time and stepping back through actions that you made on a file. Photoshop decided to take it one step further and opened up the history list to all its users, giving them more freedom over their changes. The History palette allows you to jump anywhere within your list of changes.

This chapter shows you how to get the most mileage out of the History palette and use the Snapshots feature to take the pain out of having to undo multiple edits. You'll see how to edit files selectively by undoing part of your edits with the History Brush. You'll create and save your own actions and action sets to use on several files. Finally, you'll see how to create a droplet on your desktop so that you can drag and drop several files for batch editing.

Chapter 10

213

Memorizing key commands for undoing

Whenever you undo, redo, or revert in Photoshop, you are essentially maneuvering through the History palette. You may have used these key commands in several of the exercises in the previous chapters. They all relate to the History palette; Table 10.1 is a list of History actions, the key commands, and a description of what they do.

Table 10.1. History actions, key commands, and descriptions

Action	Command	Description
Undo/Redo	⌘+Z (Ctrl+Z)	Undoes the last change or redoes the last undo
Step Backward	Mac: ⌘+Shift+Z PC: Ctrl+Shift+Z	Steps backward through undos one Snapshot at a time
Step Forward	Mac: ⌘+Option+Z PC: Ctrl+Alt+Z	Steps forward through undos one Snapshot at a time until you are at the last created Snapshot
Revert	F12	Reverts your file to the last saved version

Time-traveling with the History palette

Photoshop keeps a history of all the work you've done in your current session and stores it in the History palette. Each time you make a change to an image, Photoshop adds it to a running list of changes. Once you close the file, your history is lost. You can jump back and forth between the various changes at any time during a given session. You can create new documents from any state in your History list. You can also create Snapshots of your document. This is a quick way to store versions of your edits as you go along. Just be careful: Snapshots are cleared out when you close the file. You can create a new document from a Snapshot or any history state. The History palette has a Create New Document from Current State button. You can also right-click any of the states or Snapshots and select New Document from the drop-down list.

Now take a look at all the parts of the History palette. If it's not already visible, choose Window ⇨ History to open the palette. The palette consists of Snapshots and states for keeping track of edits one step at a time in the case of states, or several steps at once with the Snapshots. You can create a Snapshot at any point in your editing process or have Photoshop automatically create one every time you save your file.

Bright Idea!

Save a copy of your image with merged layers in two quick steps. Click the Create New Snapshot button and select Merged Layers in the From drop-down list. Right-click your new Snapshot and select New Document.

Figure 10.1 shows the History palette with a list of five states.

Figure 10.1. The History palette.

Leave mistakes in the past with one click

You are probably familiar with undoing several steps by way of the key commands or Edit menu. If you need to step back several steps, you can save your fingers some typing by clicking the step you want to revert to in the History palette.

Saving a longer history list

By default, the History palette saves up to 20 states. You can increase this number in the Preferences panel. Be warned that Photoshop eats up more memory the more states you allow Photoshop to save. The History states amount can be increased by choosing Photoshop ⇨ Preferences ⇨ General.

Watch Out!

If you select a previous state and then make a change, all the other states will be removed from the History palette.

Selective undoing with nonlinear history

You can remove specific edits to a file without losing the rest of the list by selecting the Allow Non-Linear History option from the History palette Options list. Checking this option allows you to remove single edits without affecting the other edits in the list. If you perform an adjustment on a layer and then add paint strokes to it, you can remove the adjustment without losing your paint stroke.

Figure 10.2 shows the History Options dialog box with the Allow Non-Linear History option checked.

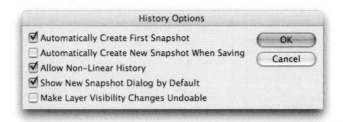

Figure 10.2. The History Options dialog box.

To enable nonlinear history through the History Options:

1. Click the little black arrow on the top right of the History palette.

2. Select History Options from the drop-down list.

3. Check the Allow Non-Linear History check box and click OK.

You can now delete a state in your History list without removing the other edits below it in the list. To delete a state, you can either click it to select it and then click the Delete button on the bottom of the History palette, or right-click the state and select Delete from the drop-down list.

Bright Idea!

Nonlinear editing comes in handy when using action sets with multiple steps. You'll be able to edit out certain steps to personalize the effect. I'll introduce you to action sets later on in this chapter.

Dragging and dropping history between files

If you perform a crop, color correction, or any other edit on a file and want to perform the same edit on another file, you can drag and drop your history state onto the other document's window, just as you would a layer or layer style. Any settings, values, or options saved with your history state will also be applied automatically on the other document.

To crop two files:

1. Open two files.

2. Select the Crop tool from the Toolbox or press the letter C.

3. Click and drag across your image to create a crop area. Press Enter to accept your crop.

4. Move your Document windows so that you can see the second file underneath the first.

5. In the History palette, click and drag your crop state onto the second file's Document window.

Voila! Instant crop. This works for just about anything that is saved in the History palette and is your first introduction to repeating actions in Photoshop on different files. The next section looks at using and creating repeatable actions to save you time when editing multiple files.

Saving History Snapshots

Your History list can fill up quickly, and sometimes being able to sort through every single brush stroke doesn't offer much of a benefit. By saving Snapshots along the way, you can keep versions of your edits in case you need to backtrack. When you open a file, Photoshop automatically creates a Snapshot of your file. You can add additional Snapshots along the way. Be careful: Just like the history list, Snapshots aren't saved once you close the file. They are only there as long as your current session lasts.

Figure 10.3 shows the New Snapshot dialog box with the From dropdown list visible.

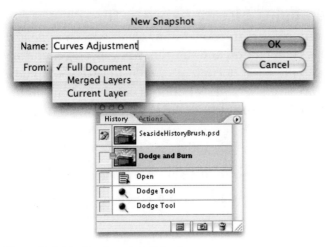

Figure 10.3. The New Snapshot dialog box.

To add and manage Snapshots of your edits:

1. Make some edits to your document. Click the Create Snapshot button on the bottom of the History palette; it looks like a camera. Give your new Snapshot a descriptive name so you'll remember what edits it includes.

2. Make some more edits and add another Snapshot.

3. Click each Snapshot or use the slider on the left side of the Snapshots list to view each Snapshot's contents.

4. You can create a new document from one of the Snapshots. Right-click it in the History palette and select New Document. This is a great feature for showing clients different edits of a design.

5. You can create Snapshots of a single layer. When you click the Create Snapshot button, choose Current Layer from the drop-down list in the New Snapshot dialog box.

Saving different Snapshots into new files can be a fast way to branch out your designs into different directions.

Bright Idea!

If you are going to run an action set with several steps, take a Snapshot before-hand. If you don't like the results, click the Snapshot to undo all the steps.

The History Brush

The History Brush allows you to travel back in time selectively by painting into the past. It works by removing any bits of history associated with the pixels that are exposed to the Brush tip. You can assign a specific Snapshot to use as your source.

In Figure 10.4, I had a photo with a bright blue sky and dramatic clouds, but the building face is in quite a bit of shadow. I wanted to enhance the building face without losing the richness of the sky. If I performed a Levels adjustment on the entire image, I'd lose that great sky. By first doing a Levels adjustment on the image and then removing some of it with the History Brush, I was able to get the best of both worlds.

Figure 10.4. Three stages of using the History Brush to remove parts of a Levels adjustment.

To remove changes selectively with the History Brush:

1. Find a photo to try out the History Brush on. Make a copy of your image layer by dragging and dropping its thumbnail on the Create New Layer button in the Layers palette.

2. Perform a Levels, Curves, or other adjustment to your copied layer.

Watch Out!

The History Brush doesn't work on Adjustment layers. You'll need to make your adjustments to the actual image layer.

3. If the palette is not currently visible, choose Window ⇨ History. Click the Create New Snapshot button on the bottom of the History palette; it looks like a little camera.

4. Set the source for the History Brush to the first Snapshot in your list. The icon looks like a brush and a circular line with an arrow (see Figure 10.5).

Figure 10.5. The History palette with Snapshots taken of three different stages.

5. Select the History Brush from the Toolbox or press the letter Y.

6. Adjust your brush diameter, hardness, and opacity as you would a regular brush. You can also use the [and] keys to adjust the brush diameter.

7. Click and drag your mouse to paint in the area where you'd like to remove your adjustment changes. The places where you paint revert to the first Snapshot of your document.

The Art History Brush

This tool lets you add texture to your photo by using any of the brush presets. In Figure 10.6 I used the colors from a History Snapshot so that when my brush is over a certain color, the brush uses that color to create texture. It's a more creative, freehand way of adding texture to your photo without using a filter. You have more control over which parts of your image you want to add texture to. You don't need to create a new Snapshot to use the tool, but you can get some fun effects by creating a funky-colored version of your image and then assigning it as the History Brush source but working in the previous Snapshot.

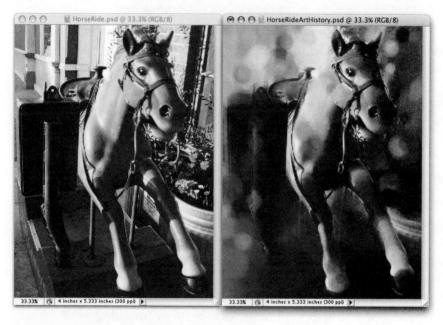

Figure 10.6. Texture added with the Art History Brush.

To add texture to a photo with the Art History Brush:

1. Open a file to paint. Create a copy of the image layer by dragging and dropping its layer thumbnail on the Create New Layer button on the bottom of the Layers palette.

2. Select the Art History Brush from the History Brush fly-out menu in the Toolbox.

3. Click the Brush Presets menu in the Options bar to view a list of brushes. Click the arrow on the top right and select Wet Media Brushes from the list.

4. Click the Append button to add them to your list of brush presets. Choose one that looks interesting to you. For Figure 10.6 I used a brush called Brush Light Texture Medium Tip.

5. Adjust the brush diameter, opacity, and style in the Options bar. You can get a little more control using the Dab or Tight Short style.

6. Begin painting. To create some nice texture, vary your brush diameter and opacity throughout your painting. Leave important areas like facial features or other details untouched.

Although it might take a little getting used to, you can get some beautiful effects when using this brush. If you like this effect, try painting from another Snapshot source. Paste a brightly colored photo into your document, and with its layer highlighted, create a Snapshot using Current Layer as the From source. Assign your new Snapshot as the History Brush source Snapshot, but click your original image's Snapshot. When you paint, the Art History Brush will use colors from the newly pasted layer.

Saving and applying your own actions

The Actions palette in Photoshop gives you a mechanism for recording several editing steps and then playing them back on new layers or documents. These steps can include anything from running a filter to painting a brush stroke. You can insert stops in your action list so that you can add an interactive piece to your actions. This comes in handy when you want to have control over settings in dialog boxes, or you want to be able to do text edits or select different layers before continuing.

Create your own action sets

Action sets are folders that help you manage and organize your actions. Once you create a set, you can then save it to your hard drive for future use or share it with other Photoshop users. There are tons of free action sets available through Photoshop support sites. See the Resources section in the back of the book for a list of places to find action sets for creating special effects or helping with common tasks.

To create your own action set:

1. Click the little black arrow on the top right of the Actions palette and select New Set from the drop-down list. The New Set dialog box you see in Figure 10.7 appears.

Figure 10.7. The New Set dialog box.

2. Name your set and click OK. The set will appear below the Default set folder. If you need to, click the arrow next to the Default set folder icon to collapse the list and give yours more room to breathe.

Record an action for performing Auto Levels and Smart Sharpen

Now that you've created your own action set, you can record an action and save it in your set. A common action you might find yourself running is one that automatically performs an Auto Levels adjustment and a Smart Sharpen filter. An action can record just about any editing task that you can think of.

To add an action for Auto Levels and Smart Sharpen:

1. Open a photo to use as your template.

2. Click the Create New Action button on the bottom of the Actions palette.

3. Name your action in the New Action dialog box and make sure your newly created set is selected in the Set list.

4. Once you click OK, Photoshop begins recording your actions. Don't panic! You can remove any unwanted ones when you are done. Notice that the Red Record button is highlighted in the Actions palette. It stays highlighted as long as you are recording.

5. Choose Image ⇨ Adjustments ⇨ Auto Levels.

6. Choose Filter ⇨ Sharpen ⇨ Smart Sharpen. Leave the settings alone for now and click OK.

7. In the Actions palette, click the square Stop button to stop recording.

8. Now click the arrow next to your new action to view its contents. Each item has an additional level of information that you can view. Expand those by clicking the arrow icon next to them. Your Actions palette should look something like Figure 10.8.

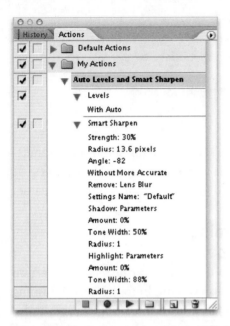

Figure 10.8. The Actions palette with a recorded action.

If you have any additional steps that you don't want as part of your action, click to highlight them and click the delete button on the bottom of the Actions palette; it looks like a trash can. To play your new action on another file, just open a new photo file, highlight your action, and click the triangular play button on the bottom of the Actions palette.

Create a droplet for drag and drop editing of multiple files

Droplets are special shortcuts or aliases that you can save to your desktop or anywhere else on your hard drive. They work similarly to regular shortcuts with the added benefit of performing a set of actions. By dropping files on top of the droplet icon, Photoshop opens the files and

Bright Idea!
Create a stop action by selecting the little black arrow in the top right of the Actions palette and selecting Insert Stop from the drop-down list. Click the Allow Continue check box to add a button to allow users to skip steps and continue.

perform actions on them. If Photoshop isn't running, it automatically starts up and performs the tasks associated with that droplet. Using the action described in the preview section, create a droplet on your desktop to use for batch editing multiple files at once.

To create a droplet for the Auto Levels and Sharpen action:

1. Choose File ⇨ Automate ⇨ Create Droplet to open the dialog box shown in Figure 10.9.

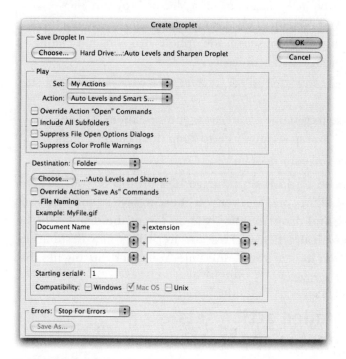

Figure 10.9. The Create Droplet dialog box.

2. Choose your Desktop or another convenient place to save your droplet. You can move your droplet anywhere you like once it's created. Give it a name so you'll remember what it does. I named mine Auto Levels and Sharpen Droplet.

3. Choose your set and action from the drop-down lists.

4. Under Destination, I recommend you save your files in another directory just to be safe. I created a folder on my desktop called Auto Levels and Sharpen.

Save Your Action Set for Future Use

Save your action set as an ATN file to use in the future or to share with others. Highlight your action set in the Actions palette and click the little arrow on the top right of the palette to open the drop-down list of options. Select Save Actions and save your file to Adobe Photoshop CS2/Presets/Photoshop Actions. Your Adobe Photoshop folder will either be in Applications on a Mac or Program Files on a PC. The next time you launch Photoshop, your custom action set will show up in the list of action sets in the options drop-down list along with the other preinstalled action sets.

---

5. You can choose to rename your files as you save them, or you can leave the File Naming settings as is to keep their current names.

6. Click OK to create your droplet.

Now all you need to do is drop image files on top of your droplet icon. Go to your desktop, or wherever you chose to save it, and find your new droplet. Drag and drop an image file on top of the droplet to run your action automatically. If you chose to save it in a new destination, open that folder and look at your edited file. You can drop any file that Photoshop can recognize.

Using preinstalled action sets to enhance photos and text

Photoshop comes with tons of preinstalled actions for adding cool effects to text and photos. There is a large set of actions that will create cool frames around your photos with the click of your mouse. There are action sets dedicated to resizing and converting your files, additional key commands for commonly used features, and another set dedicated to editing images for use in video and DVD. You can add your own actions and action sets and share them with the world of avid Photoshop users on the Web.

Action sets are groups of actions organized together in a folder hierarchy (see Figure 10.10). The list of action sets is listed in the options drop-down list in the Actions palette. You can load them just as you would styles or brush presets. When you select them from the list, you'll be prompted to either replace or append the set to your current list of actions. The sets are in collapsible folders so it's easy to load a few and pick through them. Each set you load takes memory from Photoshop, but you can always go back to the default set by selecting Reset Actions from the options drop-down list.

Figure 10.10. The Actions palette with a list of all action sets.

Applying text effects to type using action sets

Photoshop comes installed with a set of actions for performing some commonly used effects on text elements. I've displayed some of my favorites in Figure 10.11. Each one performs several steps on your text and in most cases converts your text layer to a raster image. Make sure you make copies of text layers for backup.

To try out some preinstalled text effects:

1. Create a new document.

2. Select the Horizontal Type tool and create a text element to try out the actions on. Make your font size nice and big.

3. Load the Text Effects action set by clicking the little black arrow on the top right of the Actions palette. Select Text Effects from the list.

Figure 10.11. Effects created with the Text Effects action set.

4. Click the arrow next to the Text Effects folder icon in the Actions palette to expand it.

5. Choose one of the effects to try. Avoid choosing one of the two effects that have a red icon next to them. These require both text and images. I'll cover one of them in a minute.

6. Click one of the text effects. Click the triangular Play button on the bottom of the Actions palette.

7. Photoshop automatically runs through several steps to create your text effect.

Try each one on a new text layer to see what they do. Once they are applied, you can go in and edit some of the elements, such as blending options or colors.

Bright Idea!
Try deleting some of the history states created when the action was run to personalize the effects further.

Running actions with dialog boxes

Some of the action sets have red icons next to them. This means they are interactive actions with dialog boxes that will prompt you to do some task before continuing. A few in the Text Effects action set involve both text and photos. They can be a little tricky to understand at first. I'll walk you through one of them so you can get the hang of it.

Try using the Chrome Text Effect. There are two interactive steps to the action. The first one asks you to select a photo layer. The second asks you to edit text. In Figure 10.12 I used a photo of the Vatican Museum as my text layer as well as a background image. You can use any photo source for this effect, and you can put it on any background you choose. Photoshop simply uses your photo to create a chrome texture. You don't have to create a text layer before running the effect. Photoshop will create a text layer for you and prompt you to edit it.

Figure 10.12. The Chrome Text Effect using photo and text.

To create a text effect using photos and type elements:

1. Open a photo to use as your chrome pattern. Any photo will do. Create a backup copy of your image by dragging the layer's thumbnail onto the Create New Layer button in the Layers palette.

2. With the Text Effects action set loaded, click the Chrome (photo & type) action and click the Play button to begin playing the action.

3. You will be prompted to select a photo layer. Because you've already selected your photo layer, click the Continue button.

4. You will be prompted to edit and position your type layer. Click the Stop button.

5. Your Layer palette will have a new type layer named ABC123. Double-click its thumbnail to highlight the text and edit it. This effect works best with big, bold typefaces. I used Meta-Plus Black in Figure 10.12.

6. Once you are done editing your text, click the expand arrow for the Chrome Text Effect to see its contents (see Figure 10.13). Read the list of actions until you see the one labeled "Make text layer." Select the action below it and click the Play button to continue with the actions. This time, click the Continue button when prompted to edit your text.

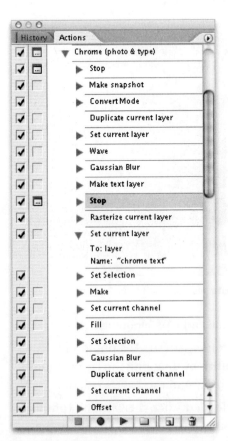

Figure 10.13. A list of actions in the Chrome Text Effect.

Now that you've gotten the hang of working with an interactive action, any of the actions with dialog boxes work in just about the same way. You are prompted to do an action, you do it, and then you find the place in the list of actions where you stopped and continue.

Running action sets on photos

The Image Effects action set has some fun combination filter effects. Many are a little on the garish side, but if you knock their opacity levels down and layer them on top of other layers, you can get some nice effects. The photo in Figure 10.14 is an example of the Fluorescent Chalk action combined with the Soft Posterize action.

Figure 10.14. Effects created with the Fluorescent Chalk and Soft Posterize action set.

To combine the Fluorescent Chalk and Soft Posterize actions on a photo:

1. Open a file to try out the Image Effects action set on.

2. Create a couple copies of your image. Drag and drop your image layer thumbnail on the Create New Layer button in the Layers palette. Turn off the visibility of all but one layer. Make sure you have highlighted the visible layer.

Watch Out!

If you are getting errors when trying to run actions, make sure you are not trying to run them on a locked background layer.

3. Load the Image Effects action set by clicking the little black arrow on the top right of the Actions palette. Select Text Effects from the list.

4. Click the arrow next to the Image Effects folder icon in the Actions palette to expand it.

5. Click the Fluorescent Chalk action and click the Play button on the bottom of the Actions palette.

6. Click the second copy of your layer in the Layers palette to highlight it, and turn on its visibility by clicking the box to the left of the layer thumbnail.

7. Click the Soft Posterize action and click the Play button on the bottom of the Actions palette.

Feel free to try out the other image effects. Many of them will merge all visible layers, so be sure to hide the visibility of a copy of your image.

Instant photo borders with the Frames action set

The Frames action set has some handy actions for creating instant borders around your photos. As with the Text and Image Effects action sets, the ones with the red icon on the left side require you to stop, perform actions, and then press play to continue. Try the Brushed Aluminum Frame on a photo. Be sure to select a photo that is a minimum of 100 pixels wide.

Figure 10.15 shows a frame added to a photo using action sets.

To create a brushed aluminum frame around your photo:

1. Open a photo to frame. Create a copy of your image layer by dragging its thumbnail on the Create New Layer button in the bottom of the Layers palette.

2. Load the Frames action set by clicking the arrow on the top right of the Actions palette and selecting Frames.

3. Click the arrow to the left of the Frames folder on the Actions palette to expand the set.

Figure 10.15. A Brushed Aluminum Frame added to photo using action sets.

4. Click the Brushed Aluminum Frame action and click the triangular play button on the bottom of the Actions palette.

5. Click the Continue button when you see the warning message about using an image that is at least 100 pixels wide.

Photoshop continues through several steps of expanding your canvas size and then cropping it. Try out some of the others by clicking the original snapshot of your image to undo your frame.

Hack

Combine several frames by continuing to run actions on your photos without undoing the previous frame. Add color by first creating a Foreground Color Frame and then surrounding it with a Wood Frame or Brushed Aluminum Frame.

Just the facts

- Save Snapshots of your work before performing multi-step operations to give yourself a quick way out.

- Selectively remove edits with the History Brush.

- Save your own actions and create a droplet on your desktop to batch-edit multiple files at once.

- Use the preinstalled action sets to add popular complex styles type and images.

- Add instant frames around photos with the Frames action set.

Enhancing Digital Photos

PART III

GET THE SCOOP ON...
Correcting color nondestructively ▪ Removing
color cast ▪ Fixing exposure problems ▪ Colorizing
black-and-white photos

Perfecting Your Photo's Color

Chapter 11

Whether you are editing digital files or scanned photos, you have a great deal of color correction tools at your disposal. Color and tonal correcting is where Photoshop really shines, and by the end of the chapter you'll be creating professional-quality images from your digital or scanned photos. You can choose to use the auto correction features, or get your hands dirty with complex and powerful color correction tools that let you adjust brightness, contrast, color balance, hue, and saturation. Using adjustment layers, you can avoid editing your original photo and compare several styles without having to work with several versions of the same file.

This chapter looks at several different ways to adjust color and tone on a photo and how to add color to a black-and-white photo. You'll discover ways to correct common exposure problems and remove color casts, and see how to get great results by adding Curves adjustment layers to photos. You'll look at correcting different parts of an image separately, and have some fun creating an old sepia tone photo effect by playing with filters and color saturation.

Tips for happy color correcting

Before jumping in, here are some tips that'll start you on the right track for creating high-quality, nondestructive color correction. The first rule of thumb is to do your corrections on a separate Adjustment layer whenever possible. You'll be able to delete or change your adjustments much easier if they are in a separate layer. Adjustment layers also afford you the luxury of easily isolating different areas of your photo for correcting in a variety of ways.

Some of the tools in this chapter, such as Shadow/Highlight and Exposure, can't be created as adjustment layers, but Curves, Levels, Color Balance, and Brightness/Contrast can all be added as separate layers. When you can't separate your corrections on a different layer, make a copy of your original image layer to keep handy.

Keep copies of your originals

Before starting any edits on your photos, don't forget to archive! Every time you make a correction to a file in Photoshop, you are losing your original data. Even if you wind up using color correction layers to avoid editing your originals, it's a good idea to make copies of all your photos before editing them. I make it a habit of creating a copy of each set of photos I take. I add the word master to my folder name so that I know it's the unedited original. I recommend you come up with a similar method for archiving your digital photos. Burning master copies onto CDs is a great way to back up your photos. Because you can't write to the CD, you can't accidentally write over the wrong files.

Edit in 8-bit of 16-bit color

Photoshop recommends that any time you are adjusting color or exposure, which you work in 16-bit mode and convert back to 8-bit mode as a final step. If you are creating professional digital photographs, you'll certainly want all the control you can get out of your files. For amateurs and hobbyists, it's really up to you and your computer's capabilities. Your file size doubles in 16-bit mode, so it may come down to a matter of free memory. If you are creating images for the Web, 16-bit mode won't buy you much. If you were planning to print high-quality images, I'd definitely recommend working in 16-bit mode whenever possible.

Professional photographers often recommend you do your editing in Lab color mode. You'll have higher control over color and fewer problems with color artifacts when adjusting color values because Lab color is device independent. Again, unless you are serious about digital photography, the choice is up to you. For most people, converting to Lab color is unnecessary.

Translating histograms

Photoshop uses histograms to display charts of image information. The Histogram palette shows us a black-and-white, or multi-channel representation of how well your darks, lights, colors, and midtones are performing. They can clue you in on how to improve your image. To understand the amount of darks, midtones, and lights, take a closer look at the Histogram palette. You'll be seeing histograms when you make color adjustments, so getting used to it will help you decipher what's happening in your image.

In Figure 11.1, I have a photo with many darks, a fair amount of lights, but very little in the way of midtones. The Histogram palette displays this information in the form of a chart. The chart runs left to right, dark to light. The mountain peak at the left represents the darks; in this case, there is a large amount of very dark shadows. The middle of my histogram represents the midtones. In this case, there are next to none; my image is split between mostly darks and lights. The right side of the image represents highlights. Because the flower is white and brightly lit, there are a lot of them. There are, however, few pure, bright whites in my image, so the histogram drops off on the far right. If I were to color correct this image, I'd try to adjust some of the darks into midtones and bring back some detail that is currently lost in the shadow.

Figure 11.1. The Histogram palette.

The Histogram palette is part of your default workspace and is located in the top set of palettes. Other tools such as the Levels dialog box take advantage of the histogram information to help you adjust your image's color and contrast. Clicking the little black arrow on the top left of the Histogram palette opens a drop-down list with several options for viewing different histogram information. You can look at the All Channels view to see both the composite histogram, as in Figure 11.1, as well as a histogram of each separate color channel in your image.

Auto adjusting color and contrast

If you are a busy person, sometimes you don't want to mess with the complicated Curves and Levels dialog boxes. In many cases, a quick auto correction is all you need to boost your image and get on to the more important things in life. Photoshop has a few menu items for automatically adjusting levels, colors, and contrast, shown in Table 11.1. They have handy key commands associated with them so you can get in and get out quickly.

Table 11.1. Auto color and contrast commands

Adjustment	PC Key Command	Mac Key Command	Description
Auto Level	Shift+Ctrl+L	Shift+⌘+L	Automatically adjusts contrast and color
Auto Contrast	Shift+Alt+Ctrl+L	Shift+Option+⌘+L	Adjusts contrast only and does not affect color
Auto Color	Shift+Ctrl+B	Shift+⌘+B	Adjusts color only and does not adjust contrast

Try out the different auto adjustments. If you prefer menu items, they all live under Image ⇨ Adjustments. If you don't like the result from an auto correction, you can always undo the correction and move on to a more involved color correction.

Brightening lights and darkening shadows with Levels

The Levels dialog box gives you tremendous control over color balance, highlights, and shadows. I think it's the most intuitive color correction option, which is why I've chosen to cover it first. It offers the easiest interface for precision adjusting your image color and contrast levels. The dialog box has an auto button, so you can try out the automatic level adjustments first. If they don't do the trick, you have the ability to adjust a composite of your image, or each color channel separately by selecting them from the Channels drop-down list.

To improve a washed-out image immediately, pull in the black point and white point markers on the bottom of the histogram preview so that they line up with the darkest and lightest points in the histogram. On images like Figure 11.2, the darks and lights are very weak. They drop off on either side of the histogram, meaning there are no true blacks or whites in the image. As long as the Preview box is selected in the Levels dialog box, you'll be able to see your adjustments in real time. Once you click OK, your adjustments will be made to your image and your histogram will update to show that you've tightened up your darks and lights.

Figure 11.2. The Levels dialog box and photo.

Hack

Reset your Levels settings in the Levels dialog box by pressing and holding the Option key (Alt) to make a Reset button appear.

To add a Levels adjustment layer:

1. Click the Add Adjustment of Fill Layer button on the bottom of the Layers palette and select Levels. The Levels dialog box appears with a histogram of your image.

2. To boost your black, click the black point slider arrow and pull it in towards the center of the histogram just a bit until you get good-looking shadows.

3. To make your whites sparkle, click the white point slider arrow on the right side of the histogram and pull it in towards the center of the histogram until you get bright whites.

4. Adjust your midtones by clicking and dragging the gray point slider to the right or left. Moving the slider to the left lightens your midtones; moving the slider to the dark makes your midtones darker.

5. If your color balance is off — say you have too much red in your image — select Red from the Channel drop-down list. Adjust the gray point slider to the right to tone down the reds. Repeat for any other colors that need adjusting.

Be careful not to overdo it when making color corrections on the color channels; they can quickly get out of control. You usually don't need more than tiny adjustments.

Mastering color adjustments with Curves

You can get good results from Levels, but if you really want control over color corrections, Curves gives you more precision and accuracy than any other color correction method in Photoshop. With Levels, you adjust highlights, midtones, and shadow with three separate sliders. With Curves, you can add up to 14 points!

To get you used to how Curves work, you'll use three points. In the photo in Figure 11.3, I adjusted with darks, lights, and midtones by adding three points along the grid and moving them just a smidgen to punch up the blacks and brighten the whites. The eyedropper tools in the bottom right of the Curves dialog box let you select white, black, or gray points in your image. In Figure 11.3, I had some nice whites to begin with, so I used the White Point eyedropper on the far right to perform some initial auto color correction.

Figure 11.3. The Curves dialog box.

In this exercise you'll adjust a photo similar to how you did with the Levels adjustment. Each photo is going to be slightly different and will need different corrections. The following instructions are generally effective with common photo problems like dull darks and dim lights. Play around with the controls to get a feel for how they work. Basically, up and to the right lightens, and down and to the left darkens.

Watch Out!

Adjusting Curves in RGB or CMYK may produce artifacts. To get the very best results, convert your image to Lab color by choosing Image ⇨ Mode ⇨ Lab Color.

Bright Idea!

Click the expand button on the bottom right of the Curves dialog box for a bigger grid.

To create a Curves Adjustment layer:

1. Open a photo to correct.

2. Click the Create New Adjustment or Fill Layer button on the bottom of the Layers palette and select Curves. The Curves dialog box appears.

3. Add highlight, shadow, and midtone points to the grid by clicking the three points along the line that meet the horizontal grid lines.

4. Adjust your shadow by clicking the last of the three points and moving it slightly down and to the right.

5. Move the top added point up and to the right to brighten the highlights.

6. Move the middle point around until you get strong midtones.

Try playing around to see what happens the more points you add. Just as in the Levels dialog box, the Curves dialog box has a Channels drop-down list so that you can adjust each color channel separately.

Changing tint and color cast

Like many things in Photoshop, there are a million ways to adjust the tint of your image, whether you are removing an unwanted color cast or adding an effect like sepia tone. This section shows you a few ways to adjust the tint in your photo.

Correcting color cast

Color cast is a common problem with digital photos in low light situations. In situations of low light, your digital camera can often miscalculate the correct white balance setting and you are left with orange-tinted photos. Most mild to moderate cases of this can be quickly corrected using the Neutralize option in the Match Color dialog box.

To remove color cast in the Match Color dialog box:

1. Open a photo with a strong color cast.

2. Choose Image ⇨ Adjustments ⇨ Match Color to open the Match Color dialog box (see Figure 11.4).

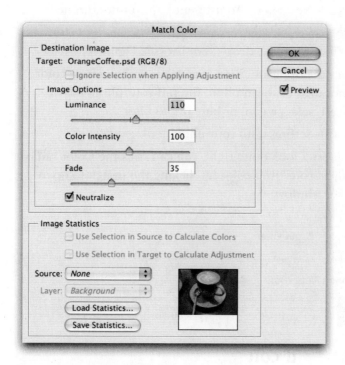

Figure 11.4. The Match Color dialog box.

3. Click the Neutralize check box to remove the color cast. Photoshop makes a best-guess effort of removing the color cast.

4. If the correction was a little too strong, you can adjust your photo further by increasing the Fade value. You may also need to fine-tune your photo's Luminance and Color Intensity settings.

I find this adjustment does wonders on just about any color cast problem I've encountered.

Another, less destructive way of removing color cast is by adding a photo filter adjustment layer on top of your photo layer. This works by layering a transparent color on top of your photo, similar to how a photo lab technician would correct color in a negative by adding colored gels to the exposure process. By adding the opposite color to your color cast, you balance out the entire photo's color.

To add a photo filter adjustment layer to correct color cast:

1. Open a photo with a strong color cast.

2. Click the Create a New Fill or Adjustment Layer button in the layers palette. It looks like a half-black, half-white circle.

3. Select Photo Filter from the drop-down list (see Figure 11.5).

4. Select a filter in the opposite color. If your photo has a blue color cast, select an orange or warm photo filter. If your photo has an orange color cast, select a cool or blue photo filter.

5. Adjust the Density setting until your photo looks correct.

6. If your color doesn't look quite right, you can click the Color radio button and adjust your filter color by clicking the swatch to open the Color Picker window.

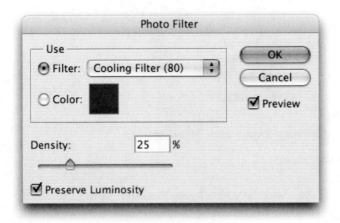

Figure 11.5. The Photo Filter dialog box.

The benefit you get out of adjusting color casts with this method is that you can always go back and adjust your Photo Filter layer, or delete the layer entirely to get back your original photo color.

Bright Idea!

If your photo is slightly overexposed, or washed out, uncheck the Preserve Luminosity setting in the Photo Filter dialog box to intensify your shadows.

Give your photo an old sepia tone look

The next time you take family photos, dress your kids up in vintage clothes. By adding a sepia photo filter and lowering the saturation level in your photos, you can create an old sepia tone look. Add some thin white lines as scratches and give your photo a slight Gaussian blur to add an aging effect to your photos. Those old photos have to look that way after lots of abuse and wear; I use the same techniques when creating an old-photo look by putting my digital files through the ringer. Figure 11.6 has had several procedures done to it to speed up the appearance of time. I've found that if you try a combination saturation adjustments and shadow/highlight adjustments to tone down your photo, you can get an old-looking photo in just a few minutes.

Figure 11.6. A photo with the Sepia photo filter and Saturation adjustments applied.

To create an old sepia tone photo:

1. Open a photo.

2. Click the Add New Adjustment of Fill Layer button on the bottom of the Layers palette and choose Photo Filter.

3. Choose Sepia Tone from the drop-down list and bump up the Density to about 100%.

4. Click the Add New Adjustment of Fill Layer button on the bottom of the Layers palette and choose Hue/Saturation.

Bright Idea!
Add a distressed edge by painting around the edge in Quick Mask Mode with a rough textured brush, and then adding a layer mask in the Layers palette.

5. Move the Saturation slider all the way to the left. Adjust the Lightness setting to about +25 to wash out your photo a little.

These adjustments alone will give you an authentic-looking photo, but adding some extra touches will really help make your photo look aged.

To add texture and scratches to your photo:

1. Click your photo layer to select it. If it is a locked Background layer, double-click its thumbnail to rename and unlock it.

2. Choose Image ⇨ Adjustments ⇨ Shadow/Highlight to open the dialog box.

3. Change the Shadow amount to 0% and the Highlights to about 50%. You want to weaken the shadows and give the photo a washed-out look.

4. Create a new layer to add some scratches. Move it to just below the Sepia Photo Filter layer.

5. Select the Brush tool from the Toolbox and choose a 1-pixel brush. Change your foreground color to white and draw some spots and scratches across your photo.

That should give you a good start on creating an old-looking photo. The more you mess with tiny adjustments to levels, blurring, noise, and grain, the older your photo will look.

Correcting exposure problems in photos

The key to getting good exposure on photos is by making sure you have strong darks, bright lights, and balanced midtones. When you take a photo, many elements can have relational effects on the exposure of your photo. If you've ever tried to take a picture of a full moon on a bright night, you'll most often end up with a photo that has a very bright moon and very dark sky. The other elements in your photo, which at the time looked so bright to the naked eye, are swallowed up by darkness.

Similar things happen when you take a photo of a person against a bright background. Much of the details of your subject winds up dark and silhouetted against the bright background. You can get back some of that detail by adjusting your photo's exposure settings in Photoshop. Following are a few ways to enhance underexposed areas of a photo and sharpen washed-out, overexposed photos.

Lightening dark photos with exposure adjustments

Due to the intense light of the sun in Figure 11.7, the midtones in the sand and water are pretty severely underexposed and much too dark. By making some adjustments in exposure, we can lighten up some of the midtones and get back some detail in the sand. The Exposure dialog box provides a few options for adjusting a photo. For Figure 11.7, I increased the Gamma setting to lighten up the grays and bumped up the Exposure setting just slightly to punch up the highlights. You can get to the Exposure dialog box by choosing Image ➪ Adjustments ➪ Exposure.

Figure 11.7. An underexposed photo and the Exposure adjustment dialog box.

The Exposure dialog box introduces a few features you may not be familiar with. Table 11.2 describes the different features and settings in the Exposure dialog box and tips for using them to get the best results in your photos.

Table 11.2. Tips for adjusting exposure settings

Setting	Description	Tips for Use
Exposure	Adjusts the highlights in a photo. The higher the exposure setting, the brighter and more highlights your photo will have.	Lower exposure to tone down photos that have a hot spot from overexposure. On dark photos, punch up the light values to bring out highlights.
Offset	Adjusts the shadows or darks of a photo.	Enrich muddy blacks on underexposed photos.
Gamma	Controls the midtones in a photo. Increasing gamma lightens them, decreasing darkens them.	Increase gamma to lighten the overall value of a photo. Decrease it to darken an overexposed photo.
Set Black Point	Assigns a black point for your photo.	Click the darkest point in your photo to have Photoshop automatically adjust all exposure levels.
Set Gray Point	Assigns a middle gray value for your photo.	Click middle values to adjust exposure automatically based on midtones.
Set White Point	Assigns a highlight value in your photo.	Boost highlights by selecting a color slightly darker than the lightest value in your photo.

You'll see many of these same controls, especially the white point and black point, throughout all of the color correction features of Photoshop.

Make adjustments to isolated areas of your photo

The photo in Figure 11.8 is getting blasting sun from behind the hill. It's completely washed out the bushes in the background and casts a nasty sun glare. The foreground isn't too bad, but it could use a little adjusting in the darks and lights.

Bright Idea!

When selecting around the outside edge of an image, switch to Full Screen mode so that you can more easily add selection points without jumping out of Photoshop by accidentally clicking the desktop.

Figure 11.8. A photo with multiple exposure problems.

Using Adjustment layers to do all of your color and tone correcting lets you correct separate parts of your image by making selections around areas to isolate them. I created a selection area around the shed and foreground, created a curve adjustment layer with mild changes, and then selected the inverse and created a curve adjustment for the background using more intense changes.

To adjust different areas of a photo:

1. Open a photo with a combination of exposure problems.

2. Using the Marquee tools, select an area of your photo to correct.

3. Click the Create New Layer icon in the Layers palette to create an empty layer to save your selection to.

4. Click the Add Layer Mask button on the bottom of the Layers palette to create a Mask out of your selection.

5. ⌘+click (Ctrl+click) the thumbnail of your layer mask to load the selection. You'll see the marching ants return.

6. Click the Create New Adjustment or Fill Layer button on the bottom of the Layers palette and select Curves from the drop-down list. Adjust your image. When you are done, click OK.

7. ⌘+click the thumbnail of your layer mask to load the selection again. Choose Select ⇨ Inverse to reverse your selection.

8. Click the Create New Adjustment or Fill Layer button and select
Curves. Adjust your image. When you are done, click OK.

You can always go back in to the Curves settings for the different
layers by double-clicking the Curves thumbnails in the layers list. In
Figure 11.9, I created a selection around the shed and foreground so
that I could adjust the foreground and background separately.

Figure 11.9. A photo with two Curves corrections on different selections.

Colorizing photos for effect

By performing Hue and Saturation adjustments on images or parts of
images, you can adjust colors by either shifting their color values in the
color spectrum or adding tints of color by colorizing them. You can boost
color saturation or change the lightness or darkness of a color.

Before getting started, consider the difference between hue, saturation, and lightness. Hue refers to the basic color information. Things are
red, green, blue, or any other color in between. Saturation controls the
intensity, or amount of tinting in a color. Pastels are lightly saturated

versions of reds, blues, and greens. Neon colors are super-saturated. The third variable to color is the lightness value. The Lightness control in the Hue/Saturation dialog box controls the amount of light in your colors. Pastels have high levels of lightness. Dark colors like navy and burgundy have lower lightness values.

Intensify a color photo with colorizing effects

The Hue/Saturation controls let you shift an image's color in the color spectrum. Blues can become greens and greens can become reds. You can also use Hue/Saturation to shift an image's color spectrum or colorize an entire image with a specific tint.

In Figure 11.10 I've colorized a photo of a purple flower with green stems. With some adjustments to the Hue settings, I've turned the purples green and the stems purple. By lessening the saturation and increasing the lightness, I can get an eerie space-flower look. If you have a photo with slightly skewed hues where your reds are a little too orange and your greens are a little too blue, you can make minor Hue/Saturation adjustments to correct color.

Figure 11.10. Hue adjustments on a photo.

Bright Idea!

Save your Hue/Saturation settings by clicking the Save button in the dialog box. Whenever you want to reuse your saved Hue/Saturation settings, click the Load button and select your saved file.

To adjust a color's Hue and Saturation:

1. Open a photo to edit.

2. Click the Create New Adjustment or Fill Layer button on the bottom of the Layers palette and select Hue/Saturation.

3. Adjust the Hue slider to shift the colors in your photo along the color spectrum.

4. Adjust the Saturation values to add or remove color saturation for your entire image.

5. Adjust the Lightness values to add or subtract light from your photo.

6. To isolate and adjust specific colors, choose a color from the Edit menu.

7. Click OK to save your changes.

Now that I've introduced you to the Hue/Saturation controls, I encourage you to play around, especially with editing specific colors. If you have objects in your photo that have strong local color, meaning the same color doesn't exist in other parts of the photo, replacing color via Hue/Saturation is the fastest way to change an object's color. I cover how to replace an object's color using the Color Replace dialog box in Chapter 7. If you can get away with doing it in a Hue/Saturation adjustment, you'll save yourself the step of having to select your object.

Add spots of color to a black-and-white photo

By isolating areas of an image, you can remove, add, or change spots of color. In the next exercise, you'll colorize a black-and-white image by adding spots of color to selected areas.

1. Open a black and white photo. If you don't have one, convert a color photo by choosing Image ⇨ Mode ⇨ Grayscale.

2. Convert your image to RGB, Lab, or CMYK.

3. Copy your image layer by dragging it on top of the Create New Layer button on the bottom of the Layers palette.

4. Select an area of your photo you would like to colorize.

5. Click the Create New Adjustment or Fill Layer button on the bottom of the Layers palette and select Hue/Saturation. A layer mask of your selection is automatically created on your new Hue/Saturation layer.

6. Click the Colorize check box to be able to add color to your image.

7. Adjust the Hue slider bar to select a color. As long as the Preview check box is selected, you'll be able to preview the color changes.

8. Adjust the Saturation and Lightness sliders to fine-tune your color. Click OK when you are done.

In Figure 11.11, I selected the bear — you can see the marching ants around him — and colorized him in a washy brown color. I might make him into a holiday card.

Figure 11.11. Adding color through the Hue/Saturation dialog box.

Hack

You can reverse this technique on a color photo by selecting the object you'd like to keep colored, choosing Select ➪ Inverse, and finally choosing Image ➪ Adjustments ➪ Desaturate.

Just the facts

- Make quick color and contrast corrections by using the auto correction commands for Levels, Curves, and Color.

- Improve the impact of your image by darkening darks and brightening highlights with Levels adjustments.

- Correct photos that are too dark or too light with exposure adjustments.

- Make separate corrections on different parts of your images by creating Curves adjustments with layer masks.

- Colorize selected areas of your images by making Hue/Saturation adjustments with the Colorize feature enabled.

GET THE SCOOP ON...
Searching for a photo ■ Viewing an instant slideshow
of your photos ■ Editing your Camera Raw photos ■
Applying the same settings to several Camera Raw files

Exploring Adobe Bridge and the Camera Raw Plug-In

O ne of the most exciting features introduced with CS2 is Adobe Bridge, a new sister application that works with Photoshop to organize and preview files. You can add metadata to your files to organize them with detailed info like location, description, date, title, and creator. If you've been using iPhoto or Picasa to organize your digital photos, you'll definitely want to consider switching over to Bridge. I love the flexible interface in Bridge, and I think Adobe has done a terrific job creating an intuitive and easy interface.

Adobe Bridge isn't just for use with Photoshop files. You can organize all of your files with Bridge and preview the contents of most image file formats. Bridge comes with a plug-in for editing Camera Raw files. Camera Raw is an exciting new digital photo format that gives you raw, uncompressed files. It is quickly becoming available on more and more digital cameras. Camera Raw's popularity is growing as more photographers switch from traditional to digital photography. It's like having a digital negative of your photos and gives you much more control over color, exposure, and light adjustments.

This chapter introduces you to Adobe Bridge and its many tools for organizing, previewing, and finding files. You'll learn how to get the clearest details and best colors

Chapter 12

from the Camera Raw window. Finally, you'll adjust several Camera Raw files at once using the Synchronize option and find out how to save settings to use on future photos.

Organizing your files in Adobe Bridge

With Adobe Bridge you have much more control over your files. By adding metadata, keywords, ratings, and labels, you can add data to make organizing and searching for specific photos so much easier. By giving you a preview thumbnail of your image file, you can quickly locate a file you are looking for.

The Adobe Bridge window in Figure 12.1 looks like a file browser window on steroids. It is much more than a file browser and can be modified in a number of ways. You can set the size of preview thumbnails, allowing you to see mini pictures of what's inside your files. Add bookmarks to your favorite photo folders and get to them quickly without having to click around in your hard drive. From within Bridge you can open multiple files at the same time and run batch processes on them, saving you time and energy for the more fun things in life.

Figure 12.1. The Adobe Bridge Standard View Mode.

Watch Out!

The bigger the thumbnail size, the slower Adobe Bridge will become. In addition, the more thumbnails there are to preview in a folder, the longer it takes Bridge to draw them all.

You can modify how the information in the Bridge window is displayed. By adjusting the slider on the bottom of the Bridge window, you can change the size of your preview thumbnails. The panels on the right side of the window can be moved, removed, and reorganized by turning them on and off in the View menu. They are draggable just like the palettes in Photoshop and can be moved up and down from the top left frame to the bottom and vice versa. The frames can be stretched and shrunk using the drag bars between them. You can add your photo folders to the favorites menu by choosing File ⇨ Add to Favorites.

Rotate several photos with the click of a button

One very simple but revolutionary feature you get by using Adobe Bridge for your file management is that you can rotate your images with one click. I tend to take a large percentage of my photos in portrait mode. Before Bridge, I had to open up the files individually in Photoshop and rotate them one at a time. Even if I set up a batch process for it, it took too much time. I used to import my photos into iPhoto just for its file rotation capabilities. No more! The rotation buttons are on the top right of the screen and are very intuitive. There is one button for clockwise rotation and one for counterclockwise rotation.

Now put Adobe Bridge to work and rotate some files by following these steps:

1. Open Adobe Bridge by choosing File ⇨ Browse.

2. Find a folder of your photos by browsing your computer files through either the Favorites or folders tab on the top left.

3. You should now have a folder of photos visible in your light box panel on the right side of your Bridge window.

4. Click a file that needs rotation to select it.

5. Click the clockwise or counterclockwise rotation buttons on the top right of your Bridge window (see Figure 12.2). You can also use the key commands of ⌘+[and ⌘+] (Ctrl+[and Ctrl+]).

Figure 12.2. Rotate buttons in Adobe Bridge.

6. To select a row of images to rotate, click the first one and then Shift+click the last one in the row. All the photos in the row will be highlighted.

7. To choose from various files in the folder, click one and then ⌘+click (Ctrl+click) several of them to add them to the selection.

The next time you open your photos, they will be rotated to the correct orientation. Using this method saves you the added step of having to save your files again once you've rotated the image.

Bright Idea!

Find photos quickly with filters. Give your kid a colored label by right-clicking the thumbnail and then choosing Label ⇨ Red. Then click the Filter drop-down list on the top right of the Bridge window and select Show Red Label to view all of your kid's photos.

Inside Scoop

Collapsing your Bridge window into Ultra Compact Mode keeps monitor clutter down while keeping Bridge handy.

Switching to a more compact view

Adobe Bridge offers two more compact views for when you don't need the other panels or when you are pressed for screen real estate (see Table 12.1). The View Mode buttons are on the top right of the Bridge window. Compact View Mode gives you a Bridge window with no left-hand panels (see Figure 12.3). Ultra Compact View shrinks your Bridge window down to a thin sliver. If you know you are going to be in and out of Bridge quite a bit, this view keeps Bridge handy while taking up minimal screen space.

Figure 12.3. Compact View Mode in Adobe Bridge.

Hack

You can have multiple Bridge windows open at the same time. Once you are in Bridge, choose File ⇨ New Window to add another Bridge window. This is a great way to drag files from one place to another without having to switch from folder to folder.

Table 12.1. The different views available in Adobe Bridge

Name	Description
Thumbnails View	A list of thumbnails and file names. Thumbnails view also shows rating, creation date, and time.
Filmstrip View	A split view with a large image in one frame and a strip of thumbnails in another bottom frame. You can control the orientation of the frames.
Details View	Shows images in a list view. You can see a preview of the image and read key file information such as date created, ratings, file size, file format, camera settings, color mode, and dimensions.
Version and Alternatives View	Displays your files in a list view and includes a column of versions and alternatives information.

View your photos as a slideshow

Let's say you just got back from your trip to Hawaii. You shot the whole trip on a digital camera and your best friend shows up, eagerly expecting to see all of your photos instantly. Adobe Bridge offers a slideshow feature for instant gratification. All you need is a folder of photos.

To view your photo folder as a slideshow:

1. Navigate to the folder where your photos are stored.

2. Choose View ⇨ Slideshow to launch a slideshow of the photos (see Figure 12.4).

   As an alternative, you can press ⌘+L (Ctrl+L).

   A translucent window appears with the key commands to control the slideshow. The three important ones to remember are:

   ▪ Press Esc to return to the Adobe Bridge window.

   ▪ Press the spacebar to play and pause your slideshow.

   ▪ Press H to hide and show the slideshow commands.

Inside Scoop

Choose Window ⇨ Workspace ⇨ File Navigation to rearrange your Bridge workspace for optimum file browsing.

The slideshow feature lets you flip through your photos using the right and left arrow keys. You can also rotate your photos right from the slideshow by using the [and] keys.

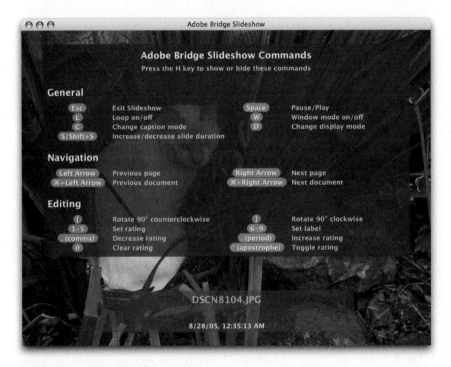

Figure 12.4. A slideshow with instructions.

Rename several files at once

Most digital cameras name their files creative names like DSCN8071.JPG. This doesn't really help you much when trying to find photos from your trip to France. Rename an entire folder's worth of files with a more suitable name by using Adobe Bridge's Batch Rename feature, shown in Figure 12.5.

Figure 12.5. The Batch Rename dialog box in Adobe Bridge.

To rename a group of files with a name and number sequence:

1. Select all the files in a folder by choosing Edit ⇨ Select All or using the standard key command ⌘+A (Ctrl+A).

2. Choose Tools ⇨ Batch Rename to open the dialog box and create the details for your renaming.

3. You can choose to rename your files in place or save copies of them in a new folder.

4. In the New File Names section, select Text from the drop-down list.

5. Type the name you want to add to your file. In Figure 12.5, I'm renaming mine with France as the beginning of the file name.

6. Click the plus arrow next to the field to create a new condition for your file name.

7. In the new condition, select Sequence Number from the drop-down list. I have over 100 photos to rename, so I'm going to select Three Digits from the drop-down list on the right side of the field. In the field I'm going to add **001**. You can just put the number 1 in the field, but I like to add the zeros so that when I view my folder as a sorted list, it will be in the right order.

8. Click Rename when you are ready to apply your new naming scheme.

You can add other things to your filename such as your camera's metadata, the date, or a different file extension. By using the preserve filename option, you can change your filename to lowercase.

Bright Idea!

Launch Adobe Bridge separately from Photoshop to use as a file organizer. Find the Adobe Bridge folder in your Applications and Program Files folder and launch it from there. Create a shortcut for the Bridge application and keep it on your desktop for easy access.

Adding metadata and keywords

Using Adobe Bridge's file browser, you can add all kinds of metadata to your file and search on that data to find photos quickly. Metadata also stores information about your camera, the creation date, and the settings used when the photo was taken. You can quickly get file information such as color mode, bit depth, resolution, and file size by viewing the contents in the File Properties section of the Metadata panel for each photo.

Adding fine details with metadata

Metadata allows you to add all sorts of information to a file such as description, location, creator, or title. You can also add copyright notices and usage terms right into your files. Metadata also stores information about the file such as:

- Date Created
- File Size
- Dimensions
- Bit Depth
- Color Mode

If your file was taken with a digital camera or other device that keeps track of metadata, each file can store information such as:

- Exposure
- ISO Speed rating
- Max Aperture Value
- Focal Length
- Camera Make and Model

While a photo is highlighted, you can click the Metadata panel to make it active, and any field that has a pencil icon next to it can be edited by clicking the pencil. The fields I find most handy for searches are

Description, Location, and Title. These live under the IPTC Core section of the Metadata panel (see Figure 12.6). By adding Paris to the location field of the photos you took during your trip to Paris, you'll be able to find them quickly in the future.

Figure 12.6. The Metadata panel in Adobe Bridge.

To add metadata to a file:

1. In the Adobe Bridge window, click one of your image files to highlight it.
2. Click the Metadata tab on the left side of the Adobe Bridge window to view its contents.
3. Under the IPTC Core section of the panel, click the Pencil icon next to the Description field.
4. Add a description to your photo.
5. Click Enter to accept and save your change.

Inside Scoop

Select multiple files to add metadata to several files at once. If some have metadata associated with them already, Bridge just appends their data.

Categorizing photos with keywords

The Keywords panel lets you add keywords to your files (see Figure 12.7). This is a handy way to organize your files into specific keywords for large categories such as family, vacation, and events. You can organize the files into sets. The Events keyword could have specific events associated with it like Thanksgiving, graduation, birthdays, and so on.

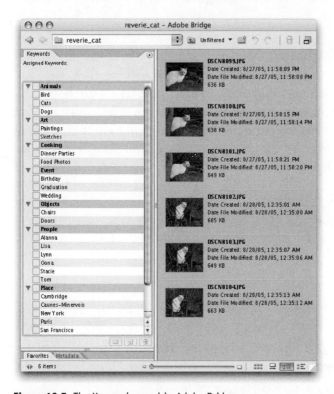

Figure 12.7. The Keywords panel in Adobe Bridge.

Watch Out!

Adding keywords and sets can quickly create a large, unmanageable list. It's better to use metadata for specific details and keywords for larger categories.

To create a new keyword set and associated keywords:

1. In the Adobe Bridge folder, click the Keywords panel to activate it.

2. Click the folder icon on the bottom of the panel to add a new keyword set. Enter a name and press Enter to accept it.

3. While your new keyword set is highlighted, click the Add Keyword button on the bottom of the panel. Enter a name for your new keyword.

You can rearrange keywords after they are created. The keyword sets have expand and collapse arrows for viewing keywords. You can move things around by clicking and dragging them up and down the list. To delete a keyword or set, click it to highlight it and click Delete on the bottom of the panel.

Finding your photos

Once you've added metadata and/or keywords to your files, you can take advantage of Bridge's powerful search tool. The search box in Figure 12.8 allows you to add multiple conditions to search your photos with. You can add as many conditions as you want and have Bridge bring you results if any or all of the criteria are met. The Find feature also lets you search sub folders.

Figure 12.8. The Adobe Bridge Find dialog box.

To create a search based on multiple conditions:

1. In Adobe Bridge, choose Edit ⇨ Find or use the key command ⌘+F (Ctrl+F).

2. Select a folder to perform your search on. If you don't know where your photos are, you can search from the main directory of your hard drive. Make sure the Include All Sub Folders check box is checked.

3. Create your first condition in the Criteria section. I am going to search All Metadata that contains "France."

4. Click the plus symbol on the right of the first condition to add another one.

5. Enter your values for a second condition. I have been tagging my travel photos with the keyword Travel, so I will search for files that have a Travel keyword associated with them.

6. Click the plus symbol again to add a third search condition.

   Because I have photos from several trips over a few years, I'm going to narrow down my results by searching only for photos that were created after 01/01/2004.

7. Choose whether you want Bridge to return files based on all or any of the criteria you've defined.

8. Click Find to begin your search.

The more folders there are to search through, the longer the search will take. Be patient if you are searching your entire hard drive. If you have a large hard drive, it might be a good time for a snack break!

Editing your Camera Raw files

Digital cameras have traditionally used JPEG or other compression versions as their standard file format. The problem with JPEG is that you lose image quality as soon as your camera saves your shot to its memory card. In compressing your image's file size, you are losing delicate details in shadows or highlights. With Camera Raw, when you perform an edit or adjustment, you are not losing image data. Similar to the idea of adjustment layers, your edits are saved separately from your image data in the EXIF data of the file or in a sidecar file. Figure 12.9 shows the Camera Raw editing window in Adobe Bridge.

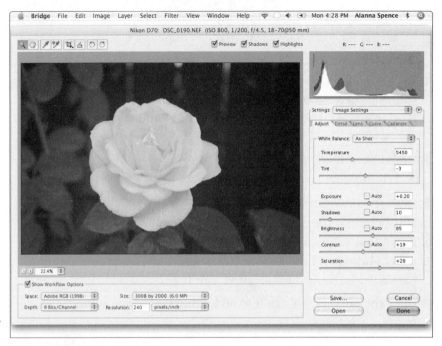

Figure 12.9. The Camera Raw editor.

The Camera Raw editor has many of the same tools you'll find in Photoshop. The toolset in Camera Raw lets you rotate, straighten, crop, and set white points (see Table 12.2).

To the left of the tools are some check boxes for previewing adjustments and viewing any clipping that may be occurring in your image. Clipping areas are highlighted in bright red or blue and indicate areas where your image is maxed out and details have been lost. Selecting these two is a handy way of checking whether you are getting the most detail out of your images. You can adjust the exposure, shadow, brightness, and contrast settings to soften highlights or lighten extra dark shadows.

Inside Scoop

Rotate your image while cropping. Make your cropping selection and hold your mouse just outside one of the corner anchor points until it turns into a rotate cursor.

Table 12.2. Tools available in the Camera Raw editor

Button	Name	Description
	Zoom	Works similar to Photoshop's Zoom tool. Press and hold the Option or Alt key to zoom out. Click and drag to zoom in to a specific area of your image.
	Hand	Use the Hand tool to move around your image when zoomed in.
	White Balance	Click a highlight in your image to set the white balance. You can also select a preset white balance setting in the Adjust tab on the right.
	Color Sampler	Lets you sample up to four spots of color and gives you a list of RGB values.
	Crop	Nondestructive crop. You can crop to a specific ratio by clicking and holding on the Crop tool icon to view the fly-out menu. Press Enter to accept a crop. To remove a crop, choose Clear Crop from the fly-out menu.
	Straighten	Click and drag along the crooked side of an image to straighten it. Straighten automatically crops your image.
	Rotate 90° Counterclockwise	Rotates your image 90° to the left. You can also press the letter L.
	Rotate 90° Clockwise	Rotates your image 90° to the right. You can also press the letter R.
	Mark for Delete	Files that are marked as delete will be moved to the Trash or Recycle Bin when you exit the Camera Raw window. This button appears only when you have multiple files open in the Camera Raw window.

The preview check boxes in the Camera Raw window are

- **Preview:** Gives you a preview of adjustment settings.
- **Shadows:** Shows you shadow clipping warnings in blue.
- **Highlight:** Shows you highlight clipping warnings in red.

Figure 12.10 shows opening a Camera Raw file in Adobe Bridge.

Watch Out!

The Camera Raw plug-in is only available to files created in Camera Raw format. If you right-click a file and don't see the Open in Camera Raw option, your camera was not set to Camera Raw Mode. See your camera's manual for instructions on changing your camera's settings.

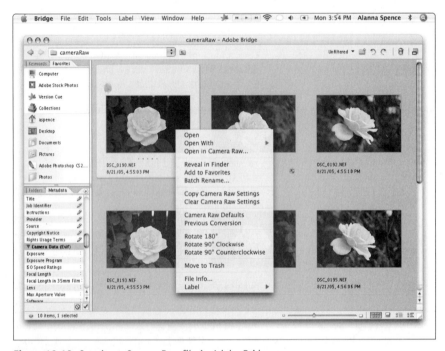

Figure 12.10. Opening a Camera Raw file in Adobe Bridge.

Perfecting your image with image settings

The Camera Raw plug-in offers five different panels of image adjustment options to perfect exposure, color, and sharpness. The next section introduces you to each panel and gives you some tips for getting the most out of your images. Before getting started with image settings, you should know a bit about the various buttons for saving and opening your Camera Raw files. Because the Camera Raw plug-in is an intermediate step between Bridge and Photoshop, you have more options than you are probably used to.

Inside Scoop

Because the adjustments you make are stored separately from your image, you can always return to your original image by selecting Camera Raw Defaults from the Settings drop-down list.

Here are descriptions of the various buttons in the Camera Raw window:

- **Save:** Similar to the Save As feature in Photoshop. You'll be able to rename your image, save it to a different location, and convert its file type.

- **Open:** Applies your changes and opens the file in Photoshop.

- **Done:** Saves your changes and closes the Camera Raw window, returning you to Bridge.

- **Cancel:** Closes the Camera Raw window without saving your changes.

Adjusting exposure, contrast, and saturation

The Adjust panel in the Camera Raw window is the first one you'll encounter when you open your image. It gives you controls for adjusting exposure settings of your photo, changing the tint and temperature of the highlight area in your photo, and controlling saturation and contrast.

Use the White Balance tool to click a highlight area of your image to adjust the white balance automatically. If you don't like the results, you can adjust them by moving the Temperature and Tint sliders. The White Balance drop-down list has several common settings for various lighting situations such as daylight, shade, and flash. Try the Auto option for each setting, and if you aren't happy with the results, adjust the slider for each setting.

Maximizing color and contrast adjustments in the Curves panel

The Curves panel in the Camera Raw window is similar to the regular Curves dialog box in Photoshop, with the added benefit of having a histogram

Hack

Press and hold the Option key (Alt) to change the Cancel button to a Reset button. Clicking Reset returns the image settings to what they were when you first opened the photo in the Camera Raw window.

Watch Out!

One drawback to the Curves panel in the Camera Raw window is that the preview doesn't appear until after you move a point and release your mouse button. Get in the habit of making small adjustments and nudge your image towards clarity.

image displayed behind it. Just like Photoshop's Curves, you can add your own points; up to 14 of them. With Curves you can get the maximum control over your image's color and contrast. Curves is by far the most powerful tool in the Camera Raw window, and you should get in the habit of visiting this panel first. You may find it's the only panel to which you really need to make adjustments. The tool automatically adds points for highlights, midtones, and shadows (see Figure 12.11).

Figure 12.11. The Curves panel in the Camera Raw window.

The Tone Curve drop-down list offers three automatic options and a custom setting for adjusting curves:

- **Linear:** The original, default straight-line curve that your image starts out with. If your curve gets out of control, select Linear to start over.

- **Medium Contrast:** Moderately boosts the darks in your image while keeping the lights the same.

- **Strong Contrast:** Darkens darks and lightens lights. Applying a Strong Contrast curve is a quick and dirty way of removing pixel noise from shadow areas.

- **Custom:** Create your own curve for maximum control. Click anywhere on the line to add a new control point.

Calibrating color in Camera Raw

The Calibrate tab in the Camera Raw window (see Figure 12.12) has many options for adjusting hue and saturation for each of the color channels as well as the shadow tint. For images with color cast problems, you can get much greater control over color adjustments in this tab.

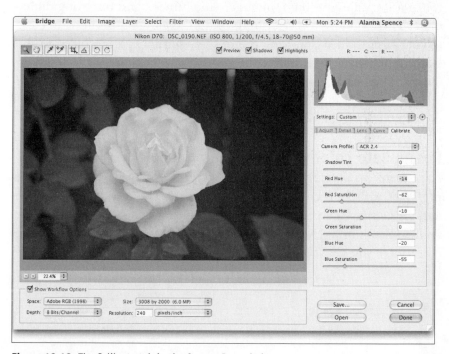

Figure 12.12. The Calibrate tab in the Camera Raw window.

To adjust your image's color with the calibrate options:

1. Right-click a Camera Raw file in Adobe Bridge and select Open in Camera Raw.

2. Click the Calibrate tab underneath the histogram thumbnail on the right side of the window.

3. Adjust the color of your shadows by moving the Shadow Tint slider to the right or left.

4. Adjust each of the Hue and Saturation sliders. Adjusting Hue changes a color from a cooler value to a warmer value. The Red Hue slider creates pinkish reds when moved to the left and orange reds when moved to the right.

When you are satisfied with your settings, click Save to save your changes and return to Bridge, or click Open to apply your settings and open the image in Photoshop for further editing.

Sharpening and removing noise with Detail

The Detail panel (see Figure 12.13) gives you options for sharpening your image, adjusting the luminance smoothness, and removing digital noise. These options are very subtle and I recommend zooming in close to your image when adjusting them. The Sharpness levels increase the contrast between dark and light pixels. The Luminance Smoothing option works well to remove grainy textures from large, bright areas of your photos, like sky. The Color Noise Reduction option takes care of digital noise that can occur in low light situations.

Fixing halo color with the Lens panel

Halo problems are rare with Camera Raw files. You may never encounter problems with halo color unless you regularly shoot with a wide-angle lens. If you see a halo of red or cyan around your image, try adjusting the Fix Red/Cyan Fringe values under the Chromatic Aberration settings to correct it. If you see a blue or yellow halo, try adjusting the Fix Blue/Yellow Fringe values.

Inside Scoop

Double-click the Zoom tool to zoom in 100%. Zoom in even closer by selecting 200%, 300%, or 400% from the Select zoom level drop-down list below the image preview.

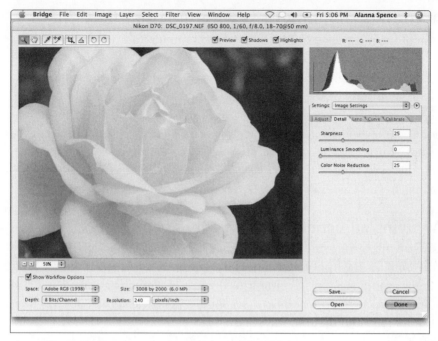

Figure 12.13. The Detail panel in the Camera Raw window.

The Vignette options in the Lens panel (see Figure 12.14) let you add a subtle dark or light cast around the outside of your image. Adjusting the Amount slider all the way to the left adds a dark cast around the edges; adjusting it to the right adds a light cast. The Midpoint setting adjusts how much of your image the vignette effects.

Figure 12.14. Vignette effects created in the Lens panel.

Applying changes to several Camera Raw files

One of the most powerful features of the Camera Raw plug-in is the ability to apply your changes to multiple files or save them to use on future sets of Camera Raw files. When you shoot a set of photos in Camera Raw mode, the odds of the entire set needing similar color correction are high. You've probably shot your set of photos in the same lighting conditions, so they will all need identical adjustments. The Camera Raw plug-in lets you apply the saved adjustments to a set of open files, or save adjustment settings for future use. You can also change the auto setting to match your camera's output better than the default auto settings.

Applying adjustment settings to a photo set

You can apply the same settings to a set of photos. If you Shift+select several Camera Raw photos at once and open them in the Camera Raw plug-in, you'll see a new column to the left of your image preview. This column lists all the opened files (see Figure 12.15). You can click any one of them to switch them in the editor.

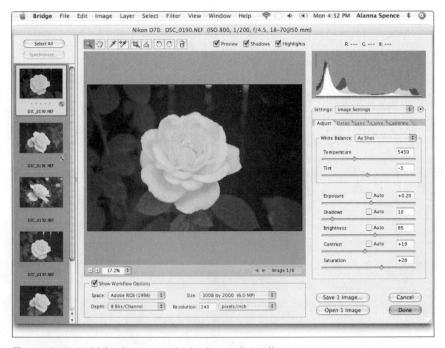

Figure 12.15. Multiple photos open in the Camera Raw editor.

Bright Idea!

Apply the default or auto Camera Raw settings to a set of photos without having to open them in the Camera Raw window. Select the files you want to adjust, right-click one of them, and select Camera Raw Defaults from the drop-down list.

To apply your current settings to a set of images:

1. Click the Select All button in the Camera Raw window.

2. Click the Synchronize button. A window appears with several options for which settings to apply. Click OK to synchronize all of your photos with the currently open photo.

Synchronize Settings is the default and synchronizes any changes you've made. You can choose to synchronize just the adjustments made on specific panels by selecting them from the Synchronize drop-down list.

Saving your settings for the future

The Camera Raw plug-in comes with default settings for auto adjustments. Each camera is going to have slight variations, and the Photoshop auto adjust defaults may not yield the best results for your camera. You can replace the default settings with your own standard set of adjustments so that you can have auto adjustments that better match the output from your camera. If you use more than one camera, or if you don't want to mess with the defaults, you can add your own sets or subsets of adjustments so that you can get consistent images no matter what camera you use. Figure 12.16 shows the Save Settings dialog box in the Camera Raw window.

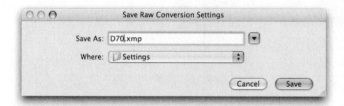

Figure 12.16. The Save Raw Conversion Settings dialog box.

The settings dialog box lives in the following places:

- **Windows:** Documents and Settings/[username]/Application Data/ Adobe/CameraRaw/Settings.

- **Mac:** Users/[user profile]/Library/Application Support/ Adobe/ CameraRaw/Settings.

The Save Settings option automatically saves any changes you've made to all five of the Image Settings tabs in the Camera Raw window. If you'd like to save settings from just one or two of the tabs, you can instead use the Save Settings Subset option (see Figure 12.17) to pick and choose from the various subsets of image settings.

Figure 12.17. The Camera Raw Save Settings Subset dialog box.

Bright Idea!

Share your settings files with other users or copy them to another computer. Search your hard drive for the settings file you created and copy it to another computer. Select Load Settings to load them into Bridge.

Just the facts

- Organize, preview, and edit your photos quickly in Photoshop's powerful sister application, Adobe Bridge.

- Add metadata, keywords, and find files based on search criteria.

- Adjust color, contrast, and exposure of your Camera Raw files in Adobe Bridge's Camera Raw plug-in.

- Adjust an entire set of Camera Raw files by opening several at once and using the Synchronize option.

- Save your own Camera Raw auto adjustments in the settings options drop-down list.

GET THE SCOOP ON...
Cropping nondestructively ▪ Creating reusable selection
sizes ▪ Adding solid color borders to photos ▪ Fixing pet
eye ▪ Rescaling images without losing picture quality

Resizing and Retouching Photos

As the technology for digital photography improves, more and more people are switching from traditional photography to digital photography. It's not hard to figure out why. There are many advantages to digital photography over traditional photography. Once you make the initial purchase of a camera and software, you don't have to worry about additional costs of film, chemicals, and darkroom equipment. If you choose to print your photos, printing technology has improved to the point where it is very difficult to tell a print made from a consumer-level digital camera from a print made using 35mm film and photo paper. With higher-end digital cameras and prints, you can't tell the difference between digital and traditional prints. There are some great options available for very affordable, high-quality printing. Places such as snapfish.com and Costco offer online printing services where you can upload your photos from home and have them delivered via mail straight to you or your friends and family.

Digital photography allows you much more freedom to experiment. Because if is easy to make backups of your digital photos, and because you aren't worrying about the cost of printing, you have much more freedom to experiment. You are free to play with exposure, colorization, creative cropping, resizing, and embellishing with artistic brush strokes.

This chapter introduces you to some cropping and resizing techniques and shows you some time-saving features that have been added in Photoshop CS2. You'll see some of the powerful photo editing tools for getting rid of red eye and removing blemishes. You'll also look at Photoshop's Liquify filter and see how to straighten a crooked nose.

Cropping photos with the Crop tool

Sometimes the greatest photo is hiding inside a larger, busier one. Many times in the heat of the moment, you forget to pay attention to composition and your subject isn't centered like you would have preferred. Cropping is a great way to focus attention on the photo's subject and remove distracting elements such as the power plug in the background of Figure 13.1.

Figure 13.1. A cropped selection made with the Crop tool.

Photoshop CS2 brings many improvements to the Crop tool. You can now set an aspect ratio and perform nondestructive crops. Table 13.1 lists the new Crop tool features and where you can access them. Some of the options are only available before you create a crop selection; some are only available after you've created an initial crop selection.

Table 13.1. Crop features and their functions

Crop Feature	Description	Feature Location
Crop to a certain size	Your image will be resized to the width and height values you enter in the Crop tool Options bar before selecting your area to crop.	Before creating a crop selection, enter a desired width and height in the Width and Height fields in the Options bar.
Crop to a certain resolution	Photoshop automatically scales the resolution of your photo while performing the crop.	Before creating a crop selection, enter the desired resolution in the Resolution field in the Options bar.
Hide the cropped area	A nondestructive cropping method. Instead of deleting the area around your crop, you can hide it outside the canvas area. You can easily uncrop your photo by enlarging your canvas size.	Choose the Hide radio button in the Options bar after creating a crop selection.
Delete the cropped area	Permanently remove the area outside the crop. Your file size will be smaller than when hiding the cropped area.	Choose the Delete radio button in the Options bar after creating a crop selection.
Control the color and opacity of the previewed cropped area	Get a good sense of your crop by changing the crop preview opacity to 100%. If the black is too distracting, change the preview color from black to white.	A color swatch and opacity setting are located in the Options bar.

Crop your photos nondestructively

Photoshop CS2's Crop tool has been improved to include a nondestructive method for cropping. The area outside your crop is hidden instead of being deleted and can be brought back by simply enlarging your canvas size again. Keep in mind that because the image data is still in your document, your file size will be larger than with the older method of deleting the cropped area. If you don't have concerns with file size, I recommend always using this method.

Inside Scoop

Use the mouse to accept or cancel a crop. Right-click inside the crop selection and choose Crop or Cancel from the drop-down list.

To create a nondestructive crop:

1. Open a JPEG photo you'd like to crop. If your file has just one layer and it is a locked Background layer, you'll need to double-click the layer's name to unlock and rename it.

2. Select the Crop tool from the Toolbox by pressing the letter C.

3. Select an area of your photo to crop.

4. Once you make your selection, the Options bar changes from displaying width and height options to displaying radio buttons for deleting or hiding the cropped area. Click the Hide radio button (see Figure 13.2).

5. Double-click inside your crop selection to accept the crop. To cancel a crop selection, click the Cancel button in the Options bar. It looks like a red circle with a slash through it.

Your document window resizes to your crop selection. If you decide to uncrop later, change your canvas size back to its original size by choosing Image ⇨ Canvas Size.

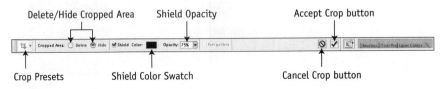

Figure 13.2. The Options bar for the Crop tool.

Crop to a specific width and height

Cropping and resizing used to be a big headache. Before the addition of this feature, shrinking and cropping was a three-step process that required a lot of eyeballing. You'd have to crop to roughly the proportions you needed, resize your image to something close to your desired size, and then adjust your canvas size to trim off any extra pixels.

Now Photoshop CS2 allows you to crop and resize in one shot, taking all the guesswork out of it and saving you time and headaches. Figure 13.3 includes height and width fields in the Options bar for the Crop tool that allow you to crop to a specific width and height. Your crop selection can be any size. The tool automatically uses constraints when you begin selecting your crop area so that it can resample your image to the crop size you entered in the width and height fields. For example, if you have an image that is 8×10 inches and you'd like to crop an area inside it and have it resized to 5×7 inches, you can create a crop of any size, within proportion constraints, and Photoshop will resize your image to 5×7 inches. Using this feature saves you two steps.

You can now change the resolution of your image while cropping. If you have a 300-dpi digital photo and you'd like to crop and resize it to 72 dpi for use on a Web site, you can now do it in one step.

Figure 13.3. Cropping to a specific size with width and height values.

Watch Out!

Avoid going from a smaller resolution to a higher one. You'll end up with a pixilated image of lower quality.

To create a 100-x-100-pixel thumbnail with a resolution of 72 dpi for use on a Web site:

1. Open a JPEG or other image file.

2. If there's just one locked Background layer, double-click the layer thumbnail to rename and unlock it.

3. Select the Crop tool from the Toolbox by pressing the letter C.

4. In the Options bar, enter 100 px in the Height and Width fields (see Figure 13.4).

Figure 13.4. A photo and the Crop tool Options bar set to 100 x 100 pixels and 72 dpi.

Inside Scoop

If you'd like to scrap your crop and start over, click any tool in the Toolbox. A dialog box appears. Click the Don't Crop button and the crop selection will disappear.

5. Enter 72 in the Resolution field and make sure pixels/inch is selected in the drop-down menu next to it.

6. Click and drag the Crop tool across your image. You'll notice the width and height are constrained to a square shape, but you can create as large or small a crop area as you like.

7. Click inside the crop area if you'd like to move your crop selection, or adjust the selection by dragging on the crop corners.

8. Once you've perfected your crop, double-click inside it to accept it.

Now, if you open the Image Size window by choosing Image ⇨ Image Size, you should see that you have an image that is 100 x 100 pixels with a resolution of 72 dpi.

Since you've come this far, I'll give you the five-second instructions on creating a JPEG file for the Web. I cover Web optimization and file types in much more detail in Chapter 20.

To save your new thumbnail as a JPEG for use on the Web:

1. Choose File ⇨ Save for Web.

2. In the dialog box that appears, select JPEG High from the Preset menu on the right.

3. Click the Save button. The Save For Web window appears (see Figure 13.5).

4. Name your file, making sure you keep the .jpg file extension, find a convenient place for it on your computer, and click the Save button.

You've now got a thumbnail JPEG ready to be added to a Web site. Resizing via the Crop tool is one way to customize your images, but if you want to keep your entire image intact, cropping doesn't make much sense. In the next section, you'll resize without cropping.

Watch Out!

When creating images for the Web, make sure your color mode is set to RGB. Choose Image ⇨ Mode ⇨ RGB Color.

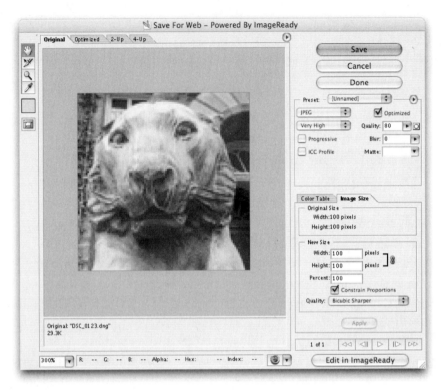

Figure 13.5. The Save For Web window.

Resizing your image and canvas size

You don't have to crop an image to resize it; and if you create a document and then later decide you need a larger canvas or smaller image, you can change it through the Image Size dialog box. If you are sharing photos with friends and family, either over the Web or through e-mail, sending a 300-dpi image is going to eat up too much bandwidth. Many e-mail servers set limits on the file size you can send in one e-mail. Many only allow attachments of up to 2MB. Chances are your friends aren't going to print out your photo on a high-resolution printer; they will just be look-ing at them on the screen. If that's the case, they will probably be looking at your images through a Web browser that displays at 72 dpi.

Figure 13.6 shows you all the options available inside the Image Size dia-log box. You have the option of changing Pixel Dimensions and Document Size. The chain icon along the right side of the Width and Height fields lets you know that the Constrain Proportions option is turned on. With this option checked, your document retains its horizontal and vertical relationship and resizes to scale.

Image Size

Pixel Dimensions: 5.49M

Width: 1600 pixels

Height: 1200 pixels

OK
Cancel
Auto...

Document Size:

Width: 5.333 inches

Height: 4 inches

Resolution: 300 pixels/inch

☑ Scale Styles
☑ Constrain Proportions
☑ Resample Image: Bicubic

Figure 13.6. The Image Size dialog box.

The Scale to Style option keeps your drop shadows and inner glow from resizing with your image. When you add a drop shadow or other style, you can control how many pixels thick it is. If you are resizing, that pixel thickness is going to change. If you want your drop shadows to be 5 pixels thick, no matter what size your image is, uncheck this option. In most cases, you'll want to keep this checked. If you aren't quite happy with the new size of your drop shadow, you can always go back in and adjust it.

The Resample Image option determines the method Photoshop uses to interpolate pixel information. If you are just starting out with Photoshop, don't worry about the Resample Image setting. It's defaulted to Bicubic and that'll give you the best results, especially when resizing photos. If you'd like to expand your techno-nerd knowledge or are planning to do professional printing or photography, keep reading.

Watch Out!

If you uncheck the Constrain Proportions check box, your image will be stretched or squished to fit the new dimensions.

When shrinking an image, you are going from a certain amount of information to less information. Think of it this way: If you have an image that is 100 pixels wide by 100 pixels high, and you shrink it to 50 by 50 pixels, you have one quarter the amount of pixels trying to display the same amount of information. Photoshop needs to make some tough decisions on how to blend many pixels down to one. It uses mathematical equations, called interpolation, to figure out how to resample data. The types of interpolation methods are listed in Table 13.2.

Table 13.2. Resampling methods used for resizing images

Method	Description	Best Use
Bicubic	Resamples your image without applying image-enhancing filters.	Good as a general-purpose photo-resampling setting.
Bicubic Sharper	Creates crisp edges.	If you have a perfect photo and want to keep all the details, use this interpolation method.
Bicubic Smoother	Creates soft transitions between pixels.	Great for lessening the amount of film grain or JPEG noise in your photos.
Bilinear	Takes a sampling of pixels in that row and uses an average of that row — takes more processing power than Nearest Neighbor.	Better for solid graphics such as vector graphics and text.
Nearest Neighbor	Quickest method — chooses color based on pixel data from its nearest neighboring pixel.	Artwork with large areas of color such as comics, illustrations, or graphics.

The general rule of thumb is to use one of the Bicubic interpolation methods for photographs. Bilinear and Nearest Neighbor may yield better results on images with solid areas of color, vector graphics, buttons, and type. Bilinear interpolation is better suited for Web and print design involving a combination of photos and graphics.

Adjusting your canvas size

Changing the canvas size means changing the area that your image sits on; it does not resize your image. If you make your canvas size smaller, you're

Bright Idea!

Add a title bar to your photos by increasing your canvas size on the top of your image.

essentially cropping your photo. If you make it bigger, you are adding space around your image. The Canvas Size dialog box in Figure 13.7 shows you all the options available for shrinking and enlarging your canvas.

Like the Image Size dialog box, you can change the units of measure for width and height using the drop-down lists. If you hate math, and you just want to add 100 pixels to the top and bottom of your image, you can click the Relative check box and enter the values you want to add. By clicking on any of the boxes in the Anchor grid, you can tell Photoshop to crop to the left, right, top, bottom, or middle. The Anchor settings in Figure 13.7 would crop equally around each side of the image. If you were to click the box below the current one, the one on the bottom middle, you'd be cropping off just the top of your image. Increasing your canvas size would add a space to the top of your image.

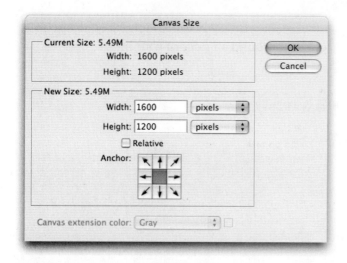

Figure 13.7. The Canvas Size dialog box.

Create a quick border by increasing your canvas size

A quick way of adding a solid color frame around your photo is by increasing your canvas size and adding a solid color fill layer.

To add a solid colored frame to your photo:

1. Open a photo you'd like to add a frame to. If your file has just one Background layer in it, double-click its thumbnail to rename and unlock it.

2. Add a solid color fill layer by clicking the Add New Fill or Adjustment Layer icon on the bottom of your Layers palette and select Solid Color from the top of the list.

3. Select a color you would like to use as your frame color, and click OK when you are done.

4. Open the Canvas Size dialog box by choosing Image ⇨ Canvas Size, or pressing ⌘+Option+C (Ctrl+Alt+C).

5. Click the Relative check box so that you can add the value you want instead of adding that amount to the existing image size.

6. Add a value to the Height and Width box. I am working with a 300-dpi image that is 1600 x 1394 pixels and I like large frames, so I'll add 400 pixels to both the Height and Width fields. If you are working with a 72-dpi image, you might want to try 100 x 100 pixels (see Figure 13.8).

7. You want your anchor setting to stay in the middle box because you want to add space evenly around all sides of your image.

8. Click OK when you are done.

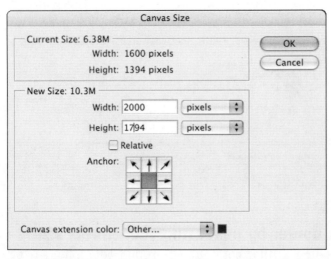

Figure 13.8. The Canvas Size dialog box with a Canvas extension color assigned.

Inside Scoop

If your document consists of one Background layer, use the Canvas Extension Color drop-down list in the Canvas Size window and pick a color for your new canvas area to save a step.

A solid colored border now surrounds your photo. If you want to edit the color, double-click the color thumbnail in your solid color layer and choose a new color from the Color Picker.

Creating rescalable photos as Smart Objects

Smart Objects are new to Photoshop CS2. They allow you to embed a high-resolution image inside your file that you can resize as much as you like without having to worry about losing image quality. Figure 13.9 shows an example of what a resized photo layer might look like after converting your photo to a Smart Object, and one that is resized as a regular layer. If you convert a 300-dpi photo into a Smart Object, you can shrink it down to Web-graphic size, save out a copy, then enlarge it again to bring it back to print quality. This saves you from having to save out the same file into duplicate files with different resolutions and sizes.

Make your own comparison. Try resizing without converting your photo to a Smart Object and then try resizing Smart Objects:

1. Open a photo with a resolution of 300 dpi or higher.

2. Making a note of its original size, resize it down in the Image Size dialog box. Choose Image ⇨ Image Size or press ⌘+Option+I (Ctrl+Alt+I), and then change your Resolution to 72 and your Pixel Dimensions to 100 x 100.

3. If you zoom in, you should have a very pixilated image.

4. Resize it to its original size by choosing Image ⇨ Image Size.

5. Adjust your zoom by pressing and holding ⌘+Spacebar (Ctrl+ spacebar) to zoom in or ⌘+Option+Spacebar (Ctrl+Alt+spacebar) to zoom out.

Inside Scoop

Smart Objects don't take up more room. Your file size is only as large as it was when you converted your image to a Smart Object.

Figure 13.9. Comparing a resized Smart Object to a regular photo.

Your image should look crummy! Now try the same steps by first converting your photo to a Smart Object:

1. Make sure you choose File ⇨ Revert to restore your photo to its original, high-resolution state.

2. While your photo layer is selected in the Layers palette, choose Layer ⇨ Smart Objects ⇨ Group Into New Smart Object. Your

thumbnail icon in your Layers palette will change slightly to include a small Smart Layers icon.

3. Repeat the previous steps.

No matter how many times you resize your image, Photoshop keeps the detailed image stored and reverts your image back to its full-resolution glory.

Editing Smart Objects

After you've converted your image to a Smart Object, you can make edits to it without having to convert it back to a raster image. When you double-click on the Smart Object in the Layers palette, Photoshop will automatically create an external file where you can edit your image to your heart's content. When you are done editing and commit your changes, Photoshop will automatically update the Smart Object in your original file to reflect your edits. You will have to keep both the Photoshop file with the Smart Object and the edited file in the same folder but you can edit it as many times as you like.

To edit a Smart Object:

1. Double-click the thumbnail of the layer you would like to edit. Photoshop will automatically create a new file that you can edit. A dialog box will appear, reminding you to save the edited file in the same folder as the file that contains the Smart Object (see Figure 13.10).

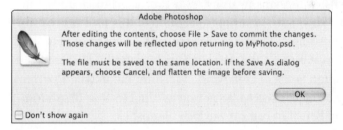

Figure 13.10. Dialog box for saving edited Smart Objects.

2. Edit the new file as you would a regular Photoshop file.

Watch Out!
Don't try to edit a Smart Object directly. If you try to make changes to a Smart Object, you will be warned that Photoshop will need to convert it to a rasterized image first. You'll lose the benefits of being able to resize it.

3. Choose File ⇨ Save and make sure you save the file in the same folder as the file with the Smart Object. Photoshop will save it to this folder by default.

4. Return to the file with the Smart Object in it. Photoshop will automatically update the edits you made in the external file.

Once you've created the editable file, you can open and edit it at any time. The Photoshop file with the Smart Object will automatically update each time you save the external file.

Performing cosmetic surgery without a doctor

Photo editing used to be a craft reserved for professional photographers and darkroom technicians. When we took birthday party photos and had them developed in a lab, we had to be content with red eye, stained shirts, pimples, and wrinkles. With the development of digital photography, you can now take matters into your own hands. Photoshop CS2 has added and improved some fantastic tools for fixing common photo problems. In this section you'll try out the Spot Healing Brush, the Patch tool, and the Red Eye tool.

Remove skin blemishes with the Healing Brush

With Photoshop's Healing Brush tools, getting rid of pock marks, moles, and wrinkles is quick, easy, and fun. Although the Healing Brush was created with photos of humans in mind, you can use it to clean up any blemished surface. If you are scanning old photos, this tool is great for removing scratches or stains. The photo in Figure 13.11 is a photo I took of a Benjamin Franklin statue on the Atlantic City boardwalk. His damaged face has been through years of sun, wind, and rain. He makes a perfect candidate for displaying the awesome powers of the Healing Brush tool.

Use the Healing Brush to remove surface blemishes:

1. Select the Spot Healing Brush tool by pressing the letter J.

2. Adjust your brush size in the Options bar at the top of the screen. You can use the [and] keys to increase or decrease your brush size in increments of 25%.

3. Click a spot you would like to remove. The Spot Healing Brush takes a sample from the surrounding area and blends your spot away.

4. To get rid of large wrinkles or cracks, click and drag the Spot Healing Brush along the wrinkle to remove it in one swipe.

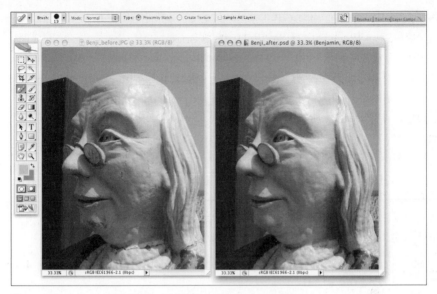

Figure 13.11. Fixing Blemishes with Healing Brush and Patch tools.

Some areas can be a little tricky, especially when you are trying to heal areas that are right next to the background of your image. The regular Healing Brush tool allows you to pick your sample area for more control.

To sample specific areas with the Healing Brush:

1. Select the Healing Brush tool by pressing Shift+J once to switch from the Spot Healing Brush tool.

2. Option+click an area you would like to sample.

3. Click and drag across an area you'd like to heal.

After just a few minutes, your subject will be looking years younger.

Tackle large problem areas with the Patch tool

As you can see in the before shot of Benjamin in Figure 13.11, his chin is beat up. He needs more than a Healing Brush to fix all that damage. The Patch tool serves as your virtual skin grafter. Selecting a good area of skin and dragging the Patch tool over the effected area blends the good and the bad together.

Bright Idea!

Use the Patch tool to cover up unwanted elements in your photos such as timestamps, film scratches, or background clutter.

To patch a large blemished area:

1. Select the Patch tool from the Healing Brush tools menu. Press Shift to toggle through the different tools in the Healing Brush fly-out menu.

2. Select an area of your subject's face that is in an ideal condition. For Benjamin, I selected an area a little bigger than a quarter, to the right of his chin.

3. Click the selection and drag it to a spot on top of the chin; the selection doesn't have to cover the spot completely.

4. Drag the selection to another part of the rough area to fix another spot.

5. Continue dragging the selection around the rough area until you've achieved good coloring and texture for the chin.

Good as new! If growing skin were that easy in real life, dermatologists would be out of business.

Performing plastic surgery with the Liquify tool

The Liquify tool is a mini application that runs inside Photoshop. It has an entirely different set of tools associated with it. Using the Liquify tool in moderation, you can turn a frown upside down, fix a broken nose, or plump up your subject's lips without collagen injections. When used a little more liberally as a creative tool, like I've done to myself in Figure 13.12, you can distort someone's face beyond recognition quickly. If you are looking for some cheap therapy, this would be a great tool to use on a photo of your boss's face — just don't say that it was my idea.

You can launch the Liquify tool by choosing Filter ⇨ Liquify; the Liquify window in Figure 13.12 appears. You can play around inside the tool as much as you want and take advantage of Photoshop's undo commands when you've gone too far; it's easy to do with this tool! Liquify also has a Reconstruct tool that removes any liquify effect you paint over. If you ever want to start over, just cancel out of the tool and start again. Once you've gotten a result you like, clicking OK applies your changes to your actual image. There are quite a few tools in the Liquify tool that are new to Photoshop. Table 13.3 explains the tools and some effective uses for each one.

Figure 13.12. The Liquify window with toolbox and options.

Table 13.3. Tools in the Liquify window

Tool Icon	Liquify Tools	Description
	Warp	Pushes pixels around. Great for fixing broken noses or adjusting expressions.
	Reconstruct	Painting over Liquified areas of your image removes their Liquify effects. Works like a sponge to remove distortions and restore parts of your image.
	Twirl	Twirls pixels around the center of the brush. To twirl counterclockwise, press and hold the Option or Alt key.
	Pucker	Moves pixels towards the middle of the brush center.

continued

Table 13.3. *continued*

Tool Icon	Liquify Tools	Description
	Bloat	Moves pixels away from the brush center. Good for plumping up lips.
	Push Left	Pushes pixels left when you drag your mouse down. Pushes them to the right if you drag your mouse up. This tool is good for slimming a person's figure by pushing their waistline slightly in towards their bodies. The preview looks quite different from the applied effect and can be difficult to gauge.
	Mirror	Works similar to a funhouse mirror.
	Turbulence	Scrambles pixels. This tool is popular with creating cloud and smoke effects.
	Freeze Mask	You can mask over an area of your photo that you do not want to liquify.
	Thaw Mask	Erases holes in your Freeze Mask. Good for isolating parts of the face like noses and eyes.
	Hand	Enables you to move around your image when zoomed in.
	Zoom	Behaves like the standard Zoom tool. Hold down the Option key (Alt key) to zoom out.

Exorcise demons by removing red eye

The dreaded red eye is caused by camera flash bouncing off blood vessels in the retinas of your subject's pupils. Some digital cameras have built-in red-eye reduction, but oftentimes it doesn't seem to make a bit of difference.

Photoshop's Red Eye tool is one of the best I've seen and is incredibly easy to use. It works by finding groups of reddish pixels and coloring them a darker color. The photo in Figure 13.13 was taken in a very low light situation. Although the subject isn't looking directly into the camera, the lighting situation was extreme enough to give her red circles for pupils.

Figure 13.13. Fixing red eye and pet eye.

To take the Red Eye tool for a spin:

1. Find a digital photo with subjects that have a red-eye problem.

2. Select the Red Eye tool from the Toolbox by selecting it from the Healing Brush fly-out menu or pressing Shift+J until it is selected. It looks like an eyeball with cross hairs over it.

3. The Options bar for the Red Eye tool is set to 50% for both Pupil size and Darken amount. These settings work fine for most photos. To get a more subtle effect, lower the Pupil size and Darken amount to about 20%.

4. Click inside the red area of one of the eyes.

5. Click inside the other eye's red area.

That's all there is to it! This tool works for most cases of red eye and is much easier than all the steps you used to have to go through in previous versions of Photoshop.

Removing the green glow from your pet's eyes

Glowing green pet eyes caused by too much flash can be a little trickier than human red eyes. In Figure 13.14, the dog's eyes are so blown out with light that there's no more detail left of his eye to repair. In severe cases like this, it's sometimes necessary to re-create the eye completely. Some animals are easier than others.

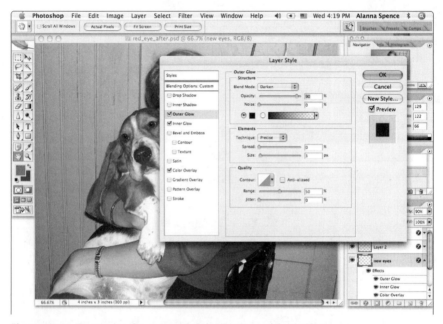

Figure 13.14. Re-creating dog eyes with Color Overlay and Outer Glow.

First get a good selection of your dog's eyes:

1. Change to the Magic Wand tool by pressing the letter W.

2. In the Magic Wand Options bar, change the Tolerance level to 30. This is a nice midrange tolerance setting for this tool. Click one of the glowing eyes to select it. If you don't like your selection, try adjusting the Tolerance level up or down.

3. Shift+click the other pupil to add it to the current selection.

4. Copy the selection by either pressing ⌘+C or selecting Copy from the Edit menu.

Watch Out!

Make sure you turn off the visibility of your layer copies so they don't cover up the one you are working on.

5. Create a new layer by clicking on the New Layer icon on the bottom of your Layers palette just to the left of the Trash Can icon.

6. Paste your selection into the new layer by pressing ⌘+P (Ctrl+P).

If you'd like, now would be a good time to save a few extra copies of your dog's eyes. Because this isn't a quick solution, you might need to try out a couple different variations. Copy your new layer by dragging it on top of the New Layer button on the bottom of the Layers palette.

Now create some realistic eyes:

1. ⌘+double-click the thumbnail of the new layer to open the layer styles for this layer.

2. Click the Color Overlay option. You should see your dog's eyes turning bright red.

3. Choose a dark color for the eye. It's sometimes a good idea to find a dark color on your pet and use the Eyedropper to select it. This usually gives you a more natural-looking color. Don't worry; your eye is going to look very funny at this point.

4. Click the Inner Glow style to select it.

5. From the Blending Mode drop-down list, choose Darken.

6. Double-click the small color swatch and change it from light yellow to a very dark navy. This gives the eye a darker outer ring and makes it look more realistic.

7. Change your foreground color to black, change your Brush size to a good pupil size, and add a dot to the center of your dog's eye.

8. Add a white highlight to your dog's eye by changing your foreground color to white and shrinking your brush size.

How did your eyes turn out? These instructions are for a worst-case scenario. Some instances of affected pet eyes aren't as severe as this one, and you may only have to follow a few of these steps to get good results. Some eye problems may only require a semitransparent color overlay.

The more you practice, the better you'll become at fixing these problems. Don't give up: As with all things Photoshop, practice makes perfect.

Just the facts

- Crop, resize, and change resolution in one step.
- Crop your photos without losing the original image.
- Convert your images to Smart Objects and keep their high-quality information no matter how many times you shrink and enlarge your document.
- Use the Healing Brush to remove blemishes from any surface.
- Fix flash problems in one click with the Red Eye tool.

Fixing Fuzz, Tilt, and Perspective

Although digital camera and scanner technology advances by leaps and bounds with each year, the human hand hasn't evolved much for hundreds of thousands of years. Even the steadiest hand can move or shake. When we think we've nailed a perfectly aligned shot, we later discover that we were off by a mile. Sometimes our cameras can distort images when working with the wide-angle or telephoto lenses. Photoshop has lots of tools for aligning, sharpening, and unwarping. Although you won't be able to perform miracles on extreme cases, you can definitely dress up most mild cases enough to pass for the stunning image you had imagined when you first took the shot.

In this chapter, you'll learn how to fix distortion problems common with wide-angle lenses by stretching and pinching images with the Distort tool. You'll see how to extend repeatable patterned images like stairs, walls, or piano keys, even when they are in two- or three-point perspective. You'll continue to explore ways of fixing common photo problems like reducing noise and cleaning up dust and scratches.

Rotating and fixing distortion

Like most digital camera owners, I have a compact consumer-range cam-era with a built-in zoom lens. I love the images I get from such a tiny, inexpensive piece of electronics. I'm willing to put up with a little distor-tion if it means I don't have to spend more money for a fancier camera. I don't want to have to deal with detachable lenses and bulkier camera bodies. Where I save in convenience and money, I pay for in some wacky distortion when trying to take photos of rectangular objects like build-ings, furniture, or paintings. The lens in my camera is a wide one, giving me a lot of options but also giving me a lot of distortion.

The photo of my painting in Figure 14.1 is both tilted slightly and dis-torted due to a fish-eye effect called *barrel distortion* created by my digital camera's lens. I didn't quite get a straight-on shot, so the right side of my painting is much shorter than the left. First fix the tilt, and then see about the distortion.

Figure 14.1. The photo before fixing rotating and warping problems.

Straightening tilted photos

The Free Transform feature not only lets you shrink and stretch your images, but you can also use it to rotate your image in tiny or large increments. You'll need to crop your image once you rotate it. In Figure 14.2, you can see the black background is rotated slightly, exposing the transparent background behind it. If the painting corner was too close to the edge when I rotated it, I might have snipped some important parts off. Make sure you do any rotations on an image before cropping it so you have some excess areas as buffers.

Figure 14.2. A photo rotated using Free Transform.

To rotate a photo with Free Transform, follow these steps:

1. Open a photo to rotate. Be sure to unlock your Background layer by double-clicking it in the Layers palette.
2. Click the Full Screen Mode with Menu Bar button near the bottom of the Toolbox. It's much easier to rotate your image if you switch to Full Screen Mode.

Inside Scoop

Press and hold the Shift key to constrain your rotation amounts to 15-degree increments.

3. Choose Edit ⇨ Free Transform or use the key command ⌘+T (Ctrl+T).

4. Move your cursor to just outside your photo until it turns into a curved line with two arrows. Click and drag your mouse to rotate your image. When you are done, press the Enter key to accept your changes.

After you've gotten your image straightened out, you can crop off any excess bits where the transparent background shows through. If you need to correct distortion, wait to do your cropping until after that's fixed as well.

Fixing barrel distortion

Barrel distortion is a common problem with digital cameras that have a wide-angle lens. It causes your image to bow out in the middle. When you are taking pictures of rectangular shapes, this becomes very apparent and can be a real pain. *Pincushion* distortion is the opposite of barrel distortion and is usually caused by telephoto lenses. The middle of your image bows in slightly, making the tops and bottoms of your image look like they are bowing out. This is most apparent when taking pictures of tall buildings or objects with vertical sides or lines.

Luckily the Distort feature of Photoshop can help correct both barrel distortion and pincushion distortion. In the next exercise, I'll show you how to correct common distortion problems like the barrel distortion you see in Figure 14.3. Be warned that just like rotation, you'll need to trim some excess off your photo after you are done. Make sure you don't crop your image before fixing distortion.

Watch Out!

You can't undo when you are in the middle of a transformation like Distort. You'll need to press Enter to accept the transformation, and then you can undo it.

Figure 14.3. A photo before distortion is corrected.

You can correct an image with barrel distortion by following these steps:

1. Open an image to correct. Be sure to unlock the Background layer by double-clicking it in the layers palette.

2. Create some guides in your image. In Figure 14.4, I framed my image using guides so that I know where to stop stretching the transform box. To add guides, first turn on Photoshop's rulers feature by choosing View ⇨ Rulers.

3. Click inside the vertical ruler and drag a guide to one side of your image. Repeat for the other side.

4. If you need to correct distortion on the top of your image as well, click inside the horizontal ruler and drag a guide to the top of your image. Repeat this step for the bottom of your image.

5. Switch to Full Screen with Menu Bar Mode. You can toggle through the modes by pressing the letter F.

6. Choose Edit ⇨ Transform ⇨ Distort. You'll see a transform box with anchors on the corners and in the middle of each side.

7. Drag the corner anchors away from your image to correct barrel distortion, or in towards the center of your image to correct pincushion distortion. Use your guides to help you. When you are satisfied with your changes, press Enter to accept them.

Now that you are done fixing distortion, your can crop your image to get rid of any areas where the background shows through, like I have in Figure 14.4. You can get rid of your rules and guides by pressing ⌘+R (Ctrl+R) to hide the rulers and ⌘+; (Ctrl+;) to hide the guides.

Figure 14.4. A photo after distortion correction.

Rotating by degrees

If you are like me, you love to take photos in portrait format, but when you open up the files in Photoshop, they're stuck on their side. If you haven't rotated your photo in Adobe Bridge (see Chapter 12), you'll need

Hack

Load the Commands Action set into your Actions palette to use key commands for rotating. Use Shift+F8 to rotate 90° clockwise, Shift+F9 to rotate 90° counterclockwise, and Shift+F10 to rotate180°. See Chapter 10 for more about loading action sets.

to know how to do it in Photoshop. You can rotate your photo 180°, 90° clockwise, or 90° counterclockwise by choosing Edit ⇨ Transform and selecting one of the rotation methods.

Creating reflections in water

The waters of San Francisco Bay are cold, murky, and choppy. There's very little reflection in the water on most days. I can pretend I'm in a more tropical locale by adding some reflections of boats to the waters around Hyde Street Pier. In Figure 14.5, I created copies of each boat separately, flipped them vertically, and then blended them into the shoreline using the Gradient tool and a layer mask.

This trick is easiest to do with photos of water that don't have a lot of reflection in them. The straighter the waterline and more horizontal the objects, the easier it is to create realistic-looking reflections.

Figure 14.5. A comparison of photos with reflections added using Flip Vertical.

To create a reflection in water, perform the following:

1. Open a photo of a water scene to create your reflection.

2. Drag your photo layer on top of the Create New Layer button on the bottom of the Layers palette to create a copy of it.

3. Select the image you'd like to use as your reflection. I just used the Rectangular Marquee tool for the boats in Figure 14.5, but you can usually get the best results by using the Lasso tool.

4. Copy and paste your selection by choosing Edit ⇨ Copy and then Edit ⇨ Paste. A new layer with your selection is automatically created.

5. With your new layer still highlighted in the Layers palette, choose Edit ⇨ Transform ⇨ Flip Vertical. Temporarily change your cursor to the Move tool by pressing and holding the ⌘ key (Ctrl) and move your object so the bottoms line up as shown in Figure 14.6.

Figure 14.6. A copied section with Flip Vertical applied.

Now that you've got a flipped copy to use as your reflection, create a Gradient mask to blend your image into the background. The reflection should be stronger the closer it is to the object it is reflecting, and weaker the farther away it gets. In Figure 14.6, I want my blend to go only as far as the sand line, so I'll need to be careful to create my gradient in between the boat and the sand line. If you've never used Quick Mask Mode, I recommend you look over Chapter 8.

To create a Gradient mask of your flipped image:

1. To select your flipped image, ⌘+click (Ctrl+click) the layer's thumbnail.

2. Click the Quick Mask Mode button in the Toolbox. It is directly under the background color swatch.

3. Select the Gradient tool. Make sure you have the first option, Linear Gradient, highlighted and that the Reverse check box is not checked. Use the default gradient called Foreground to Background.

4. Drag the Gradient tool from the edge of your waterline — or in my case, the sand line — to just past the bottom of the object you are reflecting.

5. Go back to Standard Mode by clicking the button just below the foreground color swatch button in the Toolbox. You should see a selection area where your fade will be.

6. Click the Create Layer Mask button on the bottom of your Layers palette.

Your result should look something like Figure 14.7. If you aren't happy with your gradient, you'll need to undo it and try again. Blend away any unwanted spots with the Erase tool set at a low opacity and a Hardness setting of 0%. Because my photo has three objects at different distances from the shore, I created three different reflections. I also lowered the opacity of the farthest one away to make it look more realistic.

Sharpening blurry and noisy photos

Shaky hands can ruin a perfectly wonderful photo. Many times I think I've gotten the perfect photo, only to find that my hand shook just enough to mess it up. Although you can't do much with extreme cases, blurring caused by mild camera shaking can be improved with Photoshop's Smart Sharpen filter. This tool has built-in features to automatically improve images affected by lens blur, motion blur, or Gaussian blur.

Figure 14.7. A photo with water reflections added.

Low light and digital cameras can create some funky problems with digital noise, and artifacts created by JPEG compression are compounded when your photo has low-light problems. The Reduce Noise and Dust & Scratches filters make a perfect team for removing tiny artifacts.

Smart sharpening for the shaky hands syndrome

The sharpen filters work by emphasizing the differences between pixels and giving your photo the illusion of having its focus sharpened. Photoshop can't magically fix fuzzy pixels, but it can simulate the effect by playing with light and dark values. If you zoom in close after performing a sharpen filter, you'll see all the fuzziness is still there; but when you zoom out, your image appears crisp as a new dollar bill. The Unsharpen Mask filter used to be my favorite way of improving edge detail until the new Smart Sharpen filter came along. Smart Sharpen gives you much more control over both edge sharpening and surface sharpening. It also has some handy options for improving lens, Gaussian, or motion blur problems. The photos in Figure 14.8 show a comparison between the original photo and a photo enhanced with the Smart Sharpen filter.

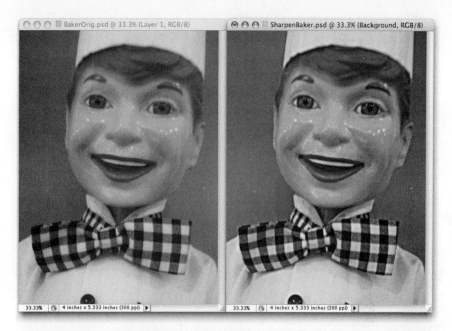

Figure 14.8. Before and after the Smart Sharpen filter.

You can enhance your photo with the Smart Sharpen Filter by following these steps:

1. Open a photo to sharpen. Create a backup of your image by dragging the layer's icon onto the Create New Layer button at the bottom of the Layers palette.

2. Choose Filter ➪ Sharpen ➪ Smart Sharpen.

3. Click the Advanced radio button to add options for controlling Shadow and Highlight sharpening separately.

4. Zoom in to an area of your image where sharpening matters most. You can use the + and – symbols or the key commands for zooming. It's important for you to zoom in close in order to get a good preview of how much sharpening you are applying to your image.

5. Adjust the Amount and Radius sliders until you get the best result you can. Radius helps Photoshop determine how large a pixel area to use to determine whether a pixel is in highlight or shadow. Amount adjusts the contrast level between dark and light.

6. Click the More Accurate check box. Photoshop takes a little more time to do a better job of removing blur. This slows down the filter, so skip it if you are in a hurry and have a slower computer.

7. Choose the Lens Blur option if your image is slightly out of focus due to camera shaking. The image in Figure 14.9 had some blur problems caused by a shaky hand in a low-light situation.

8. Adjust the Fade Amount and Tonal Width in the Shadow and Highlights tabs. Fade Amount controls the amount of sharpening in the Highlight or Shadow depending on the tab you are in. Tonal Width controls the range of tones in the shadow or highlight. A low Tonal Width adjusts only the darkest regions of the shadows or the lightest regions in the highlights.

9. Zoom out of your image to get a better sense of your changes.

10. Click OK to apply your changes to your image.

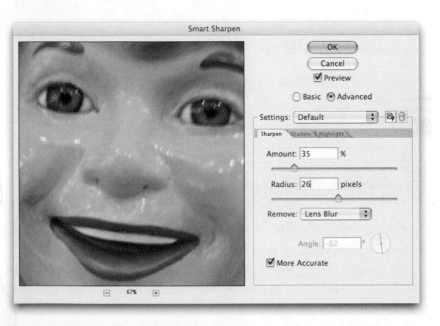

Figure 14.9. The Smart Sharpen dialog box.

If you don't like your results, try some of the other Sharpen Masks. The first two, Sharpen and Sharpen More, perform a mild overall sharpening to your image. Sharpen Edges and Unsharpen Mask focus on the high contrast areas between light and dark to bring out lines and edges.

Bright Idea!

Save your Smart Sharpen settings to use on other images by clicking the Save to Disk icon next to the Settings drop-down list.

Reducing digital noise in low-light situations

Digital photos taken in low light tend to show digital noise. Your camera can get confused and add little specks of color that weren't there. Most cameras compress images into JPEG format right in the camera. Sometimes when your camera is shrinking your images into JPEG format, you'll get areas where funky JPEG artifacts appear, especially areas that are solid, continuous colors. Photoshop has a couple mechanisms to reduce noise and JPEG artifacts. The photo in Figure 14.10 was taken in a low-light room and suffers from JPEG artifacts. In the next exercise I'll show you how to fix up your photos using the Reduce Noise and Dust & Scratches filters.

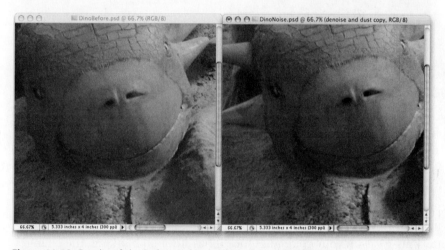

Figure 14.10. Results of the Reduce Noise and Dust & Scratches filters.

To remove digital noise and artifacts from a photo taken in a low-light situation:

1. Open a photo to edit. Make a copy of the image by dragging its thumbnail onto the Create New Layer button.

2. Choose Filter ⇨ Noise ⇨ Reduce Noise to open the dialog box that you see in Figure 14.11.

3. Click the Advanced radio button.

4. Adjust the various settings to reduce noise in your photo. Remember, less is more when it comes to doing adjustments.

5. Click OK to accept your changes.

Figure 14.11. The Reduce Noise dialog box.

Each time you make a change in the Reduce Noise dialog box, depending on how big your image is and how much memory your computer has, Photoshop takes a while to apply the changes. A small black line will flash under the preview box, letting you know that Photoshop is working away on your changes. Once it has stopped blinking, the changes can be previewed both in the dialog box and in the background of your actual file. To save time, you can turn off the Preview check box in the dialog box. You'll still get a preview inside the dialog box, but you won't have to wait until Photoshop previews your change on the entire file.

In Figure 14.11, I had a large number of colored spots from taking my photo in a low-light setting. I increased my Reduce Color Noise setting to 80% to drain some color out of the spots. Later, I'll remove them completely with the Dust & Scratches filter. I increased the Strength to 7, the

Hack

Start over without having to cancel out of the Reduce Noise dialog box and reopen it. Press and hold the Option key (Alt) while you are in the dialog box to make the Cancel button change to a Reset button. Clicking Reset restores the default settings.

Sharpen Details to 35%, and I clicked the Remove JPEG Artifacts check box. This check box helps smooth out some of the solid color areas that were affected by JPEG compression from my digital camera.

In Advanced mode, you can adjust the Reduce Noise filter per color channel for situations when you want to address the different noise problems on each color channel. If you have a set of photos with similar noise problems, you can save your settings by clicking the Save button next to the Settings drop-down list.

Use the Dust & Scratches filter to finish the job

I've gotten rid of most of the noise in my photo, but where I reduced the color noise I ended up with white and gray specks where the color once was. The Dust & Scratches filter does a great job of cleaning up what the Reduce Noise filter leaves behind. The filter works by comparing luminance values of pixels and eliminating ones that don't seem to fit. Where it finds pixels that are vastly different in value, it blends them into the surrounding pixels. The Radius and Threshold settings determine the pixel size of the area to sample and how sensitive Photoshop is to differences in light and dark values.

To smooth speckled surfaces with Dust & Scratches, follow these steps:

1. Open a photo to clean up or continue with the photo you used with the Reduce Noise Filter.

2. Choose Filter ⇨ Noise ⇨ Dust & Scratches. The dialog box you see in Figure 14.12 will appear.

3. Click and drag the Threshold slider to adjust how sensitive Photoshop is to changes in light and dark between pixels. If your Threshold level is too low, your image will look blurry. If it is too high, it won't be sensitive enough to catch subtle spots and scratches.

4. Increase your radius a pixel or two to try out different settings. Usually scratches and spots take up more than one pixel, especially if your image is 300 dpi or larger.

5. Click the + and - buttons below the preview to zoom in and out of the image.

6. Click OK to accept your changes and apply them to your actual file.

Figure 14.12. The Dust & Scratches filter dialog box.

In Figure 14.12, I found that a Threshold of 22 was just enough to take care of most of the specks while retaining a great deal of sharp detail. Any remaining spots I was able to pick off easily using the Spot Healing Brush. For more on the Spot Healing Brush, see Chapter 13.

Keeping things in perspective

Human beings have been struggling with perspective issues in two-dimensional images for nearly as long as we've held paint brushes in our hands. The first artistic attempts to depict perspective in a two-dimensional drawing can be traced back as far as Plato's time. Modifying perspective in vector-based graphics created in illustration or 3-D applications such as Adobe Illustrator or Maya is easy enough. They use mathematics to rearrange lines and fill in planes and surfaces. Working in a pixilated world adds another level of complication to the mix. Our eyes see piano keys, but Photoshop just sees a bunch of black-and-white pixels. By combining some of the same methods used in rearranging perspective lines in vector applications, Photoshop has come up with some tools that allow you to push pixels around in modified perspectives.

Widen piano keys with the Vanishing Point tool

The photo of the organ in Figure 14.13 is in perspective. The part of the organ closest to us appears larger than the part of the organ that's farthest away. I want to extend the organ so that I have more keys to play. I'd normally use the regular Rubber Stamp tool, but because the organ is going back in space, that won't work. The Vanishing Point tool has its own Rubber Stamp tool so that I can paint in perspective using a grid that I define.

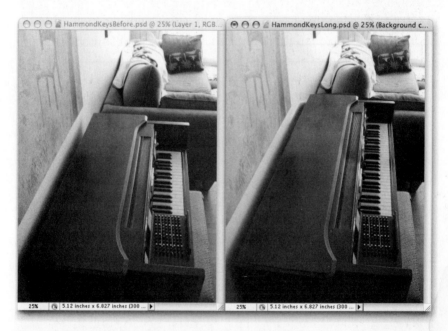

Figure 14.13. A before and after using the Vanishing Point tool.

The Vanishing Point tool works best on things with easily repeatable patterns like stairs, buildings, shelves, or floors. When you select Vanishing Point from the Filters menu, a mini application launches with its own set of tools. There is an information box inside the tool that gives you clues on how to use each of the tools. The Photoshop Help System has a great section on the Vanishing Point tool. If you know you'll be using this tool a great deal, I recommend reading it. Choose Help ⇨ Photoshop Help and type **Vanishing Point** in the search box to find a list of topics. You can find some additional exercises in the Help Center if you want more practice using the tool.

To paint in perspective with the Vanishing Point tool:

1. Open a photo that has some perspective and a repeatable surface, like stairs or flooring.

2. In the Layers palette, create a copy of the image by dragging its layer onto the Create New Layer button on the bottom of the palette.

3. Click your newly copied layer in the Layers palette to highlight it.

4. Choose Filter ⇨ Vanishing Point to launch the Vanishing Point tool in a new window.

5. Click the Create Plane tool. It should be automatically highlighted when you first launch the Liquify tool. The Create Plane tool is the second tool in the list.

6. Click around your image to create the four corners of your plane. This creates a grid that Photoshop will use as a guide. In Figure 14.14, I created a plane across the keyboard and the back of the organ.

7. After defining your grid, extend your grid by dragging the anchor points to include the entire area you want to edit. Extending your grid is an important step and gives Photoshop guidelines for how to edit your image in perspective.

8. Select the Stamp tool and adjust the Brush diameter. You can increase and decrease it by clicking the [and] keys.

9. Option+click (Alt+click) a point in your photo to select a cloning point. For Figure 14.14 I picked a spot in the keys close to the bottom of the photo. The Stamp tool shows you a preview of what you are about to paint. It's best if you choose a cloning point that is easily recognizable, like the ends of piano keys.

10. Position your mouse over the area you want to start painting and line up the preview with your photo. Click and drag your mouse to begin painting in perspective. As you move back in space, your image automatically shrinks as if moving farther away.

11. Zoom in and out to get better control of your paint brush. All the paint tools in the Vanishing Point tool work in perspective. You can use the Marquee tool to select the area you are working on and isolate it from the background of your photo.

12. When you are done, click OK to accept your changes.

Figure 14.14. The Vanishing Point tool window with grid.

If you have some areas that need cleaning up or blending, especially where the light reflections don't line up, use the Dodge and Burn tools. Because you are working on a copy, you can delete areas of your modified photo using the Lasso tool and let the original show through. In Figure 14.15 I wasn't very careful when cloning around the keys and had to sharpen up the edge of my keyboard by deleting spots. The reflections on the wood surface and keys needed some dodging and burning using an Exposure setting of about 10 and a brush Hardness of 0.

Figure 14.15. The Vanishing Point tool window after using the Stamp tool.

Copy and paste in perspective

The Marquee tool in the Vanishing Point tool creates a selection box that matches the perspective grid that you create. Instead of drawing a regular one-point perspective rectangle, the Marquee tool automatically conforms to the shape of the grid. This makes it easy to copy and paste sections of your photos. You can move or copy windows and doors, or remove them. Try this on photos of your home to experiment with remodeling options before tearing down any walls. In Figure 14.16, I decided there weren't enough windows in the building on the left. All I needed to do was launch the Vanishing Point tool, create a grid, and copy and paste the first window using the Marquee tool. Give it a try. Find a photo of a wall or building in perspective and modify the doors and windows.

Figure 14.16. Before and after using the Vanishing Point Marquee tool to copy and paste.

To add windows and doors with the Vanishing Point Marquee tool, follow these steps:

1. Open a photo. Make a copy of the image layer by dragging and dropping its thumbnail onto the Create New Layer button in the Layers palette.

2. Launch the Vanishing Point tool by choosing Filter ⇨ Vanishing Point.

3. Create a four-point grid around the area you are going to copy using the Clean Plane tool. After you've gotten the perspectives right, expand the grid. Be careful to give yourself enough extra space around the area you are copying; the Marquee tool doesn't work outside the grid.

4. Select the Marquee tool and draw a selection box around the object to copy. I've selected the window in Figure 14.17. The Marquee tool automatically conforms to the grid.

Figure 14.17. A window being selected by the Marquee tool in the Vanishing Point tool.

5. Press and hold the Option key (Alt) and then click and drag your selection to the new spot. Press and hold the Shift key to drag it in a straight line. Release your mouse button when you've placed it correctly.

6. Click OK to accept your changes and exit the Vanishing Point tool window.

If you have any areas where the lighting doesn't quite match, you can soften the abrupt lines with the Dodge and Burn tools as discussed in the last exercise.

Changing a photo's perspective

The photo in Figure 14.18 was taken at an angle. The left side of the building appears squashed due to the perspective at which it was captured. I want a straight-on shot. By using the Perspective feature with the Warp option enabled, I can stretch the left side of the photo while keeping the right side the same and give the illusion I'm adjusting the angle from which I took the photo.

Figure 14.18. A before and after using the Perspective feature.

To adjust a photo's perspective from angled to straight on:

1. Open a photo with a perspective problem you'd like to adjust. Create a copy of the image layer by dragging and dropping it onto the Create New Layer button in the Layers palette.

2. Choose Edit ⇨ Transform ⇨ Perspective. When you first switch to the Perspective tool, it defaults to the Free Transform Mode. To stretch and warp your images, you'll need to click the Warp button on the top right of the Options bar to turn on the Warp option.

3. Click and drag the corners, gridlines, and control points to warp your image. The photo in Figure 14.19 shows an example of the Perspective tool using the Warp feature.

4. Press Enter to accept your changes and apply them to the image.

You may need to crop your image because the canvas has been stretched and pinched in places. You can use the same tool to create the opposite effect by ballooning out your image for a porthole- or fish-eye-lens effect.

Figure 14.19. A photo being warped using the Perspective tool.

Just the facts

- Rotate images in tiny increments with Free Transform.
- Fix barrel and pincushion distortion by stretching and pinching images with the Distort tool.
- Add water reflections by flipping selections of images vertically and applying a gradient layer mask.
- Add windows and doors with the Marquee tool inside the Vanishing Point tool.
- Remove noise and specks caused by digital cameras in low light.

PART IV

Exploring Your Inner Artist

GET THE SCOOP ON...
Creating instant watercolors ▪ Giving your image the
look of a screen print ▪ Designing seamless patterns for
Web site backgrounds ▪ Applying several filters at once

Getting Creative with Filters

F ilters are effects that you can apply to your images to create special effects. You've been introduced to some of the more utilitarian filters such as the sharpen filters or the Extract tool. Photoshop has tons and tons of filters for adding a creative edge to your images. The filters organized under Artistic, Brush Stroke, and Sketch are aimed at transforming your images into works of art by adding paint strokes, texture, and sketch-like qualities. With the creative filters you can add artistic textures like watercolor effects, give images the look of a charcoal sketch, or create an instant painting from a photo.

You need not stop with Photoshop's preinstalled set of filters. There are many free resources for Photoshop filters available from support Web sites. Also known as plug-ins, these third-party filters offer lots of cool image effects for expanding Photoshop's capabilities. The resources section in the back of the book lists some popular Photoshop Web sites that offer free filters.

This chapter shows you how to get the most out of the Filter Gallery by combining filters or trying out and comparing several filters at once. You'll create some artistic effects using Photoshop's Artistic, Brush Stroke, and Sketch filters. You'll see how to create digital stained glass and mosaics using photos and the texture filters, and you'll learn how to install additional third-party filters to expand your collection.

Chapter 15

Getting in touch with your inner artist

The first set of filters I'll discuss are the Artistic filters. They simulate fine-art mediums by adding texture similar to brush strokes, printmaking techniques, pastels, and watercolors. Most of the creative filters are part of the Filter Gallery, a mini application that runs inside Photoshop, much like the Extract and Liquify tools. Within the Filter Gallery, you can access all the creative filters, and later on in the chapter, you'll see how to combine filters inside the Filter Gallery.

The Filter Gallery is home to the following filter types:

- **Artistic:** Colored Pencil, Cutout, Dry Brush, Film Grain, Fresco, Neon Glow, Paint Daubs, Palette Knife, Plastic Wrap, Poster Edges, Rough Pastels, Smudge Stick, Sponge, Underpainting, Watercolor

- **Brush Strokes:** Accented Edges, Angled Strokes, Crosshatch, Dark Strokes, Ink Outlines, Spatter, Sprayed Strokes, Sumi-e

- **Distort:** Diffuse Glow, Glass, Ocean Ripple

- **Sketch:** Bas Relief, Chalk & Charcoal, Charcoal, Chrome, Conté Crayon, Graphic Pen, Halftone Patter, Note Paper, Photocopy, Plaster, Reticulation, Stamp, Torn Edges, Water Paper

- **Stylize:** Glowing Edges

- **Texture:** Craquelure, Grain, Mosaic Tiles, Patchwork, Stained Glass, Texturize

That's a whole lot of filters! I won't be able to show you each and every one, but I'll discuss some of my favorites.

Create an instant watercolor

One of the most popular and creative Artistic filters is the Watercolor filter (see Figure 15.1). You can control Brush Detail for looser or tighter strokes, shadow intensity to boost contrast, and texture to modify the roughness or smoothness of the strokes. This filter works best on nature landscapes or portraits but can be used on any type of image.

To create a watercolor effect from a photo:

1. Open a digital photo. This filter alters your original image, so you might want to make a copy of the image layer first.

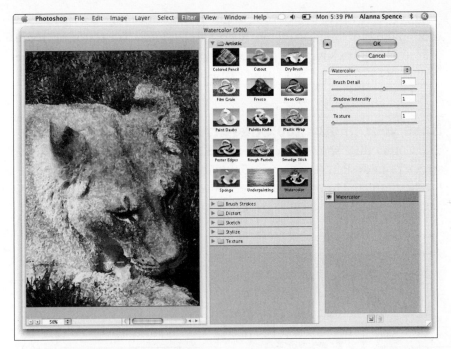

Figure 15.1. The Watercolor filter window.

2. Choose Filter ⇨ Artistic ⇨ Watercolor to launch the Filter Gallery with the Watercolor filter.

3. Adjust the Brush Detail settings. The higher the setting, the smoother and smaller the brush strokes will be. For a more painterly effect, decrease the Brush Detail amount to 1.

4. To punch up the contrast in your image, increase the Shadow Intensity setting.

5. Adjust the Texture setting. The Texture setting accentuates the edges between strokes. It makes your watercolor look more opaque, like it was painted in gauche.

6. When you are done, click OK to accept and apply your changes.

Watch Out!

Many of the Artistic filters take a little time to render the preview whenever you make an adjustment. There is a progress bar underneath the image preview to let you know how long you have to wait.

If you've made a copy of your original, you can change the opacity on your watercolor layer to blend for a subtler look. Try restoring some of your image back to its original state while leaving other areas with the Watercolor effect. Use the History Brush to blend out parts of the filter effect.

Make your photos look like screen prints

The Cutout filter simplifies colors and creates block shapes that look like screen print designs (see Figure 15.2). Simplify colors into 4 or 5 levels for the best effect. This works most effectively on images with solid shapes and high contrast.

Figure 15.2. The Cutout dialog box with a large preview.

To create a screen print look from a photo:

1. Open a photo with simple colors and shapes. Landscapes work well. Create a copy of your image layer by dragging and dropping it on the Create New Layer button in the Layers palette.

2. Choose Filter ➪ Artistic ➪ Cutout to launch the Filter Gallery and apply the Cutout filter to a preview of your image.

The drawing of the cake slice was created by tracing a photo with the Freeform Pen tool in Chapter 5.

A photo manipulated with the Dodge, Blur, and Sharpen tools to enhance the foreground. Chapter 6 includes these and other paint tools.

Masked using the Magnetic Lasso tool and a layer mask.
Chapter 7 focuses on selecting and masking techniques.

The color of the shirt was changed using the Replace Color tool.
Chapter 7 looks at the many approaches for selectively modifying color.

The face of the baby was blended into the cloud using a Gradient mask.
Chapter 8 explores methods for masking and blending images.

Selective color correction was performed on the foreground of the photo while leaving the intense colors of the sky as they were. Chapter 10 covers techniques for selectively undoing changes using the History Brush tool.

The warrior was masked using alpha channels.
Chapter 8 explores methods for masking and blending images.

A black-and-white photo was colorized using the selection tools and a Hue/Saturation adjustment.
Chapter 11 covers advanced color-correcting techniques.

The dark sand in this photo of a beach sunset was corrected with an Exposure adjustment.

Chapter 11 covers techniques for correcting tricky lighting and exposure problems.

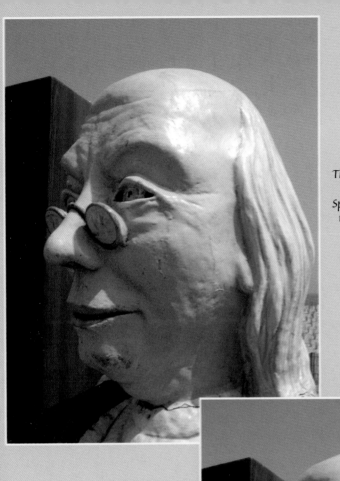

This statue was restored to its original glory using the Spot Healing Brush and Patch tool covered in Chapter 13.

The woman's eyes were corrected using the Red-Eye tool. The dog's eyes were corrected using the Brush tool with layer styles. Both techniques are covered in Chapter 13.

An extra window was added using copy and paste in the Vanishing Point tool, covered in Chapter 14.

The angle of the building was corrected using the Perspective tool, covered in Chapter 14.

The Watercolor filter was applied to the photo of a lion for an artistic touch.
Artist filters are covered in Chapter 15.

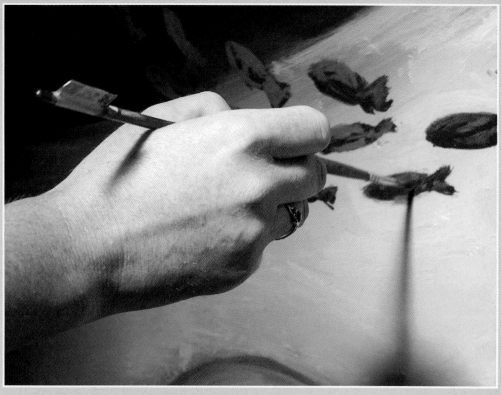

The surface of the hand was smoothed using the Surface Blur tool.
The many filters for distorting, blurring, and sharpening are covered in Chapter 16.

The Pegasus was created by combining the wings of a seagull and the body of a horse in Chapter 17. Color was corrected using the Color Replace tool. The images were blended together using the Clone Stamp tool.

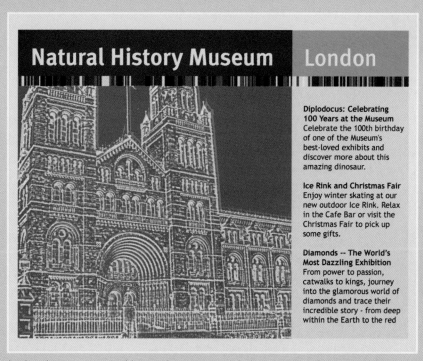

Natural History Museum London

Diplodocus: Celebrating 100 Years at the Museum
Celebrate the 100th birthday of one of the Museum's best-loved exhibits and discover more about this amazing dinosaur.

Ice Rink and Christmas Fair
Enjoy winter skating at our new outdoor Ice Rink. Relax in the Cafe Bar or visit the Christmas Fair to pick up some gifts.

Diamonds -- The World's Most Dazzling Exhibition
From power to passion, catwalks to kings, journey into the glamorous world of diamonds and trace their incredible story - from deep within the Earth to the red

This brochure was created by combining text and photographic elements in Chapter 18.
The photo was transformed into an illustration using the Photocopy filter.

Multiple filters and effects were applied to the photo of the typewriter to create a stylistic book cover in Chapter 18.

The Absurd Tales of a
Procrastinating Writer

a novel by
Alanna Spence

Inside Scoop

Enlarge your preview in the Filter Gallery window by clicking the black arrow on the top right of the filter list.

3. Adjust the Levels, Edge Simplicity, and Edge Fidelity settings. In Figure 15.2, I used a Levels setting of 4, Edge Simplicity setting of 0, and Edge Fidelity setting of 2.

4. Click OK to accept and apply your settings.

The settings are going to vary from image to image. I like the effect of a simple four-color design. This effect is similar to a Posterize adjustment but gives you more control over color. It gives you a flatter effect, giving it the look of a four-color screen print.

Creating tritone drawings with the Sketch filters

All of the Sketch filters, with the exception of the Chrome and Water Paper filters, use the foreground and background colors as their colors. You don't have to create a black-and-white charcoal drawing. You can instead go wild with color and create a charcoal drawing using bright purple and yellow, or keep it simple by using warm browns or cool blues. In Figure 15.3 I used a cream color as the background color and a dark brown for the foreground color. The Conté Crayon filter adds the color gray as the paper representation and white for highlights. The Conté Crayon filter also lets you load additional textures from the Presets/Textures folder in your Photoshop CS2 application folder.

Try the Sketch filters on a photo using your own foreground and background colors:

1. Open an image to use and drag its layer onto the Create New Layer button in the Layers palette to make a copy of it.

2. Click the foreground color swatch in the Toolbox and choose a color.

3. Click the background color swatch in the Toolbox and choose a color.

4. Choose Filter ⇨ Filter Gallery to launch it in a new window.

5. Click the arrow next to the Sketch folder to expand it. Choose one of the Sketch filters. In Figure 15.4, I'm using the Conté Crayon filter with Burlap texture.

Figure 15.3. A close up of Conté Crayon filter effect.

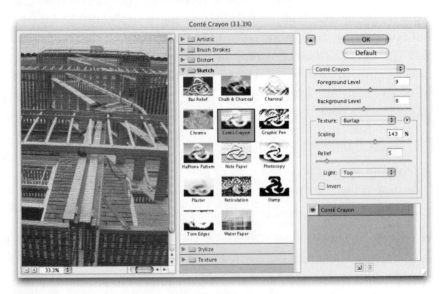

Figure 15.4. The Conté Crayon filter in the Filter Gallery.

Inside Scoop

To get a black-and-white sketch, change your foreground and background colors to white and black.

6. Adjust your settings until you get an effect you like.

7. Click OK to accept the changes and apply them.

Any of the filter icons in the Filter Gallery that are displayed in black and white take advantage of your foreground and background colors.

Turn your photo into a charcoal sketch

The Charcoal filter is a great filter for creating stunning black-and-white images. It works best for architectural or cityscape photos but will work on just about any photo with high contrast. You don't have to stick with black and white; you can apply any two colors you like by changing the foreground and background color swatches in the Toolbox. For a classic charcoal-drawing look, change the foreground color to black and the background color to white before opening the Filter Gallery window to apply the filter.

To create a charcoal drawing from a photo, follow these steps:

1. Open a photo and create a copy of the image layer by dragging and dropping it on the Create New Layer button on the bottom of the Layers palette.

2. Choose Filter ⇨ Sketch ⇨ Charcoal to launch the Charcoal filter in the Filter Gallery.

3. Adjust the settings to your liking. In Figure 15.5 I used a Charcoal Thickness of 3, a Detail of 5, and a Light/Dark Balance of 80.

4. Click OK to accept and apply your settings.

The Chalk & Charcoal filter is similar to the Charcoal filter but adds an additional chalk color so that you can assign two colors instead of one. The Charcoal is used for the darks and the Chalk is used for lights. The background color swatch in the Toolbox controls the chalk color, and the foreground color swatch controls the charcoal.

Figure 15.5. The Charcoal filter applied.

Get black-and-white images with Photocopy

One of my favorite effects is the Photocopy filter under the Sketch filters (see Figure 15.6). It works like a normal black-and-white photocopy machine by converting colors to black or white. You can adjust the Darkness settings just as you would on a photocopy machine. I like this effect on just about any image, but I think it works especially well on portraits.

To create a black-and-white image using the Photocopy filter, follow these steps:

1. Open a photo and create a copy of the image layer by dragging and dropping its thumbnail onto the Create New Layer button in the Layers palette.

2. Choose Filter ⇨ Sketch ⇨ Photocopy to launch the Filter Gallery with the Photocopy filter selected.

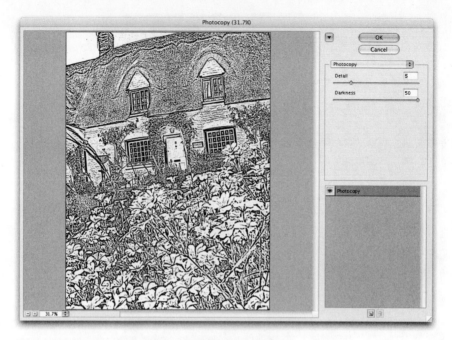

Figure 15.6. The Photocopy filter in the Filter Gallery window.

3. Adjust the Detail and Darkness settings to achieve a look you like.

4. Click OK to accept your settings and apply them to your photo.

This filter works great when you use the Fade feature. After you've applied the filter, choose Edit ⇨ Fade or press ⌘+Shift+F (Ctrl+Shift+F) to open the Fade dialog box. Lower the Fade amount to 20% or 30% and change the Blending mode to Difference. Figure 15.7 shows a photo with a Photocopy filter applied and then faded.

Bright Idea!

You can get some nice effects by layering the Photocopy filter with your original image. By applying this filter to a copy of your image layer and then selecting and deleting the white parts with your Magic Wand tool, you can get the effect of a comic book by overlaying black lines. Bump up the Darkness and Detail settings to get blacker blacks.

Figure 15.7. The Photocopy filter applied and then faded using the Difference Blending Mode.

Create nice textures with Water Paper

I love the effect you get when using the Water Paper filter on a gradient. You can get some beautiful effects to use as backgrounds for your designs. The Water Paper filter creates tiny stars across your image (see Figure 15.8). The texture looks like something you'd find in the design on an old jazz album from the '40s.

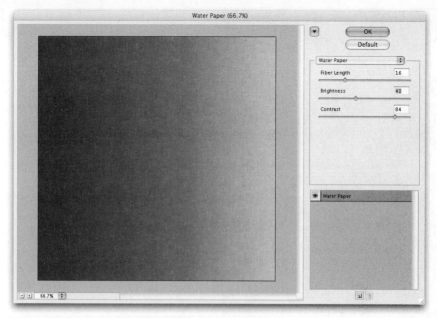

Figure 15.8. The Water Paper filter applied to a gradient.

Create abstract art from a photo

The Glass and Ocean Ripple filters give your photo the effect of being behind glass or under water in a strong current. By increasing the Distortion in the Glass filter or Ripple Size in the Ocean Ripple, you can get some nice abstract-looking art. Zooming in and cropping your image can give it an especially abstract quality. The image in Figure 15.9 was at one time a bad photo of me. I ran the Ocean Ripple filter on it and cropped off the left side of my face. Use your abstracted images as contemporary artwork or as textures for designs and collages. Because the colors are simplified, these compress nicely into JPEG format for a small enough file size to use as a Web site background.

Figure 15.9. The result of the Ocean Ripple filter.

Before continuing with this exercise, here are a couple tips for getting the best results:

▪ Because you'll be cropping to a smaller area of your photo after you run the filter, try to choose a photo that has been taken at your digital camera's highest-quality setting. If you have the ability to shoot at 300 dpi, I recommend using that setting.

▪ Images with high contrast and interesting large shapes work best.

▪ Make a copy of your file because you'll be cropping and destroying the original image.

▪ You might want to try simplifying your colors. Perform a Hue/Saturation adjustment on your image.

To run the Ocean Ripple filter on a cropped photo to create abstract artwork:

1. Open a photo, preferably at your digital camera's highest setting.

2. Choose Filter ⇨ Distort ⇨ Ocean Ripple to launch the Filter Gallery with the Ocean Ripple filter active.

3. Adjust the Ripple Size and Ripple Magnitude values to their maximum levels.

4. Click OK to accept your settings and apply them to your photo.

5. Look in your photo for an area that would make a nice abstract image.

6. Select the Crop tool and drag a crop area around a portion of your image. Press Enter to accept your crop, or click the Cancel button on the top right of the Options bar to cancel out of your crop and start over.

Applying multiple filters

The Filter Gallery allows you to try out and temporarily store the effects of different filters. You can combine filters for new effects, or pick and choose from a list that you create. On the bottom right of the Filter Gallery is a list where you can add several Filter applications. There is a visibility box for showing and hiding filter effects, allowing you to combine filters or view them separately (see Figure 15.10).

Figure 15.10. The Filter Gallery window with a list of four filter effects.

Watch Out!

Don't get too attached to all your filter previews in the Filter Gallery. After you click OK, you'll lose the list. If you want a more permanent list of filter examples, try applying different filters to layer copies of your image. Blend them by adjusting opacity levels.

To combine several filters together, open a photo and create a duplicate of the image layer by dragging and dropping it onto the Create New Layer button on the bottom of the Layers palette. Then choose Filter ⇨ Filter Gallery to launch the Filter Gallery.

Creating seamless tiles and patterns

The Pattern Maker creates tiled, seamless patterns for backgrounds you can use in your designs or Web sites. Using part of a photo or any rasterized image, you can create interesting patterns and textures. The tool doesn't give you much control over the outcome, but it's a fun tool for making nice random textures. In Figure 15.11, I used a selection from the clouds as my pattern design.

Figure 15.11. An image before and after applying the Pattern Maker filter.

To create a pattern with the Pattern Maker:

1. Open a photo or image to use as the base for your pattern and make a copy of the image layer as a backup.

2. Choose Filter ⇨ Pattern Maker to launch the Pattern Maker in a separate window (see Figure 15.12).

3. Using the Rectangular Marquee tool in the Pattern Maker, select an area to use as your pattern.

4. If you'd like your image to have a slight offset from row to row, select one of the Offset options.

5. Specify what size tiles you'd like to generate from the width and height drop-down lists, or click the Use Image Size button to create a pattern the same size as your image.

6. Click Generate to create a pattern.

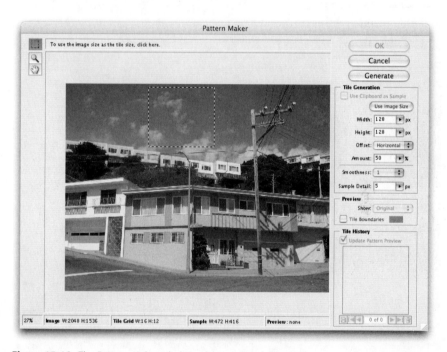

Figure 15.12. The Pattern Maker window with a source image before generating a pattern.

Inside Scoop

Increase the Smoothness to 3 for the best results.

If you don't like the results, you can keep generating patterns using different settings until you get one you like. On the bottom of the window is a small preview window that stores all of the patterns you've generated. If you decide to go with one of your earlier-generated patterns, you can click the previous button to scroll through all of the patterns you've generated.

If you are generating a tile to use on a Web site, you'll want to make the size of your document the same size you want your tile (see Figure 15.13). You'll also want to click the Use Image Size button to create one tile. You won't be able to see what your tile will look like when repeated over an entire Web page.

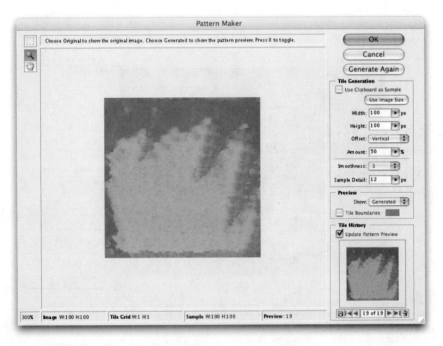

Figure 15.13. The Pattern Maker with Use Image Size button applied.

Bright Idea!

Create a pattern from scratch by running various filters on a solid color layer. The Reticulation, Note Paper, Smudge Stick, Craquelure, and Mosaic Tiles filters, among others, work well on solid colors.

Create a background pattern for your Web site

By using the Offset filter, you can create a seamless tile for use as a background pattern for your Web site. You have much more control over the image when you use the Offset filter as opposed to creating a pattern with the Pattern Maker.

The following exercise creates a translucent bubble pattern like you see in Figure 15.14. Feel free to play around with different shapes, transparencies, and colors to create your own unique pattern.

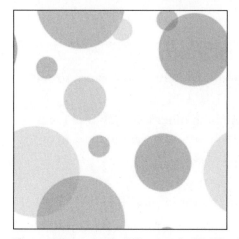

Figure 15.14. A seamless tile created with Offset filter.

To create a seamless tile with the Offset filter and the Brush tool:

1. Create a new file. If you are going to be using this as a background for your Web site, create a file with a resolution of 72 dpi. A square document of either 64 or 128 pixels will work well.

2. Select the Brush tool and change the opacity to 60%. Increase the brush size to create a nice-sized dot like you see in Figure 15.14. Change the hardness to 100%.

3. Create a new layer for your dots by clicking the Create New Layer button on the bottom of the Layers palette.

4. Click anywhere in your document to create a dot.

5. Change the size and color of your dot and create a new dot.

6. Choose Filter ⇨ Other ⇨ Offset to open the dialog box for the Offset filter (see Figure 15.15).

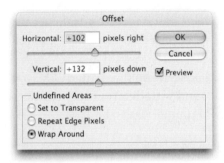

Figure 15.15. The Offset filter dialog box.

7. Be sure to select the Wrap Around radio button to create a seamless pattern.

8. Change the Offset values to something other than 0. Offset is going to shift your dots around the screen, so you'll want to have an offset value for both Horizontal and Vertical.

9. Click OK to offset the dots you've created.

10. Add another dot or two of varying size and color.

11. Now that you've used the Offset filter once, you can just repeat the last filter by choosing Filter ⇨ Offset or pressing ⌘+F (Ctrl+F).

12. Continue adding dots and applying the Offset filter until you have a tile you are satisfied with.

You can create tiles with the Offset filter using any rasterized image. Although they start out as vector objects, you can always create shapes with some of the custom shapes tools and then rasterize them. To rasterize a vector object, choose Layer ⇨ Rasterize ⇨ Shape.

Bright Idea!

You don't have to limit yourself to square tiles. You could create long vertical or horizontal strips in the same way.

Creating mosaic patterns with Textures

The Mosaic, Patchwork, and Stained Glass filters turn your image into a patterned, block-like image. Patchwork gives you a cross-stitch look by converting your image into little squares. Mosaic gives your image the appearance of tiles, and Stained Glass separates your colors into shapes that look like little panes of glass.

Create a stained glass window

The Stained Glass filter creates solid colored polygons from your photo to achieve a stained glass look (see Figure 15.16). You can control the light intensity, the size of the glass pieces, and the width of the leading or spacing between your virtual glass pieces. I've gotten the best results by adjusting the Cell Size and Border Thickness below a value of 4.

Figure 15.16. The Stained Glass filter window.

Bright Idea!

Increase your preview area by hiding the filters list in the middle panel. Click the arrow at the top of the window to toggle the middle panel on and off.

The Stained Glass filter sometimes gives photos the look of a pointillist painting by Seurat. I like using this filter on water scenes or landscapes. Try this filter out on a few different types of photos to get a feel for what appeals to you.

To make your photo look like a stained glass window, follow these steps:

1. Open a photo and create a copy of your image layer as a backup.

2. Choose Filter ⇨ Texture ⇨ Stained Glass to open the Filter Gallery window with the Stained Glass filter active.

3. Decrease the Cell Size for more clarity or increase it for a more abstract look.

4. Adjust the Border Thickness. Be careful: if you increase the Border Thickness value too much, your image will turn completely white.

5. Click OK to accept and apply your changes.

Some images work better than others. Try out a few different photos to see the various styles you can achieve with this fun filter.

Convert your image to square tiles with Patchwork

The Patchwork filter creates a grid of squares in solid colors (see Figure 15.17). It gives your photo the look of a cross-stitch pattern or woven design. It's a fun tool for creating instant pixel art from photographs. You can adjust the amount of relief for each square and get the effect of square mosaic tiles. By lowering the relief you can get a softer look. This filter works well on architecture and creates fun portraits.

To apply a square pattern to your photo with the Patchwork filter:

1. Open a photo and create a copy of your image layer as a backup.

2. Choose Filter ⇨ Texture ⇨ Patchwork to open the Patchwork filter in a new window.

Figure 15.17. The Patchwork filter window with the maximum square size and light relief settings.

3. To get the soft effect you see in Figure 15.17, increase the Square Size to its maximum amount and change the Relief value to 5.

4. Click OK to accept and apply your changes.

The Patchwork filter comes in handy if you need to create a grid pattern. By just running the filter you won't get a perfectly clean grid, but the anti-aliasing around the lines creates an appealing pattern.

To create a simple grid pattern with the Patchwork filter:

1. Create a new file with a white background.

2. Choose Filter ⇨ Patchwork.

3. Lower the Relief level to 0 and increase the Square Size to 10.

Watch Out!

When you accept your settings and exit the Patchwork filter window, your image will not look correct if you are zoomed out because the square sizes are too small. Zoom in to 100% to get an accurate display of the effect.

4. Click OK to apply your settings.

5. Double-click the Background layer containing your grid to rename and unlock it.

6. Select the Magic Wand tool from the Toolbox and change the Tolerance to 0 in the Options bar.

7. Click in one of the white squares of your grid pattern.

8. Choose Select ⇨ Similar to add the other white squares to your selection and then click Delete.

9. To add a background color behind it, choose Layer ⇨ New Fill Layer ⇨ Solid Color.

10. Select a color for your background.

11. Drag your new layer underneath the grid pattern layer so that your grid is visible (see Figure 15.18).

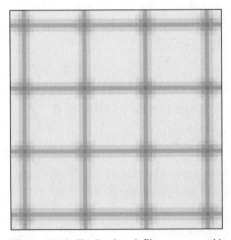

Figure 15.18. The Patchwork filter runs on a blank document.

12. If you'd like to change the color of your grid, click your grid layer in the Layers palette to highlight it and choose Image ⇨ Adjustment ⇨ Hue/Saturation.

13. Lower the Lightness value and then adjust the Hue and Saturation sliders to get the color you want.

14. Click OK to save and apply your settings.

Watch Out!
If you've created your grid on a Background layer and try to delete the white to create a transparent image, you'll replace the white with the background color. Double-click the Background layer to unlock and rename it before trying to delete the white.

You can get some interesting patterns that look like plaid and that work well when overlaid on top of other images. If you want crisp black lines with no fuzzy anti-aliasing, run a Threshold adjustment on the grid layer and move the slider over to the right until all you see are straight, crisp lines. Makes me want to do math!

Fading and blending filters for special effects
Once you run a filter on your image, you'll be able to not only fade it to any percentage from 0% to 100%, but also change the blending mode to get some nice lighting and texture effects. This option is only available immediately after you run the filter. After you perform any other task, the menu item won't be available anymore. Many of the effects can be on the extreme side; the Fade option lets you tone things down a bit and gets some more subtle effects. Figure 15.19 shows the Fade dialog box with Difference blending mode selected.

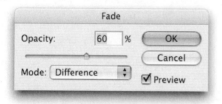

Figure 15.19. The Fade filter dialog box.

Inside Scoop
Use your keyboard's up and down arrow keys to increase and decrease the value slider in the Fade filter dialog box.

The Fade option works on all of the filters. The possibilities for fading and blending are endless, so play around with the option to find your own interesting effects. You can find more tips on Photoshop Web sites by searching for "Photoshop Fade filter" in your favorite search engine.

Just the facts

- Transform your photos into instant paintings or drawings by using the Artist filters in the Filter Gallery.
- Apply and preview multiple filters on the same image in the Filter Gallery by adding new effect layers.
- Create a seamless, repeatable pattern to use as a background image on your Web site by using the Offset command.
- Create patterned or mosaic-style images using the Texture filters.
- Use the Fade command to blend and fade your filter applications and get more subtle effects.

Adding Lighting, Blur, and Distortion Special Effects

Chapter 16

This chapter covers many of the preinstalled filters for adding lighting effects, adding blur, and distorting. The filters for blurring and adding lighting effects come in handy to enhance just about any photo. The others, such as the Stylize and Texture filters, add fun special effects to designs.

This chapter introduces you to most of the filters and gives you some pointers for getting the most out of some of the more complex ones. You'll look at some ways of adding light sources to photos with the Lens Flare and Lighting Effects filters. You'll see how to smooth surfaces while retaining details with the Blur filters. You'll create some fun graphic elements using some of the Distort, Texture, and Stylize filters. The filters in this chapter and Chapter 15 just skim the surface of all the filter effects available to you. Check the Appendix section of the book for a list of my favorite third-party filters.

Adding light with the Render filters

The Lens Flare and Lighting Effects filters are valuable tools for adding light sources to dull or dark images. These filters work well to bring out details in dark areas of a photo or add luminosity and depth to flat surfaces.

Add highlights with the Lens Flare filter

The Lens Flare filter lets you play with lighting effects and achieve a sunburst effect even on a cloudy day. The photo in Figure 16.1 shows an example of a lighting effect created with the Lens Flare filter. The tool offers four types of lens flares that enable you to adjust brightness and placement.

Figure 16.1. A photo with a lighting effect added with the Lens Flare filter.

To add lens flare to a photo, follow these steps:

1. Open a photo and create a copy of your layer by dragging and dropping it onto the Create New Layer button in the Layers palette.

2. Choose Filter ⇨ Render ⇨ Lens Flare to open the dialog box.

3. Try out the different lens types by selecting a radio button and moving the lens flare's spot around your image. You can choose from four different lens types. The Movie Prime Lens Type is shown in Figure 16.2.

Hack

Use the Lens Flare filter to add soft lighting to an image. Create a new layer and fill it with a solid color. Apply a Lens Flare with a Brightness level of 150% to 200%. On the top left of the Layers palette, change the layer's blending mode to Overlay.

4. Adjust the Brightness of your Lens Flare with the slider bar. You can have a brightness level of up to 300%, which will completely white out your image, or as low as 10% for a very subtle effect.

5. Click OK to accept and apply your settings.

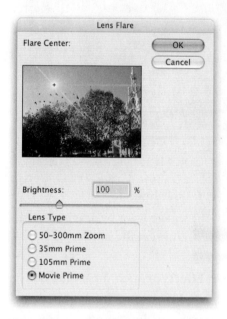

Figure 16.2. The Lens Flare dialog box with a preview of the Movie Prime Lens Type.

Try adding multiple lens flares of different types and intensities by selecting the Lens Flare filter again and placing a new Lens Flare in a different spot.

Adding a light source with Lighting Effects

With the Lighting Effects filter, you can add light sources on images that have underexposure problems in the foreground. The photo I took of

Oscar in Figure 16.3 was taken indoors, in front of a window on a bright, sunny day, which caused Oscar to be in shadow while the figures outside are bright. By adding a spotlight, I was able to take him out of the shadow and into the light.

Figure 16.3. A photo before and after the Lighting Effects filter.

To add a light source to your image, follow these steps:

1. Open a photo and make a copy of the image layer by dragging and dropping it on the Create New Layer button at the bottom of the Layers palette.

2. Choose Filter ⇨ Render ⇨ Lighting Effects to open the dialog box.

3. Using the default Light Type of Spotlight, increase the size of your light source by clicking and dragging the anchor points.

4. Increase the Exposure setting by moving the Exposure slider to the right. The higher the Exposure setting, the brighter your spotlight will be. I increased my Exposure setting quite a bit, as shown in Figure 16.4.

5. To add color to your lights, click the Light color swatch next to the Intensity slider in the Light Type section of the Lighting Effects dialog box or the Ambient color swatch to the right of the Material slider in the Properties section of the Lighting Effects dialog box.

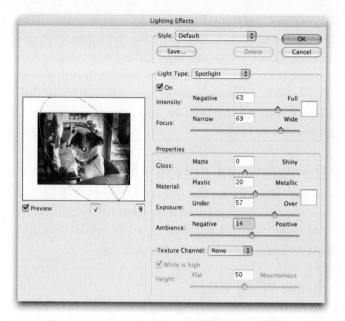

Figure 16.4. The Lighting Effects filter dialog box with the Spotlight option chosen as the Light Type.

6. Choose the other Light Type options by selecting them and increasing their size. Try out each one until you find the light types that work best for your image.

7. If you'd like to save your settings for future use, click the Save button at the top of the filter window and give your settings a name. Photoshop saves your settings in alphabetical order with the other Lighting Effects styles.

8. Click OK to accept and apply your settings.

You can add multiple light sources by clicking and dragging the light bulb icon in the Lighting Effects dialog box. You can even mix and match light types by clicking them and selecting a different option from the Light Type drop-down list.

Watch Out!

The anchor points can be a bit stubborn. Don't give up; keep clicking until you get them to move for you. Try another if one just won't cooperate.

The Lighting Effects filter has some fun presets for adding theatrical and creative lighting to your images. Many of the multiple spotlight options in the Styles drop-down list at the top of the filter's dialog box would make a nice choice for creating a collage of a stage. You might try creating a solid colored layer, applying one of the styles with multiple light sources, then lower your layer's opacity, and overlay it on top of another layer to add mood.

Blurring to accentuate an action shot

Most of the time, you want your photos to come out crisp and clean, but in some instances you want to accentuate the motion to create a more dramatic effect. The Motion Blur and Wind filters add a sense of motion to a photo by smearing or blurring the image along the surface.

Add motion with the Wind filter

The Wind filter adds streaks to your image, giving it the illusion of movement. I like this effect better than the Motion Blur because I think it gives the photo more sense of action. It is really going to depend on the image and what you are going to use it for. Motion Blur gives you a more subtle effect and might be a better option. The photo in Figure 16.5 was taken of taxidermied animals at a natural history museum. They look static even though it's a very dramatic screen. I want to add some streaks to make it look more like an action shot.

You can add motion with the Wind filter by following these steps:

1. Open an image and create a copy of your image layer.

2. Choose Filter ➪ Stylize ➪ Wind to open the dialog box.

3. Choose one of the different Methods. The Wind filter dialog box has a preview so that you can try out each one. Wind is the most subtle. The other two Methods are extreme for most images.

4. Choose a direction for your wind. You only have the options of From the Left or From the Right.

5. Click OK to accept and apply your settings.

Bright Idea!

Lessen the effects of Wind by choosing Edit ⇨ Fade Wind. In the dialog box that appears you can adjust the opacity of the filter effect and select a different blending mode.

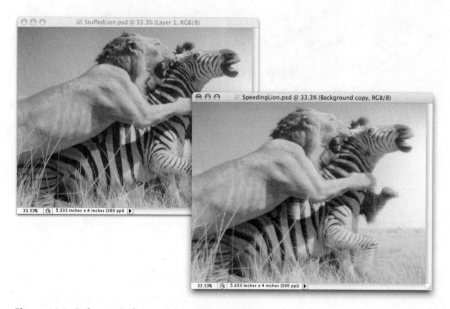

Figure 16.5. Before and after applying the Wind filter.

This is a fun tool but it doesn't offer much in the way of options. You'll find it generally works or doesn't work for a given image. Next, I'll look at some of the Blur filters as alternative methods for adding motion.

Adding Motion Blur to speedy subjects

The Motion Blur filter gives you control over the direction of your blur and allows you to adjust the radius of the blur to get a subtle or extreme effect. Limit the Blur effect to the moving objects in your photo. Use the History Brush to remove the Motion Blur effect from other parts of your image. In Figure 16.6, I've unchecked the Preview option in the Motion Blur dialog box so that you can compare the effect to the original photo.

Figure 16.6. The Motion Blur dialog box.

Soften photos with the Surface Blur filter

The Surface Blur filter softens large areas of continuous tone while trying to maintain the edges of your images. This filter is great for smoothing wrinkled or blemished faces. You can get great results by applying it
to your entire image and then editing out parts by adding a layer mask.

To add surface blur to an image, follow these steps:

1. Open a photo and create a copy of your image by dragging and
   dropping its thumbnail onto the Create New Layer icon.

2. Choose Filter ⇨ Blur ⇨ Surface Blur to open the dialog box, as
   shown in Figure 16.7.

3. Adjust the Radius and Threshold settings to smooth out your entire
   image.

4. Click OK to apply your settings to the image.

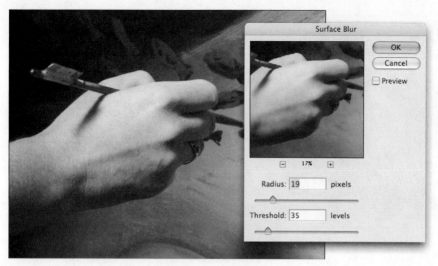

Figure 16.7. The Surface Blur dialog box and original photo.

Next, add a layer mask to selectively remove the Surface Blur effects from areas of your photo by following these steps:

1. Change your background and foreground color to black and white.

2. Click the Create New Layer Mask icon on the bottom of the Layers palette.

3. Select the Brush tool from the Toolbox or press the letter B.

4. Adjust your brush diameter and hardness in the Options bar. Lower the opacity setting to about 40%.

5. Make sure you are using black as your foreground color. If it is currently the background color, click the small arrow next to the swatches to switch the colors around.

6. Paint around areas of your image where you would like to remove the Surface Blur filter effects. In Figure 16.8, I removed the Surface Blur effect from the background and around the edges and knuckles of my hand to get back some of the details.

   If you remove too much, you can always add it back in by switching your foreground color to white and painting over the area.

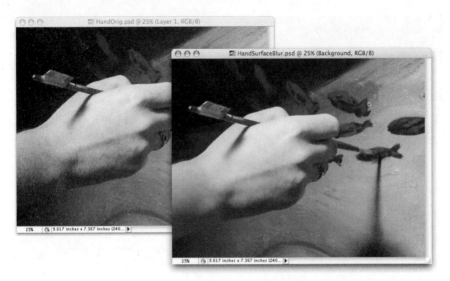

Figure 16.8. A photo before and after using the Surface Blur filter combined with a layer mask.

Your results should give you an image with smoother surface areas while retaining sharp focus on other areas. This filter is new to CS2 and is a great new addition to the Blur filters.

Blurring out the background with Lens Blur

The Lens Blur filter works along with layer masks to isolate areas of your image. You can keep the foreground or subject of your image in focus while blurring out the background, as shown in Figure 16.9.

You can create a selectively blurred image with the Lens Blur filter by following these steps:

1. Open a photo to blur, and create a copy of the image layer for backup.

2. Create a layer mask of the area you'd like to stay in focus. Create a selection using either the Lasso tool, Marquee tools, or Magic Wand tool.

3. Click the Create New Layer Mask button on the bottom of the Layers palette to add your selection as a layer mask to the copy of your image.

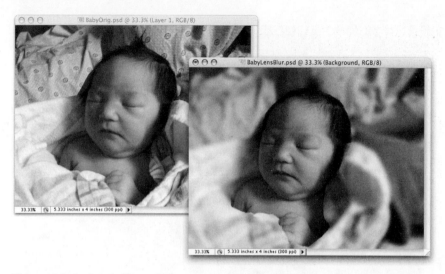

Figure 16.9. A photo before and after using the Lens Blur filter to blur out a background.

4. Click the thumbnail of your image to select it.

5. Choose Filter ⇨ Blur ⇨ Lens Blur to open the Lens Blur dialog box.

6. Select Layer Mask from the Source drop-down list.

7. Click the Invert button to keep your subject in focus.

8. Adjust the Radius value by moving the Radius slider to the right to blur out your background, as shown in Figure 16.10.

9. Click OK to accept and apply your changes.

10. Shift+click the layer mask icon in the Layers palette. A big red X appears and your background becomes blurred. This will disable the layer mask so you can see the areas affected by the Lens Blur filter.

If you'd like to soften up the areas where the blurry parts meet the foreground, try using the History Brush, set at a low opacity setting of 10% to 20%, to blend out some of the edges. The Blur tool works well to soften the hard edges.

Watch Out!

If you see a black-and-white image in the Lens Blur dialog box, you have the layer mask highlighted instead of the image thumbnail. Click Cancel, click the image thumbnail, and then relaunch the Lens Blur filter.

Figure 16.10. The Lens Blur filter dialog box using a layer mask to selectively blur an image.

Distorting, diffusing, and rippling

The Distort filters have handy tools for correcting lens distortion, diffusing light, and spherizing flat objects. I like to use some of the Distort filters to create interesting graphics elements for larger designs.

Quickly fixing lens distortion

Photoshop CS2 comes with a new filter for fixing simple barrel and pincushion distortion problems. Chapter 14 discussed a more hands-on approach for fixing distortion. I'll now show you the Lens Correction filter and how to correct typical distortion problems quickly. I prefer the control of the Warp tool to this filter, but it can be a quick solution to simple distortion issues.

The photo in Figure 16.11 has some barrel distortion problems. Instead of the sidewalks being a straight horizontal, it is bowed up. The Lens Correction filter lets me pinch my image in towards the center to alleviate any barrel distortion, or lets me stretch it out to get rid of pincushion distortion.

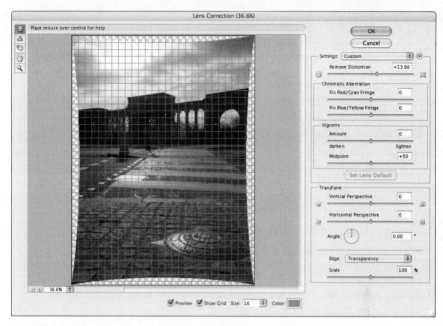

Figure 16.11. The Lens Correction filter window with correction applied to a photo.

You may not be familiar with several new tools in the Lens Correction filter. Table 16.1 lists the tools available in the Lens Correction filter and describes how to use each one to correct lens distortion and camera tilt in your photos.

Table 16.1. Lens Correction filter tools

Icon	Tool	Description
	Remove Distortion	Lets you change the pinching or bowing of your image.
	Straighten	Rotates your image. Draw a line along a tilted edge to straighten it.
	Move Grid	Allows you to reposition the grid.
	Hand	Lets you reposition your image.
	Zoom	Zooms in and out of your image. As an alternative, you can press ⌘ (Ctrl) to zoom in and Option (Alt) to zoom out.

Bright Idea!

Make your image look like you are viewing it through a porthole or rounded mirror by creating your own barrel distortion with the Lens Correction filter. Give it a circular crop by creating a circular selection with the Elliptical Marquee tool and choose Image ⇨ Crop.

The bottom of the tool gives you options for previewing your changes, showing or hiding the grid, and changing the size of the grid. You can also change the color. This comes in handy when your image closely matches the default grid color.

To perform barrel distortion on a photo:

1. Open a digital photo that needs distortion correction.

2. Choose Filter ⇨ Distort ⇨ Lens Correction to launch the tool in a separate window.

3. Choose the Remove Distortion tool from the list of tools on the top right of the Lens Correction window.

4. Pinch or distort your image by clicking and dragging the edges of the grid in the preview box towards or away from the center of the image.

5. Try adjusting the size of the grid by changing the Grid Size amount on the bottom of the window.

6. Try rotating your image slightly by using the Straighten tool.

7. Click OK to apply your changes.

Your image will probably have some transparent background showing as mine did in Figure 16.12. Use the Crop tool to remove any bowed edges.

Watch Out!

Filters won't work in Bitmap or Index Color mode. If you need images in either of these formats, first convert your image to one of the color modes — Lab Color gives you the most options — and convert to Bitmap or Index color as a last step.

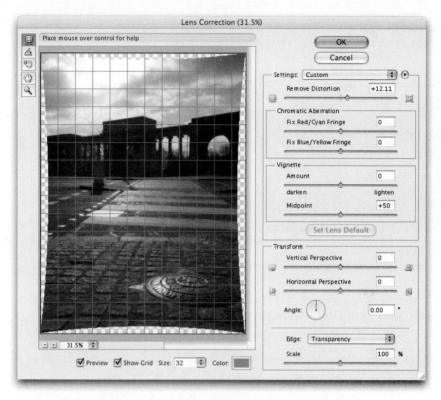

Figure 16.12. Lens Correction filter window with adjustments made to a photo.

Turn a flat surface into a globe

The Spherize filter takes a flat surface and turns it into a three-dimensional globe. Use this filter to add dents to surfaces or to make spheres. Figure 16.13 shows a close-up of a rusted metal wall before and after applying the Spherize filter.

You can create a sphere from a photo by following these steps:

1. Open a photo to use for your sphere. Close-ups of textures work well for creating a textured globe.

2. Select the Elliptical Marquee tool from the Toolbox. You can toggle to it by pressing Shift+M.

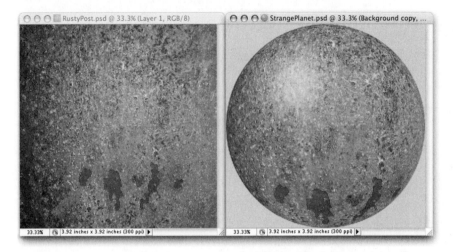

Figure 16.13. A textured surface before and after the Spherize filter.

3. Create a round, circular selection area by simultaneously holding down Option (Alt) to start your circular selection from the center out and Shift to create a perfectly round circle.

4. To create a new layer from your selection, choose Layer ⇨ New ⇨ Layer via copy. Alternatively, you can press ⌘+J (Ctrl+J).

5. Click the Visibility icon in the Layers palette to the left of the thumbnail of your image to hide the Background layer.

6. Choose Filter ⇨ Distort ⇨ Spherize to open the Spherize dialog box, as shown in Figure 16.14.

7. Set the Amount to 100% and click OK.

You'll end up with your image wrapped around a perfect sphere. You can use this filter to make a design for a holiday ornament, or wrap an image around a cylinder by using a rectangular selection and choosing either the Horizontal or Vertical Mode options in the Spherize dialog box. This is also a quick way to wrap a poster design around the photo of a telephone poll or add your own beer label to the photo of a bottle.

Bright Idea!

Add dents by reversing the Spherize effect. Select a circular shape in your image. Choose Filter ⇨ Distort ⇨ Spherize and change the Amount to a negative percentage. Add realistic light and shadow to the dent with the Lighting Effect filter.

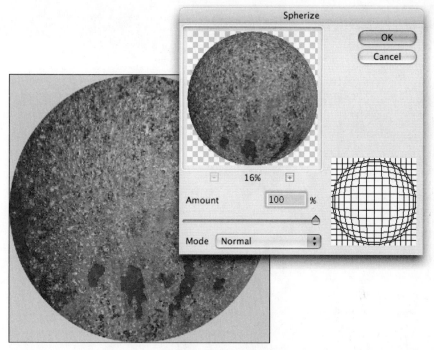

Figure 16.14. The Spherize filter dialog box with Amount set to 100% and Mode set to Normal.

Create a funhouse mirror with the Shear filter

The Shear filter gives you the ability to add distortion points along a vertical line and warp your image to the left or right, as shown in Figure 16.15.

To add a funhouse effect to a photo with the Shear filter:

1. Open a photo and create a copy of the image layer by dragging and dropping its thumbnail onto the Create New Layer button on the bottom of the Layers palette.

2. Choose Filter ➪ Distort ➪ Shear to open the Shear filter dialog box.

3. Add points along the vertical line in the center by clicking along it.

4. Click and move the points to add distortion to your image.

5. Click OK to accept and apply your settings.

Figure 16.15. The Shear filter dialog box with multiple distortion points added.

The Shear filter also comes in handy for creating interesting curving striped pattern designs. Create a new document and add several straight vertical lines in varying widths using the Brush tool while holding down the Shift key. Run the Shear filter on your stripes to create a pattern like the one you see in Figure 16.16.

Generate a countdown clock with Polar Coordinates

The Polar Coordinates filter can make the world flat once again. This filter has two options for rearranging your image. You can take a flat, two-dimensional map and wrap it around a polar center to make it round, or take a round globe and make it a flat two-dimensional map. Don't limit yourself to maps. You can make nice circular graphics with this filter. Figure 16.17 shows an example of a simple stack of lines with the two different options applied.

Figure 16.16. A wavy pattern created by applying the Shear filter to straight lines.

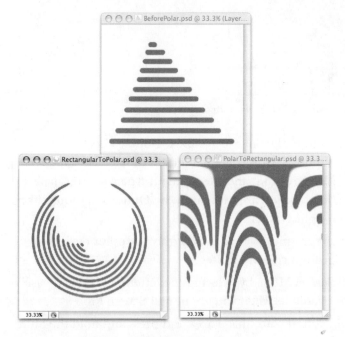

Figure 16.17. An image with different Polar Coordinates options applied using the Polar Coordinates filter.

Using lines and gradients, create the makings of a countdown clock by following these steps:

1. Create a new document. Size doesn't matter that much, but it should be square. I created an 800-x-800-pixel image at 300 dpi. That should give me a big enough image to use for both Web and print.

2. Click the Create New Layer button on the bottom of the Layers palette to create a layer to hold the gradient you are about to make.

   You'll be creating the image you see in Figure 16.18 before you run the Polar Coordinates filter.

Figure 16.18. A gradient with a line near the bottom of the image.

3. Select the Gradient tool from the Toolbox. Double check to make sure the Options bar has the first gradient selected, called Foreground to Background, and the gradient type is set to Linear Gradient. The icon for linear gradient in the Options bar looks like a simple, left-to-right gradient.

4. Change your foreground color to a dark gray (or other dark color) and your background color to white.

5. Switch to Full Screen Mode by pressing the letter F. It is much easier to create large gradients when you are in Full Screen Mode.

6. Click just to the left of your image area and press and hold the Shift key while dragging to the other side of your image area. Release

your mouse button when you get to the right side of the image. You'll see a straight line being drawn as you drag your mouse, indicating the direction of the gradient. Once you release your mouse, a gradient will be rendered.

7. Select the Line tool from the Drawing tools fly-out menu.

8. Create a line across the bottom third of your image area. If you'd like, add a stroke and outer glow to your line by right-clicking the thumbnail of your line layer in the Layers palette.

9. Shift+click the stroke and gradient layers to select them and choose Layer ⇨ Merge. You'll need to merge the layers together before applying the Polar Coordinates filter.

10. Choose Filter ⇨ Distort ⇨ Polar Coordinates. A dialog box appears with two options. Select the radio button for Rectangular to Polar.

11. Click OK to apply the filter to your image.

You should see something like the preview in Figure 16.19. This image could be used as a countdown clock or a radar screen. Add more lines to create a bull's-eye or target.

Figure 16.19. The Polar Coordinates filter dialog box with the Rectangular to Polar option chosen.

Inside Scoop

You can hover your mouse over any of the options in the Options bar to see their names.

More fun with Distortion filters

There are several more Distortion filters from which to choose. They don't appear in the list of filters available through the Filter Gallery, so don't overlook them. You'll take advantage of some of these filters to create backgrounds for collages in Chapter 17.

Other Distortion filters that add interesting effects or designs:

■ **Displace:** Distorts your image or selection using the displacement maps in Photoshop CS2/Plug-Ins/Displacement Maps. Once you click OK in the Displace dialog box, you'll be asked to find a displacement map from the Displacement Maps folder.

■ **Pinch:** This filter is similar to Spherize but with a smoother transition. The Pinch filter is great for creating porthole effects.

■ **Twirl:** Spins your image around a center point. At the higher settings, it looks like your image is being washed down the drain. This is a great tool for creating swirl patterns. Figure 16.20 shows a pattern created with the Twirl filter run on an image made up of straight lines with varying thicknesses and colors.

Figure 16.20. The Twirl filter applied to straight lines.

■ **Wave:** Distorts your image using wave patterns. You can distort your image a tiny bit or to extremes for more abstract patterns. Figure 16.21 shows a photo after running the Wave filter on it with a Sine Type selected and very high Wavelength and Scale settings.

■ **ZigZag:** Swooshes your image in a zigzag pattern from the center out. The Pond Ripples option is a quick way of adding ripples to still water.

Figure 16.21. A photo after using the Wave filter with extreme settings.

Rendering clouds and fiber texture

The Render filters include tools for creating clouds and texture like wood grain or fibers. The filters covered in this section offer quick and simple solutions for creating textures. You can blend your newly created textures with other images or use them as background textures for designs.

Add puffy clouds to clear skies

Sometimes "nothing but blue skies" isn't what you are after. You can create your own clouds and blend them into your images using the History Brush, as shown in Figure 16.22. I introduced you to the History Brush in Chapter 10. In this exercise, you'll put it to good use by blending your clouds into the horizon.

Figure 16.22. A photo before and after applying the Clouds filter and erasing with the History Brush.

You can create puffy clouds and blend them into your photo by following these steps:

1. Open a photo that has clear blue skies. Create a copy of your image by dragging the image layer onto the Create New Layer button on the bottom of the Layers palette. This is an important step; the Clouds filter will destroy your image.

2. To choose a color for your new sky, click the background color swatch and, using the eyedropper in the Color Picker window, find the darkest spot in your sky.

3. Choose a color for your clouds. Click the foreground color swatch and choose either white or a very light color in your photo. I chose a very light color in Figure 16.23.

Bright Idea!

Try another method. You can get more naturalistic or stormy clouds by using the Difference Clouds filter and then inverting the Layer by choosing Image ⇨ Adjustments ⇨ Invert. Use the History Brush to remove the effect from your foreground.

Figure 16.23. The Clouds filter applied to a photo.

4. Choose Filter ➪ Render ➪ Clouds. Your document will turn completely into clouds like those that you see in Figure 16.23.

5. Choose the History Brush from the Toolbox and increase the opacity to 100% in the Options bar. Increase the Brush Diameter to a large size.

6. Paint over the foreground to remove the clouds and restore your foreground to its original state.

7. Change the Opacity level to 20% and blend out some of the clouds from just above the horizon line of your image to make your clouds look more realistic. You can blend out certain areas so the clouds don't look as uniform.

Creating wood grain with the Fibers filter

The Fibers filter in Photoshop creates interesting, streaky, fibrous textures that can be used as backgrounds or as a layer mask to give a faded look. This filter is a great tool for making realistic wood texture, as shown in Figure 16.24.

Figure 16.24. A wood grain design created with the Fibers filter.

To create a wood grain texture with the Fibers filter:

1. Create a new Photoshop document. I created mine with a resolution of 300 dpi so that I can use it for a variety of things.

2. Select a dark wood color for the foreground color. This will be the color used for the dark streaks in your wood grain.

3. Select a light wood color for the background color. This will be the color used for the light streaks in your wood grain.

4. Press ⌘+Delete (Ctrl+Delete) to fill your layer with the background color.

5. Choose Filter ⇨ Render ⇨ Fibers to open the Fibers filter dialog box.

Bright Idea!

Add a realistic wavy pattern to your wood grain by running the Wave or Shear filter.

6. Adjust the Variance and Strength values by moving the sliders for each option to get different effects.

   The Variance slider controls the length of your streaks. The farther left you go, the longer the streaks.

   The Strength slider controls how spread out the fibers are.

7. Click the Randomize button a few times until you generate a random pattern that you like.

8. Click OK to apply the settings to your image.

The Stylize filters

The Stylize filters can be used to create interesting designs and patterns from either solid colors or photographs. Most are very creative filters with a million and one different uses and techniques. I'll try to show you some of the most popular uses for the filters to get you started. If you are interested in a particular filter, the many Photoshop support sites have great tutorials on additional effects and tricks for most of these filters. Many of the Stylize filters get better results in Lab Color Mode. One drawback is that some tools and filters, such as the History Brush, are not available in Lab Color Mode.

Diffusing light to add subtle texture

The Diffuse filter works like a traditional diffuse filter by shifting dots of color around to slightly diffuse the focus of your image. This filter is very subtle and gives your image the appearance of slightly frosted glass.

You can achieve a nice alternative to the soft-focus vignette look that was covered in Chapter 7. Create a circular marquee around your subject using the Elliptical Marquee tool, then choose Select ⇨ Inverse, and apply the filter to the background of your image. The Darken option replaces light pixels with darker ones. The Lighten option replaces dark pixels with lighter ones. The Anisotropic option retains color similarities.

Embossing your image

The Emboss filter makes your image appear to be stamped by overlaying gray with the dark outlines from your image. When used in RGB or CMYK color mode, the filter turns your image completely gray except for the edges. You can adjust the angle of the emboss shadow and increase the degree of the raised surface. In Figure 16.25, I used the Emboss filter on the entire image and then restored the baby's face and hands using the History Brush.

Figure 16.25. An image altered with the Emboss filter and then selectively restored in parts using the History Brush.

Create 3-D squares that extrude from your image

The Extrude tool reminds me of squeezing clay through the PLAY-DOH Fun Factory. It extrudes square or pyramid shapes from your image, giving it a 3-D effect. At high Depth levels of 50 or more, this tool looks like a graphic rendering of a helicopter view of a metropolis. At Depth levels below 30, it adds an interesting texture to a photo. You can either choose

Inside Scoop

To retain image color and avoid turning your image gray, switch to Lab Color Mode before applying the Emboss filter.

> **Watch Out!**
> The Extrude filter has no preview option. You'll need to render the filter in order to see what each setting will do to your image.

to use a block shape, which looks like the top view of a building, or a 4-sided pyramid shape with pointy tops. The Pixels setting controls how large you want each block or pyramid. I've seen interesting effects made by combining this filter with the Spherize filter. By Spherizing a solid-colored layer and then applying the Spherize filter to a circular selection of the extrusion, you wind up with an interesting 3-D globe. The image in Figure 16.26 was created with a solid color layer extruded using the Random setting in the filter window. After running the Extrude filter on the image, I applied the Glowing Edges filter to enhance the edges created by the Extrude filter.

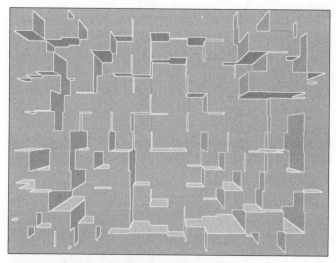

Figure 16.26. The Extrude filter applied to a solid color layer and then combined with the Glowing Edges filter.

Accentuate your image edges with Trace Contour

The Trace Contour filter works best in Lab Color Mode. In RGB or CMYK, you'll end up with strange, multicolored lines. In Lab Color, you'll get nice, dark, traced outlines around the edges of your image. After you've applied the Trace Contour filter, change your blending mode to Multiply.

To add an outline to your image:

1. Open a photo.

2. Choose Image ⇨ Mode ⇨ Lab Color.

3. Create a copy of your image by dragging and dropping the image thumbnail onto the Create New Layer button in the Layers palette.

4. Choose Filter ⇨ Stylize ⇨ Trace Contour to open the Trace contour filter dialog box.

5. Adjust the Level setting until you like the contour lines around your image.

   When you add the Trace Contour filter, your image is going to turn mostly white with some dark lines. You'll change the blending mode in a minute to make the contours blend in with your image.

6. Click OK to accept and apply your settings.

7. Select Multiply from the Blending Mode drop-down list on the top of the Layers palette.

The result you get by combining your regular layer with a layer enhanced with the Trace Contour filter is a punchier image with strong outlines. The photos in Figure 16.27 show an image before and after using the Trace Contour filter set to a blending mode of Multiply. Remember to convert your image to Lab Color Mode before using this filter for the best outcome.

Figure 16.27. The Trace Contour filter in Multiply blending mode.

Just the facts

■ Correct common lens distortion problems quickly with the Lens Correction filter.

■ Add light sources to photos with the Lens Flare and Lighting Effects filters.

■ Create a sense of motion with the Blur and Wind filters.

■ Design your own patterns and graphics with the Distort filters.

■ Wrap a photo or design around a sphere or cylinder with the Spherize filter.

GET THE SCOOP ON...
Creating a collage from several photos ▪ Combining
and blending parts from several photos ▪ Creating a
personal greeting card ▪ Combining several photos
into a panorama

Combining Images and Creating Collages

I f you haven't figured it out already, Photoshop is much more than a photo editing program. It is a powerful design tool for combining many different design elements including but not limited to type, illustration, and photographic images. Think of Photoshop as a fridge full of ingredients. The possibilities of what you can create are endless. The next two chapters introduce you to a few of my favorite recipes. I hope they inspire you to come up with your own creations.

This chapter shows you how to create collages and combined photos using many of the tools discussed in previous chapters. You'll see how to mask images and blend them together into one object, and you'll create a personal greeting card for the holidays using family photos. You'll also try out the new Photomerge tool for creating panoramas from a series of photos.

Creating a photo collage

It's quick and easy to combine several images together to create a collage of a family trip, holiday party, or other adventure. By using Smart Objects, you can resize and rearrange your photos to find the perfect arrangement without having to worry about losing image quality. By adding a stroke to each image using Blending Options, you

Chapter 17

can create a postcard effect. I used the type-on-a-path feature to add my own text to the graphics in Figure 17.1. The circular photo in the center is a simple elliptical selection converted into a layer mask.

Figure 17.1. A collage of photos converted to Smart Objects.

Create a large document canvas for your collage

This project involves several parts, which I've broken up into different tasks. You'll first need to create a new Photoshop document as the base for your collage. If you plan to print your collage, try to use scanned images with a resolution of 300 dpi, or the largest setting available on your digital camera. For my collage, I was working with 300-dpi images, so I created a letter-sized document, landscape orientation, at 300 dpi. If your images are only 72 dpi, set the resolution of your new file as 72 dpi. For this exercise, I'll create a file in RGB color mode. If you choose to print it on a professional, photo-quality printer, you can always convert it to CMYK later down the road and adjust colors as you need.

You can create a large canvas for your collage by following these steps:

1. Choose File ⇨ New to open the New dialog box, shown in Figure 17.2.

2. Set the document Width to 11 inches and the Height to 8.5 inches.

3. Enter 300 in the Resolution field.

4. Select RGB Color from the Color Mode drop-down list and then select 8 bit from the Bit Depth drop-down list.

5. Set the Background Contents to Transparent.

6. Click OK to create your new file.

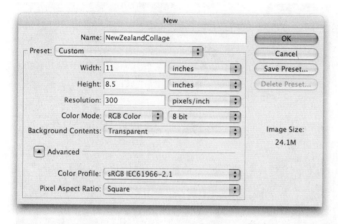

Figure 17.2. A letter- and landscape-sized document at 300 dpi in RGB color mode.

Combine several images into one document

Next, copy all of the photos you want to use into the new document. Be aware of document size. You'll want to copy only images that won't need to be enlarged. Stretching images larger than their original size is going to result in low-quality images. You'll be converting your images to Smart Objects before resizing them, so for now just paste them into the new document. If your images are large, say as large as the document you've created, you might want to shrink them a bit before copying them, just to save on file size. Leave a little bit of wiggle room by keeping them slightly larger than you think you'll need.

To copy and paste photos into your new document:

1. Open each of your photos and choose Select ⇨ All, or press ⌘+A (Ctrl+A).

2. Choose Edit ⇨ Copy, or press ⌘+C (Ctrl+C).

3. Paste each of your photos into the new document by choosing Edit ⇨ Paste or pressing ⌘+P (Ctrl+P).

4. Repeat for each image you want to use in your collage. You should end up with a file that looks something like Figure 17.3.

Figure 17.3. Several photos pasted into one document.

Bright Idea!

Give your layers meaningful names so that you can find things easily. You can increase the size of the thumbnails in your Layers palette. Click the black arrow on the top of the Layers palette and select Palette Options. Choose the largest thumbnail size.

Convert your images to Smart Objects

The new Smart Objects feature allows you to shrink and enlarge an image as many times as you want without losing image quality. You can resize your images as easily as resizing a vector graphic.

Convert photos to Smart Objects for limitless resizing by following these steps:

1. Click one of the thumbnails of your photos in the Layers palette to select it.

2. Choose Layer ⇨ Smart Objects ⇨ Group Into New Smart Object.

3. Repeat for each photo layer.

Your Layer thumbnail icon will include a small document icon in the lower right corner to indicate it is now a Smart Object (see Figure 17.4).

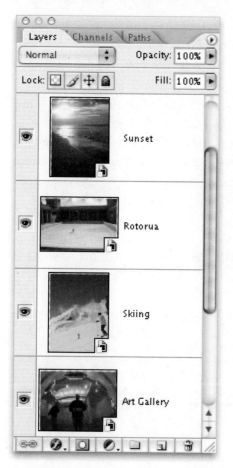

Figure 17.4. A list of layers that have been converted to Smart Objects in the Layers palette.

Inside Scoop

You can right-click a layer name to open a list of options and select Group Into New Smart Object.

Create a circular mask around an image

For the center image, create a circular image mask to add some pizzazz to the collage. The shape you use doesn't have to be a circle. Try creating masks from the shapes available in the Custom Shape tool.

To create a circular layer mask, follow these steps:

1. Select the layer of the image you'd like to mask into a circular shape.
2. Select the Circular Marquee tool from the Marquee tools fly-out menu. You can press Shift+M to toggle through the Marquee tools.
3. Press and hold the Option key and then click and drag from the center out to create a circular shape for your mask.
4. Click the Create New Layer Mask icon on the bottom of the Layers palette.

Your image will be masked with the circular selection. You can move your image separate from the layer by clicking the image thumbnail in the Layers palette. To move the layer mask separately from the image, click the mask thumbnail. Once they are selected, you can move them around with the Move tool.

Create type on a curve

Now add some type to your image by creating a circular path that mimics the masked circular photo and adding type on a curve. If you've used other shape tools for your image mask, you can use the same shape tool to create type on a curve. Shapes that have sharp points don't work as well as rounded corners. Figure 17.5 shows an example of type on an elliptical path.

Bright Idea!

You can add a stroke to your circular image by choosing Layer ⇨ Layer Style ⇨ Stroke. This is an alternative to right-clicking the thumbnail icon and selecting Blending Options.

Watch Out!

Moving text around a shape can be tricky and takes a little getting used to. If you mess up, undo your changes and try again. Pay special attention to the cursor icons.

Figure 17.5. Type on an elliptical path.

You can add type on a curve by following these steps:

1. Select the Elliptical Shape tool from the Shape tools fly-out menu. You can toggle through the shape tools by pressing Shift+U.

2. Click the Paths button on the far left of the Options bar. The button looks like a rectangle with a pen tip.

3. Press and hold the Option key (Alt), and then click and drag to draw an ellipse from the center out.

4. Select the Horizontal Type tool from the Toolbox. You can press the letter T to highlight it.

5. Click the path to place your cursor and enter your text.

6. To move your text around the circle, press and hold the ⌘ key (Ctrl) and hover your mouse over the text until the cursor changes to a text insert icon with a right or left black arrow. Then click and drag to move the text around the path.

Add outlines to your photos using Blending Options

To give your collage a travel postcard look, add solid strokes to each of the photos. You might consider adding drop shadows instead of strokes. Try out a few options to find a look you like.

To add a Stroke to layers:

1. Right-click one of the layers and select Blending Options from the drop-down list.

Inside Scoop

Temporarily disable Layer Styles by right-clicking the effects icon next to your layer and selecting Disable Layer Effects. The icon looks like an *f* in a black circle.

2. Click Stroke to check its check box and view the options as shown in Figure 17.6.

3. Click the color swatch to choose a new color.

4. Increase the pixel width. As long as the Preview check box is checked, you'll be able to preview your changes in your document.

5. Click OK to apply your settings. Instead of having to repeat these steps with each layer, copy and paste the layer styles.

6. Right-click the same layer and select Copy Layer Style.

7. Right-click another layer and select Paste Layer Style.

8. Continue pasting the layer style for the remaining layers.

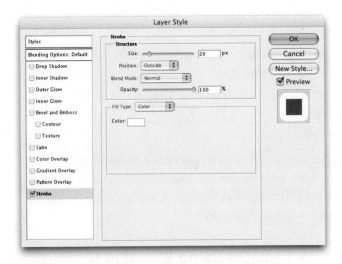

Figure 17.6. The Stroke panel in the Layer Style dialog box.

Adding eyeballs to vegetables

I combined the images of eyes and pumpkins in Figure 17.7 by simply copying and pasting circular selections of the eyes and then blending them with the Stamp tool. I added a dark area around them by creating an Outer Glow using darker colors and changing the blending mode to Darken or Multiply. The eyebrows were simply copied pieces from other areas of the pumpkin photo. I feathered the edges slightly so that they would blend into the background better. Using Flip Vertical and the Free Transform tool, I was able to copy each of the eyeballs and eyebrows and switch their orientation.

If you have an old chair or other favorite object that you consider to have anthropomorphic qualities, here's your chance to give it even more life.

Figure 17.7. Combined images using feathering and blending.

To add eyeballs to inanimate objects:

1. If you have a digital camera, take a picture of your eye. If you don't have a digital camera, any photo with a close-up shot of eyes will do.

2. Open a photo of some sort of inanimate object.

3. Open your eyeball photo.

4. Make a rough selection of an eyeball. Copy and paste it into your other photo. You'll probably need to resize it once you paste it.

5. Choose Edit ⇨ Free Transform or use the key command ⌘+T (Ctrl+T).

6. Press and hold the Shift key and drag the corner anchors to adjust the size of your eyeball.

7. Position it into place. You can use Free Transform again to rotate it.

8. Perform any needed masking with your masking method of choice. I used the Quick Mask Mode to create a selection and created a layer mask from the selection. See Chapter 8 for more instructions on masking.

9. Choose Edit ⇨ Transform ⇨ Flip Horizontal (or Flip Vertical depending on the orientation of your original eyeball).

10. Press and hold the ⌘ key (Ctrl) to temporarily change your cursor to the Move tool and drag your new eyeball into place.

11. Right-click each of the thumbnails of your eyeballs in the Layers palette and choose Blending Options from the drop-down list.

12. Click Outer Glow to check the check box and view its options.

13. Change the Blending Mode to Darken.

14. Click the color swatch and click a dark area of your photo.

15. Increase the Spread and Size. This helps blend your eyeball into the object behind it. It might depend on the individual image, so use some liberties here to get the right effect.

You should have a good start now. In Figure 17.8, I've isolated the elements that I added to my original pumpkin photo.

I was able to add fake eyebrows by creating a selection of a dark area in the pumpkin photo using the Lasso tool. To bend it into an eyebrow shape, I used the Edit ⇨ Transform ⇨ Warp tool. You may want to add a feather to the eyeballs or eyebrows to soften their edges. By ⌘+clicking the thumbnail in the Layers palette and choosing Select ⇨ Feather, you can designate how many pixels thick you'd like your feathering to be.

Bright Idea!

Take this project to the next level by adding other facial features. Give your subject lips and place a thought bubble above them.

The eyes on the right side of Figure 17.8 were blended into the pumpkin using the Clone Stamp tool. I lowered the opacity of the Clone Stamp tool as I got closer to the eyes so that they look like they are blending into the pumpkin behind them.

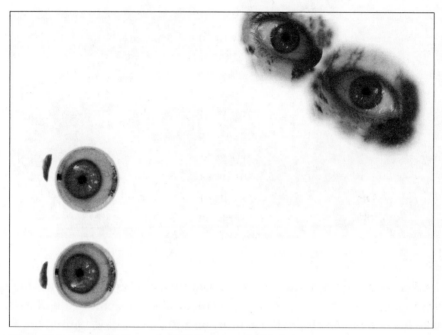

Figure 17.8. Newly added layers isolated from the original photo.

Creating your own mythical creatures

How many times have you picked up one of those spoof newspapers and wondered, How did they create that photo of a half boy, half donkey? The simple answer, dear friend, is layer masks and the Clone Stamp tool. These two techniques, plus a couple of free hours, are all you need to create your own creatures. This section shows you how to blend parts from various animals together into one mythical creature. You'll also get some tips on correcting color and blending so the separate parts appear to be from the same beast. The Pegasus in Figure 17.9 was created from stock photos of a horse and a seagull.

Figure 17.9. Combining images of seagull wings and a horse to create a Pegasus.

By masking each of the creatures from their backgrounds, I was able to piece their parts together into one creature. I changed the tint of the seagull wings to match the horse by using a Replace Color adjustment. I blended the wings into the body of the horse using the Clone Stamp tool. The horse was masked using a combination of techniques including the Select Color Range feature and the Quick Mask Mode. If you haven't done so yet, read Chapter 8 to get an understanding of the various masking techniques.

The photos of the horse and seagull in Figure 17.10 were gathered from a stock photo Web site. For a list of my favorite stock photo Web sites, see the appendixes. The photo of the building is a photo I took during a trip to Cambridge. I used the Clone Stamp tool to remove the man from the lawn in Figure 17.10. I decided to crop out the river; it made the photo look modern and I wanted to emphasize the dreamlike, timeless quality of the building in the background.

Figure 17.10. Three photos used for the Pegasus picture.

Create a mask from a modified channel

The bird was created by making a threshold adjustment on one of the channels. I found the channel with the most contrast, duplicated it, and converted it to black and white using a Threshold Adjustment. I had to do some minor editing in Quick Mask Mode, but this method saved me tons of time.

To create a mask using a channel:

1. Click the Channels palette tab behind your Layers palette. If it's not visible, choose Window ⇨ Channels.

2. Find the channel with the most contrast between foreground and background.

3. Click and drag the chosen channel onto the Create New Channel button on the bottom of the channels palette. Your newly copied channel will automatically be selected.

4. Choose Image ⇨ Adjustments ⇨ Threshold.

Watch Out!

If you weren't able to get a clear distinction between foreground and background, choose another masking method. The channel masking method only works on photos where the foreground image can be isolated easily from the background image.

5. Adjust the settings until you have the most amount of difference between foreground and background. Figure 17.11 shows the Threshold dialog box and a preview of what my Threshold will look like.

6. Click OK to apply your Threshold adjustments.

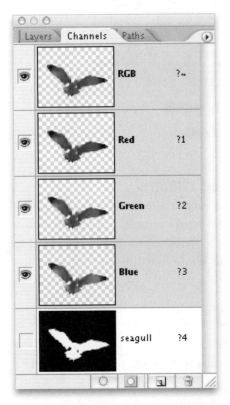

Figure 17.11. The seagull blue channel with a Threshold Adjustment applied.

You should now have a straightforward black area to use as a mask. You can use a variety of selecting and paint tools to clean up your selection.

To create a Layer Mask from a selected channel:

1. You'll want your foreground to be white and your background to be black. You can quickly swap them by choosing Image ⇨ Adjustments ⇨ Invert.

2. ⌘+click your new channel's thumbnail in the Channels palette. Photoshop selects the white areas of your channel.

3. Click the top, composite channel to restore your image. It will be called RGB or CMYK depending on your color mode.

4. Click the Layers tab to switch back to the Layers palette.

5. Click the Create Layer Mask button on the bottom of the Layers palette. Figure 17.12 shows my seagull photo after applying a layer mask.

Figure 17.12. The seagull image with layer mask applied.

Bright Idea!

You can feather your selected channel for a softer look before adding a layer mask by ⌘+clicking your modified channel to create a selection, and then choosing Select ⇨ Feather. Add a feather of 1 to 4 pixels.

Your edited channel is still available if you ever need to tweak the image and create a new layer mask. When used on the right image, this method is quick and accurate.

Create consistent colors across multiple layers

The wings of the seagull were very blue compared to the warm, light brown of the horse. In order to adjust the colors of the wings, I used the Replace Color feature, and then fine-tuned with a Brightness/Contrast and Levels adjustment.

To replace the color and adjust the brightness of an image:

1. Place the image of the layer you are adjusting next to the image to which you are blending it. The Replace Color tool has a preview feature so you'll be able to compare them more easily when they are right next to each other.

2. Make sure the image you are adjusting is highlighted in the Layers palette.

3. Choose Image ⇨ Adjustments ⇨ Replace Color. The dialog box that you see in Figure 17.13 appears.

4. Click the second Eyedropper tool on the top of the screen. This tool has a plus sign (+) next to it and means that it will add any areas that are clicked on to the previously selected color. Click and drag across the area you want to change. I clicked and dragged all across the white parts of the wing but left the black tips alone.

5. Move the Hue slider to change the color cast.

6. Adjust the Saturation levels. I raised mine slightly to bring out the color more.

7. Adjust the lightness levels. I lightened mine up a little to try to match the horse's coat.

8. Click OK to apply your settings to the highlighted layer.

Inside Scoop

Adjust the Opacity settings of the Clone Stamp and other paint tools by pressing a number on your keyboard. 1 = 10%, 5 = 50%, and so on.

Figure 17.13. The Replace Color dialog box with Hue adjustments.

Your image is probably not perfectly blended with your other image. If you look again at Figure 17.13, you'll see that the wing is still much darker than the horse. If you need to, perform other adjustments like Brightness/Contrast, Curves, or Levels. I was able to get the two parts close in color by adjusting the Brightness/Contrast and lightening the midtones by performing a Levels adjustment.

Blend images together using the Clone Stamp tool

After I corrected the color of my wing, I made a copy of it and flipped it horizontally by choosing Image ⇨ Transform ⇨ Flip Horizontal, so that I'd have a mirror image for the other side of the horse. To blend the wing into the body of the horse as shown in Figure 17.14, I used the Clone Stamp tool at an opacity setting of about 50%.

Figure 17.14. Wings blended into the horse using the Clone Stamp tool.

To blend two layers together with the Clone Stamp tool:

1. Click the Create New Layer button to keep your blends separate from your parts.
2. Select the Clone Stamp tool from the Toolbox. You can press the letter S to highlight it.
3. Change the Opacity to 50% in the Options bar.
4. Adjust the brush size by typing the] key to increase the brush diameter and [to decrease it.
5. Option+click (Alt+click) an area to select it as the source for your image cloning.
6. Click and drag your mouse over an area to blend the colors together.

I made several passes with the Clone Stamp tool, first blending colors from the wing into the coat of the horse, then blending colors from the horse into the edge of the wing.

Hack

Flatten your image into one layer to use in other documents. Click the Create New Document from Current State button in the History palette. In the new document, choose Layer ⇨ Merge Visible.

Design a personal greeting card

Next time the holidays roll around, why not create your own personal greeting card using family photos? In Chapter 20, I cover some online printing services where you can order your own greeting card designs. To get you started, I've created the design shown in Figure 17.15 that you can easily adapt to your own photos.

Figure 17.15. A greeting card design blending photos together using a gradient mask.

The photo of the child inside the ornament was copied and pasted using an Elliptical Marquee tool selection. I resized the circle to match the size of the ornament using the Free Transform tool. I then created a gradient mask to blend the outer edges of the child's face by using the Gradient tool in Quick Mask Mode.

To create a circular selection of a photo:

1. Open a photo to use for your circular selection.

2. Select the Elliptical Marquee tool from the Toolbox. You can press Shift+M to toggle through the Marquee tool fly-out menu until you have highlighted the Elliptical Marquee tool.

3. Press and hold Shift+Option (Alt), and then click and drag from the center out to create a perfectly circular selection.

4. If you need to reposition the selection area, you can use the arrow keys on your keyboard or click and drag the selection area.

5. Choose Edit ⇨ Copy or use the key command ⌘+C (Ctrl+C).

6. Click the Create New Layer button on the bottom of the Layers palette.

7. Choose Edit ⇨ Paste or use the key command ⌘+P (Ctrl+P). Figure 17.16 shows an image that has been copied and pasted using a circular selection.

Figure 17.16. A circular image copied and pasted using the Elliptical Marquee tool.

Bright Idea!

You can distort your image to make it look like it is wrapping around the ornament by choosing Filter ⇨ Distort ⇨ Spherize and setting the Amount to 100%.

You can turn off the visibility of the original layer to see your new circular image. You now have a circular selection that you can use as your photo ornament.

If you have a photo of an ornament, follow along and create a gradient mask around your circular photo to blend it into the ornament photo.

To create a gradient mask for your circular image:

1. Open the photo of your ornament and the circular photo you just created.

2. Click and drag the layer thumbnail of your circular image onto the photo with the ornament.

3. Choose Edit ⇨ Free Transform to resize your image to fit your ornament. If you press and hold the Shift key while dragging the Free Transform corner points, your circle maintains its proportions.

4. In the ornament file, ⌘+click (Ctrl+click) the thumbnail of your circular photo to create a selection around the photo and highlight the layer.

5. Click the Quick Mask Mode button in the Toolbox. Your screen will turn pink.

6. Select the Gradient tool from the Toolbox. You can press the letter G to highlight it.

7. Click the Radial Gradient button in the Options bar.

8. Check the Reverse check box in the Options bar.

9. Click and drag from the center of your circular image to just outside of it.

10. Click the Standard Mode button in the Toolbox. This returns you to the regular mode. You should see a circular selection slightly smaller than your circular image, as shown in Figure 17.17.

11. Click the Add Layer Mask button on the bottom of the Layers palette.

Figure 17.17. A circular selection created by applying a radial gradient to a photo in Quick Mask Mode.

If your gradient didn't turn out quite like you'd hoped, undo the last two steps and try again. The Gradient tool takes a little getting used to. The rest of the design I'll leave up to you. Here is a description of how I created the rest.

The star shapes were created using the Custom Shape tool. They come preinstalled with Photoshop. I changed the opacity on the larger shapes to add some dynamic shapes to the background. Because the

Inside Scoop

You can temporarily disable layer masks by Shift+clicking the layer mask thumbnail. A red X will appear over the layer mask thumbnail. Shift+click it again to enable it.

photo of my ornament was on a solid white background, I created a selection of the red ornament using the Magic Wand tool with a Tolerance setting of 50, and overlaid it on top of the large star shape so that it would recede into the background.

The text was added using the Horizontal Type tool and a font that I found on a free font Web site. See the resources section in the back of the book for a list of font Web sites.

Stitch several photos together

I can't tell you how many times I've taken a series of photos in 360 degrees hoping that someday I'd get around to the complicated task of blending them into one giant panorama. The problem is my free time is a very precious commodity. I could rarely justify the time that it used to take me to sew several images together, and when I did, my results were poor at best. When I first tried the new Photomerge feature in Photoshop CS2, I was giddy with excitement. Even photos that I had taken without the aid of a tripod were sewn together with near flawlessness.

The Photomerge feature in Photoshop stitches several photos together by overlapping matching areas. You can let Photoshop take a crack at arranging photos, or turn off autopilot and arrange them yourself. The panorama created in Figure 17.18 was made up of several photos.

Figure 17.18. A panorama created by stitching several photos together with Photomerge.

The Photomerge window is comprised of a large Workspace panel for previewing your work, a smaller Lightbox panel with images that Photoshop could not place, and a row of tools to help you merge your photos. Table 17.1 describes the Photomerge tools and shares tips for using each one.

Table 17.1. Tools available in the Photomerge window

Tool Icon	Tool Name	Tips
	Select Image	Click and drag images around the screen to arrange them.
	Rotate Image	Rotate any image inside the Preview window by clicking and moving it with your mouse.
	Select Vanishing Point	Sets the vanishing point image. Works only when you have Perspective selected from the Settings radio buttons. The outline around the image turns blue when it is the vanishing point source.
	Zoom	Zooms in and out of the preview window. Press and hold Option (Alt) to zoom out.
	Move View	Moves the entire set of images at once. This command comes in handy when you have several rows of images to piece together.

Try out this tool on a set of photos that you've taken. If you don't have a set handy, and you have a digital camera, try creating a set. Stay in one place and use a tripod if you have one. Take a series of photos that slightly overlap each other. Upload your photos to your computer and place them in a separate folder on your hard drive.

To create a panorama from a series of photos:

1. Create a folder of images that form to create a panorama.

2. In Photoshop CS2, choose File ⇨ Automate ⇨ Photomerge to open a dialog box that will ask you which folder of files to use, as shown in Figure 17.19.

3. Click the Browse button and find your folder of images.

4. Check the Attempt to Automatically Arrange Source Images check box.

5. Click OK to begin Photoshop's process of merging images. This process takes a while, especially if you are using large files. Be patient. Photoshop tries its best to merge all of your images into one. You may get a dialog box telling you that it could not merge all of the images.

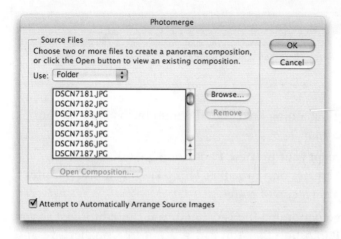

Figure 17.19. The Photomerge dialog box.

6. Click OK in the dialog box that warns you Photoshop could not place all of the images. You'll be taken to the Photomerge tool window, as shown in Figure 17.20.

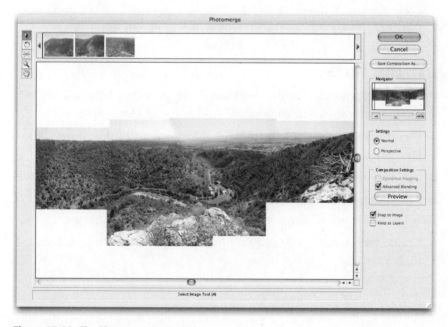

Figure 17.20. The Photomerge tool window.

Inside Scoop

When Snap To Image is selected, you can double-click a thumbnail in the Lightbox to have Photoshop automatically place it.

7. Click and drag remaining images in the thumbnail area into your image to place them.

8. Click OK to accept your preview. Photoshop goes through each image file and creates one large file. This takes one to five minutes to generate, so get a cup of coffee.

Once your large panorama file is created, you can edit it just as you would any other Photoshop file. You can resize it to a smaller size and e-mail it to friends and family or place it on a Web site.

If you are using Adobe Bridge as a file organizer, creating panoramas is even easier. You can launch Photomerge directly from Adobe Bridge by selecting the images you want to use and choosing Tools ⇨ Photoshop ⇨ Photomerge.

Select Keep as Layers to keep the images separate. This is a great idea if some of your images need color correcting to match other images.

Just the facts

■ Create a photo collage by combining several photos into one document. Add a stroke to each photo and add text elements.

■ Blend layers together by feathering selections and using Inner Glow blending options using the background color.

■ Create a greeting card design using family photos.

■ Combine elements of several photos into one image by masking, color adjustments, and blending using the Clone Stamp tool.

■ Create panoramas from several photos with the new Photomerge tool.

GET THE SCOOP ON...
Creating a professional business card design ▪ Designing
a brochure with text and graphics ▪ Layering multiple
images with opacity settings ▪ Creating resizable vector
art from low resolution photos

Designing Stunning Graphics

Chapter 18

This chapter shows you some simple and versatile designs created by combining some of the techniques discussed in previous chapters. You'll create a simple business card design, and using the Picture Package automation tool, I'll show you how to lay out several copies of your business card on a printable letter-sized page that you can print on your home printer. Using filters and opacity settings, I'll show you how to create attractive images for brochures, CD covers, or other designs.

When designing for print or Web, the one thing I can't stress enough is moderation. The old adage "less is more" is a wise philosophy to live by. Try to use no more than two or three typefaces. Take advantage of the regular, bold, italic, and black options available with most fonts instead of reaching for a third or fourth font. When choosing a color palette for your design, stick with two or three main colors, and base any secondary or highlight colors on the main ones by choosing lighter or less-saturated versions of the same color. Try not to use more than one or two bright colors in a design. Choosing a bright color and a more subdued color usually keeps you out of trouble. The best way to increase your design chops is by paying attention to the designs around you. If you like a certain design, try to figure out what it is that you are drawn to. Is it a certain color scheme, layout, or image that appeals to you? Try to incorporate these elements into your designs.

Creating a business card with custom brushes

You can add special touches to a simple business card design by using the Custom Brush tool and taking advantage of the many brush options for scattering the brush strokes. The business card design in Figure 18.1 was created using the Butterfly Custom Brush Tip Shape. I played with the settings for Shape Dynamics, Scattering, and Color Dynamics to create a random pattern using a variety of colors based on the foreground and background colors. Using duplicated type layers of varying font sizes, I layered the logo type for an interesting look. You can create a custom shape from any image; see Chapter 5 if you'd like to create a custom shape using your company logo or other graphic.

Figure 18.1. A business card created with custom brushes and text elements.

I've broken the steps for this project into a few manageable chunks. You'll first create a file the size of a standard business card. You'll then see how to customize the brush tip settings to get a random, scattered look using multiple colors and opacity settings. You'll add some text elements to finish the design. Lastly, you'll see how to create a custom layout

Bright Idea!

There are hundreds or thousands of free and affordable custom brush tips available on Photoshop enthusiast sites. Search for "Photoshop brushes" in your favorite search engine. You can use them as painting tools or clip art. Great for use in collages, too.

in the Picture Package automation tool so that you can print an entire letter-sized sheet of your business cards on your home printer.

You can create a new file the size of a standard business card by following these steps:

1. Choose File ⇨ New.

2. Select inches from the unit of measure drop-down list next to the Width field.

3. Enter **3.5** in the Width field and **2** in the Height field.

4. Set the Resolution to 300. Select RGB from the Color Mode drop-down list and White from the Background Contents field. If you are planning to print your design on a laser printer, select CMYK as your color mode.

5. Click OK to create your new file.

Next, design your business card. You'll customize the brush flow settings of one of the brush tips and add text elements to your card. Once you've created your card, I'll show you a trick for creating a page full of business cards that you can print on your home printer.

To set up the options for your Custom Brush Tip Shape:

1. Select the Brush tool from the Toolbox or press the letter B.

2. Click the Brushes tab in the Palette Dock on the upper right side of your screen. This expands the Brushes palette to display all the Brush options.

3. Click Brush Tip Shape to view all the available brush tips.

4. If you'd like to add more brushes to the list, click the black arrow on the top right of the palette and select one of the presets from the list. When prompted, click Append to add a preset to your current list.

5. Choose a brush tip to use for your business card design. I'm using the Butterfly brush tip.

6. Click Shape Dynamics. Set the Minimum Diameter value to 10%. The higher the level, the more uniform the brush tip size will be. For this exercise, we'll create a varied brush tip size.

7. Click Scattering. In the Scatter Options shown in Figure 18.2, set the Scatter to 600%. Set the Count to 1 and the Count Jitter to 50%. The Scattering option controls the randomness and spread of the brush strokes.

8. Click Color Dynamics. Set the Foreground/Background Jitter to 50%. This causes the brush to use the foreground and background colors equally. Set the Hue Jitter to 5% and the Saturation Jitter to 15%. This gives you some variation in color.

9. Click Other Dynamics. Setting the Opacity Jitter to 90% gives you a great deal of variation in the opacity of each brush stroke.

10. Click Wet Edges and Smoothing. These aren't necessary, but I especially like the effects created with the Wet Edges option.

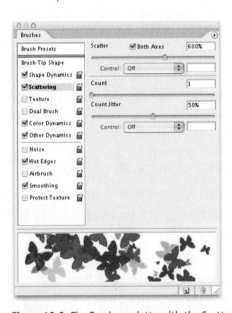

Figure 18.2. The Brushes palette with the Scattering options visible.

Inside Scoop

Click and drag the Brushes tab onto your screen to remove it from the Palette Dock and add it to your viewable palettes.

Next, you'll use your custom brush settings to paint a swatch of patterned brush strokes across your business card. You can then add text elements to complete your card.

To add a design using your custom brush tip:

1. Choose a background and foreground color by clicking each swatch and picking a color. Your brush tip is going to paint colors in between the two. I used a dark brown and dusty light green in mine.

2. Press the] key to increase your brush diameter, or press the [key to decrease the diameter.

3. Click and drag your mouse cursor across the screen to add your design. You may need to undo and try again until you get a result you like.

4. Add some extra touches by increasing your brush diameter quite a bit and adding one or two stamps to your design. The larger butterflies on the right side of the card were created with a large brush diameter setting by repeatedly clicking to create one butterfly at a time. Figure 18.3 was created with two different brush diameters.

5. Select the Type tool from the Toolbox or press the letter T.

6. Add your information, such as name, title, address, and telephone, to the business card. Use the Character and Paragraph palettes to format your text. Use colors that go well with your brush pattern.

Figure 18.3. An effect created by using the Butterfly brush tip with scattering and color options.

Bright Idea!

To get some ideas for your business card design, start paying special attention to business cards you come across in your daily life. Search the Web or browse the design section of your local bookstore for design ideas.

7. To get the layered text effect you see in Figure 18.1, create a text layer and then click and drag it onto the Create New Layer Icon to duplicate it. Change the font size and color in the Character palette.

8. Change the opacity setting for the larger font by adjusting the Opacity field in the Layers palcttc.

You now have your very own business card design. If you are taking the design to a professional printer, be sure to read Chapter 19 for prepress tips. Next, I'll show you a quick tip for creating a full page of business cards to print on your home printer.

You can create a custom Picture Package layout to print your business card to your home printer by following these steps:

1. Choose File ⇨ Automate ⇨ Picture Package to open the setup screen.

2. Click the Layout Edit button below the Layout Preview on the bottom right of the screen. The Edit Layout dialog box appears.

3. Type a name for your layout and choose 8.5" x 11.0" (or fill in the paper size to which you'll be printing).

4. Click one of the images (referred to in the Edit Layout window as an Image Zone) in your preview and change its dimensions to 3.5 x 2 inches for a standard business card size, or choose your own size.

5. Remove any other image zones in the preview by clicking them and clicking the Delete Zone button.

6. Option+click (Alt+click) your resized image zone and select Duplicate from the drop-down list.

7. Click and drag your new zone into place.

8. Repeat steps 6 and 7 until you've created a layout similar to Figure 18.4.

9. Click Save. You'll be asked to enter a filename for your newly created layout. Once it's created, you'll return to the main Picture Package window.

10. Click OK in the Picture Package window to accept your settings and generate a new document using the layout you created.

Bright Idea!

Use guides to help you place crop marks or position your business card layout for printing on perforated cards. Choose View ⇨ Rulers to display rulers. Click and drag from the rulers onto your design to add guides. See Chapter 2 for more information about Guides and Rulers.

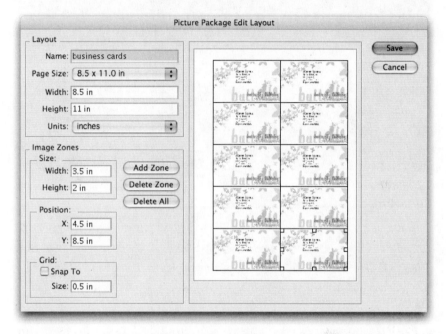

Figure 18.4. A custom Picture Package dialog box with a layout for business cards.

You can now print your business card design to your home printer using a nice card stock. You might want to add some cutting guides with the Line tool between each card to make cutting easier. There are also some perforated business card papers on the market. The trick is lining up your layout to the perforations.

Combining photos and text into a brochure design

You can create a simple yet powerful brochure design with a photo, some creative filters, and the right combination of colors. The brochure created in Figure 18.5 was an imaginary brochure I created for the Natural History Museum of London. I used a photo I had taken on a trip to

London as the main image and then added color and text to complete the design. This could be the outside of a brochure or the beginnings of a Web site design.

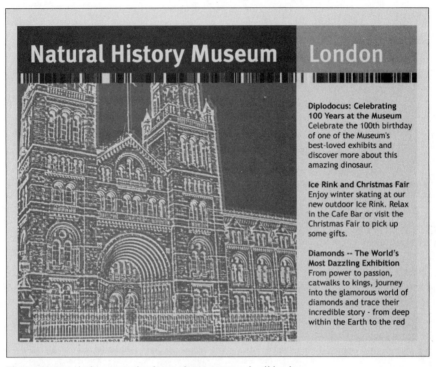

Figure 18.5. A design created using a photo, text, and solid colors.

I liked the look of light lines on a dark background. I chose a chocolate brown for the background color and a grayish powder blue for the header text and the foreground lines of the image. Of course, your photo sources are going to vary, so be creative with your design. The steps of this project can be altered to suite your photo and design; you can use any of the Sketch filters and get similar looks. I'm partial to the look you get with the Photocopy filter.

You can create a design using a photo and the Photocopy filter by following these steps:

1. Open a photo to use as your main design. Buildings work well with this filter.

2. Make a backup copy of your image layer by dragging and dropping it on the Create New Layer button on the bottom of the Layers palette.

3. Choose a light foreground color and a dark background color.

4. Choose Filter ⇨ Sketch ⇨ Photocopy. The Filter Gallery launches with the Photocopy filter options visible. Adjust your settings to achieve the look you want.

5. Click OK to apply your filter settings to your photo. You should have achieved an effect similar to Figure 18.6.

Figure 18.6. A photo with the Photocopy filter applied using a light foreground color and a dark background color.

You now have the main image for your design. Next, you'll enlarge your canvas area and add some different colored boxes to hold your text.

Watch Out!
You may need to resize your image to fit the page size for which you are creating. Images that have been manipulated with the sketch filters are a little more forgiving when it comes to enlarging. Watch out for pixilation when enlarging your image; try to avoid enlarging your original if possible.

To create the layout for a letter-sized brochure design, follow these steps:

1. Choose Image ⇨ Canvas Size. Assuming your image is smaller than 11 x 8.5 inches, increase your canvas Width to 11 inches and Height to 8.5 inches.

2. Click the box on the bottom left of the placement thumbnail as shown in Figure 18.7. This increases the canvas space above and to the right of your image.

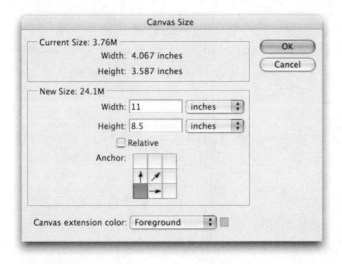

Figure 18.7. The Canvas Size window with image placement.

3. Choose Foreground from the Canvas extension color drop-down list. If you'd like to choose another color, click the swatch and choose a new color using the Color Picker window.

4. Click OK to extend your canvas.

5. Select the Rectangle tool from the Toolbox or press the letter U.

6. Click the Shape Layers button in the Options bar.

7. Click the foreground color swatch and choose a new color for the title background. I'm using a dark brown.

8. Click and drag a rectangle above your image.

9. Click the foreground color swatch to choose a new color for the subtitle area of your design.

10. Click and drag a rectangle for your subtitle background.

11. Click the foreground color and choose a color for the main text area of your design. Because the text in this area is going to be smaller, be sure to choose a very light or very dark color so that your text is more legible.

12. Click and drag a rectangle for the background of your main text.

You should have something like the design in Figure 18.8. All that's left for your design is the multicolored band underneath the title and the text elements for title, subtitle, and main content.

Figure 18.8. The brochure design after adding block shapes with the Rectangle tool.

Finally, add some text elements to your design. If you are unfamiliar with Photoshop's type tools, I recommend reading through Chapter 9 before continuing. The title and subtitle use regular point type. The main

Hack

Create a striped graphic larger than you need and add a layer mask to resize it. You'll be able to reuse it for other designs more easily.

content text was created using paragraph type, so that the text would wrap around the bounding box nicely without my having to adjust paragraph breaks every time I resized the text.

To add point and paragraph type to your design:

1. Choose Window ⇨ Character to display the Character palette.

2. Select the Horizontal Type tool from the Toolbox or press the letter T.

3. Click the color swatch in the Character palette and select a color for your title.

4. Change the font face and size in the Character palette.

5. Click the title area and enter your title text.

6. If you need to adjust the font size and face, highlight the text and change the elements in the Character palette.

7. Press Enter when you are satisfied with your text.

8. Click the Subtitle area and add text. Change the font face, color, and size if you need to.

9. Click and drag to create a large paragraph text box on the right-hand content column of your design. Leave room on the top, bottom, and sides so your text doesn't go all the way to the edge of the content box. Figure 18.9 shows the bounding box around the content text.

10. Change the font size and font face, and then add content to your paragraph text box. You can choose to make some of the type bold, such as the content headers. Highlight any text you would like to change and modify any of the settings in the Character palette.

You now have a basic design for a brochure. To add extra dimension to mine, I duplicated the photocopy image and moved the copied layer slightly. I lowered the opacity of the second layer so that it was barely visible.

The band of multicolored stripes was created with the Brush tool. I made a simple rectangular selection in a new layer with the Marquee tool. The lines were created with the Brush tool with varying thicknesses and colors. I pressed and held the Shift key to keep my brush strokes straight. I used variations of colors that were used in the other elements of my design to keep the colors cohesive.

Watch Out!

Be careful how you overlay images. The Layers palette displays the layers from top to bottom. Before declaring your work done, zoom in and make sure all the corners match up correctly and there are no mistakes in overlapping.

Figure 18.9. Paragraph text with a visible bounding box.

Figure 18.10 is a snapshot of the Layers palette from the finished design. I added extra padding around the outside of my design by including an additional solid color background. This might make a nice layout for the front page of a Web design.

Combining filters and adjustment layers

In the next project, you'll create a layered design with multiple effects and styles. You can create a great-looking design by running different filters and effects on copies of the same layer and then blending them together by adjusting each layer's opacity setting. The design in Figure 18.11 was created by duplicating the same photo layer and applying different effects to each copy. I blended them together by adjusting opacity settings.

In this design, you'll layer several copies of the same image one on top of the other. You'll run some different filter effects and adjustments on the images to create an interesting look. With all the projects in this chapter, get creative and try different effects to come up with your own unique designs.

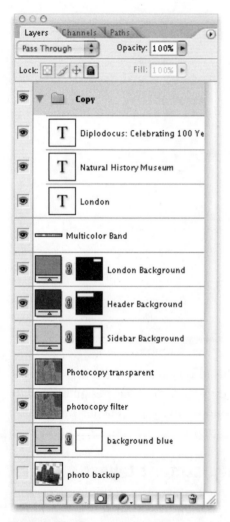

Figure 18.10. The Layers palette for the brochure.

Figure 18.11. A book cover design created with multiple filters and adjustment layers.

You can create a halftone dot effect with Halftone and Threshold by following these steps:

1. Open a photo to use for your design.

2. Create a copy of your image layer by dragging and dropping it on the Create New Layer button on the bottom of the Layers palette.

3. Choose Filter ➪ Sketch ➪ Halftone Pattern. The Filter Gallery appears with the Halftone Pattern filter applied to a preview of your image.

4. Increase the dot size by moving the Size slider to the right until the dots are fairly large.

5. Click OK to apply the filter to your image.

6. With the same image selected in the Layers palette, choose Image ⇨ Adjustments ⇨ Threshold. Your dots are going to turn black and white. Adjust the settings until you have some interesting dots happening in your image. You're going to lower the opacity quite a bit, so this image will help add texture to your image.

7. Click OK to apply the Threshold settings.

8. Click and drag to lower the opacity on your halftone image layer to 20% in the Layers palette. Your original image should show through and look similar to Figure 18.12.

Figure 18.12. A halftone image layered at 20% opacity over the original photo.

Bright Idea!

You can get a nice plaid effect by first using the dot Pattern Type and then running the filter a second time using the line Pattern Type. The circular Pattern Type creates interesting effects by drawing concentric circles from the center out.

The next few steps add a photo filter adjustment layer to your design. I actually used two photo filters on this image. The first photo filter was called Sepia; the second photo filter was called Underwater. The two balanced each other out to give my image a washed-out look, like an old color photo from the '60s.

To add photo filters to your design to simplify colors:

1. Create another copy of your original image layer. Drag and drop its thumbnail onto the Create New Layer button.

2. Choose Filter ⇨ Stylize ⇨ Solarize. There are no options to worry about with this filter. It just does what it does. Make sure your newly solarized image layer is below the halftone image layer.

3. Choose Layer ⇨ New Adjustment Layer ⇨ Photo Filter. Two dialog boxes appear, one after the other. Enter the name of your layer in the first dialog box; you'll be using the Sepia filter, so you can call it **sepia**. In the second layer, select Sepia from the drop-down list of filters.

4. Click OK to add your new adjustment layer to the Layers palette.

The rest of the design is straightforward. I created the transparent band of color for the book title by selecting a rectangular area and then creating a new solid color adjustment layer. If you have an active selection, the solid color layer automatically creates a mask of your selection. You can always resize the selection area layer by performing a Free Transformation (choose Edit ⇨ Free Transform) on the layer. The Layers palette in Figure 18.13 shows a list of all the layers associated with this design.

I added texture to the text by using the grunge text trick discussed in Chapter 9. I used an old sidewalk as my source photo to get small scratches and clumps in the texture. I ran a Threshold adjustment on the sidewalk and copied only the black parts of the image into a new layer of my design file. I then selected the black specks by ⌘+clicking (Ctrl+clicking) the layer thumbnail and added a Layer Mask using the selection.

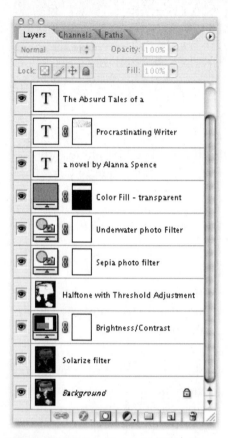

Figure 18.13. A list of layers for the book cover design.

Creating resizable graphics from low-resolution images

The next project is going to differ greatly depending on what photo you use. This technique works especially well on high contrast portraits. You can use any low-resolution photo from the Internet as a base for your

Bright Idea!

If you are working from a color photo, convert it to black and white by choosing Image ⇨ Adjustments ⇨ Desaturate.

design. Because I don't have a reference to the images you might be using, I will show you how I created the design in Figure 18.14 and hopefully the same or similar steps will work for your image.

By applying a Posterize adjustment to your image, you'll be simplifying the color or shade of your image to about four different colors. The key to this project is to find a Posterize level that gives you the best descriptive interpretation of your image using simple blocks of color.

When applying the Posterize adjustment, pay special attention to important details and shapes such as eyes. The photo in Figure 18.15 is a public domain photo of Joan Vollmer that I'll be using as my source photo. This image is in 72 dpi, and I'll need to create vector art to use in my 300-dpi design. In this exercise, I use Select ⇨ Similar to add similar blocks of color to the selection. You may find that the different colors are too similar, even with your Magic Wand set to a Tolerance of 0. If this is the case, you can Shift+select other areas to add them to the selection.

Figure 18.14. An image created with Posterize and Paths.

You can create vector art from a low-resolution photograph by following these steps:

1. Open a photo in Photoshop to use as your image source for the vector art you'll create. The low-resolution photo I used for this example is shown in Figure 18.15.

2. Drag and drop the image thumbnail onto the Create New Layer icon in the Layers palette to make a copy.

3. Choose Image ⇨ Adjustments ⇨ Posterize. A dialog box appears. Your image will appear in simplified colors.

4. Adjust the Levels value by using the up and down keys on your keyboard or typing in a new value. You'll usually get the best results from values between 3 and 8. I was able to get the most interesting shapes around the eyes by using a level of 7 on my photo.

Figure 18.15. The source photo for the posterized vector graphic.

5. Click OK to accept and apply your changes.

6. Switch to the Paths palette. If it isn't currently visible on your screen, choose Window ➪ Paths.

7. Click the black arrow on the top of the Paths palette and choose Select.

8. Select the Magic Wand tool from the Toolbox or press the letter W.

9. Change the Tolerance to 0 in the Options bar.

10. Click the darkest area of your posterized image.

11. Choose Select ➪ Similar to add the other dark spots to the selection.

12. Click the Make Work Path from Selection button on the bottom of the Paths palette. It is the circle icon with anchor points protruding from the sides. This creates your first path.

13. Double-click the path name and rename it **Darkest**.

14. Click in the open area of the Paths palette to deselect the newly created path.

15. Repeat steps 10 to 14 for the three remaining color values. Be sure to give them descriptive names like medium-dark, medium-light, and highlight. You should end up with four paths similar to Figure 18.16, representing the various shades in the photo.

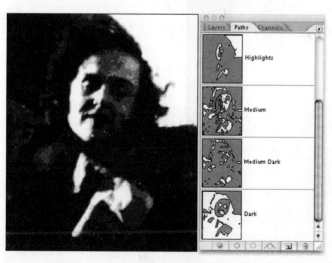

Figure 18.16. The Paths palette with four paths representing four levels of color.

Inside Scoop

Check the Only Web Colors check box on the bottom of the Color Picker to limit your color palette and make choosing a color shade easier.

16. Choose Image ⇨ Image Size to open the dialog box for resizing your image. My design will be used for CD cover art, so I want it to be a minimum of 5 x 5 inches with a resolution of 200. Be sure to keep the Constrain Proportions check box checked.

17. Click OK to resize your image. You'll probably have to zoom out a bit since you've substantially increased the size of the image.

Now that you've created and enlarged paths that represent each shade of your image, fill in each path with color and create a single layer of your image that you can convert into a Smart Object. You'll work from dark to light to compensate for any areas that may have overlapped.

You can add solid color fills to your paths and convert your image to a Smart Object by following these steps:

1. Choose Layer ⇨ New ⇨ Layer or use the key command ⌘+Shift+N (Ctrl+Shift+N).

2. Click the foreground color swatch and choose a color for your darkest color.

3. Click the path for your darkest color areas in the Paths palette to highlight it.

4. Click the Fill Path with Foreground Color button on the bottom of the Paths palette. It looks like a circle filled with gray.

5. Repeat steps 2 to 4 for the remaining paths. You should end up with an image similar to Figure 18.17.

6. Choose Layer ⇨ Smart Objects ⇨ Group Into New Smart Object.

After you've converted your image to a Smart Object, you'll be able to resize it without having to worry about losing image quality. You've now

Bright Idea!

Because each image is going to differ greatly, you may need to add more than four colors or try to posterize your image with another Levels settings to get the best results.

got a cool poster-style graphic from a low-resolution photograph that you can use as a design element. The steps may seem long, but once you get the hang of it, you can create a great-looking graphic from a low-quality photo in a couple of minutes.

The three apples and the crown image in Figure 18.18 were created from low-resolution clip art in the same way. Instead of creating a multi-colored image, I used a Threshold adjustment to convert the image to black and white. I selected all the black areas and saved them as a path.

I layered the image of Joan with an illustration of an apple by lowering the opacity of the apple layer. Both the illustrated apple and the image of Joan were masked using a layer mask. I layered some of the text by duplicating the original text layer and increasing the font size of the second layer. I decreased the copied layer's opacity so the text would blend in with the background.

Figure 18.17. An image created with colored paths from a posterized image.

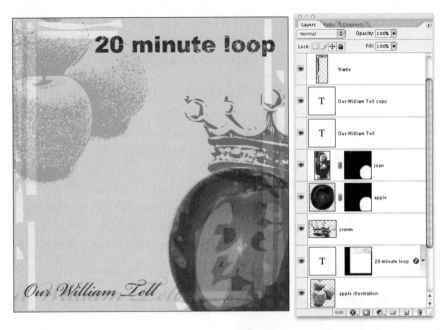

Figure 18.18. The finished design and the list of layers that comprise the different elements of the design.

I hope the design examples in this chapter have sparked your creativity and you are busily conjuring up new designs.

Just the facts

- Use the Picture Package Automation tool to lay out several business cards onto one printable page.

- Create a simple brochure by converting a photograph to a two-color drawing using the Sketch filters. Use complementary colored blocks around the photo to frame your text elements.

- Design with multiple layered images by adjusting opacity and blending modes.

- Create rescalable vector art from a low-resolution photo by posterizing the image down to four or five shades and then creating paths from the various shades of color.

Preparing for Print or Web

GET THE SCOOP ON...
Printable sizes from digital cameras ▪ Choosing the
best paper for your inkjet printer ▪ The best methods for
converting to CMYK ▪ Preparing files for 4-color offset
printing ▪ Ordering prints online

Printing Your Work

We've all experienced the moment of frustration when we've spent so much time perfecting the color in an image only to find that when we print it, we get a muddy printout that is much darker than the on-screen image. Creating color on your computer monitor is an entirely different ballgame than printing inks onto paper. There are many factors at play here. You need to consider your monitor color, paper stock, your printer choice, and a handful of other variables. Getting the colors you see on your screen to print perfectly is not a simple task, but I hope to point you in the right direction to get the best image quality you can from your prints. Photoshop has spent a great deal of time developing its printing technology, and it makes the process of going from screen to print painless. With just a little extra attention, you can transform your prints from good to great.

This chapter shares some wisdom about resolution, color mode, and printer types. You'll learn some pointers for getting the best color out of your home printer and for preparing your files for a professional printer. You'll also learn some easy online options for printing your own custom stamps, greeting cards, or standard-sized photo prints.

Chapter 19

Understanding megapixels and printing

If you are planning on printing from a digital camera, you should know a thing or two about what size prints you can get from the various pixel ratings available in digital cameras. The pixel rating refers to the number of megapixels your camera is capable of capturing. A megapixel is equal to one million pixels. So if you have an image that is 1200 pixels wide by 1600 pixels high, your image is made up of just under two million pixels (1,200 × 1,600 = 1,920,000). The camera in Figure 19.1 is a consumer-level camera with an integrated lens.

Figure 19.1. A digital camera with an integrated lens.

Most printers get the best quality out of images that are a minimum of 240 dpi (dots per inch). The most commonly used resolution for printing is 300 dpi. Whatever the pixel rating on your camera is, try to shoot at the highest setting possible. Even if you don't intend to print your images, you may find that you want to later. You can't add details to a photo after it's taken. Shooting at the highest settings gives you more options for printing or any other project you may find yourself involved in — like for example, writing a Photoshop book!

I have a 3-megapixel camera. At its highest setting, I can get images that are 2048 x 1536 pixels. At a resolution of 300 dpi I can get a high-quality image that is roughly 5 x 7 inches. If I halve the resolution to 150 dpi, and keep the same pixel proportions, I can get a medium-quality image

Bright Idea!

If you are interested in digital photography and want more help finding the right camera, check the appendices for books specializing in digital photography.

of about 13.5 x 10.25 inches. Trying to stretch my image any farther than that will not produce the greatest results. The lower the resolution, the fewer dots per inch available to render the image. This means less information for your printer to display, resulting in images that look pixilated or blocky. Table 19.1 lists some of the high-quality print sizes you can get from various pixel ratings.

Table 19.1. Digital camera printing resolutions per megapixel	
Megapixels	**Printable Size**
8+	Up to 20-x-30-inch high-quality prints. Most 8-megapixel (or higher) cameras offer Camera Raw file format capabilities for professional image quality.
6 to 7	11-x-14-inch high-quality prints. 20-x-30-inch medium- to high-quality prints. Some 6- and 7-megapixel cameras offer Camera Raw capabilities for professional image quality.
4 to 5	Medium- to high-quality 8-x-10-inch prints.
2 to 3	High-quality 4-x-6-inch prints, medium- to high-quality 5-x-7-inch prints.

Finding the right printer

With computer electronics becoming cheaper, better, and more accessible, there's no reason you can't find yourself an affordable inkjet or laser printer for your home. This section covers some basic information about finding the right printer and choosing the best paper for your budget and needs.

Purchasing a home printer

For getting near-photo-quality results with a relatively low number of prints, you can't beat an inkjet printer. They can range from $50 to $1,000, and most produce fantastic results. Most have drivers that prefer to print in RGB color so you don't have to monkey around with changing color modes. Inkjet printers are great for personal use or small businesses not planning to print a high volume of pages per month.

Epson, Canon, Kodak, and HP make great consumer-level inkjet printers. I advise you find a computer store where you can compare prints in person. Most companies provide print samples for you to compare. You may even be able to print your own photos from some of the models that offer memory card slots. When shopping around, be sure to bring your digital camera's memory card with you so that you'll be ready to put a printer to the test.

The ink and paper can eat up your wallet quickly, so they are best used for making a small number of prints. I wouldn't recommend mass-producing fliers on an inkjet printer. For larger jobs, you are much better off investigating the many affordable color laser printers available on the market. Many are targeted towards personal and home business use. Color laser printers typically range from $300 to $3,000 and the ink cartridges last much longer than inkjet cartridges. For even larger jobs, like mass mailings, postcards, and brochures, consider using a low-cost color copier or a 4-color offset printer. Towards the end of the chapter, I've listed some of my favorite postcard and business card printing places. The photo in Figure 19.2 illustrates the sometimes-painful expenses you can run up against when printing large numbers of color prints on an inkjet printer.

Figure 19.2. Color Inkjet cartridges can eat up your wallet.

Watch Out!

When shopping for printers, check the cost per page, or CPP for short. The average cost per page for laser printers is between $.03 and $.08 a page. Inkjet printers average at $.20 to $.30 a page for color and $.03 to $.06 per page for black and white.

Don't skimp on paper

Inkjet cartridges use wet ink to produce images. The printer produces ink dots that blend slightly while wet to produce a near-photo-quality image. You want a paper with enough absorption for the inks to stick to it. If you tried to print on a shiny plastic sheet, you'd end up with a mess of ink. On the other hand, most cheap photocopier-quality papers are too porous. They soak up the inks like a sponge and your image turns out blotchy, wet, and smeared. They are typically so thin that your paper warps from the moisture of the inks.

Fortunately, there are more and more paper options for inkjet printers. The cheapest option is a ream of standard white paper that is made especially for inkjet printers. It is very similar to photocopier paper but is much smoother and is made from a heavier paper stock. This paper is fine for printing files with mostly text or simple graphics; it works fine when you just need a proof of your image. At the time I wrote this book, you could pick up a packet of 500 sheets for between $5 and $10.

On the other end of the spectrum are the glossy photo-quality papers. These can be pricey but yield the best results for printing photographic images. Their surfaces are much smoother and produce the sharpest images. Many are archival quality, boasting a life of 25+ years. The non-archival papers typically last five to eight years before fading and deteriorating.

My recommendation is that you keep a minimum of two paper types handy. Use cheaper paper for text or proofs, and more expensive paper for final output of photographic or graphic work. The best thing to do is to try out several options. Keep notes on what papers you liked or didn't like. There are so many papers available now, it's hard to keep track. Table 19.2 lists the various types of paper available for inkjet printers. The average prices were based on the available prices at the time I wrote this book and may vary.

Inside Scoop

I've had great success with smooth card stock paper. It works well for printing business cards or graphic images.

Table 19.2. Types of paper available for inkjet printers

Paper Type	Description	Price Range
Glossy paper	Use for photos and designs with photo elements. Range from semi-gloss to high gloss. Some are available in acid-free archival quality for prints that last 25+ years. Most non-archival papers have an estimated life of six to eight years.	$.25 to $2 a sheet. The average cost is about $.50 a sheet.
Matte paper	Works well for files with a mixture of photos and text. Low-cost multipurpose papers work well for brochures, e-mails, and rough proofs. Some heavyweight versions work well for photos and fine art.	Multipurpose papers start at $5 to $10 for 500. Average cost is $.10 to $.20 a sheet. The photo-quality or heavy-weight papers can run as much as $1 to $2 a sheet.
Specialty paper	Includes paper for greeting cards, business cards, self-adhesive sheets, transparencies, and photo stickers.	Prices vary widely and can range from $.10 to $3 a sheet.
Art paper	Many professional art paper companies now make fine art papers with a special coating designed for inkjet printers. These papers work well for fine art and photography. High quality, archival paper. Many different textures are available.	Starts at $1 a sheet, up to $5 a sheet.

Use the right printer driver

Your printer needs special software called *printer drivers* to produce the best-quality image. Be sure you are using the latest drivers available for your printer. Check your printer manufacturer's Web site and look for a section called software, downloads, or drivers. Some printer manufacturers make drivers for an entire series of printers. If you can't find your exact model, look for software for that series. For example, I have a

Canon i450 printer. The software for my printer is located under the I Series printer drivers.

Choosing a printing option

If you look under the File menu item as shown in Figure 19.3, you'll see several more printing options than you will usually see in most applications. Photoshop offers options for simple printing using a standard print dialog box, or you can choose from more advanced printing options that give you much greater control over color management.

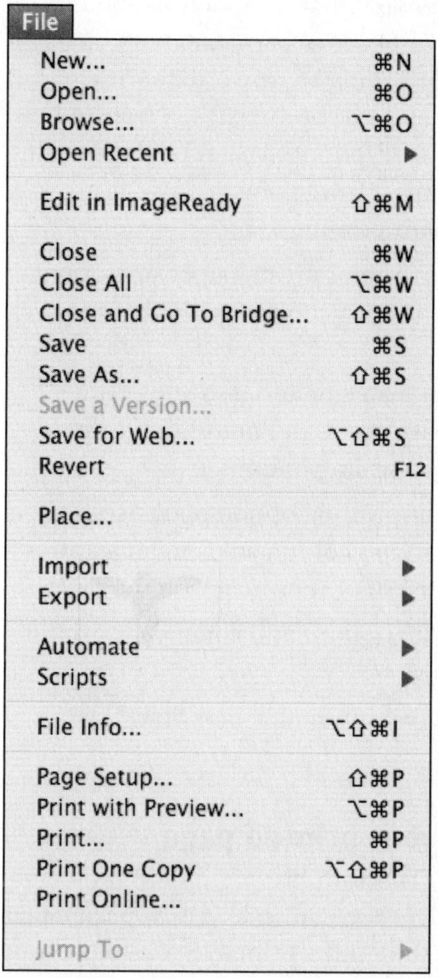

File	
New...	⌘N
Open...	⌘O
Browse...	⌥⌘O
Open Recent	▶
Edit in ImageReady	⇧⌘M
Close	⌘W
Close All	⌥⌘W
Close and Go To Bridge...	⇧⌘W
Save	⌘S
Save As...	⇧⌘S
Save a Version...	
Save for Web...	⌥⇧⌘S
Revert	F12
Place...	
Import	▶
Export	▶
Automate	▶
Scripts	▶
File Info...	⌥⇧⌘I
Page Setup...	⇧⌘P
Print with Preview...	⌥⌘P
Print...	⌘P
Print One Copy	⌥⇧⌘P
Print Online...	
Jump To	▶

Figure 19.3. The bottom of the list shows menu items associated with printing in Photoshop CS2.

> **Hack**
>
> If you are in the habit of using the ⌘+P (Ctrl+P) key command but want to use Print with Preview as your printing option of choice, you can edit Photoshop's key commands. Choose Edit ⇨ Keyboard Shortcuts. Click the key command field you want to change and press and hold the keys you'd like to use. Click Accept to save your changes.

I recommend that you use the Print with Preview option, even if you don't take advantage of all the options available. The biggest advantage you get with Print with Preview is the ability to see how your image is going to fit on your page. This business of pixels, resolution, and document size can be difficult to translate into actual page size. With the Print with Preview option, you have one less thing to worry about. It also has the fantastic option of scaling your image to fit the page, a feature I use quite a bit. The following list is a description of each of the printing options and what features you can expect from them.

The File menu items associated with printing are

- **Page Setup:** Lets you choose your printer driver, paper size, orientation (landscape versus portrait), and scale. Also accessible from the Print dialog boxes.

- **Print:** Bypasses Photoshop's print manager and uses your printer driver features only. You won't have access to Photoshop's color management features or advanced scaling options.

- **Print with Preview:** Make this your printing option of choice. This option takes advantage of Photoshop's color management features and previews the scale and placement of your image on the page.

- **Print One Copy:** Uses the last print options and completely bypasses any print dialog boxes.

- **Print Online:** Lets you order prints from Kodak Easy Share by uploading JPEG files.

Scaling your artwork to fit your printed page

One of the fantastic features of the Print with Preview option is the ability to scale your artwork to fit the page. You can scale it to a specific percentage or allow Photoshop to fill the entire printable area with your image. You can move your artwork around the page or use the centering feature. This next exercise steps through a quick and basic printing test. The exercise in the following section includes some of the color management options in Print with Preview.

To print your document scaled to the paper size:

1. Open the document you would like to print in Photoshop.

2. Choose File ⇨ Print with Preview. The dialog box you see in Figure 19.4 appears with a thumbnail of your image on the left.

3. Click the Page Setup button. You'll be taken to a dialog box where you can choose paper size and printer driver.

4. Select your printer driver from the Format For list.

5. Select the paper size you want to use.

6. Select the paper orientation that fits your image best.

7. Click OK to return to the Print with Preview dialog box.

8. Check the Scale to Fit Media box. Your thumbnail will enlarge to fit the entire preview box, minus the default print margins used by your printer.

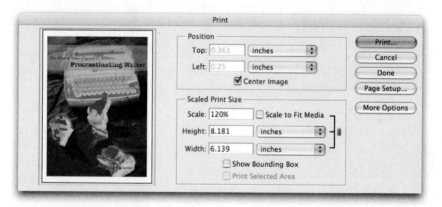

Figure 19.4. The Print with Preview dialog box.

Hack

Speed up printing times by flattening layers. Your inkjet printer isn't a Postscript printer, so there's no benefit in keeping your layers separate, which increases your printing time. Choose Layer ⇨ Flatten Image and then save your flattened image as a separate file. Make sure you don't write over your original file.

Getting good color from your inkjet printer

By letting Photoshop take over the color management side of printing, you'll usually get better results. There are just a few changes you'll need to make. This exercise works for both inkjet and laser printers.

Use Photoshop's color management features to get the best color prints possible from your inkjet printer:

1. Open a document to print.

2. Choose File ⇨ Print with Preview. A dialog box appears with a thumbnail of your image on the left.

3. Click the More Options button to display the color management panel. If you see a button that says Fewer Options, you don't need to click anything. The dialog box in Figure 19.5 is the Print with Preview window with all options viewable.

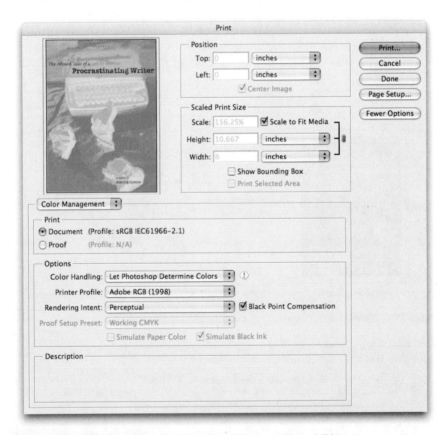

Figure 19.5. The Print with Preview dialog box with more options visible.

4. Choose Color Management from the drop-down list directly below the image preview.

5. Choose Let Photoshop Determine Colors from the Color Handling drop-down list.

6. Choose Adobe RGB (1998) from the Printer Profile drop-down list. If you are using a Laser printer, choose a color profile for your printer model.

7. Click the Print button. You will be taken to the Print dialog box where you can adjust your printer settings.

8. Choose your printer from the Printer drop-down list.

9. Choose Color Options from the drop-down list below the Presets list. It should currently read Copies & Pages. If Color Options is not listed, choose Color Management. The options in this drop-down list are going to vary from one printer to another. Figure 19.6 shows the Color Options panel for a Canon i450 inkjet printer.

10. Choose None from the Color Correction drop-down list.

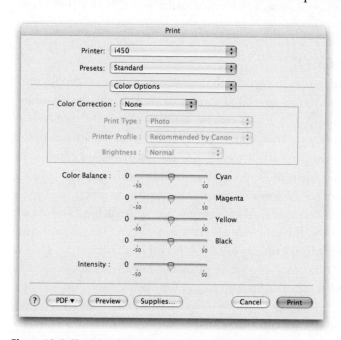

Figure 19.6. The Print dialog box with Color Options visible.

11. Click the drop-down list below the Presets list and choose Quality & Media. Your printer driver might have it listed as something different.

12. Choose the type of paper you'll be printing to from the Media drop-down list.

13. Click the Print button to begin printing.

The two important things here are that you are allowing Photoshop to take over the color correcting by choosing color correction in Photoshop's print dialog box and then disabling the printer's color correcting in the regular Print dialog box, and that you changed the media option to match your paper. Different papers absorb inks differently. Your printer's driver has special software to help correct for this.

Printing in CMYK color mode

You'll need to convert your file to CMYK color mode if you are planning on printing to a laser printer or sending your files to an offset printer. This section covers some basic techniques for getting the best color conversions. I'll also give you some tips for preparing your files for delivering to a professional printing shop.

Converting to CMYK

The RGB color mode can use colors that aren't available in CMYK color mode; it's important to pay special attention to your image details when converting. Photoshop has an excellent built-in converter, but you'll want to double-check your image after you convert it and make any color corrections before sending it off to the printer. Most digital photos do fine when converted from RGB to CMYK. Graphics with very light colors are the most in danger of less-successful conversion, so keep your eyes peeled for light-colored areas. Always save your original file. The more you convert your color, the more image data you lose. Never go back and forth between color modes unless you have no other choice.

The default CMYK color profile is probably not the best choice for your needs. SWOP stands for Specifications for Web Offset Publications and is for use on printers that produce magazines. You are probably going to be printing your images on a sheet-fed offset printer. Before converting, it's important you change your color profile settings.

To convert your color profile settings:

1. Choose Edit ⇨ Color Settings. You'll see the Color Settings dialog box with the default setting of U.S. Web coated (SWOP) v2 selected for CMYK.

2. Change the CMYK drop-down list to U.S. Sheetfed Coated v2, shown in Figure 19.7.

3. Click OK.

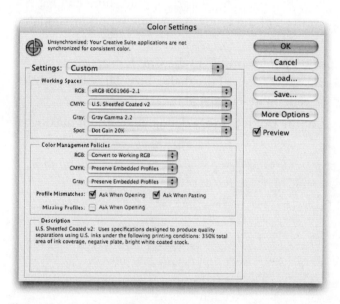

Figure 19.7. The Color Settings dialog box with U.S. Sheetfed Coated selected as the CMYK value.

You are now ready to convert your image to CMYK.

To convert your image to CMYK:

1. Choose Image ⇨ Mode ⇨ CMYK.

2. Check your image carefully for any additional color correction needs.

3. Make color adjustments using Curves or Levels adjustments.

4. Choose File ⇨ Save As and save your converted image to a new file, leaving your original intact.

Installing a color profile for a CMYK laser printer

Most inkjet printers don't have their own color profiles; they usually just use the sRGB color profile. When you are printing to a laser printer or other CMYK printer, you'll want to get the latest color profile or ICC file for that printer.

If you installed your printer using the software that came with it, your color profile is probably available. First check to make sure you have a color profile installed in your computer.

To check for your printer's color profile:

1. Launch Photoshop.

2. Choose Edit ⇨ Color Settings. The dialog box that you see in Figure 19.8 appears with all of the Color Management options available to you.

3. Look for your printer's color profile in the CMYK drop-down list under the Working Spaces area of the dialog box. The color profiles for my printer are called Phaser 8400 Standard Paper.

4. Click Cancel to exit the Color Settings dialog box without making any changes.

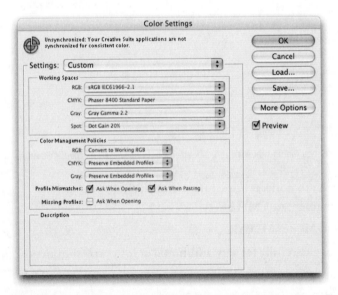

Figure 19.8. The Color Settings dialog box with the printer's color profile selected.

If you found your color profile, great! If not, try downloading and installing the latest drivers for your printer. Visit your printer's Web site for the latest. If your driver software doesn't come with its own installer, here is where you should install your printer's ICC files:

Watch Out!

Your changes will not take effect until you restart all of your Adobe applications. After installing color profiles, be sure to restart any open Adobe applications.

- **Windows:** Right-click an ICC file and select Install Profile. You can also copy the files by hand into the WINDOWS\system32\spool\ drivers\color folder on Windows XP or the WINNT\system32\spool\ drivers\color folder on Windows 2000.

- **Mac:** Copy the ICC files to the /Library/Application Support/ Adobe/Color/Profiles/Recommended folder.

Soft-proofing colors

Photoshop gives you a way to get a sneak peak of how your image will print on various printers. The results from screen to print are going to vary depending on the paper you print to and how accurate your monitor colors are.

To soft-proof your image before printing, follow these steps:

1. Choose View ⇨ Proof Setup ⇨ Custom. The dialog box in Figure 19.9 appears.

2. Select your printer's color profile from the Device to Simulate list. Some printers, such as the Tektronics Phaser, offer a variety of paper choices.

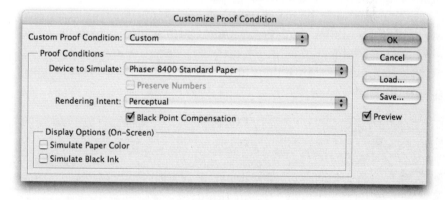

Figure 19.9. The Customize Proof Condition dialog box.

Bright Idea!

Install the color profile of the professional printer you'll be printing to in order to take full advantage of soft-proofing.

3. Click OK. The View ⇨ Proof Colors options automatically activate.

4. Choose View ⇨ Proof Colors to turn off color proofing.

The soft-proofing features also let you preview what each color plate will look like. To preview each individual plate, choose one of the working plate options under View ⇨ Proof Setup.

Finding a printer and preparing files

The most important thing that I can stress about getting the best printing results from a professional printer lies in developing a solid professional relationship with the printer. Get to know them. Ask them questions. Most professional printers would prefer getting the chance to educate you on preparing your files correctly before you hand them in. Giving them the chance to help you first will save the both of you headaches, keep you on schedule, and get the best results possible.

If your printer isn't responsive to your questions, find another printer. Either they won't give you instructions because they don't know what they are doing, or they are simply uncooperative with beginners. Neither of these scenarios is going to get you the professional quality prints you deserve. It's your money; spend it wisely!

On the other side, be nice to your printer technician. During a typical week, they encounter panicky customers with wildly unrealistic schedules, unexpected technical problems with printers, and are often sleep-deprived and cranky. Give them the benefit of the doubt and they will return the favor.

Bright Idea!

If your printing place has a Web site, they probably offer guidelines for preparing files. Read the guidelines first. You'll be more knowledgeable when you need to talk to your printer, and they'll appreciate the effort.

Choosing a printer type

There are many different options for professional color printing. The most common and affordable options are printers that offer a 150-lpi (lines per inch) resolution with a mix of CMYK inks. They produce halftone dots by combining the four inks. These prints are most commonly found in postcards, greeting cards, and most four-color promotional materials like flyers and business cards. They are reasonably priced; 500 postcards with four colors on the front and black and white on the back will run you about $99. They typically have a quicker turnaround of two to five days. Photographic-quality printers such as color Linotronic printers or AGFA color printers produce photo-quality images at around 1200, 2500, or 3000 dpi. These prints are more expensive and have longer turnaround times. They are suitable for printing small runs of fine-art-quality prints. The photo in Figure 19.10 is of a four-color offset printer.

Figure 19.10. A four-color printing press.

Getting a quote

You have several things to think about before getting a quote from your printer. Be prepared by writing out a list of your needs before you approach a printing place. You'll need to consider your requirements for the following:

Watch Out!
If you are printing a postcard that you intend to mail out, you'll want to consider the cost of the stamps. Oversized postcards require first-class stamps, and the extra cost can add up quickly.

■ **Deadline:** Allow yourself some wiggle room. If you have good communications with your printer, mistakes can be minimized, but always assume Murphy's Law will strike when you least expect it.

■ **Budget:** Your budget is going to help determine the quantity, paper stock, color format, and coating. Know your limits before talking to a printer so that you don't walk away with more than your wallet can handle.

■ **Paper stock:** Consider what thickness or texture of paper you want.

■ **Paper size:** Custom-sized paper costs a great deal more than standard-sized paper. Consider this when you are designing your work. Talk to your printer beforehand to get a list of available standard print sizes.

■ **Quantity:** The amount of copies you need combined with your budget will probably be a determining factor in which printer option you choose.

■ **Glossy or Matte:** You may have the option of choosing between glossy, matte, or satin (somewhere in between the two). Ask to see samples of the various paper types and textures. If you can't go directly to the printer, they may be able to mail you paper samples.

■ **Embossing:** There are two types of embossing methods. The traditional involves running the paper over raised metal plates. The raised-ink method adds several coats of ink to raise the surface. Contact your printer for instructions on how to prepare images for embossing.

■ **Proof:** Whenever possible, ask for a printing proof. When you get your proof, check for not only color but also layout, content, typos, and missing elements.

Can I use color text?

When a color printer tries to print text with a combination of printing inks, the printer needs to make several passes over the same text area. You may get colors that don't perfectly match up together, and this becomes more apparent with smaller font sizes. It's best to avoid printing colored text smaller than 12 points. To be safe, if you are using colored text, ask the printer for a proof before running off hundreds of copies.

Bleed and trim

If you have images that you want to extend all the way to the edge of your document, you'll want to "bleed" the image beyond the crop marks. Most printers recommend a bleed of .125 inches (⅛ of an inch). Some four-color printers are gang run, meaning multiple documents are printed alongside each other. The printer cuts your images to slightly smaller than the printable area to ensure that no images overlap each other.

Because your printouts may shift during the cutting process, be sure to keep any text or important elements that you don't want to be trimmed .125 inches inside the crop line. This will ensure they aren't accidentally snipped off.

Preparing final artwork — saving to EPS or TIFF

When delivering your files to the printer, you will probably be asked to convert your document to EPS or TIFF format first. This saves the printer the hassle of dealing with Photoshop file versions or having to install font faces. Instructions are going to vary from printer to printer, so be sure to ask your printer for guidelines if you haven't been supplied with any.

Using rich blacks for text

When using black type that will be printed on a CMYK printer, it's recommend that you use rich blacks instead of the regular black. Create a rich black swatch in your Swatches palette for convenience. Rich black is 45 Cyan, 35 Magenta, 20 Yellow, and 100 Black. The Color Picker window in Figure 19.11 shows the CMYK settings for rich back.

Watch Out!
When saving your file in TIFF format, you'll be asked if you want to use LZW compression. Most printing places advise you not to use this option. If you need to compress your files, use a zip or Stuffit program after you've saved your file.

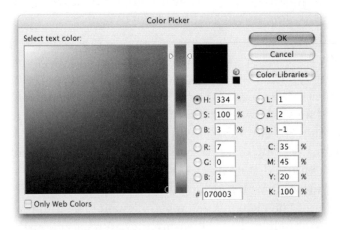

Figure 19.11. The Color Picker window with CMYK rich black settings.

Ordering prints online

Many places offer very affordable prints from digital files. The Print Online menu item automatically takes you to a Kodak Easy Share interface where you can order prints from a currently-opened JPEG file. The Kodak Easy Share system lets you choose from a variety of paper sizes and types, and you can order single or multiple copies of your images. It's quick and painless, and the print quality matches that of traditional photo prints from film. The first time you select the Print Online option, you'll be prompted to set up a new account. You'll need to be connected to the Internet. Figure 19.12 shows you the Registration page that appears when you first choose File ⇨ Print Online.

Once your account is created, you'll be able to quickly order prints from open JPEG files. If you are currently in a Photoshop file and want a print, Photoshop asks you if you'd like to create a JPEG and takes care of the rest for you. This is a handy option and removes some of the steps involved with other online ordering systems. I'm still not totally sold on

Hack

Once you create a login through the Print Online feature, you can use the same login to access your account through a regular browser by going to KodakGallery.com.

this feature and tend to go straight to the Web site where I can upload multiple files at once.

I personally have had great success with the Costco online print ordering. Costco.com has collaborated with Snapfish.com, and you can either have your prints mailed directly to you or pick them up at a Costco location of your choice. You can choose from several different print sizes and paper options. The Web page in Figure 19.13 shows you some of the printing options available. The prints are very cheap. At the time I wrote this book, a single 4-x-6-inch print cost a measly $.12. The SnapFish.com Web site also gives you the option of picking up your prints at a Walgreen's of your choice.

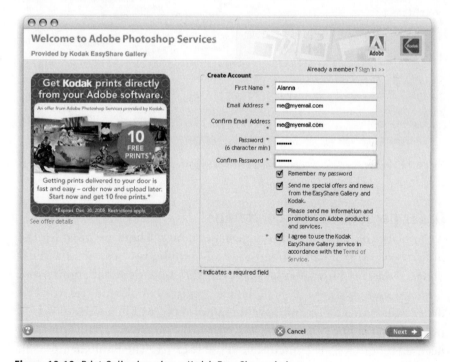

Figure 19.12. Print Online launches a Kodak Easy Share window.

Bright Idea!

Send prints directly to your friends or relatives by changing the shipping address to their mailing address. Most places let you add several shipping addresses. Go to the account settings area of the Web site and look for address book options.

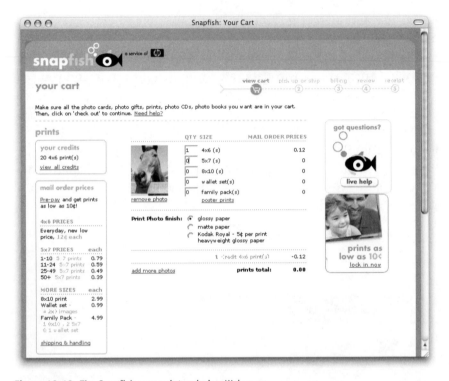

Figure 19.13. The Snapfish.com print ordering Web page.

Order personal postage stamps

A few places online offer custom postage stamps. These are great for the holidays or everyday use. The process is simple; you just need a JPEG image. You can order stamps in seven different denominations from postcard stamps to priority mail stamps. In just a couple minutes, you can order your own stamps and have them delivered within a week. For U.S. postage, make sure the place you are ordering from is an approved licensed vendor for the United States Postal Service. The PhotoStamps.com Web site is shown in Figure 19.14.

Inside Scoop

There is a free Mac downloadable application for creating PhotoStamps available on the Web site. It works with iPhoto and gives you more options for border color and image placement.

Figure 19.14. The PhotoStamps.com setup page for creating custom stamps.

The cost can run high. The price for one sheet is slightly more than twice the face value of the stamps. The more you order, the lower the cost per stamp. The image area of the stamp is about 1.1 inches. These are great fun if you don't mind spending the extra money.

Print a postcard or greeting card

Several places online offer professional-quality greeting cards and postcards from your original art. They provide Photoshop templates for you; all you need to do is follow the instructions and upload the files. They double-check the files, and you can have them shipped to you or you can pick them up if you are local. Table 19.3 is a list of places I've had great success with. I recommend you check out printers in your area and help support your local economy.

Table 19.3. Recommended online postcard-printing places

Printer	Services	Web Site
Modern Postcard	Flat postcards, folder postcards, business cards, catalogs, sales sheets	ModernPostcard.com
Rocket Postcard	Postcards, business cards, posters	RocketPostcards.com
4by6	oversized postcards, business cards	4by6.com

Prices for standard postcards run about $99 for 500 postcards with four colors on the front and black only on the back. You usually have to order a minimum of 500 cards. Before you create your design, be sure you have downloaded the correct templates and have thoroughly read the guidelines.

Just the facts

- Scale your image to fit your paper size in the Print with Preview dialog box.
- Use Print with Preview and allow Photoshop to handle color management for optimal color results.
- Choose a paper made especially for inkjet printers for the best image quality from your home inkjet printer.
- Change your default CMYK color profile to one that matches your target printer to get the best color conversion.
- Order prints of your photos from online services like Costco, Kodak Easy Share, and Snapfish.

GET THE SCOOP ON...
Resizing and optimizing photos for the Web or e-mail ▪
Saving graphics in GIF format ▪ Creating a simple
Web page from start to finish ▪ Removing fringe
from transparent GIFs

Preparing Images for the Web

I mageReady is a sister application for creating images and HTML for the Web. It comes installed with Photoshop and uses much of the same tools. With ImageReady, you can design and generate browser-ready HTML pages and graphics, all without having to learn a single line of HTML code.

The Web is still a relatively low-bandwidth delivery method for information. It's best if you can keep your total page size as small as possible by using image files sparingly and compressing images as much as possible while keeping an acceptable quality. There are a few browser-standard file formats that are used to display images, and each of them optimizes a bit differently.

You don't have to be an optimization expert to create images for the Web. Photoshop and ImageReady come with several excellent presets for quick and painless optimization. This chapter covers optimization techniques for quickly optimizing files using the presets or for squeezing and shrinking your file sizes for optimum performance. I'll show you how to use the slice tools and how to generate HTML from your sliced images.

465

Choosing a file type for the Web

There are three basic choices for the types of image files you can optimize for the Web. The various types offer different compression algorithms and therefore work better on certain types of images.

The different types of Web-compatible optimization file formats are

- **GIF:** Best used for images with large blocks of solid color such as comic book–style illustration and text and line art with little gradations.

- **JPEG:** Best suited for photographs or images with lots of gradients and colors.

- **PNG:** Developed to replace the GIF format, PNG was introduced a few years ago but has been slow to catch on. GIFs can store only up to 8 bits of information per pixel. PNG can support 8-bit or 24-bit color and handles transparency much better than GIF.

Optimizing photos in JPEG format

You've just uploaded your latest set of photos from your digital camera. You are so excited about a few of them; you want to share them with your friends through e-mail immediately. However, sending full-sized digital photos through e-mail is not such a great idea. If you shot the images using your camera's highest setting, the files are probably too large to send. The dimensions of your image are also probably not very user friendly. By shrinking both the dimensions and color data, you can achieve great looking, e-mail friendly photos.

No-fuss resizing and optimization photos

If you have a digital camera, this might be the most common activity you find yourself doing in ImageReady or Photoshop. If you just want to resize and optimize one or two files, here's the quick and simple method:

1. Open a photo in ImageReady.

2. Choose Image ⇨ Image Size. The Image Size dialog box appears.

3. Change the dimensions of your image to something more manageable. I like to shrink my images to somewhere between 450 and 600 pixels wide. Images this size can be viewed on nearly any monitor without forcing your viewer to scroll.

4. Click OK to apply your changes.

5. Open the Optimize palette. If it's not visible on your screen, choose Window ⇨ Optimize. The Optimize palette is the one you see in Figure 20.1.

6. Choose JPEG High from the Preset drop-down list in the Optimize palette.

7. Click the Optimize tab above your document window to preview the setting.

8. Choose File ⇨ Save Optimized As. A Save As dialog box appears.

9. Choose a location to save your file and give it a name.

10. Make sure Images Only is selected from the Format drop-down list.

11. Click Save.

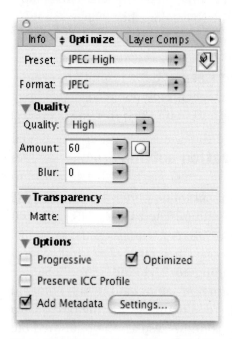

Figure 20.1. The Optimize palette with JPEG options.

Save your file as you normally would any file. You now have a smaller version of your photo that can be easily e-mailed to friends and family.

Bright Idea!

Share your photos with the world by signing up for a photoblog Web site like Flickr.com, My-Expressions.com, or photos.yahoo.com. Most photoblogs offer free limited memberships and very affordable advanced memberships.

Additional JPEG settings and what they mean

There are several other settings for JPEG optimization in the Optimize palette. Here is a list of what they are and what they do:

- **Quality:** There are five standard settings for Quality: Low, Medium, High, Very High, and Maximum. Choosing one of these options changes the value in the Amount field. You can fine-tune the value field by adjusting the slider or entering a new amount in the text field.

- **Blur:** Does exactly what it sounds like. It blurs your image. This comes in handy to blend away JPEG artifacts created when you need to shrink your JPEGs substantially to meet file size restrictions. Use in moderation, if at all.

- **Matte:** You can't create transparent JPEGs, but on images that have transparent areas, you can control what colors they will change to. Without selecting a different Matte color, the transparent parts of your image change to solid white.

- **Progressive:** The Progressive check box adds low-resolution versions to your image that load while the higher-resolution image is loading. This option may increase file size and won't work on some browsers.

Comparing multiple optimization settings for the best option

The tabs along the top of your Document window offer different viewing options for comparing optimization settings. The 2-Up and 4-Up options in ImageReady allow you to compare different settings on the same file. By clicking either 2-Up or 4-Up, you can then click each window separately and adjust the Optimization settings for that window. You'll be able to compare up to 4 different Optimization settings at the same time, as shown in Figure 20.2 and choose the one that gives you the best quality with the lowest file size. Each of the windows displays the optimized file size you'd get with the various settings.

Hack

Change the Document information on the bottom of each panel by clicking the down arrows below each window and choosing a new option. You can view estimated download times, optimize information, or optimize settings.

Figure 20.2. The 4-Up option comparing three different JPEG Quality settings.

Optimizing graphics in GIF format

The GIF format is great for images with large blocks of solid colors and text. Anything that is not a photo and doesn't have any gradients in it will probably optimize best as a GIF image. GIFs typically give you much smaller file sizes than JPEG because the images are simpler. The next section covers the options available for GIF optimization. The options are quite different from JPEG options, as you can see in Figure 20.3. Once you understand the GIF options, you'll be able to use nearly the same set of options when creating PNG files.

Saving a simple GIF

Optimizing an image as a GIF is more complex than when optimizing a JPEG image. There are more options available for saving GIFs, so there are more options to worry about. You can always just use one of the presets; they work well when you aren't concerned with getting the smallest file size possible. When you are delivering images to clients, sometimes size matters a great deal. In those cases, knowing all the tricks to getting the smallest file possible is essential. You'll start with a basic image with a text element and a solid background.

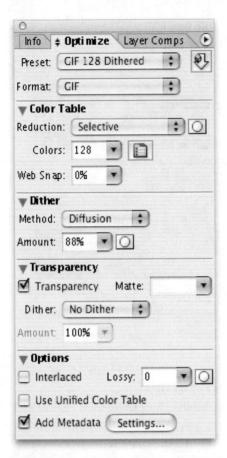

Figure 20.3. The Optimize palette with GIF options.

To create a simple GIF to use for the following exercises, perform these steps:

1. Create a simple banner ad in ImageReady. Choose File ⇨ New to create a new document that is 300 pixels wide by 100 pixels high.

2. Add a solid color background. Click the background color swatch to choose a color. Automatically fill your layer with the current background color by pressing ⌘+Delete (Ctrl+Delete).

3. Add a text element. Choose the Type tool, click anywhere inside your document, and enter some text.

4. Press Enter to accept your new text addition. You can move your text by pressing and holding the ⌘ key (Ctrl) and then clicking and dragging your text to a new location.

Now that you've created your example file, look at some of the options for optimizing GIFs. Figure 20.4 shows a banner ad I've created along with the Optimize palette.

Figure 20.4. A banner ad with the Optimize palette and GIF options displayed.

Because the file you created is comprised of a solid background and a text element, optimizing it as a GIF is going to give you the best results. My image in Figure 20.4 has some vector graphics, which also do best with GIF optimization. Pay special attention to soft edges around type, gradients, drop shadows, or other layer styles when optimizing images as GIFs. If the GIF settings are too low, you will start to see jagged areas in your image.

You can optimize your GIF using the Optimize palette by following these steps:

1. Open your newly created file from the previous example in ImageReady.

2. Bring the Optimize palette to the front. If it is not visible on your screen, choose Window ⇨ Optimize.

3. Select GIF from the Format drop-down list. The GIF options will be displayed.

4. Click the Optimize tab on the top of your Document window to preview your optimization settings.

5. Choose the various choices in the Reduction drop-down list to preview their effects. The Reduction options tell Photoshop what

method to use when reducing the number of colors in your image. With such a simple image you won't be able to tell much difference between the methods. Here is a breakdown of how each reduction method optimizes color:

- **Perceptual.** Reduces colors based on colors to which the human eye is more sensitive.

- **Selective.** The best option for the Web. Similar to Perceptual but with a preference for Web-friendly colors.

- **Adaptive.** Takes an even sampling of all the colors. Usually not as good a quality as Selective, but this method can shave off a few extra bytes from your file size.

- **Restrictive (Web).** I recommend not using Restrictive reduction. This option shifts your colors dramatically and tries and force them into the 216 Web-safe color palette. The Web-safe color palette is very rarely used any more.

6. Choose a Dither method. Dithering helps ImageReady blend colors together when reducing the color palette. Here are the descriptions of each Dither method:

- **No Dither.** Doesn't apply a dithering method. Use this option whenever you can. Dithering doesn't work well on most images.

- **Diffusion.** Produces random patterns of dots.

- **Pattern.** Uses a uniform pattern of dots.

- **Noise.** Similar to Diffusion. Usually the best Dither option if you need to use dithering.

7. Choose the number of colors in your image. This is where you can really shave off file size without losing much detail. For simple images, such as text on a solid background, you can reduce colors down to as much as 4. Be careful with anti-aliased text: If you cut down the palette too much, the edges of your text will look jagged.

The Options panel in the Optimize palette

I've shown you the most commonly used options for optimizing GIF files. A couple fewer common options can come in handy.

Here are some additional features to consider when optimizing your image as a GIF:

- Interlacing produces a simplified preview of the image so that the viewer sees a simplified version of the image while the main image is loading. Not recommended in most cases because it increases file size.

- The Lossy option allows you to remove detail from your image in order to decrease file size. Comes in handy when all other options fail and you don't mind losing some image quality.

Avoiding halos and fringe with transparent GIFs

If you are using anti-aliased graphics, and you plan to place them onto a colored background, you'll need to add a Matte color to your image so that ImageReady knows what color to use to remove the anti-alias fringe from your image. The two options under the GIF settings are Transparency and Matte as shown in Figure 20.5.

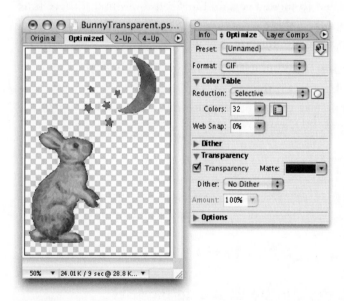

Figure 20.5. A transparent GIF with Matte color selected to match the background color of a Web site.

Watch Out!

The transparency feature affects only images with transparent areas. Be sure you can see the gray-and-white checked pattern somewhere in your image to take advantage of the transparency feature.

Here is a list of descriptions for the transparency settings:

▪ **Transparency:** When this box is unchecked, the transparent parts of your image will be filled in with the Matte color. Check this box to retain transparency.

▪ **Matte:** When Transparency is selected, choose a Matte color that matches the background color of your Web site in order to remove color fringe from the edges of your image. When transparency isn't selected, the image will fill in any transparent areas with the Matte color.

Optimize to file size

When you really need to meet a certain file size requirement, there is an option in the Optimize palette to optimize to a specific file size.

To optimize to a specific file size, follow these steps:

1. Open the file you would like to optimize in ImageReady.

2. Click the black arrow on the top of the Optimize palette and choose Optimize to File Size from the drop-down list. The dialog box that you see in Figure 20.6 appears.

Figure 20.6. The Optimize to File Size dialog box.

Bright Idea!

This option works well when you've created a Web site that needs to be under a certain size. With images that have multiple slices, the options on the bottom of the Optimize to File Size dialog box will be highlighted. Specify that you want the file size to be the equivalent of all the slices.

3. Enter the desired file size in bytes.

4. Choose whether you want ImageReady to choose an optimization method automatically.

What is happening with PNG?

The Portable Network Graphic or PNG format was created as an alternative to the GIF format. It offers many more features than GIF and is especially excellent with transparencies. PNG files can display many more colors than the limited 256-color palette available to GIF and are much better at compressing image data. Sadly, this format has been very slow to be adopted. When it was first introduced, most Web browsers didn't support it. As I write this book, nearly 100 percent of all browsers support most features of PNG, and Photoshop has gradually increased its support of PNG and resolved most of its known software bugs relating to PNG. Slowly, applications seem to be focusing more attention on PNGs; and as enthusiasm grows, support will surely follow.

The PNG-8 options are identical to the GIF options, and PNG-24 has just a small subset of the GIF options. I suggest trying out different settings and comparing them to the results of GIF optimization with the same settings. In Figure 20.7 I'm comparing a transparent image with Selective Reduction and a color palette of 32 colors. I was able to shave off an additional 1K when optimizing with PNG-8. If you have a graphic-heavy Web site, the extra savings can add up to quite a bit.

Watch Out!

Although PNG-24 gives you the best image quality, the file size is substantially larger. Use this option sparingly on Web sites.

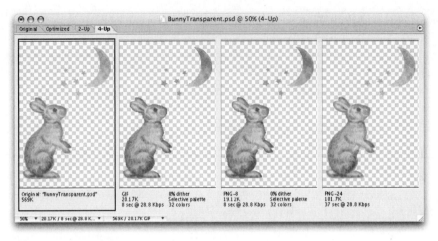

Figure 20.7. A comparison between GIF and PNG optimization.

Slicing layouts for Web sites

This book spends very little time in the realm of Web design. It's a complicated world that I could fill up several books talking about. I'm going to attempt to introduce you to the world of HTML and slicing graphics in just a few short pages. If you are interested in Web design, I encourage you to seek out books that focus on the Web-design side of things. The following pages cover the basics for slicing and generating Web pages using ImageReady's built-in HTML source generator.

The Web pages you'll be creating here will be automatically coded in HTML for you. HTML is a mark-up language for displaying text and graphics in a Web browser. If you've ever viewed the source of a Web page or have experience with HTML development, you know that Web pages consist of nothing more than a lot of code. There is code that handles the organization of the page, code that references images, and code that links to other Web pages. You won't need to write any HTML code, but it's important to understand what is being generated for you. HTML organizes Web pages like jigsaw puzzles made of squares: Everything fits into a grid. What may look like a curvaceous, elegant design, HTML reduces to a grid of boxes. When designing slices, this is an important concept to understand. I'll start you off slowly with a cool pre-installed action in ImageReady that will do all the hard work for you.

Create a simple Web page with the Make Web page action

ImageReady has a handy action for creating a generic Web site layout, which you'll take advantage of in this next section. After all, it will be much easier to explain ImageReady's slicing tools if we have something to start with.

To create a Web site using the Make Web page action:

1. Launch ImageReady.

2. Create a new document. It doesn't matter what size you make it; ImageReady will automatically resize it when you run the action.

3. Open the Actions palette. If it is not visible on your screen, choose Window ⇨ Actions.

4. Click the Make Web page action to highlight it.

5. Click the play button on the bottom of the Actions palette. ImageReady will busily create a generic Web page for you. Give it a minute or two to finish. When complete, you should have a Web page that looks something like Figure 20.8.

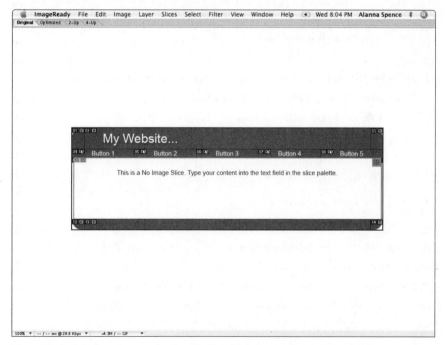

Figure 20.8. A Web page created using the Make Web page action in ImageReady.

Bright Idea!

Change the color of the blue header and footer boxes or add a pattern using layer blending options. To change the color, double-click the color swatch thumbnail in the Layers palette for the header and footer graphic and choose a new color from the Color Picker.

When ImageReady created this Web site, it automatically created slices for each image. To preview the Web page so you get an idea of how your page is being created, choose File ⇨ Preview In and choose a browser of your choice from the list.

The top of your browser window displays your shiny new Web page. The bottom half of the screen displays the HTML that was ImageReady generated. You can close your browser window and return to ImageReady. I just wanted to show you what your page looks like before we begin monkeying around.

Customize the Make Web page template

Now that you have your basic Web page design, you can modify it any way you like. In this section, I'll get you started with some basic modifications. The first thing I'd like you to do is increase the header area. This will be an easy introduction to modifying slices.

To enlarge the blue header area of your Web page:

1. Increase the canvas size of your image. Choose Image ⇨ Canvas Size. Change the Height to a minimum of 500 pixels.

2. Click OK to resize your canvas.

3. Find the layer for the header. Click the Visibility icon next to the two masked solid-color fill layers to determine which is the top and which is the bottom.

4. Click the layer to highlight it.

5. Choose Edit ⇨ Free Transform.

6. Drag the anchor point on the top of the shape to enlarge it to the size you want.

7. Click the Slice Selection tool in the Toolbox. It is the second tool in the second row. You can press the letter O to highlight it.

8. Click inside the main header area to select the slice. The blue outline around your header will turn yellow.

Inside Scoop

Resize several slices at once by Shift-clicking all of them and then resizing by dragging the anchor points of just one slice.

9. Click and drag the slice's top anchor to match the new size of your header.

10. There are three slices associated with the header bar. Click each of them and resize them.

Now when you preview your Web page, you should have a larger header area. If your images look strange, check to make sure your slices are perfectly aligned on top. If you'd like to change the text or font in your header, go ahead and make your changes the same way you'd change text in Photoshop.

Add images and text to your Web page design

Next you'll add an image to your Web page and create a new image slice for it.

To add an image slice to your Web page design:

1. Turn off the visibility for the layer entitled "This is no image slice." It will get in your way if you leave it there, and you don't need it.

2. Drag and drop, or copy and paste, an image from another file into your Web page file.

3. Choose Edit ⇨ Free Transform or use the key command ⌘+T (Ctrl+T). Resize your image so that it fits between the header and footer. Press and hold the Shift key while dragging the corner points to constrain proportions while resizing.

4. Select the Slice Selection tool from the Toolbox or press the letter O.

5. Click inside the green box in the main white part of your Web page design. This is a non-image slice, so you want to move it over a bit to make room for your image.

6. Click the anchor on the left side of the box and move it over, making room for your image.

7. Select the Slice tool from the Toolbox. You can press the letter K to highlight it.

Watch Out!

Image names shouldn't have spaces in them. Make sure you keep the Name field space free. It's okay to use spaces in the Alt field or Status Bar Message field.

8. Draw a slice around your image. Your Web page should look something like Figure 20.9.

9. View the Slice palette. If it is not visible on your screen, choose Window ⇨ Slice.

10. With your new slice still highlighted in yellow, make sure Image is selected in the Type drop-down list.

11. Give your image slice a name. This will be the name of the image file when ImageReady generates the HTML and images for your Web page.

Figure 20.9. An image slice around a new image and the Slice palette.

To preview your changes and make sure everything still lines up, choose File ⇨ Preview In and select your favorite browser from the list. Next, do something about the text that reads "Type your content here."

To add text to a non-image slice:

1. Click the Slice Select tool in the Toolbox. You can press the letter O to highlight it.

2. Click inside the green highlighted box in the middle of your Web page.

3. View the Slice palette. If the palette is not visible on your screen, choose Window ⇨ Slice.

4. Replace the text that reads "Type your content here" with whatever you like. The text entered into this box is HTML text and visible only when you preview your page in a browser or generate your page as HTML and images.

5. Choose File ⇨ Preview In and select your favorite browser to view your new text addition. Figure 20.10 shows the text that I added to my design.

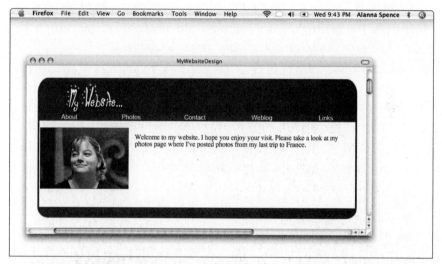

Figure 20.10. A Web page design with HTML text previewed in a browser.

Unfortunately, as far as formatting text goes, I can't help you change font faces or sizes without teaching you how to code HTML. If you want to avoid HTML, you can always produce a Web site entirely using images; it will just load much slower than a Web page using HTML text. I've added some HTML resources in the appendixes of the book if you'd like to learn about HTML.

Add links and customize optimization settings

Next, change the text of the buttons and give them some links. Since you've had plenty of text editing practice, I'll skip those steps. Before starting the next exercise, go ahead and edit the text layers for your buttons.

Watch Out!
You can't use the same name for different graphics on the same Web page.
Watch out for duplicates.

To add links to your buttons:

1. Click the Slice Select tool in the Toolbox or press the letter O.

2. Click one of the slices surrounding one of the buttons.

3. View the Slice palette. If it is not visible on your screen, choose
Window ⇨ Slice. The Slice palette looks like Figure 20.11.

4. Change the name of your button to something more meaningful. I
like to name my buttons the same name as the text.

5. Add a URL for your button. If it is pointing to another Web site, use
the full URL, starting with http://. If you are planning to point to
another page within the same Web site, you can use a filename like
about.html. Be careful; your pages will all need to be in the same
folder if you set up your links like this.

6. Repeat these steps for the remaining buttons.

Figure 20.11. The Slice palette with the Name, URL, and Alt fields filled out.

Now that you've added text and images and edited your buttons,
you're finally ready to move on to optimization. Most of the image slices

in your design are going to be GIFs. The photo you added needs to be saved as a JPEG.

To set up image slices for optimization:

1. View the Optimize palette. If it is not visible on your screen, choose Window ⇨ Optimize.

2. Click the Slice Select tool in the Toolbox. You can press the letter O to highlight it.

3. Click one of the solid blue slices.

4. Shift-click the remaining solid blue slices, including all of the button slices to add them to the current slice selection as you see in Figure 20.12.

5. Choose GIF 32 No Dither from the Presets drop-down list in the Optimize palette. This means your images will be optimized as GIF files using 32 colors and no image dithering. This option works well for your Web page because the buttons and header have very few colors in them.

Figure 20.12. A Web page design with selected slices ready for GIF optimization.

Bright Idea!

Get maximum file savings by optimizing each image differently. In the case of your Web page design, you can get away with less than 32 colors for the solid colored slices but not with the button and header slices.

6. Click the Optimize tab on the top of your document window. This previews your optimization settings. If you don't like the image quality of just 32 colors, try changing the setting to GIF 64 No Dither or GIF 128 No Dither. This makes your files larger but gives you better image quality.

7. Click the slice for the photo you added.

8. Choose JPEG Medium from the Presets list.

9. Click the Optimize tab to preview your settings. You can click back and forth from the Original tab to the Optimize tab to compare image quality, or use the 2-Up tab to see both at once.

10. If JPEG Medium isn't giving you the image quality you want, try JPEG High.

Your optimization settings are all ready to go. The only step that remains is generating the HTML and creating the image slices. If you'd like to do any other modifications to your design, now would be a good time to do them. You can always preview your progress by choosing File ⇨ Preview In and choosing your browser of choice.

Generate HTML and image slices for your Web page

You've successfully modified the header and buttons on your Web site, added your own photo, and added some simple HTML text. You're finally ready to generate your HTML and images. ImageReady creates a folder with images and an HTML file that you can then upload to a Web server. You can always view your Web page locally by dragging the HTML file onto a browser window.

To generate HTML and images from ImageReady:

1. Open your Web page design in ImageReady.

2. Choose File ⇨ Output Settings ⇨ Saving HTML.

3. Deselect the check box for multiple files as shown in Figure 20.13. This option creates multiple files for each of the buttons. Since we haven't created any new content for these files, we'll just want to save one HTML file.

4. Choose File ⇨ Save Optimized As. A dialog box appears.

5. I recommend you create a separate file for your Web site. Choose your new file in the Save As dialog box.

6. Make sure HTML and Images is selected from the Format drop-down list and that All Slices is selected in the Slices drop-down list.

7. Click Save to generate your images and HTML.

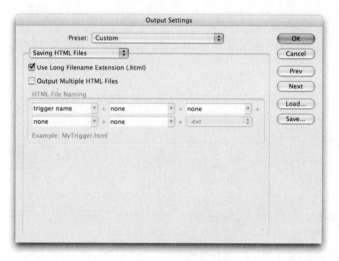

Figure 20.13. Saving HTML options in the Output Settings dialog box with the Saving HTML Files options visible.

You can try out your new Web page by dragging and dropping the HTML file onto a browser window. You've just completed a basic Web page from start to finish. I wish I could spend more time showing you some of ImageReady's Web design features. Be sure to check the appendixes for books and resources on HTML and Web design if you are interested.

Bright Idea!

Now that you've gotten your basic template set up, save out your file to create additional Web pages and link them using the navigation buttons. If you use the same images, choose HTML only when you generate your file.

Optimizing single images from Photoshop

You don't have to jump to ImageReady every time you want to optimize an image. Photoshop has a Save For Web feature that is a subset of ImageReady's optimization features. If you are just interested in optimizing a single graphic, using the Save For Web feature works just as well and will save you from having to jump back and forth.

ImageReady offers you many more options than Photoshop. If you tend to save only individual files as JPEG or GIF and do most of your work in Photoshop, the Save For Web feature is probably all you need. If you plan to do a lot of designing for the Web, you'll probably find yourself gravitating to ImageReady.

In Photoshop's Save For Web option under the File menu, you'll find some tabs: Original, Optimized, 2-Up, as you see in Figure 20.14, and 4-Up. The right-hand side shows the options to save files as JPEG, GIF, PNG-8, or PNG-24.

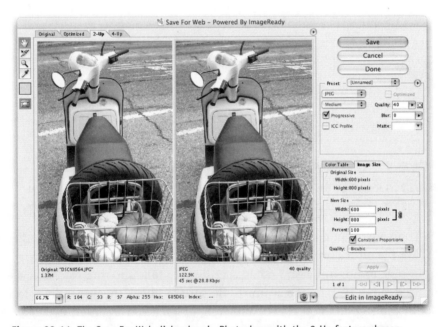

Figure 20.14. The Save For Web dialog box in Photoshop with the 2-Up feature chosen.

Just the facts

- Optimize images that contain solid colors and text or graphics as GIF.

- Optimize photos and images that contain gradients in JPEG format.

- Add a matte color that matches the background of your Web site to blend the edges of transparent GIFs.

- Use the Optimize to File Size option when you need your files to be a specific size.

- Create a simple Web page using ImageReady's Make Web page action and modify it to fit your needs.

- Optimize images straight from Photoshop with the Save For Web feature.

GET THE SCOOP ON...
Creating multi-framed animations with text and
graphics ▪ Getting smooth transitions between frames ▪
Saving your animations as SWFs

Creating Animated GIFs

Chapter 21

Animated GIFs are a great way to add pizzazz to your Web site. They make great buttons and can emphasize important content on a page by drawing the viewer's eye with motion graphics. One thing to keep in mind when creating animated GIFs is that some graphics look great as GIFs and others don't. GIFs work well with text and vector graphics, or any image that has large flat areas of color and not very much gradation in color. Photos end up looking choppy as GIFs, and the file size will be much larger than vector graphics. The image examples in this chapter were all created with the Freeform Pen tool by tracing photos. Even the crocodile head was traced from a photo of a drawing. I cover how to create graphic illustrations from photos in Chapter 5 if you are interested in creating your own.

In this chapter you'll create some animations in ImageReady. You'll start out with a simple multi-frame animation and then add image maps and tweening for smooth transitions between frames. Most of the projects in this chapter are cumulative and build on the previous section. Be sure to save your work so that you can use one example for another exercise. I'll show you how to save your animation as a SWF file to save on file space, and you'll create rollover buttons for a Web site.

Building a multi-framed animation

Animations are image files that display different information at different times. You can create both animated GIFs and Flash SWF files from ImageReady. You can create artwork in Photoshop and then use the Jump To ImageReady button to switch over and finish your animation.

The first few sections in this chapter deal with the Animation palette. This palette lets you create multi-framed animations and control things like the delay between frames, fades between frames, and the amount of times an animation plays before stopping. Table 21.1 outlines the different features in the Animation palette.

Table 21.1. Animation palette buttons and features

Button	Description
Delay Setting	Sets the amount of time a given frame will be displayed.
Looping options	Controls the amount of time an animation plays. Set the loop to forever, once, or a specified number of times.
Previous Frame	Goes to the previous frame in the animation.
First Frame	Goes to the first frame in the animation.
Play/Stop	Plays or stops the animation.
Next Frame	Goes to the next frame in the animation.
Tween	Creates intermediate frames in between two frames.
Duplicate Current Frame	Makes a copy of the currently highlighted frame.
Delete Current Frame	Deletes the currently highlighted frame.

Create a multi-framed animation

Start out by creating a simple multi-framed animation similar to the one you see in Figure 21.1. Vector graphics and text work best with animated GIFs, so take some time to gather up some fun elements for your animations. ImageReady works a little differently than Photoshop, so I'll walk you through a couple of the basic steps.

Figure 21.1. A single frame of an animation created in ImageReady.

To create the first frame of a multi-frame animation:

1. Create a new 300-x-100-pixel file.

2. Add some image and text elements to your new file.

3. To create a solid background color, click the Create New Layer button. Click the Add Layer Style button and select Color Overlay. Choose a color by clicking the color swatch and keep the opacity at 100%.

4. ImageReady automatically tries to place elements for you by snapping them to other objects. When working with such a small file, I find this option just tends to get in my way. You can turn off the Snap To option by choosing View ➪ Snap.

5. Before creating a text layer, choose View ➪ Show ➪ Text Selection so that the Type tool works more closely to Photoshop's Type tools.

6. Select the Type tool from the Toolbox and create a text element.

7. Add some clip art or other artwork to your banner. If you like, create an image by drawing something with the Custom Shape tool in Photoshop and copying it over to ImageReady.

Now that you have created your first frame, you can start adding new frames. Frames work by controlling the visibility of layers. In the next exercise, you'll add some additional text layers and display different text per frame. The images in Figure 21.2 display the content in six different frames. Open the Animation palette to see your first frame. You'll be

---

Watch Out!

You can't drag and drop layers between Photoshop and ImageReady. You can, however, copy and paste them. Be careful to think about scale and resolution differences.

building your multi-frame animation from the single-frame animation you created in the previous exercise.

Figure 21.2. Six frames that make up a single animation.

You can add more frames to your animation by following these steps:

1. In the Animation palette, change the delay of your first frame from 0 seconds to 2 seconds. The delay setting is just below the frame thumbnail.

2. To create some copies of your text layer and change their text to use in different frames, drag and drop the text layers onto the Create New Layer button in the Layers palette. Double-click the thumbnail of each one to select it and modify the text.

3. Drag and drop your frame thumbnail onto the Duplicate Current Frame button about four times to make some copies of it.

4. Change the visibility of elements in each frame. Click the first frame and turn off all layers you don't want to show. Repeat with each frame by clicking them and turning layers on and off.

5. Try out your animation by clicking the Play button on the bottom of the Animations palette. Click the Stop button to stop it.

6. Make adjustments to frames by clicking them and adjusting the visibility of various layers. Each of the frames in the Animation palette in Figure 21.3 have different layers visible.

Bright Idea!
Don't forget to save your work. Before you save an optimized version of your animation, make sure you save a PSD file. Optimized files lose all layer data.

Figure 21.3. Artwork, Animation palette with multiple animation frames, and Layers palette.

Add a link to your animation

You can have ImageReady create the HTML code needed to add a link to your animation. In this section you'll be assigning a URL to your animation in the Slices palette. You'll then save and generate an HTML file to go with your animation. ImageReady automatically creates a slice of your entire document when you create a new file, so you won't have to add a new slice for this exercise. The next section shows you how to add multiple links in a banner.

You can add a link to your banner by following these steps:

1. Open the Slice palette. If it is not visible, choose Window ⇨ Slices.

2. Select Image from the Type drop-down list.

3. Enter a name for your slice. This will be the name of your image files. Some servers don't like spaces in file names, so use an underscore (_) instead of a space or use initial caps for new words like those that I've done in Figure 21.4.

Figure 21.4. The Slice palette with an image slice.

4. If you'd like your link to automatically open in a new browser window, select _blank from the Target drop-down list.

5. Add text to the Alt field. This text is used on computers or browsers that can't show images. It's good practice to add alt tags to all of your Web images.

6. If you'd like to add a message to the status bar on the bottom of your browser window when someone mouses over your banner, click the Status Bar Message expand arrow and add your text.

7. Your slice is ready for prime time. To preview your banner ad in a browser, choose File ⇨ Preview In and select your favorite browser from the list. You can add browsers to the list by choosing File ⇨ Preview In ⇨ Edit Browser List and then finding your browser application either in Program Files on a PC or Applications on a Mac.

ImageReady previews your animation with a preview of the HTML code below it. If everything checks out okay, you are ready to save your animated GIF. Choose File ⇨ Save As Optimized and then select HTML and Images from the Format drop-down list.

> **Hack**
>
> Entering mailto: followed by an e-mail address in the URL field (make sure there are no spaces) spawns an e-mail program. The e-mail address automatically is added to the To: field.

Change the number of times an animation plays

The Animation palette defaults to playing an animation forever. When creating marketing banner animations for display on other Web sites, many places require that your animation play only a certain number of times. To change the number of times an animation plays, select Other from the Looping Options drop-down list and enter a number in the Set Loop Count dialog box, as shown in Figure 21.5.

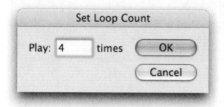

Figure 21.5. The Set Loop Count dialog box.

Add several links to one image with image maps

The Image Map tools in ImageReady let you add links to selected areas of an image. Similar to slices, you can add links to vector-based areas. The difference between the two is that slices create separate images with anchor tags. Image maps don't create separate images per map. You can have as many maps on a single image as you want. ImageReady creates the image map code for you. When you create an image map, you are assigning a link to mapped coordinates in your image.

There are three Image Map tools in the fly-out menu. The Rectangular Image Map tool looks like a square with a pointing finger. Clicking on it will reveal the fly-out menu for the Image Map tools.

The Image Map tools include:

■ **Rectangular Image Map:** Draws rectangular image maps. Press and hold the Shift key to draw perfect squares or the Option key (Alt) to draw your rectangle from the center out. Figure 21.6 shows an animation with two rectangular image maps.

- **Circular Image Map:** Creates circular image maps. Press and hold the Shift key to draw perfect circles or the Option key (Alt) to draw your circle from the center out.

- **Polygon Image Map:** Creates any shape you like by clicking from point to point. Press and hold the Shift key to constrain the tool to 15-degree increments.

- **Image Map Select:** Lets you select and modify the shape and size of image maps.

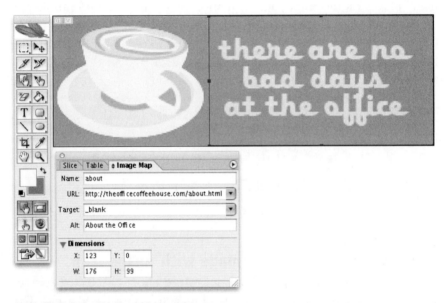

Figure 21.6. An animation with two image maps.

Using the same animation you created in the last couple of sections, add image maps so that you can have several links in one image.

To add an image map to your animation:

1. Remove the edited slice so the browser doesn't get confused over which link to use, and then click the Slice Select tool on the Toolbox, or press the letter O to highlight it.

2. Click your image to highlight the slice and click the Delete key to remove it.

3. Select the Rectangular Image Map tool from the Toolbox or press the letter P to highlight it.

4. Draw a rectangle over part of your image to create an image map.

5. Open the Image Map palette. If it isn't currently visible, choose Window ⇨ Image Map.

6. Give your image map a name, URL, target, and alt text.

7. Draw another rectangular image map over your animation.

8. Enter information for your second image map.

9. To resize your image map, choose the Image Map Select tool to the right of the Image Map tools in the Toolbox. You can press the letter J to highlight it.

10. Click your image map to highlight it. Click and drag the resizing points to change the area of your image map. You can also use the Dimensions option in the Image Map palette to adjust the size.

After you have all of your image maps defined, try them out by choosing File ⇨ Preview In and selecting your favorite browser. ImageReady will launch a browser window and you'll see a preview of your animation with a preview of the HTML code generated for your animation, as shown in Figure 21.7. Don't worry, the HTML code won't be visible when you use your final design.

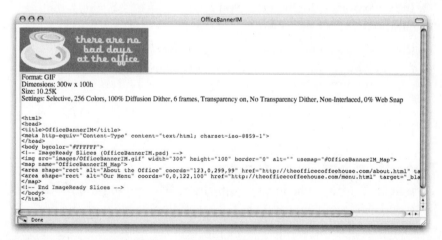

Figure 21.7. A preview of animation with two image maps.

Watch Out!
Try not to overlap image maps. If there are two maps assigned to an area, the browser usually goes with the second one in the list. If you are seeing strange behavior with your links, check to make sure there are no overlapping image maps.

Exporting animations to Flash SWF files

You can now create Flash SWF files right from ImageReady without having to learn anything about the Flash application. Animations created in ImageReady can be exported as SWFs and keep all of their functionality. Saving as SWF allows you to embed JPEGs and even QuickTime movies. When you are working with vector graphics and text, the SWF format can shave off quite a bit of your file size. For animations with tweens, using the SWF format can save you even more file size. There is one drawback to consider when choosing to use Flash SWF files over GIF animations: For viewing SWFs on a Web site, users will need to install a Flash plug-in on their browser. GIFs don't require any additional software to be installed but are generally larger. As Flash has become more and more popular, many browsers automatically come with Flash installed. If you know your users may not have the ability to see Flash movies, you might want to play it safe and choose GIF format.

Try saving your animated GIF as an SWF file by following these steps:

1. With your animation file open, choose File ⇨ Export ⇨ Macromedia Flash SWF.

2. In the export dialog box that you see in Figure 21.8, check the Generate HTML check box.

3. Click OK to choose a place to save your files.

4. Create a folder for your SWF and HTML files and click OK to generate it.

5. To view your new SWF file in a browser, find the files you just generated and drag and drop the HTML file in a browser window.

Tweening between frames

Tweening lets you transition between frames by adding interim frames between keyframes. You can fade text in and out or change the position of text to make it appear as it is floating across the image.

Fading elements in and out with tweening

Because I can't show you an animation in a book, Figure 21.9 shows an example of the keyframes in my animation with some tweening frames in between. I kept the logo in the same place and tweened out the coffee cup and subtitle, and then added the cake and new subtitle. In the next exercise, you'll try fading out elements and fading in new ones.

Macromedia® Flash™ (SWF) Export

Export Options   (OK)

☑ Preserve Appearance   (Cancel)

SWF bgcolor: [▼]

☑ Generate HTML

☐ Enable Dynamic Text

Embed Fonts: [None   ▲▼]

[AB | ab | # | ʷⁿ]

Extra: [   ]

Bitmap Options

Format: [Auto Select   ▲▼]

JPEG Quality: [80 ▼]

Figure 21.8. The Macromedia Flash (SWF) Export dialog box with the Generate HTML checkbox selected.

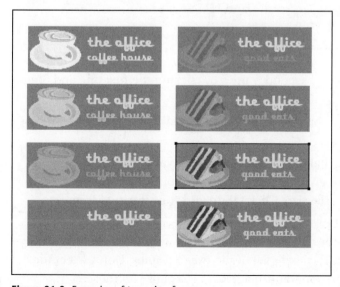

Figure 21.9. Examples of tweening frames.

Watch Out!

Watch file size when tweening. You can quickly increase the size of your file by ten times or more when adding complicated tweens. Consider exporting your animation as an SWF instead. See the section on SWFs in this chapter.

You can create a tweened animation by following these steps:

1. Create a new file or use the animation you created earlier in the chapter.

2. You'll need three frames to create your tween. The first frame is the beginning of your animation. The last frame is the end of your animation. The middle frame is going to be the frame you use to fade elements in and out. Leave this frame empty except for a background color, or leave one element in place as I did in the example in Figure 21.10.

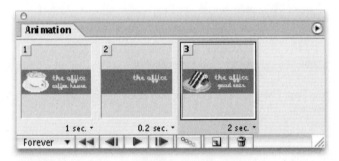

Figure 21.10. Three animation frames to be tweened.

3. Select the first and second frames by clicking the first one and Shift-clicking the second one.

4. Click the Tween button. It looks like several boxes layered on top of one another.

5. The Tweening dialog box appears. The default settings are fine. Five frames will give you a smooth transition. Consider three or four to save on file size. Click OK to add your tweened frames to the Animation palette.

6. You'll see five more frames added to your animation. Change their duration by Shift-clicking all of the tween frames. Don't select the original frames; you want ImageReady to pause on those.

Bright Idea!

Add another tween to fade the last frame out before the animation starts over. Create a blank frame at the end of your animation and create a tween between it and the frame before it.

7. In one of the selected frames, select 0.1 seconds from the Delay drop-down list on the bottom of the frame.

8. Next, create a tween from the middle frame to the last frame.

9. Select the last two frames in the animation and click the Tween button on the bottom of the Animation palette.

10. Click OK in the Tween dialog box to create your tweening frames. Your Animation palette will automatically show the newly created tweening frames like you see in Figure 21.11.

11. Change the delay between tweened frames by Shift-selecting them and choosing 0.1 seconds from the Delay drop-down list.

12. If you like, increase the delay on the first and last frame. I like to have my important frames on-screen for at least two seconds.

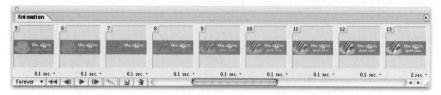

Figure 21.11. The Animation palette with tweening applied between frames.

Preview your new animation by choosing File ⇨ Preview In and select the browser of your choice. You may need to slow down the tweened frames a bit or add more time to the key content frames. Make any adjustments you need before saving your animation. Once you are ready, save it by choosing File ⇨ Save Optimized As and choosing HTML and Images from the Format drop-down list. To see your live version, drag and drop the HTML file on a browser window.

Reversing frame order

You can quickly copy a fade-out created with tweening and create a fade-in. This exercise shows you how to reverse several frames and gives you some practice in moving animations around the Animation palette.

Inside Scoop

⌘+click (Ctrl+click) animation frames to select them individually without selecting the frames in between.

To create a reverse tween, follow these steps:

1. Create an animation frame with text and/or image elements and another frame with no elements.

2. Shift-click both frames to select them and click the Tweening button on the bottom of the Animation palette. Click OK in the Tween dialog box to add several tweening frames.

3. Create copies of the tweened frames. Select all of the tweened frames by Shift-clicking them and click the Duplicate Current Frame button on the bottom right of the Animation palette.

4. While the new frames are still highlighted, click and drag them to the right of the last frame.

5. Now click the arrow on the top right of the Animation palette and select Reverse Frames to change their order, as shown in Figure 21.12.

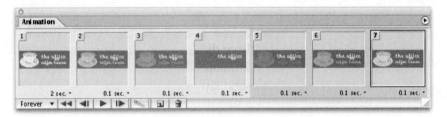

Figure 21.12. The Animation palette with reversed tweening frames.

You now have an animation that fades in and out by taking advantage of the Reverse Frames feature of the Animation palette. You also dragged and dropped frames to rearrange them just as you can with layers in the Layers palette.

Creating an animated button

The Web Content palette lets you create rollover states for Web site buttons. ImageReady creates all the code for you so you don't have to mess around with JavaScript or HTML. Rollover states work similarly to animation frames. Each state has different layer visibility. Figure 21.13 is an example of three states of a rollover button created in ImageReady.

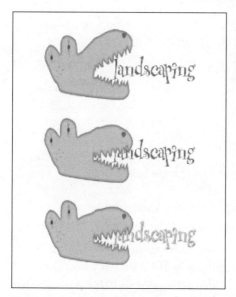

Figure 21.13. Three rollover states of a button.

To create three button rollover states:

1. Create artwork and text for three different button states. You can reuse your artwork from the animated GIF or try something new. An easy option is to create three text layers with different layer styles. Choose Layer ⇨ Layer Style ⇨ Blending Options to add drop shadows, stroke, or other blending options to your text.

2. Open the Web Content palette. If it isn't visible on your screen, choose Window ⇨ Web Content.

3. Click the Create Rollover State button on the bottom right of the Web Content palette. ImageReady automatically adds an Over state. Click the button two more times. You'll want a rollover state for over, out, and down, like the example in Figure 21.14. If you need to, change the states by right-clicking the state name and selecting a different state from the drop-down list.

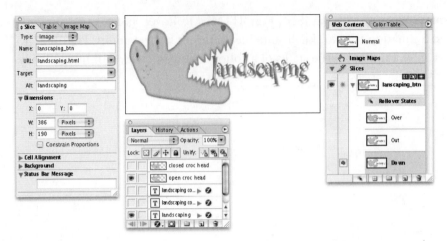

Figure 21.14. The Web Content palette with three rollover states added.

4. Click the Over state. This state appears when you mouse over the image. Change your layer visibility for the Over state.

5. Click each of the other two states and change the layer visibility for that state. Down determines what image will be shown when the mouse button is depressed. Out is the resting or inactive state when there is no mouse interaction with the image.

6. To preview your button, choose File ⇨ Preview In and select your browser of choice. ImageReady will launch a browser window with a preview of your button similar to the one you see in Figure 21.15.

If your button works how you like it, you can save the image and HTML or continue designing buttons for your Web site. When you are ready, choose File ⇨ Save As Optimized and choose HTML and Images from the Format drop-down list.

Creating an animation with a transparent background

You can give your GIF a transparent background by removing any background or solid color layer and selecting the Transparency check box in the Optimize palette. If your GIF is going to be used on a color background, you can take an extra step of adding a matte color to avoid the dreaded color fringe around your image.

Figure 21.15. A preview of the button with a rollover state and HTML code created by ImageReady.

To create a transparent GIF:

1. Open an image to use as your transparent GIF.

2. If you need to, turn off the visibility of any solid color layers or white background layers.

3. Open the Optimize palette. If it is not visible on your screen, choose Window ➪ Optimize.

4. Check the Transparency check box.

5. Open a file that has the background color you are going to place your GIF on. Click the Foreground swatch to open the Color Picker and choose the color with your eyedropper. In the Color Picker window, copy the six-character value in the field labeled #. This is the hexadecimal value of your color. It's the easiest way to copy a color value when you can't use the Eyedropper tool.

6. Go back to the file with your transparent image. Click the Matte color swatch to open the Color Picker.

7. Paste the hexadecimal color value of your background color into the # field and click OK. Figure 21.16 is an example of a transparent GIF with matte color added to avoid fringe.

8. To save your image, choose File ⇨ Save Optimized As.

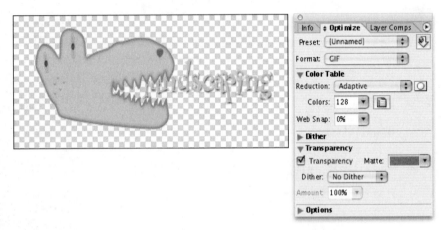

Figure 21.16. The Optimize palette and an image on a transparent background.

You can drag and drop the image onto a browser window to test it out, or, if you have a Web site, add it to a file using the background color to check for fringe. ImageReady uses the Matte color to blend the edges of your image instead of using white.

Just the facts

- Create a multi-framed animation in the Animation palette by controlling layer visibility separately in each frame.
- Add multiple links to one image by adding rectangular, circular, or polygon image maps.
- Fade images in and out to create smooth transitions between animation frames by adding tweening.
- Create rollover buttons for your Web site design with the Web Content palette.
- Save your animations as SWF files and generate the necessary HTML code by exporting them.

Going Beyond the Basics

PART VI

GET THE SCOOP ON...
Calibrating your monitor ▪ Correcting skin tones with
advanced Hue/Saturation adjustments ▪ Setting your
own Auto Color defaults ▪ Whitening and brightening
teeth and eyes

Exploring Advanced Color Calibration and Correction

Chapter 22

I would be off my rocker if I thought I could teach you everything there is to know about advanced color calibration and correction in one chapter. Countless books on the market cater to advanced color techniques for Photoshop, digital cameras, and printing. I'll spend some time in this chapter introducing you to a few key concepts for achieving professional color. If you want to get serious about color, I've listed many books in the appendixes that go into color much more thoroughly than I can in this overview-style book.

In this chapter I'll show you how to calibrate your monitor using software calibrators. For those of you who are serious about color, I'll give you some pointers on purchasing a hardware monitor calibrator. I'll give you two easy methods for finding and removing out-of-gamut colors. I'll show you some more advanced techniques for correcting color in digital photos by taking advantage of some little-known and underutilized features of Photoshop CS2. I'll also show you some advanced techniques for color correcting portraits, enabling you to get bright teeth, sparkling eyes, and glowing skin for your images.

509

Watch Out!

If you are using a CRT monitor, be sure to let your monitor warm up for 30 minutes or more before calibrating. Your monitor color will be slightly different when it is "cold."

Calibrating your monitor

There are two types of monitor calibrators. The type I'll cover most in this section is monitor calibration software. It is fast, free, and simple, but it doesn't offer much in the way of accuracy. It improves your monitor color but is less than perfect. The second option, monitor calibration hardware, gives more accurate results and is a good device to purchase if you are considering a career as a professional digital photographer. For the rest of us, I recommend trying a quick software monitor calibration and then getting on with your life.

I hate to be the one to break it to you, but monitor calibration is not a magical solution for creating perfect color. It will definitely not solve your home printing dilemmas. The honest truth is, the monitor calibrating software that comes on your computer, in most cases, can offer nothing more than a fractional improvement in image quality from computer to printer. For better tips on getting good color prints, see Chapter 19.

Having burst your calibration bubble, I say a little software calibration couldn't hurt you; and if your monitor is unbalanced, it just might help you a great deal. So let's look at color calibration on Mac OS X and Windows machines using free software.

Calibrating monitors on a Mac

The calibration tool in the Display control panel does a decent job at calibrating your monitor by having you go through a series of small adjustments. If you are calibrating an LCD monitor, be sure you have your screen adjusted as you usually have it and be conscious of room lighting. Is there a lamp off that you usually have turned on? Do you do most of your intense color work late at night with all the lights out and the shades closed?

To calibrate your Mac monitor:

1. Open System Preferences by clicking the System Preferences button in the dock.
2. Click the Displays control panel to open it. The Displays control panel defaults to the Display options.

3. Click the Color button on the top of the Displays control panel to access the screen shown in Figure 22.1.

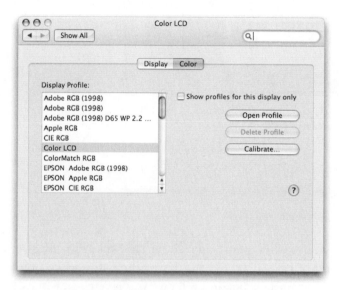

Figure 22.1. The Color options in the Displays control panel.

4. Click the Calibrate button. The Display Calibrator Assistant appears.

5. Click the Expert Mode check box.

6. Click Continue and proceed through the next five steps. The Assistant will tell you exactly what to do. You are trying to match up the grays between the pinstriped background and the apple icon. Squinting your eyes (or taking off your glasses!) helps you determine whether the grays are matching.

7. Click Continue to proceed to the Target Gamma screen that you see in Figure 22.2.

8. Adjust the slider bar in the Gamma screen to choose a Gamma as shown in Figure 22.2. I recommend sticking with the Mac Standard Gamma of 1.8. See the "Choosing the Right Gamma Setting on a Mac" sidebar for more information.

9. Click the Continue button to proceed to the Target White Point screen.

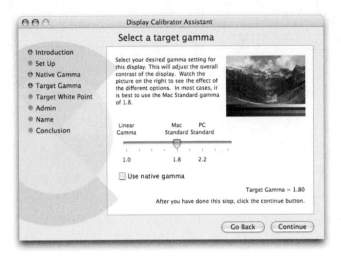

Figure 22.2. The Target Gamma options.

10. Check the Use native white point check box. This will probably give you a white point of D65 (6500 Kelvin). Using the native white point option is probably your best bet and will give you nice clean whites without a yellow tint. The lower the White Point setting, the warmer (more yellow) your whites will be.

11. Click the Continue button once you've selected a white point. The next screen asks you whether you want to share your calibration settings with other computer users.

12. Check the Allow others to use this calibration checkbox to allow anyone who has a separate login account on your computer to choose your calibration settings. Unless your calibration settings somehow involve secret government documents, it's probably safe to check the box.

13. Click Continue to move along to the Name screen.

14. Give your calibration settings a name. If you are mobile like I am and use multiple monitors, you might want to include something about the monitor in the name.

15. Click Continue to save your calibration setting and view a conclusion of your settings similar to what you see in Figure 22.3.

Inside Scoop

Apple.com has a great instructional movie on how to calibrate your display. Go to Apple.com and search for Calibrating Your Display.

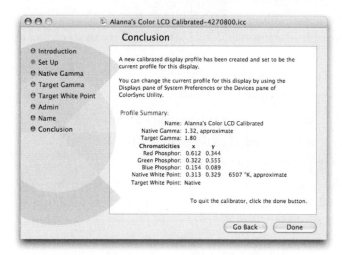

Figure 22.3. The Conclusion screen in the Calibration Assistant.

Your monitor colors should now be pretty well adjusted. If this solution doesn't solve your color problems, I'd recommend thinking about a hardware calibrator.

Choosing the Right Gamma Setting on a Mac

The Gamma settings that you set in the Displays control panel will determine the amount of contrast of your screen color. Apple recommends you use a milder Gamma of 1.8. PC monitors typically use a Gamma of 2.2. If you know your images will mostly be viewed on the Web, you might want to consider a Gamma of 2.2. I've heard professional digital photographers swear by 2.2 and that it gives them more control over shadows. Being a Mac purist, I stick with 1.8. If I am designing a Web site, I will often switch to a Gamma of 2.2 temporarily to make sure it will look okay on most PCs.

Calibrating monitors on a Windows machine

The Adobe Gamma control panel is a software calibration utility that comes free with Adobe Photoshop. It is automatically installed when you install Photoshop. It's not as useful as the Apple calibration software, but it'll do in a pinch. It goes through a few quick steps that ask you to make personal judgments about colors, which probably doesn't do much good at all if you are color blind. However, let's look and I'll try to steer you in the right direction.

To calibrate a monitor on a Windows system:

1. Choose Start ⇨ Settings ⇨ Control Panels.

2. Double-click the Adobe Gamma control panel to launch it.

3. Choose the Step by Step Wizard radio button. This will lead you through the steps of creating a calibration profile.

4. Read the instructions for each screen, and click Next when you are ready to proceed. You'll be taken to a screen asking you to name your calibration profile.

5. Enter a name for your profile in the Description field.

6. To save some time, click the Load button and check to see if you have a preinstalled .icc profile for your monitor. If not, you might want to check your monitor manufacturer's Web site for an .icc profile. It will give you more accurate color.

   The wizard will ask you to adjust the brightness and contrast of your monitor using the buttons on the front of your monitor.

7. Click Next when you are done adjusting your monitor brightness and contrast.

8. Click Next to continue to a Gamma correction screen. You'll see a screen similar to Figure 22.4.

9. Uncheck the box labeled View Single Gamma Only.

10. Adjust the red, green, and blue sliders until the center square matches the outer square as closely as possible.

11. In the White Point section, choose the White Point Hardware that matches your monitor. The most common setting is D65.

12. The last screen gives you the option of comparing your monitor color before and after your calibration settings. Try each setting.

13. Click Finish to complete your new calibration profile.

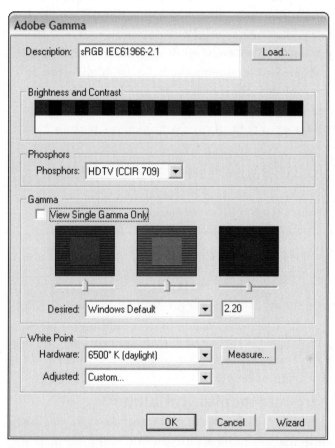

Figure 22.4. The Gamma correction screen in the Adobe Gamma Wizard.

Hack

If your monitor profile is not shown in the list of Phosphors, Ian Lyons of computer-darkroom.com recommends you use either Trinitron or P22-EBU. You can tell a Trinitron monitor from other monitors by the two barely visible lines that run horizontally across your monitor. If you don't see these lines, choose P22-EBU.

Can I Calibrate for Web Design?

Monitor calibration offers little to no help in creating 100-percent accurately represented color Web graphics. All monitors are different, and they display different colors depending on the lighting in the room. If you are using an LCD monitor, the colors differ depending on the angle of your screen. If the monitor- and light-inconsistency problem isn't enough, you have the human eye to contend with. Everyone sees color differently, and how we see color changes as we age. Even if you achieve the colors you want on your own monitor, you have no control over your viewer's monitor. My advice to you is:

- Calibrate your monitor using either software or hardware calibration.

- View your designs on a few different monitors (LCD and CRT) and operating systems to make sure you aren't totally off target.

Beyond that, don't lose any sleep over it.

Remember to recalibrate your display profile if your lighting conditions change. This method performs a system wide calibration for your monitor so your colors will be corrected for all applications, not just Photoshop.

Picking out a hardware monitor calibrator

As I mentioned earlier, there are hardware calibrators that give you much more accurate results than software calibrators do. Even then, if you really want accurate color, you'd need to calibrate at different times of the day or work in a completely controlled room with no natural light. If your work involves professional digital photography, I'd definitely recommend looking into hardware calibrators, which are USB devices that pick up ambient light in the room to give you the most accurate calibration possible.

Hardware monitor calibrators range from around $200 to $6,000. Companies that make calibrators are LaCie, Monaco, GretagMacbeth, Sony, and ColorVision (shown in Figure 22.5). I'm the first to admit that

I am no hardware calibration expert. My advice to you is to spend some time researching product reviews on the Internet or check out some of the advanced digital photography books listed in the appendixes.

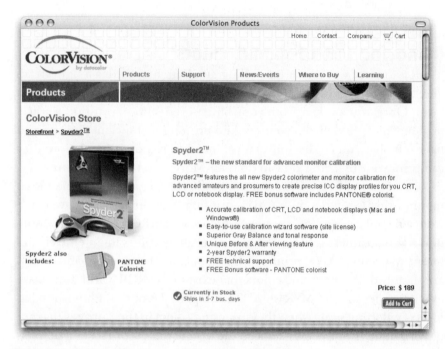

Figure 22.5. The ColorVision Spyder2 USB monitor calibrator.

To help steer you in the right direction, here are a few key products I've been recommended:

- **Monaco Optix XR Pro:** Offers great bang for your buck and performs with the best of them. Visit the Monaco X-Rite Web site for more information (www.xritephoto.com).

- **ColorVision Spyder2 Pro Studio 2.0:** Many professional digital photographers swear by this software/hardware combo. It retails for about $300. The ColorVision Web site (www.colorvision.com) is shown in Figure 22.5.

- **Sony Artisan Monitor:** If you are in the market for a monitor, I've heard fantastic reviews of the Sony Artisan monitor. It comes with a built-in calibration "puck" and retails for between $1,500 and $2,000. You can find out more on the Sony Web site (b2b.sony.com).

Bright Idea!

The Digital Photography Review Web site offers some in-depth reviews on popular monitor calibrators. Visit www.dpreview.com and look under the reviews section.

Removing out-of-gamut colors

It's not a pretty scenario after pulling an all-nighter under a tight deadline. You drop your files off to your local printer before collapsing into a heap. Once you awaken from your blurry-eyed stupor, you find a voicemail on your phone from your favorite printing technician. She says you have out-of-gamut colors and that you need to remove them before they can print your file. How do you do that? Moreover, what is a gamut?

Out-of-gamut issues occur when you are viewing an image on an RGB monitor that is intended for CMYK printing. Your image may have come from a digital camera, or scanners, which also use RGB color. Since monitors, digital cameras, and scanners create their colors in an entirely different way from CMYK printers, the color palettes for RGB and CMYK are slightly different. Some colors that exist in the RGB world don't have exact matches in the CMYK world. To compensate for this, Photoshop has tools for alerting users when they are using colors in their images that are out of gamut. If you've ever noticed the icon in the Color Picker that looks like an exclamation point in a triangle, you've probably wondered what it's for. It serves as a warning that if you use the color that is currently selected, it might not print well on a CMYK printer. That's all fine and good when you are creating a design from scratch; but if you are using digital photos, there is no way of telling your camera to please stick to CMYK-safe colors. No worries; you'll just need to make a couple of quick adjustments.

To use the Sponge tool method for removing out-of-gamut warnings, follow these steps:

1. Choose View ⇨ Gamut Warning. The areas of your photo that have out-of-gamut colors turn gray. I've changed my gamut warning color in Figure 22.6 so you can more easily see where I have gamut warnings. The sky in this photo is almost entirely out of gamut.

Figure 22.6. A photo with gamut warning visible.

2. Select the Sponge tool from the Toolbox. It is listed under the Dodge tool fly-out menu. You can press Shift+O a couple of times to toggle to it.

3. Change the brush diameter of the Sponge tool either by adjusting the value in the Options bar or typing the [or] key.

4. Brush over the gray areas with the Sponge tool until the gray areas disappear and your image color returns. If the default gray gamut warning color is too hard to see, you can change it through the Gamut Warning settings in Photoshop ⇨ Preferences ⇨ Transparency & Gamut.

Hack

Avoid out-of-gamut colors when using the Color Picker. If you choose a color that displays the out-of-gamut icon (looks like an exclamation point in the top right of the Color Picker), click the exclamation point and Photoshop will pick the nearest safe color.

The second option for removing out-of-gamut colors works well when the offending colors can easily be identified as belonging to a particular color channel. If you have colors that can't be categorized quite so easily, I'd recommend sticking to the first option.

Here is the Hue and Saturation method for removing out-of-gamut colors:

1. Choose View ⇨ Gamut Warning.

2. Click the Create New Fill/Adjustment Layer button on the bottom of the Layers palette.

3. Choose Hue/Saturation from the drop-down list.

4. Choose the color from the Edit menu that most closely matches the out-of-gamut color. In Figure 22.7, I chose Blues because my gamut warnings are all in the sky.

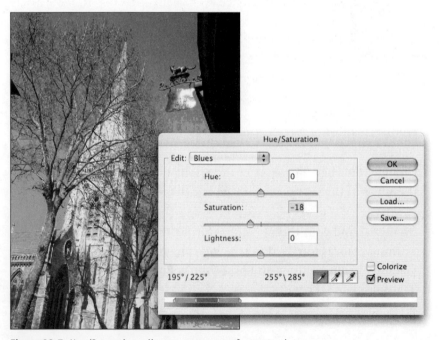

Figure 22.7. Hue/Saturation adjustments on out-of-gamut colors.

Bright Idea!

To change the gamut warning color, choose Photoshop ➪ Preferences ➪ Transparencies & Gamut. Under the Gamut section, click the color swatch to open a Color Picker window. Choose your new gamut warning color. It's best to pick a zany, garish color that you won't typically find in your image.

5. Click the grayed-out gamut warning area with the Eyedropper tool.

6. Lower the Saturation slider until the gray, out-of-gamut warning color disappears.

Sometimes this method under saturates other parts of your image, so it won't work for all occasions. When it does work, it sure beats having to sponge down the out-of-gamut areas of your image.

Changing the default Auto Color settings

Chapter 11 discussed the auto color correction options located under the Image ➪ Adjustments menu. These use some default Photoshop settings to correct colors, or levels. These settings work well for some images and not so well for others. Most of your images probably come from the same source and have similar color characteristics from image to image. Wouldn't it be nice if you could customize the settings to suite your source? There is a little-known feature in Photoshop that allows you to customize the default settings so you can get better results when using Auto Colors or Auto Levels.

You can save your own auto color correction settings by following these steps:

1. Open an image. Any image will do.

2. Choose Image ➪ Adjustments ➪ Levels.

3. Click the Options button. The Auto Color Correction Options dialog box that you see in Figure 22.8 appears.

4. Click the Find Dark & Light Colors radio button.

5. Check the Snap Neutral Midtones check box.

6. Check the Save as defaults check box.

Don't click OK just yet; you have to adjust a couple more things first.

The default clipping percentages of .1% for both highlight and shadow can be a bit harsh. You can adjust them to even smaller increments.

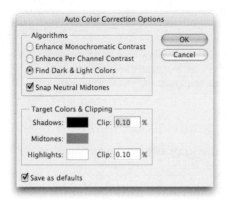

Figure 22.8. The Auto Color Correction dialog box with new default settings.

7. Try adjusting the clipping percentages to 0% for Shadows and some-where between .02% and .05% for Highlights. A much lower setting on the highlights helps avoid the floodlight effect that is so common with the default auto correction settings.

The three color swatches in this dialog box represent the target values for shadow, highlight, and midtone. You can click each swatch and change the colors in a Color Picker window like you see in Figure 22.9. Generally speaking, the default shadows are too dark and the lights are too starkly white, so you should soften the blacks and warm up the whites a tad. While you're at it, also soften up the midtones. This is my own recipe and I tend to like warmer, softer colors. Feel free to use your own measurements.

8. Click each color swatch in the Auto Color Correction Options dialog box and change their values to the following:

- Set the Shadows to R: 16, G: 16, B: 16
- Set the Midtones to R: 133, G: 133, B: 128
- Set the Highlights to R: 245, G: 245, B: 235

9. It's safe to click OK now. You've managed to tweak every option in this semi-hidden feature.

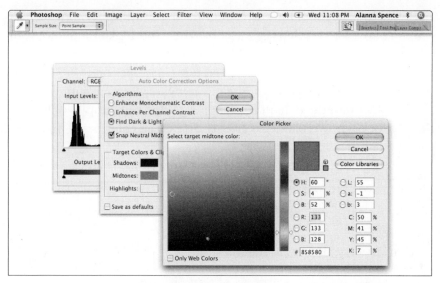

Figure 22.9. The Auto Color Midtones target value changed in a Color Picker window.

Try out your new settings on a few different images. You may need to fine-tune your settings to find an auto correction that serves your needs. These settings won't fix every image: Lighting situations are going to vary from photo to photo. Even if you can use this on only 50 to 75 percent of your images, you'll still save tons of time; and if you wind up using Auto Colors or Levels regularly, your colors will probably be more consistent from photo to photo.

Creating healthy skin and sparkling whites

Humans are the toughest subject to color correct. Skin tone is a very delicate thing. If the color is slightly off on the photo of a flower, who's to know; but add a slightly green tint to a human face and you have problems. The surface of people's skin has so many variations; it's often tough to fix problem areas without messing up the whole picture. Chapter 11 introduced you to some basic techniques for color correcting using Curves Adjustments. This section takes it one step further by selecting and correcting specific colors. I'll show you some pro tips for whitening and brightening eyes and teeth, as well as how to save your own auto curves settings.

Before you begin color correcting, fix the Eyedropper tool so your sampling area has a little wiggle room. When you look at a photo, your eyes automatically blend several different colors together into one shade. The impressionists and pointillists used this phenomenon to create spectacular paintings. A nice effect creates punchier, more exciting colors. The problem with the default Eyedropper setting is it samples only a single pixel of color. We want it to give us an average color based on a sampling of many colors.

To change the sample size of the Eyedropper tool, follow these steps:

1. Click the Eyedropper tool in the Toolbox to highlight it.

2. Choose 3 by 3 average from the Sample Size drop-down list in the Options bar.

That was easy; now on to the fun stuff.

Adjusting skin tones

The photo in Figure 22.10 has some tricky color problems in the nose, eyelids, and under the eyes. There is a strong red hue over these areas. Trying to correct the entire image would throw off other colors in the photo. By using the Eyedropper tool in a Hue/Saturation adjustment layer, you can isolate the strong reds and tone them down.

Figure 22.10. A photo with oversaturated reds around the nose and cheeks.

To tone reds down:

1. Open a photo that needs color correction.

2. Click the Create New Fill/Adjustment Layer icon on the bottom of the Layers palette.

3. Select Hue/Saturation from the drop-down list.

4. Choose a color channel from the Edit drop-down list. I chose the Red channel for mine since my color problems are mainly with red hues.

5. Click inside a problem area in your image.

6. Adjust the Saturation value. To take some of the sting out of the color, move the slider to the left.

7. Adjust the Hue. The reds in my image were a little on the purple side. I adjusted the Hue slider so that my reds were warmer with a bit of orange in them.

8. Adjust the Lightness slider to the right to lighten up the value of the color.

9. If there are areas that weren't adjusted as much as you like, continue the process of clicking them with the Eyedropper tool and adjusting their settings.

10. Click OK when you are done with your adjustments.

Because you performed your Hue/Saturation adjustments in a separate layer, you can adjust the Opacity setting for the adjustment layer to tone down your effect a bit. For the girl's face in Figure 22.11, I sampled three or four different areas and adjusted them until I got a result I was happy with. The girl no longer looks sunburned and has a healthy, warm glow to her skin.

Whitening and brightening teeth

Most people over the age of 16 start to show some coffee or tea stains in their teeth. It's just a fact. Everyone knows those whitening toothpastes and gums are no match for strong coffee. The next time your friends complain about your taking photo evidence of their poor oral hygiene, tell them about this nifty trick. They'll be showing you that toothy grin in a moment.

Figure 22.11. The Hue/Saturation dialog box using the Eyedropper tool.

To whiten and brighten teeth in a portrait, follow these steps:

1. Open a photo that includes some teeth that could use a little whitening.

2. Select the Magic Wand tool from the Toolbox or press the letter W.

3. Click an area of tooth in your photo. You may need to adjust the tolerance settings in the Options bar to get a good selection area.

4. Press and hold the Shift key and then click another area of tooth to add it to the selection.

5. Continue Shift-clicking each tooth until they are all selected. You don't want all of the teeth selected. Leave some of the shadow areas unselected to achieve a more natural look.

6. Choose Select ⇨ Feather. This softens the edges of your selection.

7. In the Feather dialog box, set your Feather Radius to 2 pixels.

8. Choose Image ⇨ Adjustments ⇨ Hue/Saturation to open the dialog box you see in Figure 22.12.

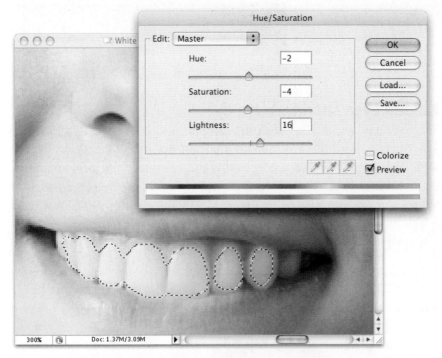

Figure 22.12. The Hue/Saturation dialog box and a close-up of teeth.

9. To hide your selection lines temporarily, press ⌘+H (Ctrl+H). Your teeth will still be selected but the marching ants will be hidden from view. This makes it so much easier to get an accurate preview of your adjustments. To unhide the selection lines, press ⌘+H (Ctrl+H) again.

10. Decrease the Saturation levels a tad. You probably don't need to go any lower than a value of –10.

11. Increase your lightness values. Don't increase them too much or your teeth will look unnaturally white. Stay under a value of 20.

12. To remove a yellow tint, lower the Hue value just a touch. A value of between –1 and –5 should do the trick.

13. Click OK to accept your settings.

Your subject now has sparkling white teeth that aren't sensitive to ice cream or other cold foods. Lucky ducks!

Inside Scoop

If you overdid your tooth whitening, you can fade your adjustments immediately after you make them by choosing Edit ⇨ Fade and decreasing the opacity.

Making eyes sparkle

Subtle enhancements to eyes can really bring out the best in a portrait. The Sharpen tool lets you quickly sharpen up areas like eyelashes and highlights to make eyes sparkle. In this exercise you'll perform an adjustment on a feathered selection and add crispness to eyelashes with the Sharpen tool. The photos in Figure 22.13 show a portrait before and after whitening teeth and eyes. It also shows the subtle improvements you can get by sharpening the pixels around the eyes.

Figure 22.13. A before and after photo of color correction on eyes and teeth.

To enhance your subject's eyes, follow these steps:

1. Open a portrait photo. Make sure you pick a photo that shows the whites of someone's eyes. This trick also works for whitening teeth, so you can reuse the same photo as the last exercise if you like.

2. Select the Sharpen tool from the Toolbox. It is located in the Blur tool fly-out menu and looks like a white triangle. To toggle through the fly-out menu items under the Blur tool, press Shift+R.

3. Change the Strength setting in the Options bar to about 20%.

4. Adjust your brush diameter so that you can easily target areas around the lashes and highlights. You can use the [and] keys to enlarge or shrink your brush diameter.

5. Paint around the lashes of your subject's eyes. If there is a visible highlight in the eyes, paint around the edges to enhance it. Don't overuse this tool; it works best in moderation.

6. To whiten the subject's eyes, select the Magic Wand tool from the Toolbox, or press the letter W.

7. Select an area in the whites of your subject's eyes. You might have to adjust the Tolerance settings in the Options bar. Usually a Tolerance setting of between 8 and 16 works well for eyes.

8. Press and hold the Shift key and click another area of the whites to add it to the selection until you have selected all of the whites of your subject's eyes.

9. Choose Select ⇨ Feather. Enter a Feather Radius of 2 pixels to soften the edges of your selection.

10. Click the Add New Fill or Adjustment Layer button on the bottom of the Layers palette.

11. Choose Brightness/Contrast from the drop-down list. A new layer is automatically created with a mask of your selection, and the Brightness/Contrast dialog box that you see in Figure 22.14 appears.

Bright Idea!

If you have any unsightly red veins you'd like to tone down, try the Desaturate tool. It is located in the Dodge tool fly-out menu. If your desaturated veins are still too visible, lighten them up with the Dodge tool. Choose Highlight from the Range drop-down list and lower the exposure to about 10%.

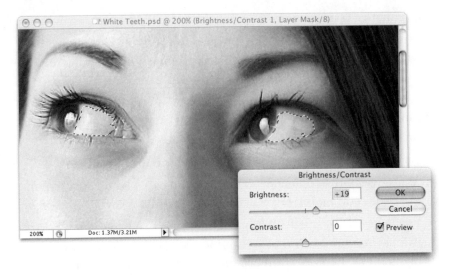

Figure 22.14. The Brightness/Contrast dialog box and a close-up of eyes.

12. Adjust the Brightness setting. Try to keep the value below 20; otherwise, your subject's eyes will look unnatural.

13. Click OK to accept and apply your changes.

If the whites look a little too bright, you can lower the opacity setting of your Adjustment layer to blend it with the original image. The great thing about this method is that you can double-click the adjustment layer thumbnail at any time and readjust your Brightness/Contrast settings.

Advanced shadows and highlights

You may be familiar with the Shadow/Highlight adjustment tool, but did you know it has an advanced options mode? The default dialog box for Shadow/Highlight has two simple controls. It automatically makes judgments on what is a shadow and what is a highlight. I don't know about you, but that seems a little presumptuous. Most people wind up overlooking this tool and head straight for Levels or Curves. A little-known secret is a big, wonderful world for fine-tuning the lightness, shadow, color balance, and midtones of your photos. The bottom of the Shadow/Highlights adjustment dialog box has a sneaky little check box that displays many more sliders when checked. The options it offers let you control what you consider shadow and what you consider highlights, allowing you to get much more control over your images. The before and after example in Figure 22.15 shows how you can target shadow and highlight areas to bring out more detail.

Figure 22.15. A photo before and after performing Advanced Shadow/Highlight adjustments using advanced settings.

To perform advanced Shadow/Highlight adjustments on a photo, follow these steps:

1. Open a photo.

2. Choose Image ⇨ Adjustments ⇨ Shadow/Highlight.

3. Check the Show More Options check box on the bottom of the Shadow/Highlights dialog box. The extended list of options that you see in Figure 22.16 appears.

4. Under Shadows, adjust the Amount and Tonal Width values. The Amount value controls how much light appears in your shadows. The higher the value, the lighter the shadows. The Tonal Width value controls the brightness value of the colors in your shadows.

5. Adjust the Radius value to control how many levels of dark are considered to be in the shadow area of your image.

6. Under Highlights, adjust the Amount to between 15% and 20%. It will probably look too dark; you are going to fix that in the next step.

7. Adjust the Tonal Width. The lower the value, the lighter the highlight areas. In most cases, adjusting this level to just above 0% will add some richness to your highlight areas. This option comes in handy on images with highlights that look washed out.

Hack

You can use your Tab key to tab through the value fields. Adjust the values by using your keyboard's up and down arrows.

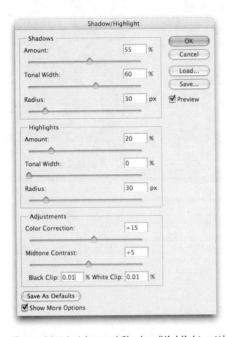

Figure 22.16. Advanced Shadow/Highlight settings.

8. Adjust the Highlights Radius value to adjust the amount of colors Photoshop considers highlight colors in your image.

9. Adjust the Adjustments value to boost colors and contrast in your midtones.

10. Click the Save As Defaults button. This button saves your new settings as default settings so that they are automatically applied whenever you perform a Shadow/Highlight adjustment. Clicking this button also means that the advanced settings options will be automatically visible.

Just the facts

- Use Adobe Gamma on a Windows machine or the Color panel of your Displays control panel on a Mac to calibrate your monitor color.

- For the most accurate monitor color possible, purchase a hardware monitor calibrator such as the ColorVision Spyder2 or the Monaco Optix XR Pro.

- Remove out-of-gamut colors using gamut warning and the Sponge tool, or use the Hue/Saturation adjustment tool to selectively desaturate them.

- Create your own default settings for Auto Color and Auto Levels adjustments.

- Get more control over shadows and highlights by enabling the advanced features of the Shadow/Highlight adjustment tool.

- Get great skin tones by using the Eyedropper tool and isolating specific colors in the Hue/Saturation adjustment tool.

- Brighten and whiten teeth and eyes using feathered selections and masked adjustment layers.

Creating and Using Automation Scripts

One area where Photoshop excels is in automation. Because the Photoshop user community is so large and Adobe is so receptive to its user's comments, suggestions, and projects, many cool automation tools have been added over the years. One of my favorites is the Web Photo Gallery creator. It creates a mini HTML Web site using various templates. You can then add it to your pre-existing Web site if you have FTP access to your server, or burn it to a CD to share with friends. Anyone with a Web browser can view it and you have some nice options for customizing colors and content.

You'll be spending half your time in Photoshop and half in ImageReady. Be sure to read Chapter 20 to get a solid foundation in ImageReady. The most important point to remember is that ImageReady is an application designed for creating images for the Web or digital media. All images created in ImageReady are created as 72-dpi files.

This chapter shows you how to create a PDF to share several images in a single file. You'll create an action for adding copyright text to images and batch-process that action on a folder of images.

535

Creating print and Web designs using automation tools

Photoshop has several tools for automating the creation of printable documents and Web sites. All the tools are located under the File ⇨ Automation menu. This section looks at some of my favorites and I'll show you how to get the best results from the various options associated with them.

Creating a Web photo gallery

If you are looking for a fast way for creating Web sites from a folder of digital photos, The Web Photo Gallery might be the answer to your prayers. I use this automation tool all the time when I need to get photos up on the Web fast. It makes a great tool for organizing design comps for clients. With just a couple of clicks, you can take a folder of images, create a mini Web site with all of your photos, and include copyright text or other information in each image. The photo gallery options let you pick from several different styles or layouts and give you control over colors and text. You can then upload the Web site to your Web server if you have one or burn it to a CD to share with friends. Anyone with a Web browser can view it from a CD or hard drive without having to connect to the Internet, and you have some nice options for customizing colors and content.

The Web sites created using the Web Photo Gallery have large photos, thumbnails, an index or home page, and individual pages of each large image. This feature comes in handy when you have several design ideas you want to share with a client and you don't want to monkey around with creating a Web site or other presentation design from scratch. Figure 23.1 shows a Web photo gallery created with Photoshop CS2.

To create a mini Web site with Web Photo Gallery, follow these steps:

1. You'll need to create two folders before generating your photo album. Create a source folder that holds all of the photos you'd like to include in your photo gallery. Create a second, empty folder in which Photoshop can create your Web photo gallery. You can create them anywhere on your hard drive.

2. Open Photoshop and choose File ⇨ Automate ⇨ Web Photo Gallery. A large dialog box appears.

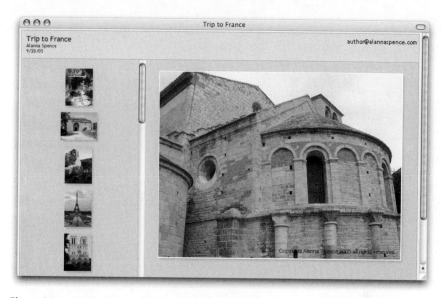

Figure 23.1. A Web photo gallery previewed in a Web browser.

3. Choose a template for your Web site from the styles drop-down list. In Figure 23.1, I used Simple – Vertical Thumbnails. You can preview what each style will look like in the thumbnail on the right side of the dialog box.

4. Under Source Images, choose Folder in the Use drop-down list and click the Choose buttons to first select your source folder and then the Web gallery folder you created in step 1.

5. Step through each panel under the Options drop-down list. Each style has different options available to it. For example, Simple-Vertical lets you change only banner color; it doesn't allow you to change background or link colors. If one of the options you need is grayed out, try selecting another style.

6. You don't need to fill out everything, just the elements you'd like to add or change.

7. Select a size for your full-sized images in the Large Images panel, as shown in Figure 23.2. Choose a JPEG compression quality. For high-quality images, choose between 8 and 12. If you are very low on space and don't mind losing a little image quality, choose Medium quality. For my photos, 9 tends to give me quality images and shaves off a little in file size.

Figure 23.2. The Web Photo Gallery dialog box.

8. Choose a thumbnail size for the image previews. I like thumbnails that are either 75 or 100 pixels. Otherwise they are too small to be recognizable.

9. The Security panel shown in Figure 23.3 offers you some nice options for adding copyright text to your images. If someone downloads your JPEGs, each will have copyright information on them. Add a copyright blurb by selecting Custom Text and adding your own text. Change the position and size. I like to lower the opacity of my text to 60% or 80% so it doesn't interfere with my image too much.

10. When you have finished modifying all the panels, click OK to generate your Web photo gallery.

The generating process takes some time, so have patience. Photoshop opens and resizes each one of the images for your gallery. The more images, the longer it will take. When Photoshop is done, it automatically launches your gallery in a browser window.

Bright Idea!

If you are comfortable with editing HTML, you can add your own Web gallery style by creating your own template files. Visit the Adobe Help System topics on Web Photo Gallery for more information.

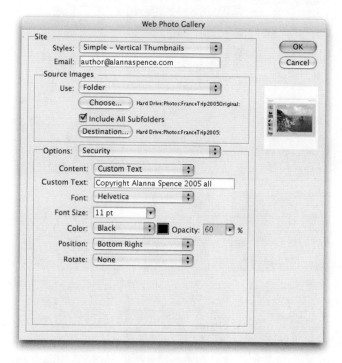

Figure 23.3. The Web Photo Gallery dialog box with Security panel visible.

Generating contact sheets of your photos

The Contact Sheets automation script takes a folder of images and creates a page full of thumbnails that you can print out or use in digital form. If you like having physical printouts of your photos, keeping a binder of all your digital photo folders can be a great way to stay organized. Figure 23.4 shows a document of thumbnail images created with the Contact Sheet II automation tool.

Figure 23.4. A document created with Contact Sheet II.

To create a contact sheet of your photos, follow these steps:

1. Choose File ⇨ Automate ⇨ Contact Sheet II.

2. The tool by default creates a contact sheet that will fit on an 8.5-x-11-inch piece of paper. Change the document width and height settings if you are printing on larger or smaller paper. Remember to consider page margins.

3. Choose a color mode for your document. Most inkjet printers prefer documents in RGB. Color laser printers prefer documents in CMYK.

4. Adjust the number of images per column and row. Your image thumbnail sizes are automatically resized based on the number of columns and rows.

5. To adjust the vertical and horizontal spacing between images, uncheck the Use Auto-Spacing check box. You can use any unit of measure that Photoshop accepts. Enter the value followed by *in* for inches or *px* for pixels.

6. You have the option of including the filename underneath each thumbnail. Having the filename associated with a thumbnail image makes it easier to find the images later, even if the folders are moved around.

7. Click OK when you have finished changing your settings in the Contact Sheet II dialog box as shown in Figure 23.5.

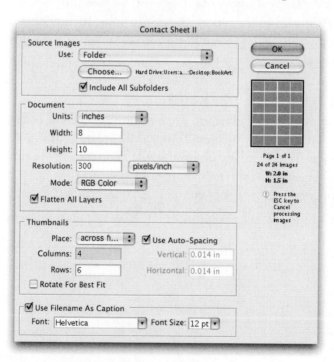

Figure 23.5. The Contact Sheet II dialog box.

Bright Idea!

Create a contact sheet from the currently selected files in Adobe Bridge. In the Source drop-down list, choose Selected Images from Bridge. Arrange your photos in the order you'd like them displayed in your contact sheet.

Photoshop opens, copies, and resizes each of the images in your set and creates a single Photoshop file with a grid of your images. If you unchecked the Flatten All Layers check box, you can rearrange your images.

Create a grid design using contact sheets

A creative way to use this tool is to make tiled design from several square photos, similar to the design shown in Figure 23.6. Create a folder of images that have been cropped to perfect squares. Be sure to uncheck the Flatten All Layers check box so you can move things around. Remove some of the images and add text elements. Also make sure your document proportions match the number of images you have in your design. If you create a 5 x 5 grid, you'll need to make sure your document is a square, like 8 x 8 inches; otherwise, Photoshop automatically creates spaces in between your images.

Printing out a picture package

With printers getting better and cheaper, you can now get a great home printer that prints photo-quality images. To instantly create a printable page with various photo sizes like the one you see in Figure 23.7, you can use the Picture Package automation tool. The tool has several options for laying out different combinations of common photo sizes for wallets and frames.

Figure 23.6. A design created with Contact Sheet II.

Figure 23.7. Differently sized images created using the Picture Package automation tool.

To share photo prints by generating a Picture Package, follow these steps:

1. Open the photo file you'd like to use.

2. Choose File ➪ Automate ➪ Picture Package.

3. Select Frontmost document from the Use drop-down list.

4. Choose a photo set from the Layout drop-down list. I used the second option in the list for Figure 23.8, which gives me one 5-x-7-inch image, two 2.5-x-3.5-inch images, and four 2-x-2.5-inch images per page.

5. In the Label section, you can add custom text to your image, like copyright information or details about the photographer. You can change the font size, color, and opacity of the font. You can also rotate the text if you prefer a vertical positioning. Figure 23.8 shows the Picture Package dialog box with label information added.

6. Click OK to generate your Picture Package file.

Photoshop creates a new document with the various image sizes. If you deselected the Flatten All Layers check box, you can rearrange the images after the file is generated, or use them in other files by copying and pasting.

Figure 23.8. The Picture Package dialog box.

Bright Idea!

Use this feature to print out business card designs. Click the Edit Layout button to create your own custom layout and fill your page with 2-x-3.5-inch images.

Create a PDF presentation of your photos

A great way to send photos to friends and family is to create a PDF presentation of all your photos. Most people have Acrobat Reader preinstalled on their computers, so all they need to do is double-click the file to open it. It's about as foolproof as you can get if you want to share a set of photos with the computer-challenged. A set of 24 Photoshop files, sampled down to 72 dpi each, will be about 5.5MB. Be careful with file size: If you don't sample down, your files can be 54MB for 24 300-dpi images. You have options of creating either a presentation, which automatically launches a slideshow, or a multi-page PDF document that your friends and family can thumb through using easy navigation buttons.

To create a PDF presentation, follow these steps:

1. Choose File ⇨ Automate ⇨ PDF Presentation.

2. Click the Browse button to choose source files from your computer's hard drive. Shift-click to select multiple files in a row. To selectively choose certain files in a list, ⌘+click (Ctrl+click) each file. Click the Open button to add them to the Source Files list.

3. Choose your output options. Multi-Page creates a regular PDF file with navigation buttons to view each page. Presentation creates a file that automatically launches in Slideshow mode. If you choose this mode, you need to tell your friends to use the Escape key to exit the slideshow.

4. Click the Save PDF button, give your PDF file a name, and choose a handy place to save it.

5. A large window launches with the various options for creating your file. Most of the settings are fine as is, except for the Compression settings.

6. Click Compression to open the Compression panel.

7. If you will be e-mailing this PDF, you need to make sure your file size is as small as possible. Under Options, make sure Bicubic Downsampling

To is selected and both the fields show 72 pixels/inch, as shown in Figure 23.9. This shrinks any images down to 72 dpi when they are larger than that.

8. If you don't care about file size and want the best images possible, keep the "for images above" field set to 300 or turn off downsampling by selecting Do Not Downsample from the drop-down list.

9. You can add a password to your file that is required either when someone tries to open the file, print it, or modify it. If you'd like to add a password, click Security to view the panel.

10. When you are done modifying your settings, click Save PDF to generate your PDF file.

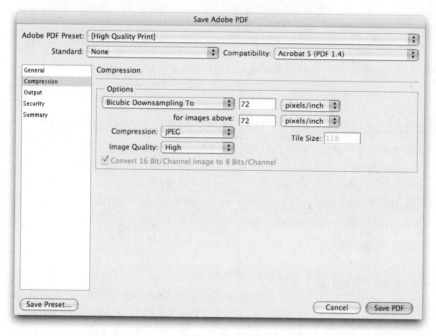

Figure 23.9. The Compression panel in the PDF Presentation tool.

Try out your new PDF file. Find it on your hard drive and double-click it to launch it in Adobe Acrobat. If you selected the Presentation option, you can escape out of the full-screen slideshow by pressing the Esc key. When not in slideshow mode, there are navigation buttons on the bottom of the screen to click through the pages like the ones you see in Figure 23.10. To launch slideshow mode again, press ⌘+L (Ctrl+L).

Figure 23.10. APDF file created in Photoshop and launched in Adobe Acrobat.

Running actions in batches for speed editing

Actions can be recorded for just about any activity in Photoshop and played back on new files. Photoshop gives you a couple of options for processing multiple files. Chapter 10 covered Droplets; this chapter looks at the Batch automation tool. Batch works similar to Droplets but is more immediate than creating a droplet and then dropping files onto it. Batch lets you run actions on one or many files right then and there.

Adding copyright text to photos

You can create an action to automatically add copyright information to your photo. Using an action to do this ensures that all of your copyright text has the same font face, size, color, and placement. Once you create your copyright action, you can save it and use it on future sets of photos.

If you don't have your own action set saved, I encourage you to create one. If you just add action sets to the default set, they will be erased if you reset the Actions palette. Saving your own set ensures that even if you reset your Actions palette, you can reload your action set and get your actions back.

To create an action set, follow these steps:

1. Click the arrow on the top right of the Actions palette and select New Set from the drop-down list.

2. Give your set a name and click OK. Your new set will now appear in the Actions palette.

3. Save your set to your hard drive.

4. Click your set name to highlight it and then click the Actions options arrow on the top right of the palette.

5. Select Save Actions to open a dialog box and choose a location for your ATN file.

6. Save your new action set file to the Adobe Photoshop CS2/Presets/ Photoshop Actions folder.

You can now safely add your own actions without worrying about losing them. If you ever need to load the set again, click the options arrow on the top right of the palette and select your set from the list of sets at the bottom of the drop-down list. Now that you have a place to save your action set, create an action for adding copyright text. Figure 23.11 shows my photo after recording all the steps in my action.

To add an action for copyright text, follow these steps:

1. Open a photo.

2. Click the Create New Action button on the bottom of the Actions palette. Give your action a name like Add Copyright and click OK. Photoshop automatically starts recording once you create your action.

3. Select the Horizontal Type tool from the Toolbox or press the letter T to highlight it.

4. Click wherever you'd like to add your text and type your copyright text. Change the font face, size, and color. Press Enter when you are done.

5. If you like, change the opacity of the text layer to something lighter. I chose 60% in Figure 23.11.

6. Click the square Stop button on the bottom of the Actions palette.

7. Click the arrow next to your new action to view its contents. If there are any extra actions that snuck in, delete them by clicking them and clicking the Delete button on the bottom of the Actions palette.

Watch Out!
Make a habit of testing out any new action on one or two files before running it on an entire set of files. Open another file to try out, click the action to highlight it, and press the triangular Play button to run your action.

Figure 23.11. A new action for adding copyright text to a batch of photos.

Now that you've got your action recorded and tested, you can create a droplet of your action to drag and drop files onto, or you can run a batch process on an entire folder or a set of opened documents.

Batch processing and renaming

Batch processing lets you skip the step of creating a droplet and gets down to business. You can select an entire folder and its contents to run an action on. Batch processing gives you all of the same options that droplets have, with the added bonus of being able to choose from a couple different options for selecting files to edit.

Inside Scoop

Perform an action on all opened documents by selecting Open Documents from the Source drop-down list.

To start a batch process, follow these steps:

1. Choose File ⇨ Automate ⇨ Batch. The Batch dialog box that you see in Figure 23.12 appears.

2. Select your action set and action that you created in the last section from the top of the Batch dialog box.

3. Choose Folder from the Source drop-down list.

4. Click the Choose button to find and select the folder you would like to batch process.

5. Check the Suppress File Open Options Dialogs and Suppress Color Profile Warnings check boxes. Photoshop uses the default color profile or the last used option when these are checked.

6. Choose Folder from the Destination drop-down list and select a folder in which Photoshop will save your edited files. It's always good practice to save your batch-processed files to a new place so you don't accidentally overwrite your original files.

7. To add a serial number to the end of your filename, in the second field under File Naming, select 4 Digit Serial Number. In the third field, select extension so that Photoshop will add a .psd file extension to your filenames.

8. In the Starting Serial# field, enter 0001 to give Photoshop a number to start with. Figure 23.12 shows an example of how to add a serial number to your files.

9. Click OK to begin your batch process.

Photoshop opens and adds copyright text to your files, and then saves them to your destination folder with a four-digit serial number added to the name.

Add frames to several photos at once with droplets

Chapter 10 briefly introduced droplets, but did you know you could use them with any of the action sets that come preinstalled with Photoshop? Before running the Web Photo Gallery automation tool, why not add a frame to your set of photos first?

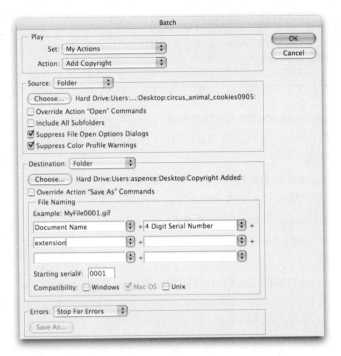

Figure 23.12. The Batch dialog box with options for renaming a file to include a serial number.

To add photo frames by dragging and dropping files, follow these steps:

1. Make sure you have the Frames action set loaded in your Actions palette. If it isn't listed in the list of actions, click the black arrow on the top right of the palette and choose Frames from the bottom of the drop-down list. Click the Append button to add it to your current list of actions.

2. Choose File ➪ Automate ➪ Create Droplet to open the dialog box you see in Figure 23.13.

3. Click the Choose button to name your droplet and choose where to save it.

4. Select the Frames set and choose the Brushed Aluminum Frame, or any other frame style you'd like to use.

5. Click the Suppress File Open Options Dialogs and Suppress Color Profile Warnings check boxes to have Photoshop ignore them. The default settings will be used instead.

Bright Idea!

Take advantage of the file naming option to give your digital photos a better name. Select None from the first Text Naming field, add a serial number to the second one, and add a file extension in the third field.

6. Under the Destination settings, select Folder from the drop-down list and choose a folder in which to save your framed images. This way you'll avoid writing over your original files.

7. Click OK to create your droplet.

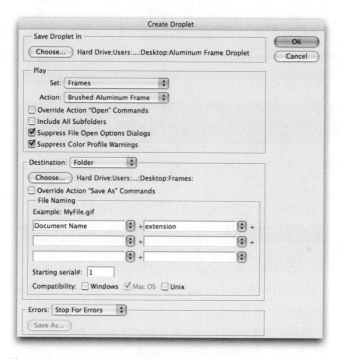

Figure 23.13. The Create Droplet dialog box.

Now, any file you drop on top of the droplet icon automatically opens in Photoshop and performs the set of actions associated with the action you selected.

Getting the most out of ImageReady actions

ImageReady has some advantages and additional features that aren't currently part of Photoshop. There are a few preinstalled actions for creating commonly used design elements and simple templates for Web sites. In ImageReady you can add conditional steps to actions so that you can require certain criteria before performing a task. ImageReady also has a couple of fun text effects for creating flaming or freezing text.

Creating instant Web page templates

If you are in a hurry, ImageReady has an action for creating an entire Web page template with the push of a button. Once it's created, you can change colors, add drop shadows or other effects, and modify text to suit your needs. The action creates a simple design with rounded corners and solid colors, with a few navigation buttons along the top like the example you see in Figure 23.14. The slices for each graphic element are created for you. This section assumes you are familiar with the topics covered in Chapter 20 and are familiar with ImageReady's tools for creating slices.

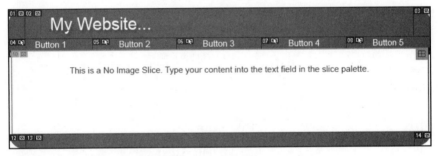

Figure 23.14. The Make Web page action in ImageReady.

To create and modify a Web site design using the Make Web page action, follow these steps:

1. Create a new file in ImageReady. It doesn't matter what size you make it. ImageReady will automatically resize it.

2. Click the Make Webpage action in the Actions palette and click the triangular Play button.

3. ImageReady generates a Web page. Be patient; this will take a minute or two. Now that your template is created, modify some colors and text.

Bright Idea!

Add a drop shadow to your Web site design. Increase your canvas size. Add a white rounded rectangle behind your design with a corner radius of 20px and add a drop shadow to it. You'll need to adjust your slices to include the drop shadow.

4. Double-click the layer named My Website to select the header text. Add your own text and modify the font and color if you like.

5. Double-click each of the color swatches in the two shape layers on the bottom of the Layers palette and change their colors.

6. Rename each of the buttons and delete some if you need to.

7. Add text to the content field. Be careful to adjust your slices if you make changes to or move the images.

8. When you are done editing, choose File ⇨ Save Optimized As and choose HTML and Images from the Format drop-down list. Select a folder to save your Web page and images to.

You now have a basic Web page. To see how it would look on a Web server, find the HTML file that was created and drag and drop it onto a browser window.

Adding flaming or freezing text

ImageReady has a couple more popular text effects installed in the Actions palette. You can use them just as you would any other text action by creating a text layer, clicking the action to highlight it, and clicking the Play button. Figure 23.15 is an example of the Flaming Text and Frozen Text actions available in ImageReady.

Photoshop users love their flaming text effects. If you want to create even cooler flaming text, try searching the Internet for "Photoshop flaming text." You can also check the Resources section in the back for some popular Photoshop tutorial sites.

Inside Scoop

Stretch the flames or icicles by selecting the layer and choosing Edit ⇨ Transform ⇨ Scale.

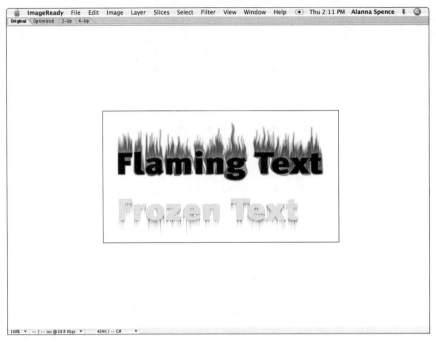

Figure 23.15. The Flaming and Frozen Text actions applied to type in ImageReady.

Creating slide frames for thumbnails

ImageReady includes four different actions for creating slide frames for displaying thumbnails on Web sites. The two slide frames in Figure 23.16 are called Metal Slide Gallery Button and Metal Slide Thumbnail. You'll need to create a new ImageReady file before playing the action. It doesn't matter what size your file is; ImageReady will take over and resize it for you.

Creating conditional actions in ImageReady

ImageReady has an added actions feature that is not in Photoshop. You can now add conditions to actions to have Photoshop perform certain checks before continuing with the action. With a conditional step, you can check an image's aspect ratio and whether it has a portrait or landscape orientation. You can check image width or image height against image size criteria like greater than, less than, or equal to. There are conditional statements for a layer's count, type, or name. In the next exercise, you'll add a condition that only tries to resize an image if it is larger than 600 pixels wide.

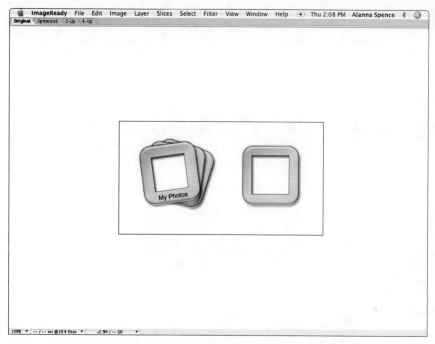

Figure 23.16. A Metal Slide Gallery Button and Thumbnail created with actions.

To add conditions to an action in ImageReady, follow these steps:

1. Open ImageReady either by launching it like any other application or by clicking the Jump to ImageReady button on the bottom of the Toolbox in Photoshop.

2. Open the Actions palette. If it's currently not visible on your screen, choose Window ⇨ Actions.

3. Click the Create New Action button on the bottom of the Actions palette and give it a name.

4. Click the script button on the bottom left of the Actions palette and choose Create Conditional.

5. Create a condition for Image Width that is less than 600.

6. Select Skip from the Perform the following action drop-down list and enter 1 for the number of steps to skip.

7. Click OK to add your condition to your action. You are still in record mode, so continue adding to your action.

Hack

Use Conditionals to find files with certain traits or specific layer names. Choose Beep from the Perform the following action drop-down list to have Photoshop alert you when it's found the condition you have defined. This is great for finding a specific text layer in a sea of files.

8. Choose Image ⇨ Image Size and enter 600 in the Width field, as shown in Figure 23.17. Click OK to add your image sizing to the action.

9. Click the Stop button on the bottom of the Actions palette to stop recording your new action.

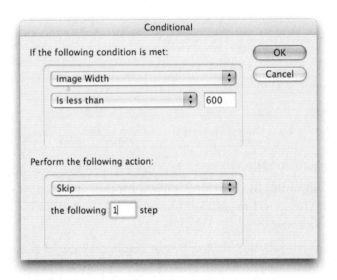

Figure 23.17. The Conditional dialog box with a condition for Image Width less than 600 pixels.

This is a good way of resizing several images at once, while avoiding accidentally enlarging an image that is smaller than the target size. By creating a droplet using your newly created action, you can quickly resize an entire folder by dragging and dropping files on top of the droplet icon.

Just the facts

- Create a mini Web site of your images by running the Web Photo Gallery automation tool on a folder of images.

- Create a printable page of varying photo sizes by using the Picture Package automation tool.

- Share several images in one file by creating an Adobe Acrobat PDF file.

- Add frames to a set of photos by creating a droplet using one of the Frames actions.

- Add consistent copyright text by creating an action that adds a text layer.

GET THE SCOOP ON...

Saving multiple design versions with Layer Comps ▪
Managing project files with the Bridge Center ▪
Trying out stock photos before you buy ▪ Tracking
file version history

Managing Your Designs

K eeping track of large Photoshop files and multiple designs can get tricky. You may need to create several versions of a design to show a client. In older versions of Photoshop, this meant saving out multiple files, all with different design elements. Inevitably, the client ends up wanting pieces and parts from various files, and it's your job to figure out where you put what. If you are working with multiple designers, sharing files can often lead to accidentally losing versions of designs if the wrong file versions are used. Photoshop has heard the cry of the frustrated designer and stepped up to the plate, offering many useful tools for running a tight ship.

This chapter introduces you to some of Photoshop's features for managing files and designs. These tools were designed with professional designers in mind and are powerful aids in presenting multiple design ideas or helping maintain version history of design files. We'll take a peak at Adobe Stock Photos, a new feature in Adobe Bridge that gives you the ability to try out and edit stock photos (so that when it's time to shell out the cash you know you're buying the right image). I'll show you some advanced features of Photoshop and Bridge for managing and tracking files. If you aren't yet familiar with Adobe Bridge, I encourage you to look through Chapter 12.

Chapter 24

Saving layer comps

The new Layer Comps feature in Photoshop is a lifesaver if you do any sort of design work that involves having to save different versions of your designs. You no longer have to deal with the headache of managing several files with slightly different design elements. Layer Comps lets you save different sets of information such as layer visibility and location, and it lets you save layer blending options.

Layer Comps are also a good reason to start getting used to doing all of your image adjustments on adjustment layers instead of applying changes directly to your image layer. You'll be able to turn adjustment layers on and off, making the task of saving different versions painless and quick.

The Web site design in Figure 24.1 is the first of several design comps I'd like to show my client. I'm going to first add this version in my layer comps file and then create alternative designs.

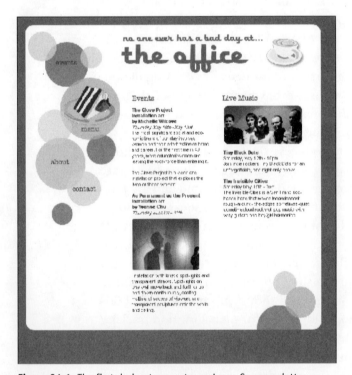

Figure 24.1. The first design to save to my Layer Comps palette.

The Layer Comps palette is similar to the History palette in that it keeps track of different changes you've done to your document. The main difference and benefit with Layer Comps is that they don't actually alter any of the artwork in your document. They are merely keeping track of layer visibility, layer styles, and layer placement. Unlike History snapshots, they are permanent, so you can return to them even after you've quit and relaunched Photoshop.

To save your first design comp to the Layer Comps palette, follow these steps:

1. Open your design file.

2. Bring the Layer Comps palette to the front. By default, it is stored in the Palette dock. You can click and drag its tab outside of the palette dock for easier access. If it's not visible on your screen, choose Window ⇨ Layer Comps.

3. Click the Create New Layer Comp button on the bottom of the Layer Comps palette. The dialog box shown in Figure 24.2 appears.

4. Enter a descriptive name and comments for your Layer Comp.

5. Check the boxes for layer Visibility, Position, and Appearance. With these three checked, Photoshop keeps track of any changes you make to the positioning of your layer, any layer styles you add or change, and which layers are visible or hidden.

6. Click OK to save your new layer comp.

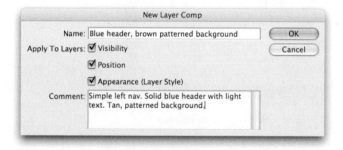

Figure 24.2. The New Layer Comp dialog box.

You are now free to change your design for the next layer comp version. Layer comps remember changes made to layer visibility, blending options, and layer position, so you can get away with many of your changes

Watch Out!

Layer Comps won't remember color changes to layers or other edits. If you are changing color or running filters on a layer, you'll need to create a copy of the layer first and save a different combination of layer visibility with each layer comp.

without having to manage different copies of layers. For my second design comp, I changed the header graphics, background color, and replaced the navigation with a simpler design. Figure 24.3 shows my second design comp.

Figure 24.3. A second design comp for the Layer Comps palette.

After you've made a few changes to your design and you are ready to save another layer comp, simply repeat the previous steps. I've created three different versions of my design and saved them all to the Layer Comps palette. Figure 24.4 shows my list of layer comps.

Figure 24.4. The Layer Comps palette.

The icon to the left of the current layer comp shows you which layer comp is being used. To switch layer comps, click the empty box next to the layer comp you'd like to use. Photoshop automatically changes layer visibility, the positioning of layers, and any changes made to layer styles like drop shadows, color overlay, or stroke.

The Layer Comps palette has a few more options available through the black arrow on the top right of the palette, as shown in Figure 24.5. Many are represented in the buttons along the bottom of the palette, but a couple of them are extra features that you shouldn't pass up.

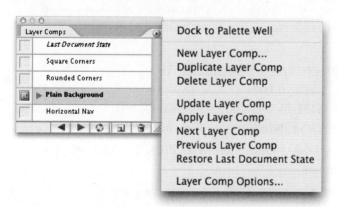

Figure 24.5. Layer Comps palette options drop-down list.

The Layer Comps palette options are

- **New Layer Comp:** Creates a new layer comp based on your document's current state.

- **Duplicate Layer Comp:** Makes a duplicate of the currently highlighted layer comp.

- **Delete Layer Comp:** Permanently removes the layer comp from the Layer Comps palette. Performs the same task as the trash icon on the bottom of the Layer Comps palette.

- **Update Layer Comp:** Updates the currently selected layer comp with any changes you've made. Performs the same task as the button with circular arrows on the bottom of the Layer Comps palette.

- **Apply Layer Comp:** Applies the settings from the highlighted layer comp. Performs the same task as clicking the box in the left column of the layer comp.

- **Next Layer Comp:** Steps down through the list. Performs the same operation as the right arrow button on the bottom of the palette.

- **Previous Layer Comp:** Steps up through the list. Performs the same operation as the left arrow button on the bottom of the palette.

- **Restore Last Document State:** If you accidentally switch to an older layer comp before creating a new one, you can restore your last document state with this option.

- **Layer Comp Options:** Allows you to update the information you entered in the Create New Layer Comp dialog box.

Save your layer comps to separate files

After you've created several layer comps, you can quickly create a set of PDF, JPEG, PSD, or TIFF files to share with your clients.

To save your layer comps to separate files, follow these steps:

1. Choose File ⇨ Scripts ⇨ Layer Comps To Files. The dialog box in Figure 24.6 appears.

2. Click the Browse button to select a destination for your files.

3. Enter a name in the File Name Prefix field. Photoshop fills in the suffix based on the file type you select.

4. You can choose to save only the selected layer comps or the entire set with the Selected Layer Comps Only check box.

5. Choose a file type from the drop-down list. I've included a detailed list of file types and their options later on in this section if you need help deciding.

6. Click Run to create your new files.

Layer Comps To Files

Destination:

| Desktop/WebsiteComps | Browse... | | Run |

File Name Prefix:

| bm_website | | Cancel |

☐ Selected Layer Comps Only

File Type:

| PDF ▲▼ |

☑ Include ICC Profile

PDF Options:

Encoding: ○ ZIP ◉ JPEG

Quality: 8

Please specify the format and location for saving each layer comp as a file.

Figure 24.6. The Layer Comp To Files dialog box.

Saving files as PDF or JPEG is probably the easiest option to use if you plan on sending your comps around to one or more people for review. In the next section, I'll show you how to create a Web site for your layer comps using the Web Photo Gallery introduced in Chapter 23.

Each one of the file types gives you the option to save your current color profile with the file. It's up to you whether you include it or not. If exact color isn't a priority, unchecking it can cause less confusion if one or more people will be looking at the files. Table 24.1 lists the various file types and their options as listed in the Layer Comps To Files dialog box.

Hack

The PDF File Type option in the Layer Comps To Files dialog box creates a separate PDF file for each layer comp. Create a single PDF, including slideshow options, by choosing File ➪ Scripts ➪ Layer Comps to PDF.

Inside Scoop

Select multiple layer comps by Shift-clicking them in the Layer Comps palette.

Table 24.1. File options available though Layer Comps To Files dialog box

File Type	Options	Description
BMP	Bit Depth	File format used on the Windows operating system only.
PDF	Zip or JPEG, JPEG Quality	This option saves each layer comp to a separate PDF file.
JPEG	Quality	Viewable in a variety of applications including Web browsers.
PSD	Maximize Compatibility	Users with older versions of Photoshop will more likely be able to open your file. Increases file size.
Targa	Bit Depth	Used for video and color MS-DOS applications.
TIFF	Image Compression, JPEG Quality	Commonly used for printing or file compatibility between applications.

Create an instant Web Photo Gallery from layer comps

There is a script for creating a Web Photo Gallery from a set of layer comps. This script creates a Web site using the Web Photo Gallery option covered in Chapter 23. By uploading a Web gallery of layer comps, you can instantly show clients your design revisions without having to worry about e-mailing large files through slow Internet connections. Just upload the files to your Web site and send the URL to your client. The Web Photo Gallery works on any browser, so you can view it locally or use it for a meeting presentation.

I've created a Web Photo Gallery using the style Simple – Vertical Thumbnails. Figure 24.7 shows the main page of the final Web site generated by Photoshop.

Hack

The dialog box for this script automatically uses the last used style from the regular Web Photo Gallery automation tool. To use a different style, enter the exact name of the style in the Layer Comps To WPG dialog box.

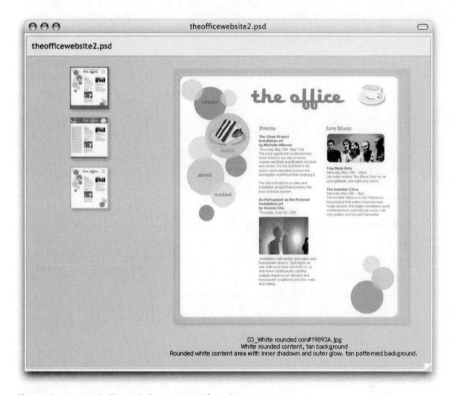

Figure 24.7. A Web Photo Gallery created from layer comps.

To create a Web Photo Gallery from layer comps, follow these steps:

1. Open a file with several saved layer comps.

2. Choose File ⇨ Scripts ⇨ Layer Comps to WPG. The dialog box in Figure 24.8 appears.

3. Click the Browse button to choose a destination for your Web Photo Gallery. This script creates multiple files and folders, so I recommend creating a main folder for your Web Photo Gallery.

Watch Out!

Photoshop uses the last settings that were used for the Web Photo Gallery Style. If you need to change colors, fonts, or other attributes, you'll need to run the regular Web Photo Gallery through File ⇨ Automate ⇨ Web Photo Gallery, make your changes, and run the script.

Figure 24.8. The Layer Comps To WPG dialog box.

4. Photoshop automatically picks the last style used in the Web Photo Gallery automation tool. If you prefer to use a different style than the one listed, enter the name of another style.

5. You have the option of creating a Web Photo Gallery from all layer comps or just the selected ones.

6. Click Run to generate a Web Photo Gallery from your comps.

Photoshop creates a Web Photo Gallery in the location you specified and automatically launches your new Web site in a browser window. In your destination folder, you'll find a main index page and folders for the link pages, large images, and thumbnails. You can then upload it to a Web server or burn it to a CD. This script is great when you need to quickly put together a presentation of your layer comps.

Exploring the Bridge Center

The Bridge Center is a new feature included with Adobe Bridge. It is only available for people who own the entire Adobe Creative Suite CS2. It has some handy features, and I'd recommend looking into it if you are a Creative Suite CS2 owner. Figure 24.9 shows the Bridge Center in Adobe Bridge.

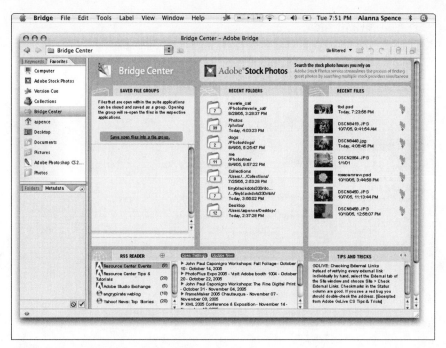

Figure 24.9. The Bridge Center in Adobe Bridge.

To access the Bridge Center, click the Bridge Center in the Favorites panel of Adobe Bridge. If it's not there, you'll need to change your Adobe Bridge Preferences.

To add the Bridge Center to your Adobe Bridge Preferences, follow these steps:

1. Launch Adobe Bridge by either choosing File ⇨ Browse from inside Adobe Photoshop or by launching the Bridge application from your hard drive. The Bridge folder is located in your Applications folder (Program Files folder).

2. With Adobe Bridge open and active, select Bridge ⇨ Preferences or press ⌘+K (Ctrl+K). The dialog box in Figure 24.10 appears.

3. Click the Bridge Center check box under the Favorites Items section.

4. Click OK to exit the Preferences window.

Bridge Center will now appear in your Favorites panel every time you launch Bridge. You can click it to view the Bridge Center panel.

Bright Idea!

The Bridge Center has some handy features for calibrating color across all of your Creative Suite applications. Click the Color Management button on the bottom of the Bridge Center window.

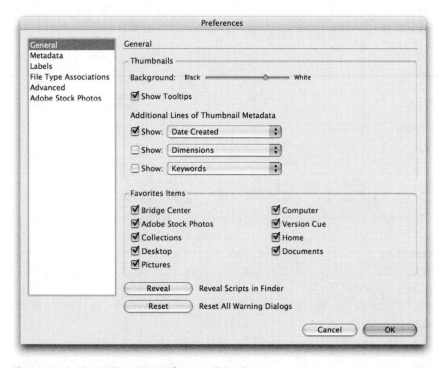

Figure 24.10. The Adobe Bridge Preferences dialog box.

Saving file groups in the Bridge Center

Adobe Bridge has a special panel for viewing recent files and folders, saving your own file groups, viewing RSS feeds, and getting the latest tips and tricks for the products in the Adobe Creative Suite. The Bridge Center keeps track of recent files and folders used not only in Adobe Photoshop, but also for users who own the entire Adobe Creative Suite. It also keeps track of recent activities in any of the Creative Suite applications.

One very handy feature in the Bridge Center is the ability to save file groups. These groups can consist of any type of file, and the files can live in separate folders. If you are working on a Web site for a company and have several files that you need open at the same time, you can add them to a file group by clicking the group in the Bridge Center. All the associated Creative Suite applications will launch with the files in the file group. The files don't need to live in the same folder. You can point to a logo file in another folder instead of creating copies of files all over your hard drive. This sets up a sort of dotted-line association with files. File groups can be created from any open Creative Suite files.

To create a file group from open files, follow these steps:

1. Open several files that you'd like to add to your file group. If you own the entire Creative Suite, you can open files in other programs such as Illustrator or GoLive. If you just own Photoshop, try opening a file in ImageReady and a file in Photoshop.

2. Open Adobe Bridge by choosing File ⇨ Browse from inside Photoshop.

3. Click the Bridge Center shortcut in the Favorites panel.

4. Click the link that reads Save open files into a file group.

The Bridge Center creates an item with a suitcase icon that lists how many files are associated with it (see Figure 24.11). By clicking it and then clicking Open this file group, you can reopen all of the files in your file group.

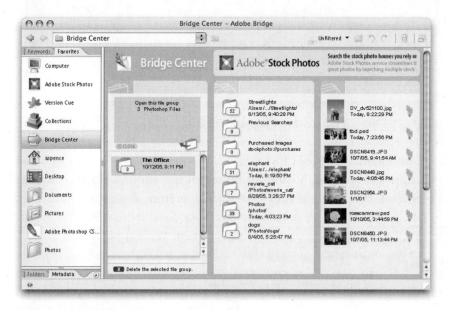

Figure 24.11. The Bridge Center with a file group.

Watch Out!

You cannot add files that have unsaved changes. Be sure to save your files before creating a file group. Bridge automatically closes all of your files when it first creates the file group.

Once you create a file group, you can't edit it. If you need to change it, you'll need to delete it and create a new one. A delete button appears when you have selected a file group from the list.

Adobe content and RSS feeds

The bottom panels of the Bridge Center shown in Figure 24.12 offer content about Adobe products, including tips and tricks for Photoshop and other Adobe products. The RSS Feeds panels show content only if you are connected to the Internet. It feeds information from the Adobe Web site straight to your computer and has information about Adobe events, tips and tutorials, and information about downloads like filters and actions.

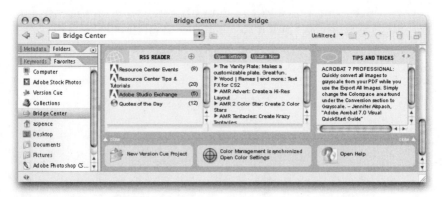

Figure 24.12. The RSS Feeds and Tips and Tricks panels in the Bridge Center.

You can add your own RSS feeds to the Bridge Center. With so many Photoshop support Web sites out there, it's not surprising that you have many Photoshop-specific RSS feeds to choose from. Check the Resources

Watch Out!

The RSS feeds are available only when you have access to the Internet. If your RSS Feeds panel is empty, check your Internet connection, or try clicking the Update Now button above the middle panel.

Hack

The Bridge Center checks for new info only every 4 hours. To change the refresh interval for RSS feeds, click the Open Settings button in the panel to the left of the RSS Feeds panel and enter a new number of hours.

guide in the back of the book for a listing of popular Photoshop support Web sites.

One popular Photoshop Web site that has an RSS feed is PhotoshopSupport.com. At the time I wrote this book, there was a handy orange-and-blue XML feed link on the right-hand side of the page. Clicking it takes you to a page with information and a link that you can use as an RSS feed. Many Web sites have XML or RSS orange buttons with URLs for adding RSS feeds to your own applications or Web sites. You can find many more by searching for **Photoshop RSS feed** in your favorite search engine.

To add an RSS feed to the Bridge Center, follow these steps:

1. You'll first need an RSS feed link. Go to PhotoshopSupport.com and find the XML Feed button on the right-hand side. Click it to go to the RSS Feeds information page. Copy the URL for subscribing to the Photoshop Blog News Feed.

2. Open Adobe Bridge and click the Bridge Center in the Favorites panel. Click the + symbol on the top of the RSS Feeds panel.

3. A dialog box appears with a field for adding a URL for an RSS feed. Paste in the URL you copied and click OK.

The Bridge Center now automatically fetches the latest news from the RSS feed. You can add any RSS feed you want. They don't necessarily have to be Photoshop related. I added a Quote of the Day RSS feed to mine.

Exploring Adobe stock photos

Adobe has collaborated with several stock photo companies to bring its users access to a huge library of stock photography. By opening Adobe Bridge, you have instant access to this library. It allows you to pop comp files right into your designs, and once you decide they are what you really want, gives you an easy way to purchase and use them. It also remembers previous searches, downloaded comps, and purchased images. You pay a price for convenience, but sometimes when you are under a deadline,

Watch Out!
You need to be connected to the Internet in order to use Adobe Stock Photos. If you click the Adobe Stock Photos link in the Favorites panel of Adobe Bridge and nothing happens, check to make sure you have an Internet connection.

convenience is worth a lot. Some of its providers are Photodisc, Comstock Images, DigitalVision, ImageShop, and Amana. I'm sure more providers will follow suit soon enough.

To perform a search in Adobe Stock Photos, follow these steps:

1. Launch Adobe Bridge from within Photoshop by choosing File ⇨ Browse.

2. Click the Adobe Stock Photos link in the Favorites panel in Adobe Bridge. The welcome screen appears.

3. Type something in the search box on the top of the screen and click the Start Search button. The button looks like a pair of binoculars. Figure 24.13 shows the search results from a search on *elephant*.

4. Right-click an image and select Download Comp.

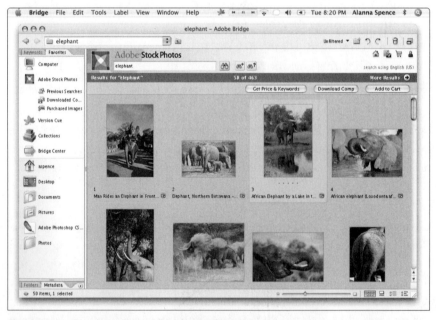

Figure 24.13. Search results in Adobe Stock Photos.

5. Click the Downloaded Comps link below the Adobe Stock Photos link in the Favorites panel of Adobe Bridge.

6. Double-click a file to open it in Photoshop. A low-resolution 72-dpi version of the file opens in Photoshop.

7. Try out your file. You can make any changes you want to the file.

8. Return to the Downloaded Comps panel in Adobe Bridge when you are ready to purchase a high-resolution version of the image.

9. Click the image to highlight it and click the Add to Cart button. Adobe Bridge adds the item to your shopping cart.

10. Click the Shopping Cart icon on the top right of the Adobe Stock Photos window. The screen that you see in Figure 24.14 appears.

11. Step through the checkout process as you would any other Web site shopping cart.

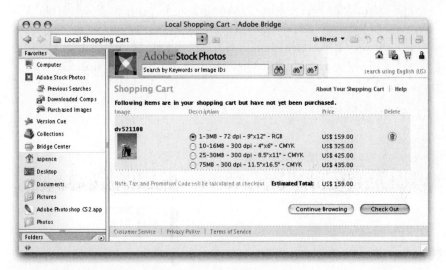

Figure 24.14. The Shopping Cart screen in Adobe Stock Photos.

 Watch Out!

Be sure to save your login information in a safe place so you don't lose it.

The first time you purchase a stock photo, you'll be asked to create a new account. The checkout process for subsequent purchases will be much faster. Replace your newly purchased high-resolution image with the low-resolution comp file.

Tracking changes in Version Cue

Version Cue offers the ability to track and control changes for a project, as well as keeping track of assets and revision changes. Version Cue ensures that co-workers don't accidentally write over your files, and it keeps a backup of your designs at different snapshots of the project. Version Cue is a concurrent versioning system, which means multiple people can work on the same file without stomping on each other's changes.

Adding a new project

Using Version Cue starts with creating a new project. Your project is where you'll manage all of your files and versions. Version Cue also handles file sharing if you are sharing your projects among several people. Figure 24.15 shows the New Project window in Adobe Version Cue.

Figure 24.15. The New Project window in Version Cue.

To create a new project in Version Cue, follow these steps:

1. Launch Adobe Bridge by choosing File ⇨ Browse.

2. Choose Tools ⇨ Version Cue ⇨ New Project.

3. Add a Project Name and Project Info. Select the Share this project with others check box if other people will be connecting to your project.

Now that you've created your project, you can add Photoshop files to it.

> **Inside Scoop**
>
> Version Cue has its own Help system. While in Adobe Bridge, choose Help ⇨ Version Cue.

Add a Photoshop file to your Version Cue project

Once you've gotten your project set up, you'll need to add Photoshop files to it. You can do this in Adobe Bridge by dragging files from other folders into your projects folder.

To add a Photoshop file to your project, follow these steps:

1. Open Adobe Bridge by choosing File ⇨ Browse.

2. In the Folders panel, scroll down and click the arrow next to Version Cue to expand it. You should see your project folder in the list.

3. Find your Photoshop file and drag it into your project folder.

Now, whenever you work on your file, the menu item File ⇨ Save Version As is available to you. You can now start saving different design edits to the same file.

The Version Manager

Each time you perform modifications to your design and you want to save them, you can select File ⇨ Save As Version. Once you have two or more versions, you can use the Version Manager window as shown in Figure 24.16 to change the current version or view older versions.

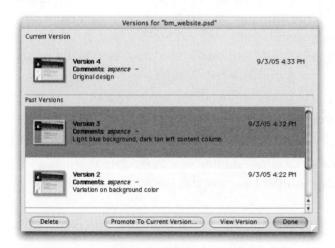

Figure 24.16. The Version Manager window in Adobe Bridge.

Inside Scoop

Use the Versions and Alternatives view in Adobe Bridge to see all of your versions in one big frame.

To view the Version Manager window, follow these steps:

1. Open Adobe Bridge by choosing File ⇨ Browse.

2. In the Folder panel, double-click Version Cue, and then double-click your project. You should see your Photoshop file or files in the main lightbox frame now.

3. Right-click the Photoshop file you'd like to mange. Select Versions to open the Version Manager window.

The Version Manager has a few buttons on the bottom of the screen for deleting versions, promoting versions to the current version, or viewing any of the versions available. Each one of them asks you to add a comment to your change.

Administering your project

If you right-click a project folder in Adobe Bridge and select Edit Properties from the drop-down list, you can gain access to Version Cue's advanced Administration interface that is shown in Figure 24.17. The Administration interface is a browser-based application that lets you add and edit users, remove old versions, create new projects, and manage your workspace preferences where you can add FTP and http proxies. When you first launch the Administration tool, both your user name and password defaults to "system."

Launch the Administration tool and add a new user by following these steps:

1. In Adobe Bridge, click Version Cue in the Folders panel.

2. Right-click your project in your main Bridge lightbox.

3. Select Edit Properties from the drop-down list.

4. Click the Advanced Administration button in the Edit Properties window. A browser window launches and the Administration tool appears.

5. Log in to the tool by entering the default user name and password of system.

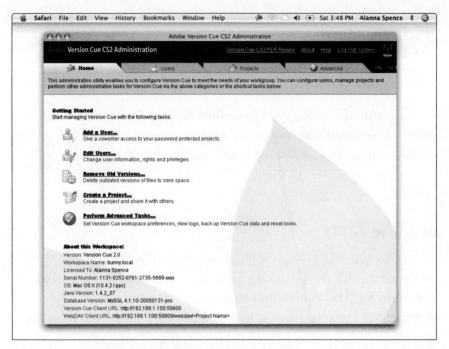

Figure 24.17. The Version Cue Advanced Administration tool.

The homepage of the Administration tool appears, as shown in Figure 24.17.

To create a new user for yourself, follow these steps:

1. Click the Add a User link.

2. Select System Administrator in the Admin Access Level drop-down list.

3. Add a user name and login. The User Name field can be your full name. The Login field can be anything you want, like a nickname or your first name.

4. Add a password and enter the same password in the Verify Password field to ensure there were no typos.

5. You can add contact information like phone or e-mail. Entering an e-mail in the E-Mail field allows you to take advantage of Version Cue's e-mailing capabilities when you want to send out comps to several users on your project.

6. Click Save when you are done.

Watch Out!

Login names and passwords are case sensitive. Be careful when choosing them and make sure you save your login information in a secure place so you don't forget it.

Make sure you change the password for the System Administrator before you begin sharing with other users or they will be able to log in as administrators. Look at the other tabs in the Administration tool. The Projects tab gives you an option of backing up your projects for safe-keeping.

Just the facts

- Share different design options with your clients using Layer Comps.
- Create a quick presentation of your layer comps by using the Layer Comps To WPG automation script.
- Try out stock photos before buying them with Adobe Stock Photos.
- View your recently edited Adobe files with Adobe Bridge.
- Keep track of revision history with Version Cue.

GET THE SCOOP ON...
Taking advantage of variable pressure brushes
with graphics tablets ■ Finding the right scanner ■
Straightening and cropping multiple scanned photos
at once ■ Copying files from your digital camera into
Bridge ■ Installing Camera Raw plug-ins from digital
camera manufacturers

Adding Plug-ins and Hardware Devices

Chapter 25

N ow that you've become a Photoshop whiz, it's time to tempt you with more options for toys. If you have a birthday or other gift-giving holiday approaching, be sure to earmark pages and circle some of the gadgets in this chapter, and then leave the book conveniently open to the appropriate page for your loved one to find.

Photoshop has some added benefits for taking advantage of hardware devices such as scanners and graphics tablets. Graphics tablets allow you to paint using a pressure-sensitive stylus to vary line thickness. This chapter covers the use of graphics tablets with Photoshop and some of the added benefits you get by using a tablet instead of a mouse. I'll cover scanner plug-ins and standard scanner settings and features. We'll look at Camera Raw plug-ins available through digital camera manufacturers, and I'll show you how to install and use third-party plug-ins for importing images from hardware devices.

Using graphics tablets

Graphics tablets are an excellent addition to your Photoshop setup, especially if you are interested in exploring the more creative aspects of the program. You not only get better control over paint tools by using a more natural tool, you get the added benefit of pressure control. You can create strokes that go from fat to thin by adjusting the amount of pressure you use with the pen. Most tablet pens come equipped with an eraser tip on the back for easy, natural erasing. Many manufacturers ship their tablets with wireless mice that work with the tablets so that you have the optional mouse without having to deal with more wires.

The examples in this chapter were created with a Wacom Intuos 2 (4-x-5-inch) graphics tablet. Each tablet is going to be a little different in regards to software drivers and options, but the basic settings are very similar. The graphics tablet in Figure 25.1 is an example of a tablet with both pen and mouse options.

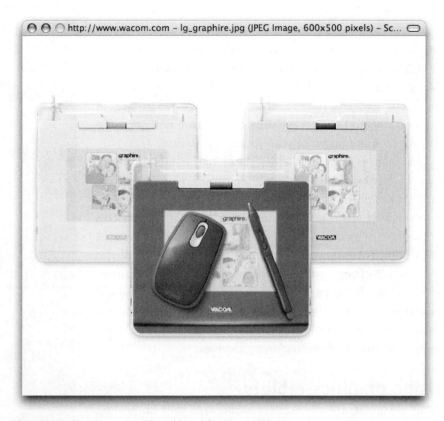

Figure 25.1. The Wacom Graphire tablet with a pen and mouse.

Choosing the right graphics tablet

The most common tablet manufacturer is Wacom (pronounced wah-kum). Other companies that make graphics tablets include Aiptek, Nisis, Addeso, and Trust. Of the currently manufactured graphics tablets, I only have experience with Wacom tablets, and I think very highly of them. If you are looking for a tablet, don't base your decision on low price; many other graphics tablet manufacturers have come and gone. Wacom is and has been the market leader for a good reason. I've tried many other tablets over the years, and all the ones that I have experience with are no longer on the market.

Since I haven't tried some of the newer tablets, I can't say with certainty that Wacom is the best option for you. Others may very well have caught up to Wacom's performance and high standards. My advice is don't be lured by low prices: Try before you buy and see for yourself. A poor performer will only wind up in your closet or in the junk pile at your next garage sale. Many Web sites, such as PC Magazine, Macworld (shown in Figure 25.2), ZDNet, and Consumer Guide, offer product reviews.

Figure 25.2. A product review on MacWorld.com.

Inside Scoop

Get a larger tablet if you can afford it. The larger the tablet size, the more control you'll have over your brush strokes.

Adjusting your tablet settings

For this example, I'll be showing you the control panel that comes with Wacom tablets. Other graphics tablet manufacturers will have similar software. The Wacom tablet comes with special software for adjusting the various settings available for the tablet. The first step in setting up your tablet is to install the tablet software either from the CD-ROM or from a download through the Wacom Web site. Check with your graphics tablet manufacturer for installation instructions. For Wacom users, you'll find the Wacom Tablet control panel you see in Figure 25.3 listed among your other control panels. Visit the Wacom Web site for the latest software drivers.

The Wacom Tablet control panel has several options for adjusting the tablet settings. You can control the sensitivity of the pen tip and eraser. You can also change the default button assignments for the tip and other buttons on your pen. By adding Photoshop to the list of applications, you can control the settings for Photoshop separately from other applications. If you use Adobe Illustrator, you might want to add it to the list as well so you can fine-tune your settings when using Illustrator. Since the

Handwriting Recognition in Mac OS X

Mac OS X comes installed with Ink, a handwriting-recognition control panel that works with the Wacom tablets. You can choose to use Ink in all applications, or use the Ink pad, a special scratch pad utility to write out text and then send it to your currently active application. Ink pad also has a sketch setting that allows you to create a small sketch that can be copied and pasted into an application. This is a handy way to add your signature to a digital document. See the Ink control panel for more information.

Bright Idea!

The Wacom Web site has a set of special brushes for Photoshop users. Go to the support section of www.wacom.com to download the latest.

graphics tablets drivers are different for each tablet, and the software is updated often, the best thing to do is check the Web site for the latest user manual for your tablet.

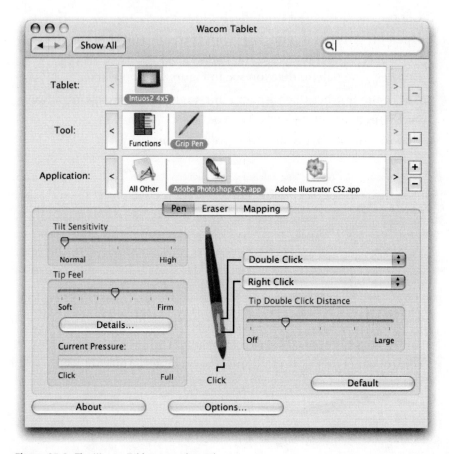

Figure 25.3. The Wacom Tablet control panel.

Controlling brush flow with tablet brush settings

The Shape Dynamics panel in the Brushes palette has three options for using pen pressure. You can have the tablet respond to brush diameter, pen angle, and roundness. You'll need to select these options to take advantage of pressure sensitivity.

You can change brush options following these steps:

1. Create a new Photoshop file to try out your graphics tablet with the Brush tool.

2. Choose the Brush tool from the Toolbox.

3. Open the Brushes palette. If it is not currently visible in your workspace (by default it's in the palette dock), choose Window ⇨ Brushes. The palette that you see in Figure 25.4 appears.

   Any of the brushes that display a thin-to-thick line are taking advantage of pen pressure from your tablet.

4. Choose one of the brushes with pressure sensitivity.

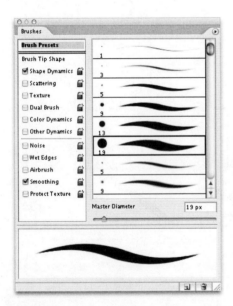

Figure 25.4. The Brushes palette with Presets list.

5. Using your pen and tablet, draw some lines. Vary the pen pressure to try out the tablet features. In Figure 25.5, I've drawn using different pressure to get a varied line.

6. Click Shape Dynamics in the Brushes palette. This panel has three drop-down lists that have options for pen pressure.

7. Choose Pen Pressure from the Control drop-down list, as shown in Figure 25.6.

8. Adjust the Roundness jitter and the Minimum Roundness to get different effects. The lower the settings, the more jagged the line will be.

9. Try out your new settings. Don't forget to save your settings if you want to keep them.

10. To save your new brush setting, click the black arrow on the top right of the Brushes palette and choose Save Brushes from the drop-down list.

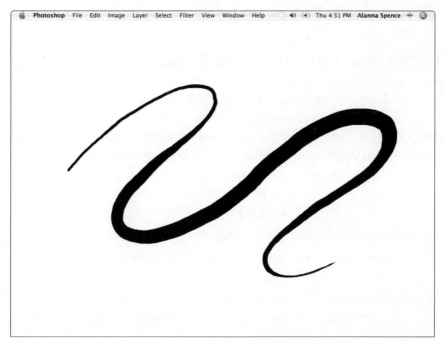

Figure 25.5. A line with varying thicknesses created with a graphics tablet.

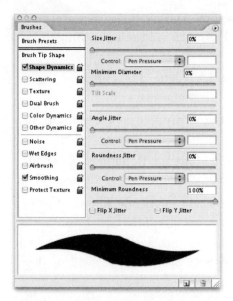

Figure 25.6. The Brushes palette with Shape Dynamics set to Pen Pressure.

Tracing from paper sources with graphics tablets

Some tablets have a transparent sheet that can be lifted in order to place a piece of artwork underneath for tracing. This is a great way to create vector art or even freehand drawings using the Brush tools. Graphic designers commonly trace hand-drawn art as a way to translate ideas and sketches into digital art. Tracing takes a little getting used to, so I've included some tips to get you started on the right track. The illustration in Figure 25.7 was created by tracing a photo of a cityscape.

Here are tips for tracing from photos of drawings:

■ Make your canvas size much bigger than you need.

■ Switch to Full Screen mode and zoom in so your canvas takes up most of the screen.

■ Use many layers. The more layers you use, the easier it will be to remove mistakes and the harder it will be to accidentally paint over other areas.

■ Play with line thickness and opacity for interesting effects.

Bright Idea!

Use a digital photo as the source for creating a digital painting. Open a photo in Photoshop and create new layers to paint on top of your image. Use a combination of thin, solid lines and thick, lower-opacity paint strokes. When you are done, turn off the visibility of your photo layer.

Figure 25.7. Tracing a photo with a graphics tablet.

Picking out a scanner

If you are in the market for a scanner, you might feel a little intimidated by all of the options out there. I'll do my best to help you make the right decision for your needs. I encourage you to read product reviews online. Along with the same Web sites I recommended for graphics tablet reviews, CNet, PC World, and Business Week offer product reviews on scanners. Also, read the consumer reviews on the bottom of the scanner product pages on Amazon.com.

Finding flatbed scanners

These are the most common types of scanners and there are multitudes of them on the market. Flatbed scanner prices can range from $50 to $5000. You can get a great scanner for under $200 that will serve just about any purpose you can dish out at it, similar to the scanners shown in Figure 25.8.

Figure 25.8. Epson scanner models on the Epson Web site.

Watch Out!

Many scanners have two scanning resolutions listed. The first one is the actual scanning resolution of the scanner's optical reader (CCDs). Pay attention to this one. The second number refers to the interpolated resolution. This mean the scanner interpolates or converts the scanner's true resolution to the interpolated resolution. It's splitting pixels.

Here are tips for finding the right scanner:

- **Stick with scanners that can scan 2400 dpi at the very least:** Similar to digital cameras, the better the light sensor, and the more data the scanner is able to pick up. You'll also have more options for enlarging images. I recommend finding a scanner that will do up to 9600 dpi.

- **Scanning bed dimensions:** Many scanners only allow for letter-sized scans. If you know you'll be scanning from various sources, you might want to look at scanners with larger scanning beds. Many have enough space for legal-sized paper and some can hold images up to 11 x 14 inches. Because the image sensor is bigger, they tend to cost a little more.

- **User-friendly software is vitally important:** I have had many scanners from many different manufacturers over the years. The single most important aspect that made me love or hate them was the user-interface experience. Even though you'll be using a Photoshop plug-in, you'll still be using the scanner manufacturer's interface. Before you shell out cash on a scanner, go to a store and try out the software. Even if the computer store is using the stand-alone scanner application and not the Photoshop plug-in, the interfaces are usually identical.

- **Consider bit-depth:** A device that can pick up 48-bit color is going to be able to detect much more color quality than a 24-bit scanner.

- **Read product reviews on Web sites or in magazines:** You can learn everything you need to know about potential scanner purchases by reading consumer reviews. They offer invaluable advice, and most reviews will really put the scanners to the test. If you are presented with a 2400-dpi scanner that has a 5-star rating and a 9600-dpi scanner with a 2-star rating, go with the first one. Make sure you understand who is doing the reviewing and who writes that person's paycheck. The ZDNet Web site at `reviews-zdnet.com` is a good place to start. They list scanner reviews by price range, manufacturer, or scanner type, and you can sort by Editors' rating as shown in Figure 25.9.

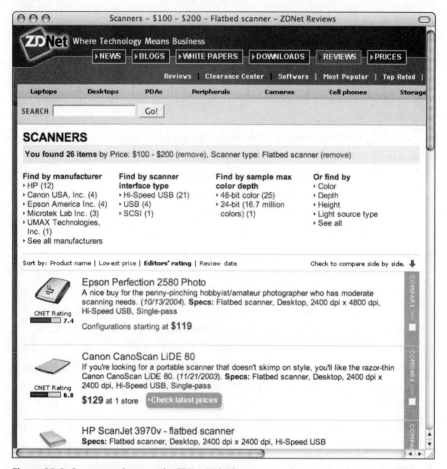

Figure 25.9. Scanner reviews on the ZDNet Web site.

- **Don't judge a scanner by its speed:** In scanners, quick doesn't always mean good. Slow and steady doesn't always win the race, but it usually picks up more details along the way.

- **Consider an all-in-one printer/scanner/copier:** I have an HP PhotoSmart 3310, and aside from the less-than-desirable slide-scanning capabilities, I think my all-in-one is the cat's meow. Epson and HP make some great models with fantastic photo-quality printers that start at about $200. The scanners on them range from 2400 dpi to 9600 dpi.

Scanners with slide or film scanning features

Don't be duped: You cannot get decent-quality slide or film scans on a flatbed scanner. I have searched the world high and low for a decent film scan from a flatbed scanner. At this moment in time, they do not exist, at least not in my price range. If you really need to scan slides and film, I recommend looking at specialized slide/film scanners.

Here are some recommendations for slide and/or negative scanners:

▪ **Nikon makes great a slide/film scanner series called Coolscan:** The retail prices start at around $500 and will give you fantastic color scans that can be used in professional work. You can visit the Nikon Web site that you see in Figure 25.10 at www.nikonusa.com. Photographer LeeAnn Heringer says this scanner is top notch.

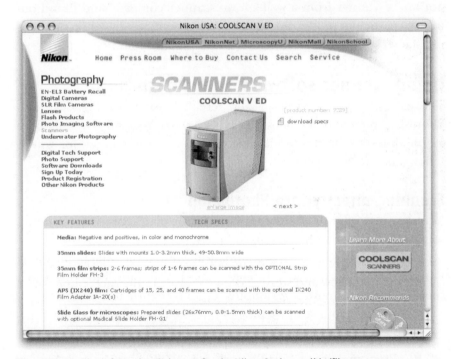

Figure 25.10. The information Web page for the Nikon Coolscan slide/film scanner.

Inside Scoop

Look for a scanner that includes Digital ICE technology. This feature does a fantastic job of automatically reducing surface scratches and dust without sacrificing image quality.

- **Konica Minolta has a series of slide/film scanners called DiMage:**
  This series starts at a slightly lower price point. Fine artist Anna L.
  Conti uses a DiMage for scanning color slides. She has used the scans
  for printing enlarged Giclee prints and enlarged 4-color prints of her
  paintings. The Konica Minolta Web site at www.konicaminolta.net
  has detailed specifications on what film sizes the scanner takes.

- **Go the rental route:** Check professional photography stores in your
  town for slide/film scanner rentals. Spend a weekend scanning in all
  of your old slides and avoid having to buy one more piece of equipment. This is also a great way to try before you buy.

If you are in the market for a scanner, make sure the scanner you are
interested in has a plug-in available for your platform. I mistakenly did
not buy a scanner from a well-known scanner company and found out
that my particular model did not have, nor would ever have, a plug-in for
my Mac. It's still sitting in my closet gathering dust bunnies.

Using scanner software with Photoshop

The examples in this section were created using the HP Scan Pro
Photoshop plug-in that comes with HP scanners. Your software might be
a little different, but the similarities should be close enough for you to
follow along with my steps.

Scanning directly into Photoshop

Most scanners offer plug-in software so that you can access your scanning
software from inside Photoshop. Although your scanner software probably has an installer, it may not automatically install the plug-in into your
Photoshop directory, as seen in Figure 25.11. You'll need to copy it to a
specific directory in order for Photoshop to recognize it.

You can copy your scanner plug-in into the following directory:

- **Mac:** Applications/Adobe Photoshop CS2/Plug-Ins/Import/Export
- **PC:** Program Files/Adobe Photoshop CS2/Plug-Ins/Import/Export

Changing scale and resize settings

Most scanner software has an option for scaling. This is a great feature
for enlarging small images without having to mess with image resizing. If

you are using an HP scanner, the scaling feature is hidden in a menu item. To change the scaling of your scans, choose Basic ⇨ Resize to open the Resize dialog box you see in Figure 25.12.

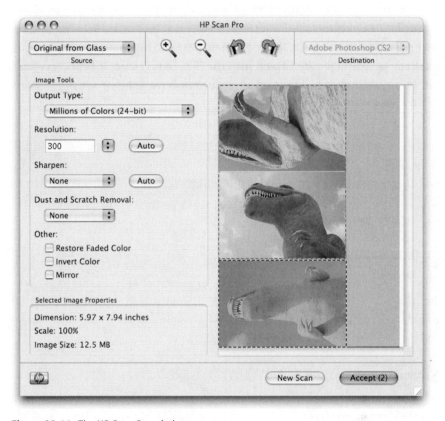

Figure 25.11. The HP Scan Pro window.

Figure 25.12. The Resize dialog box in the HP Scan Pro plug-in.

Scanning text into Photoshop

Your scanner probably comes with a feature to scan text and convert it to type layers. This is a great way to convert old paper documents you have lying around. This method of scanning, called *optical character recognition,* or OCR, tries to guess all the letters in your document and convert them into editable text. No OCR program is perfect, but many can boast an accuracy percentage rate of well into the 90s. In any case, it beats retyping the entire document. The Canon scanners have built-in OCR software like the one you see in Figure 25.13.

Figure 25.13. The OCR settings dialog box for the CanoScan scanner plug-in.

Straighten and crop crooked scans

Placing photos straight on a scanner is an art in itself. The moment you think you've gotten things lined up perfectly, you close the lid of your scanner and your images move around from static cling. Photoshop has a very handy automation tool for fixing this problem. It automatically straightens and crops all of the images in your scan.

To straighten and crop scanned images, follow these steps:

1. Launch Photoshop if it is not already open.

2. Choose File ⇨ Import and choose your scanner plug-in from the list of Import plug-ins.

3. Place several photos on your scanner and close the lid.

4. Perform a new scan preview. Your scanner plug-in window should look something like Figure 25.14.

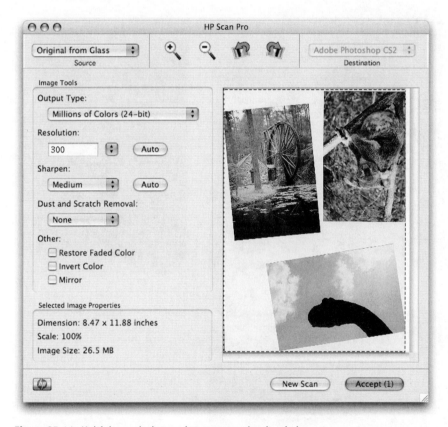

Figure 25.14. Multiple crooked scans in a scanner plug-in window.

5. Select the entire preview as your scan area. If you are using software such as HP Scan Pro that automatically creates selection areas around your photos, you can remove them by clicking them and hitting the

Delete key on your keyboard, and then drag a new selection box around the entire scanning area.

6. Click the Accept (or equivalent) button to perform the final scan. Your scanned image will be imported into Photoshop.

7. Choose File ➪ Automate ➪ Crop and Straighten Photos. Photoshop straightens and separates your multiple images into separate files like those that you see in Figure 25.15.

Figure 25.15. Files created from the Crop and Straighten automation script.

Bright Idea!

You can change the default scan settings by visiting the preferences for your scanner software. If you are using an HP scanner, launch the plug-in and choose HP ScanPro ⇨ Preferences. The HP Scanner lets you control the settings for best-quality scaling, resolution, and automatic color correction.

You can now save each of your files or perform any edits you'd like on them. This tool works well for artwork that has straight edges. It won't work so well on oddly shaped pieces of paper or images on white backgrounds that match the white of the scanner lid. You may need to do a little extra trimming, but for the most part this is a great way of quickly scanning in large numbers of images without having to spend time cropping and straightening each one.

Using digital camera software features

Most digital camera manufacturers have their own photo management software and some even have their own Photoshop plug-ins for Camera Raw editing. I'll cover a few options on the market right now and give you some experience with installing and using plug-ins for cameras.

Uploading from your digital camera into Bridge

Most digital cameras have photo organizing software similar to Adobe Bridge. There are some decent photo-managing applications on the market, but in my opinion, the only one you need is Bridge. If you are going to be doing most of your work in Photoshop, Bridge should be the image manager of choice because it works so seamlessly with Photoshop. You don't need to use your camera manufacturer's image managing software. You'll need to install the drivers for the camera, but the applications that come with it are optional. In most cases, your camera mounts on your desktop or computer just as a hard drive would, and you can drag and drop your files into any folder you create on your hard drive. Your camera should automatically show up in Bridge like the one you see in Figure 25.16. You can get to it either by double-clicking the Computer icon in the Favorites panel or by navigating to it in the Folders panel.

You aren't limited to just one Bridge window. To make copying images from one place to another easier, you can open an additional window like the one I've done in Figure 25.17. That way you can copy from one folder to another without having to navigate through Bridge or scroll through a large list in the Folders panel.

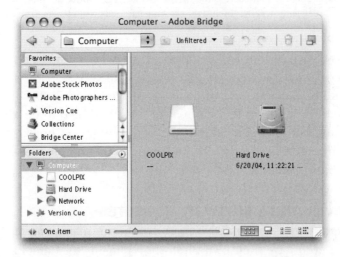

Figure 25.16. A digital camera icon mounted on the Desktop.

Figure 25.17. Two Bridge windows.

Hack

Here are some useful key commands for Bridge. ⌘+T (Ctrl+T) toggles the visibility of file information. ⌘+\ (Ctrl+\) cycles through the different views.

To open multiple Bridge windows, follow these steps:

1. Open Bridge by choosing File ➪ Browse from inside Photoshop.

2. Once in Bridge, choose File ➪ New Window to create a new window.

3. You can resize the windows by clicking and dragging the resize handle on the bottom right of the Bridge window.

4. Navigate to the window you'd like to view or create a new folder by clicking the New Folder icon on the top right of the Bridge window.

5. Switch to Compact View by choosing View ➪ Compact Mode or by using the key command ⌘+Return (Ctrl+Return).

Use multiple windows to copy images from your digital camera to your hard drive.

Camera Raw plug-ins for your digital camera

Some digital camera manufacturers are starting to release their own versions of Camera Raw editing tools. I looked at the recent version of Nikon's Camera Raw Photoshop plug-in and I wasn't impressed. As you can see in Figure 25.18, there are very few options for adjusting exposure and light. The preview window is very small and the zoom feature has minimal functionality. You might be interested in this plug-in if you don't want to mess with the complexity you get in Photoshop's Camera Raw utility.

This market is still very young, and I suspect that by the end of 2006 the options for editing Camera Raw will skyrocket. My advice to you is to try out the software that comes with your camera. Check your manufacturer's

Watch Out!

If Bridge doesn't recognize your DNG or Camera Raw files, your Camera Raw plug-in may need updating. See the Adobe Web site for the latest Camera Raw plug-in. If that doesn't work, try running your images through Adobe's DNG file converter. It will take other file formats such as NEF and convert them to DNG files that Adobe can recognize.

Web site a minimum of every six months for updates and new software options. Who knows what the future holds for Camera Raw software? Check the folder where your camera software was installed for Photoshop plug-ins. They are often an under-documented feature.

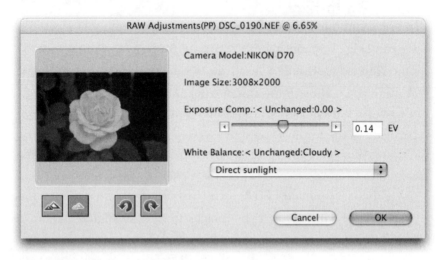

Figure 25.18. The Nikon Camera Raw plug-in.

Installing third-party plug-in filters

Plug-ins are mini applications that work inside Photoshop and offer additional features like image filters, import/export, file formats, and automation tools. Many makers of Photoshop plug-ins offer 30-day free trials so you can try before you buy. I've downloaded a few from the most popular plug-in makers to show you. If you go to the Adobe Web site and navigate to the Photoshop page, you'll find a link along the left side of the page that will take you to a plug-ins page as shown in Figure 25.19. The appendixes in the back of the book list many sites where you can find plug-ins.

The types of plug-ins that I'll show you in this section are additional filters that add special effects to images or enhance photos. The plug-in developers will have specific instructions for installing their plug-ins, and many of them have installation programs. During the installation process like the one you see in Figure 25.20, you'll be asked to locate your Photoshop plug-ins folder.

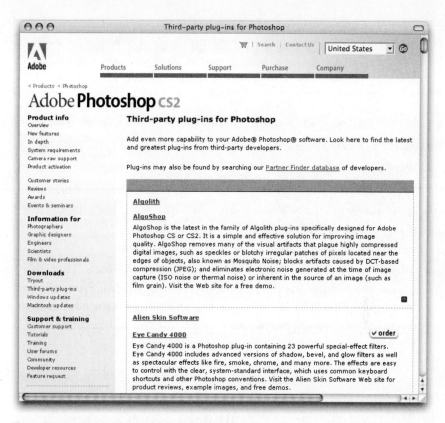

Figure 25.19. The Photoshop plug-ins page on Adobe.com.

Figure 25.20. A Photoshop third-party plug-in installer dialog box asking for the location of the plug-ins folder.

Watch Out!

Avoid purchasing old plug-ins that may not work on the latest version of Photoshop. Make sure you buy plug-ins that support your current version of system software and that are Photoshop CS2 compatible.

You can find your Photoshop plug-ins folder in the following location:

- **Mac:** Applications/Adobe Photoshop CS2/Plug-Ins
- **Windows:** Program Files/Adobe Photoshop CS2/Plug-Ins

Once you've installed your plug-ins, you'll need to restart Photoshop. The next time you launch Photoshop, you'll find your new plug-ins listed at the bottom of the Filters menu.

A few popular plug-in makers are

- **Alien Skin:** A popular plug-in for creating special effects. They also have advanced photo-editing plug-ins for restoring and retouching scanned photos. The Xenofex package has plug-ins for adding light-ning strikes, creating burnt paper edges like those that you see in Figure 25.21, and simulating crumples and cracks.

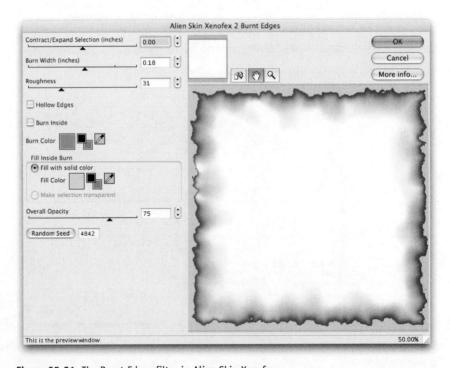

Figure 25.21. The Burnt Edges filter in Alien Skin Xenofex.

- **OnOne Software:** Makers of Genuine Fractals, PhotoFrame, Mask Pro, and Intellihance Pro. If you find yourself using Photoshop's contact sheets for printing multiple image sizes on one sheet, you might want to look at Genuine Fractals. It offers more options and control than the Contact Sheets feature in Photoshop. Visit onOneSoftware.com for a free 30-day trial.

- **Digital Film Tools:** Plug-in products include 55mm, Digital Film Lab, Light!, and Ozone. All are very cool, high-end digital photography filters for enhancing color and light and traditional lens filter simulation. Visit digitalfilmtools.com for more information.

- **Vertus Fluid Mask and Fluid Color:** The Fluid Mask plug-in is well worth the investment if you plan to do a lot of masking. It works much like the Extract tool but automates much of the process and offers you many more tools. The plug-in window in Figure 25.22 gives you three different views and a whole host of tools.

- **Auto FX:** Makers of AutoEye, DreamSuite, and Photo/Graphics Edges. Plug-ins range from photo-enhancing tools to digital effects. Visit AutoFX.com to download and try out demo versions of their plug-ins.

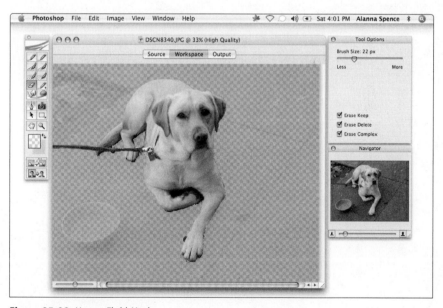

Figure 25.22. Vertus Fluid Mask.

Just the facts

- Check product review Web sites for ratings, examples, and details about graphics tablets.

- Change pressure-sensitivity features in the Brushes palette to get the most out of your graphics tablet.

- When shopping for a scanner, pay attention to the true resolution capabilities and not the interpolated resolution.

- Copy images from your digital camera into Bridge by opening multiple Bridge windows.

- Visit the Photoshop section of Adobe.com for a list of third-party plug-ins.

- Try before you buy. Most plug-in developers offer free 30-day trials of their products.

GET THE SCOOP ON...
Bookmarking Help topics ▪ Searching for specific
keywords or phrases ▪ Purchasing expert help ▪ Adding
Web sites and tech support contacts to your Help Center
▪ Finding resources on the Adobe Web site

Expanding Your Photoshop Knowledge

Photoshop is a big program. Taking the Photoshop plunge can feel like a daunting task. Over the years it has evolved from a simple photo-editing tool to a multipurpose application for digital photography, Web design, print design, and even video editing. With so many things to learn, how do you know where to start?

The good news is that Adobe has spent a great deal of effort on supplying users with some powerful tools for learning and expanding their knowledge of Photoshop. Within the application itself, the Help documentation gives you access to some easy-to-read, straightforward tutorials. All are accessible either from the Help menu or from the Welcome Screen. This screen appears each time you launch Photoshop and gives you quick access to some of Photoshop's most useful tutorials. Much of what is on the Welcome Screen can be found in the Help documentation. Adobe has used the Welcome Screen to highlight some of the most-used areas of their documentation.

Photoshop is an ever-expanding, complex application, and with each new release, Adobe adds many great features. I think it's valuable to get into the habit of trying out new tutorials every now and then, even if you consider yourself a seasoned veteran. This chapter introduces you to some of the most useful tutorials available with the application and goes over some additional resources available from the Adobe Web site.

Bright Idea!

To resize the panels in the Help Center, click and drag the resize button in the middle of the divider bar between the left and right panels.

Getting around the Adobe Help Center

The Adobe Help Center comes with all Adobe products and has a wealth of information about Adobe products, from simple tool descriptions to advanced tutorials. There is something for everyone in the Help Center. I encourage you to make it your first stop for finding answers. The Help Center is also a bridge to more extensive online help. The Expert Support button accesses a subscription-based technical support system. The More Resources button gives you a list of free online resources available through the Adobe Web site. If you have Internet access, clicking any of the links in the More Resources panel launches your default browser and brings you to the related Web page.

Explore the Help topics through the Contents and Index tabs

There are three tabs along the left-hand side of the Help Center window, as shown in Figure 26.1. The main Contents tab lists the Help Topics by subject in hierarchical menus. You can click any of the arrows next to a subject to see the subtopics associated with it. Clicking the arrow again collapses the list. Clicking the Help items with document icons next to them opens a page with information or instructions on performing a specific task. Many of the Help items have hyperlinks that take you to similar topics for more information.

The second tab in the Help Center window is an index list of all of the Help topics. It has expandable and collapsible topics and displays the same information as the Contents tab, but is organized alphabetically. It just offers an easier way for you to find a specific subject quickly.

Bookmark your favorite Help topics

The Help Center allows you to bookmark specific topics so you can find them easily in the future. You can bookmark a topic, subtopic, or content item.

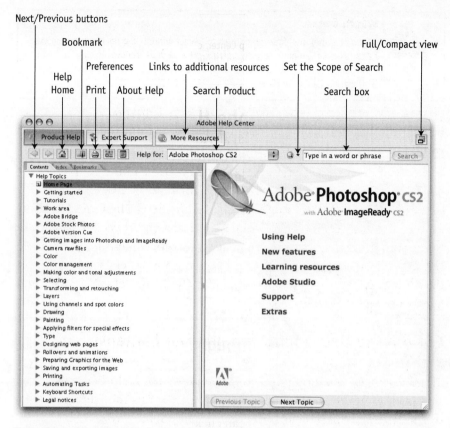

Figure 26.1. The Adobe Help Center welcome screen.

Follow these steps to bookmark a topic, subtopic, or page:

1. Navigate to the Help topic or page you'd like to bookmark.

2. Click the small Bookmark button above the Bookmarks tab in the Help Center window. It looks like an open book with a bookmark.

3. To return to a bookmarked item, click the Bookmarks tab in the Help Center to display your list of saved bookmarks as shown in Figure 26.2.

4. Click the bookmarked item you'd like to see.

If your bookmark list gets long and disorganized, you can change the order of items by clicking them and then using the up and down arrows on the bottom of the panel. The two other buttons on the bottom of the Bookmarks panel allow you to rename your bookmarked item or delete

Watch Out!

If you see only one panel in your Help Center window, you may have accidentally clicked the Compact View button. To view both the navigation and content panels, try clicking the Full/Compact View toggle button on the top right of the Help Center window.

it from the list. You won't be deleting the item from the Help Center; you'll just be removing it from the Bookmarks list.

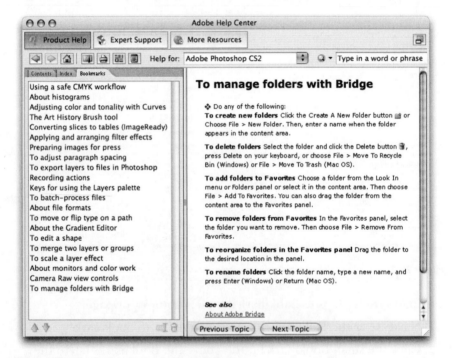

Figure 26.2. The Bookmarks tab in the Help Center.

Quickly find answers with the search feature

The search box on the top right-hand side of the Help Center is a quick way to find specific subjects. The little black arrow on the left-hand side of the search box lets you specify whether you want to search for help topics throughout all of Adobe's products or just for a specified Adobe product such as Photoshop.

To search for specific text in the Help Center, follow these steps:

1. Enter a keyword or phrase relating to Photoshop in the search box.

2. Press Enter. The Help Center populates the left panel with a list of related topics.

The Help Center window that you see in Figure 26.3 shows the search results for the keyword "clone." If nothing is found, the Help Center displays <No search results found>.

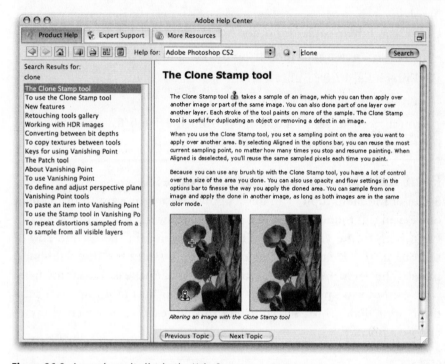

Figure 26.3. A search results list in the Help Center.

The search feature defaults to topics related to the currently active application. The Help Center is for all Adobe products. You can search for keywords or phrases related to the products.

To search Help topics for Adobe products, follow these steps:

1. Click the small arrow to the left of the search box.

2. Choose Search All Help from the drop-down list.

3. Enter your text as you would for a regular search.

4. Press Enter to begin your search.

Inside Scoop

To return to the main Help menu, click the house button in the second row of buttons in the Help Center.

You can find a Help topic on other Adobe products such as Bridge, Version Cue, or ImageReady. If you have the Adobe Creative Suite, you can also search for Help topics on Illustrator, InDesign, GoLive, and Acrobat.

To search help topics for other Adobe products, follow these steps:

1. Choose a new application from the Help for drop-down list.

2. Enter a keyword or phrase in the search box.

3. Press Enter to begin your search.

You'll need to select Photoshop from the Help for drop-down list when you'd like to return to the Photoshop help.

Print out Help content for easy access

Some of the Help topics can get lengthy. You might want to print them out so you can follow along without having to switch back and forth from Photoshop to the Help Center. The Print button in the second row of buttons in the Help Center prints out the contents of the right-hand panel. The Help Center automatically excludes the left column from your printout to save on paper. Clicking the print button opens a standard print dialog box, like the one in Figure 26.4, in which you can choose a printer.

Print
Printer: Phaser 8400DP (8e:7c:ce)
Presets: Standard
Copies & Pages
Copies: 1 ☑ Collated
Pages: ⦿ All
○ From: 1 to: 1
(?) (PDF ▼) (Preview) (Supplies...)   (Cancel) (Print)

Figure 26.4. The Print dialog box for Help content panels.

Bright Idea!

Save color ink by printing Help topics in black and white. In your Print dialog box, find the setting for grayscale printing. It is usually listed under color or paper settings. For Canon inkjet printers, look under Color Settings. For HP printers, look under Paper Type/Quality.

Subscribing to Expert Support

Once you become more acquainted with Photoshop, you may find that you have some tough issues that you can find solutions to through the Help Center or Adobe Web site. You may want to consider getting an annual subscription to Expert Support. This technical support service provides a higher level of support by offering an affordable annual subscription. Members get to talk to senior technical support specialists, enjoy extended service hours, and don't have to wait on hold as long as the rest of us. Annual memberships for single products start at $159. Adobe offers group rates or multi-product support subscriptions as well. Visit the Expert Support panel in the Help Center as shown in Figure 26.5 for more information.

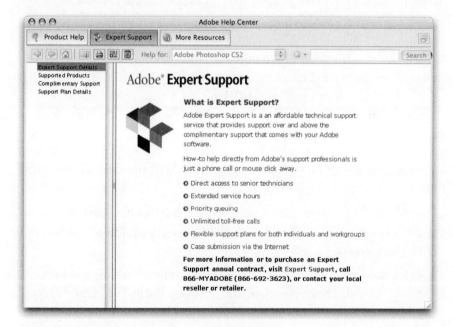

Figure 26.5. The Expert Support panel in the Help Center.

Adding contacts and Web sites in More Resources

The More Resources section of the Help Center has a handy panel where you can save contact information for tech support specialists or useful Photoshop Web sites. Keeping a Photoshop-specific contact list that's accessible from inside Photoshop ensures your important support contacts won't get lost. I've added some of my favorite Photoshop Web sites and contact information for tech support specialists in Figure 26.6.

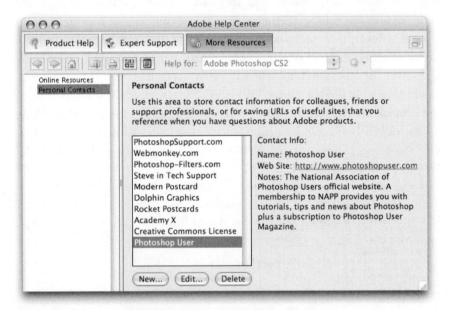

Figure 26.6. The Personal Contacts panel in the Help Center.

To add your own Photoshop contacts and Web site links, follow these links:

1. Click the More Resources button on the top of the Help Center.

2. Click the Personal Contacts link on the left-hand side of the Help Center window.

3. Click the New button. A pop-up window appears asking you for name, e-mail, phone number, and Web site information, and has an additional field for notes. None of the fields is required, so you can fill out as many or as little as you want.

4. Click OK to add your contact to the list.

Bright Idea!

Check for software updates for all of your Adobe products through the Help Center. Choose Adobe Help Center ⇨ Preferences and click the Check for Updates button. The Help Center automatically compares the versions of your Adobe products to the currently available versions. You will need to be connected to the Internet.

You can access your contact information by clicking the contact name in the list. You can edit or delete the contacts at any time through the buttons below the contact list.

Get up and running with How To

The How To Tips, on the top of the Contents Navigator, offer some helpful tutorials for real-world scenarios. Here you can learn how to create art for use in other programs such as Flash or InDesign, how to set brush pressure sensitivity when using a digital tablet, or how to create a custom paintbrush. In How To Customize and Automate, there are a couple of subtopics related to customizing your work area. If you are going to be using a particular tool frequently, I recommend reading the Customize tool presets subtopic on how to save your tool options. For example, if you are doing a digital painting and you want to have your paintbrush automatically set to a certain brush size and opacity, being able to save this information can be a big timesaver. Each of the main How To menu items that you see in Figure 26.7 has between five and ten links to tutorials. These tutorials are available through the Help Center. The How To links just provide a quick and easy way to get to them fast.

Create Your Own How Tos to Share

You can create your own How To file in HTML and send it to friends. The file needs to live in Adobe Photoshop CS2\Help\ Additional How To Content in order for Photoshop to recognize it. Knowing a little HTML will be a big help, but you can use one of the other files as a template. To find out more about how to create your own How To, choose Help ⇨ How to Create How Tos ⇨ Create your own How To Tip.

Figure 26.7. How Tos in the Help menu item.

Training resources on the Adobe Web site

Adobe's company Web site at www.adobe.com has a ton of resources with links to user groups, forums, and additional training resources. Go to www.adobe.com, and in the top navigation select Products ⇨ Digital Imaging and then click the Adobe Photoshop CS2 link. On this page you'll find links to Adobe Studio, the NAPP (National Association of Photoshop Professionals) Photoshop Learning Center, and a Photoshop blog. If you select Training from Support in the top navigation, you'll find even more information about online training, instructor-led training, books, videos, and seminars, as seen in Figure 26.8.

Bright Idea!

To sign up for support announcements, go to Support ⇨ Announcements and subscribe to e-mail announcements for Photoshop. You'll receive e-mails on product news, special offers, How Tos, and new plug-ins.

Figure 26.8. The Training page on Adobe.com.

Adobe-authorized training centers

You can obtain a list of Adobe-authorized training centers in your area. Most of these centers offer group onsite or offsite classes by an Adobe Certified instructor. Most places I researched tended to offer a beginner-to-intermediate-level course and an advanced course. The workshops are usually two full days and are in the $700 range.

I would recommend the beginner-to-intermediate course to anyone who needs to get up to speed fast, or who is feeling a bit overwhelmed with the learning curve. I would recommend the advanced class only after you have carefully read the curriculum and think you could get benefit out of it. I noticed the definition of advanced curriculum seemed to vary greatly from place to place. To find instructors in your area, click

Watch Out!

Authorized training centers are private companies and are only affiliated with Adobe through a certificate program. Their quality and price may vary. Shop around for the best prices and most valuable workshops.

the instructor-led training link on the Training page of Adobe.com. A search page like the one you see in Figure 26.9 appears, asking you for product and location details.

Figure 26.9. The instructor-led training search page.

Exploring tutorials on Adobe Studio

Adobe Studio is a Web site dedicated to training and support resources for Adobe products. On the site you'll find free tutorials, training and support resources such as lists of classes, information on print design and production, and a page where you can buy new OpenType fonts from the Adobe Type Library. The main page at http://studio.adobe.com, which you see in Figure 26.10, has a handy search box for finding tutorials and help on different topics. You can search for keywords or phrases across all of Adobe's product line, or limit your search to a single Adobe product. Figure 26.10 shows the Adobe Studio Web site for Photoshop.

Resources available through the Adobe Studio Web site are

- **Tips & tutorials:** Video- and text-based tutorials on popular features of Photoshop.

- **Featured stories:** Customer profiles of professional designers and photographers.

- **Feature stories:** Interesting profiles of creative people such as designers and artists using Adobe products.

- **Adobe Studio Exchange:** Free downloads of filters, actions, brushes, shapes, styles, tutorials, and more.

Figure 26.10. The Tips & tutorials page on Adobe.com.

Inside Scoop

Tips and tutorials for ImageReady, Bridge, Camera Raw, or Version Cue will be listed with Photoshop.

Hack

You can have answers to your forum posts go directly to your regular e-mail account. Click the preferences link on the top of the forums page and click the Email Address Settings link. Enter your regular e-mail as your contact e-mail address. Click the radio button below labeled Your email address.

Find answers on Adobe forums

Photoshop users are some of the more generous creatures on the planet. If you have a tough question, the Forums section of the Adobe Web site at www.adobeforums.com might be a good place to look for answers. The forums are user-supported message boards where people give and receive advice on tricky problems. You'll need to register first. Registration is free and gives you access to the entire archive.

There are separate forums for Macintosh and Windows Photoshop users. The Photoshop for Windows Users forum is shown in Figure 26.11 and lists both general topics and Windows-specific topics. Both the Windows and Macintosh forums have the same basic information towards the top of the page, covering updates and frequently-asked questions, and displaying a link to the Photoshop Knowledgebase. The second half of the page is a list of questions asked and answered by Photoshop users.

Finding classes at local colleges

Many local community and state colleges and most art schools offer beginner-to-advanced courses in Adobe Photoshop. Oftentimes they are a fraction of the cost of Adobe Certified Training Centers, and depending on the teacher, can be just as good or better. I found a listing of Community Colleges in California on the California Community Colleges (www.cccco.edu) Web site. 50states.com (www.50states.com) has lists of colleges in every state.

Watch Out!

My local community college has the Photoshop classes listed as Digital Imaging classes and only lists Photoshop in the course description. Try looking under Computers or Graphics Communications.

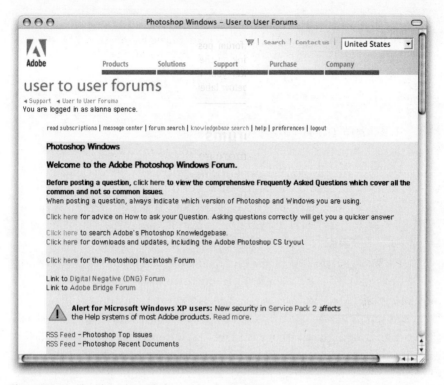

Figure 26.11. The Photoshop Windows user to user forum.

Just the facts

- Use the Content or Index tabs in the Help Center to browse topics. Find information on specific keywords or phrases through the search box on the top right.

- Bookmark or print Help topics using the buttons on the top of the Help Center.

- For additional technical support resources, click the Expert Support button in the Help Center. Annual subscriptions to Expert Support provide a higher level of technical support with extended hours and shorter waits on the phone.

- Visit http://studio.adobe.com for QuickTime videos of new features, tips and tricks, and other training resources.

Troubleshooting and Tips

Photoshop FAQ

The following FAQs provide answers to common issues or questions you may come across while using Photoshop CS2. If you read the FAQ and still have unanswered questions, try the forums section on the Adobe.com Web site. The forums are user supported bulletin boards and you can usually get responses to questions within a day.

Workspace, tools, and palettes

How do I select the contents of a layer?
⌘+click a layer thumbnail to select all of its contents.

How do I move a masked image to another file?
If you want to move a masked layer into a new document, apply the mask first to combine image and mask. Choose Layer ➪ Layer Mask ➪ Apply.

When I try to use a tool on my image nothing happens.
There may be a selection marquee around part of your image. If that is the case, you will be able to make edits only on the area inside the selection. To deselect and allow for editing on the entire image, press ⌘+D (Ctrl+D). You can also choose the Rectangular Marquee tool and click inside your document to deselect.

Other causes for tools not working properly may be attributed to one of these factors:

- You do not have the correct layer selected. Click the layer you would like to work on in the Layers palette.

- The layer you are working on is hiding underneath another layer. If there are elements from other layers covering up the layer you'd like to work on, click the visibility icon for the other layers to hide them temporarily.

- Your opacity settings for the current tool may be set too low. Check the opacity settings in the Options bar.

- Your blending mode might be set to something that won't work for the color you are using. Check the Blending Mode value in the Options bar. Try using Normal as your Blending Mode to see if that's the problem.

When I try to run a filter on my image, nothing happens.

You may be trying to run a filter on a Background layer. If the name of the layer you are working on is displayed in italics, it is a Background layer. You'll need to convert it to a regular layer first. Double-click the thumbnail of your Background layer in the Layers palette and a dialog box will appear where you can change the name of the layer. You don't need to add a new name if you don't want to. By default, Photoshop names your converted layer "Layer 0." Click OK. Your layer is now a normal layer.

My Toolbox and palettes have disappeared.

Try pressing the Tab key to toggle your Toolbox and palettes on and off. Photoshop gives you the ability to hide your Toolbox and palettes temporarily any time you want. You may have accidentally hidden them by hitting the Tab key.

I still don't see any palettes.

Choose Window ⇨ Workspace ⇨ Default Workspace to reset your Toolbox and palettes to the default that was used when you first installed Photoshop.

Most of the menu items are grayed out.

Most probably you are working in Lab color, Index color, or bitmap mode. Some of the tools work only in RGB or CMYK color mode.

Why does my cursor display cross hairs instead of the appropriate tool icon?

Check your Caps Lock key. When it is depressed, your cursor turns into cross hairs. This feature is great for getting into tight spots of your image but makes other tasks more difficult.

The resize handles in the Free Transform or Scale tool are off the map.

Switch to Full Screen mode so that you can view the Free Transform or Scale tool handles even when they expand outside your image canvas. Type the letter F to toggle between screen modes.

I can't resize my Crop or Marquee tool.

Check the Options bar to make sure you don't have fixed-size information entered. In the Marquee too, be sure Normal is selected from the Style drop-down list. In the Crop tool, make sure there are no values entered for Width or Height.

Can I change the color of my workspace when I'm in Full Screen mode?

Yes you can change it to any color you like. The two different Full Screen modes can have separate colors.

To change the workspace color:

1. Select the Paint Bucket tool. It is in the Gradient tool fly-out menu in the Toolbox.

2. Click the foreground color swatch and choose a new color.

3. Switch to Full Screen mode. You can toggle through screen modes by pressing F.

4. Shift-click inside the workspace area to fill it with the foreground color.

5. If you'd like both of the Full Screen modes to be the same color, switch to the other mode and Shift+click inside the workspace area to fill it with the foreground color.

Whenever I try to zoom on a Mac, a Spotlight window appears.

The Spotlight application on Mac OS X uses the same key commands that Photoshop uses for zooming. You'll need to disable or change the keyboard shortcuts for Spotlight.

To change the Spotlight options:

1. Launch System Preferences by clicking on its icon in the Dock.
2. Click Spotlight to view the preferences.
3. Uncheck the two check boxes on the bottom of the screen for Spotlight keyboard shortcuts. If you like, you can select a new keyboard shortcut from the drop-down menus to the right of the check box items.

Is there a way to hide the selection lines temporarily without losing my selection?

Sure! Just choose View ⇨ Show ⇨ Selection Edges to toggle them on and off. An even faster method is to turn off all extras using the key command ⌘+H (Ctrl+H).

The Clone Stamp tool isn't working.

There are a couple of common problems that you may be encountering:

■ You need to take a sample of your image before painting with the Clone Stamp tool. Press and hold the Option (Alt) key and click the area you'd like to clone. Then paint as you normally would.

■ If you are using a multilayered image and want to clone into a new layer, be sure you've selected the Use All Layers check box from the Options bar.

How do I get Photoshop to accept my crop or free transform?

You can either click the check button in the Options bar or press Enter. To cancel out of a crop or transform, press ⌘+. (Ctrl+.) or click the Cancel button in the Options bar. The Cancel button looks like a red circle with a slash through it.

I can see my image or text in the Layers palette but it doesn't show up on my screen.

There could be a variety of things going on here:

- The order of layers matters. Make sure the layer in question is listed above other layers in the Layers palette.

- Make sure the layer's visibility is turned on. You should see an eyeball icon to the left of your layer's thumbnail.

- Check to make sure the opacity setting for your layer isn't set too low. Click the layer to highlight it and check the Opacity value on the top right of the Layers palette.

When I try to move and place images or text, they move slightly from the spot where I want them.

Try choosing View ⇨ Snap To ⇨ None. Your elements may be snapping to a grid or other layer, causing them to shift slightly from where you want them to go.

Type

Nothing happens when I try to change my font face or size.

You need to highlight the text in your type layer before formatting the fonts. Double-click the type layer's thumbnail to select all of the layer's contents automatically.

Photoshop is giving me a warning message about rasterizing type. What is this?

You may come across this warning message when trying to apply a filter or perform other tasks on a type layer:

"This type layer must be rasterized before proceeding. Its text will no longer be editable. Rasterize the type?"

Because type is vector-based, you won't be able to run filters on type layers unless you first convert them to raster graphics. Once converted, you won't be able to make any changes to the type fonts, sizes, or formatting. Be sure to make a backup of your type layers before performing filters on them so that you have an editable backup copy of your text.

Font Preview isn't working in the Font drop-down list.

Font Preview is a new feature of CS2. If you are using an older version, you won't be able to preview fonts in the drop-down list.

For Photoshop CS2 users, check your Type preferences. Choose Photoshop ⇨ Preferences ⇨ Type. Make sure the Font Preview Size check box is selected. You can choose a larger preview size if you like.

I can't edit my text, and the thumbnail in the Layers palette is no longer the letter T icon.

You probably ran a filter or action that required you to convert your text to a rasterized image. Photoshop will warn you when it is rasterizing a type layer, but who really pays attention to those dialog boxes anyway? If you haven't closed your file since it was converted, you can revert to a previous state by navigating through your changes in the History palette. If your file has been closed and reopened, I'm afraid you'll need to re-create your type layer to edit it.

I have installed many fonts, but some of them are not showing up in the font list.

Photoshop has a limit on the amount of fonts it can list. You'll need to uninstall some of your fonts. Try using a font management tool such as Font Book, Suitcase, or FontAgent Pro.

Color modes and file formats

When I convert my image from RGB to CMYK, the colors change drastically.

You may need to change your CMYK color profile. If you are printing to a specific printer, see the printer manufacturer's Web site for the current color or .icc profile. See Chapter 19 for more details on changing your CMYK color profile defaults.

My color picker lets me choose only black, gray, or white.

You are probably in Grayscale mode. Choose Image ⇨ Mode ⇨ RGB to convert your file.

Can I use a CMYK image for the Web or e-mail?

You won't be able to display CMYK images on the Web. You'll need to convert your image to RGB. Choose Image ⇨ Mode ⇨ RGB. Be sure to make a backup first!

I saved my file as JPEG and now my layers are gone.

Always save your master files as Photoshop (.psd) files. You will lose layer data when saving to most other formats.

Error and warning messages

I am getting an error message that says my scratch disk is full. What is this?

Your scratch disk refers to the free space on your computer that Photoshop uses as extra memory. Many functions take up a great deal of memory, so Photoshop takes advantage of free space on your hard drive to store data temporarily. If you have more than one hard drive, you can set up Photoshop to use extra hard drives as scratch disks. To modify your scratch disk settings, choose Photoshop ⇨ Preferences ⇨ Plug-ins and Scratch Disks. If you do not have an extra drive to use, you'll have to free up memory on your hard drive by deleting files.

How do I turn off or remove the grids, guides, and rulers?

You can choose to hide one or all of the options, and you can move or delete guides one at a time. Here are the options:

- To turn off all of the grids, guides, and ruler options, choose View ⇨ Extras. The command key is ⌘+H (ctrl+H).

- Choose View ⇨ Show and choose one of the options in the list.

- Delete or move a guide by pressing and holding the ⌘ (Ctrl) key while clicking and dragging the guide off the screen. Your cursor will change to the Guide Move tool when you are directly over the guide. You can move guides the same way.

Adobe Bridge and Camera Raw

Can I increase the font size in the metadata panel?

Click the arrow at the top right of the Metadata panel and choose Increase Font Size.

Do I really have to right-click Camera Raw images in Bridge to open them in the Camera Raw window?

You can change your Bridge preferences so that all Camera Raw images automatically open in the Camera Raw window.

To change your Camera Raw file preferences:

1. From within Bridge, choose Bridge ⇨ Preferences.
2. Click Advanced on the left-hand side.
3. Check the box next to Double-click edits Camera Raw settings in Bridge.
4. Click OK to save. Now all of your Camera Raw files will open in Camera Raw, and other image files will open directly in Photoshop.

I can't open my image in Camera Raw.

The Camera Raw plug-in only works on images that have been shot in Camera Raw mode on your camera. Check the metadata for your image file in Adobe Bridge. If the Document Kind does not say Camera Raw, it is not the right format. See your camera's manual for help in changing your capture settings.

Files from my digital camera aren't recognized as Camera Raw.

You may be using an older version of Adobe Camera Raw. See the Adobe Web site for a free upgrade. If that doesn't fix your problem, you may need to upgrade the firmware on your camera. See your camera manufacturer's Web site for a list of available upgrades or contact their customer service.

When I plug in an external device, it doesn't show up in the folders panel.

You can refresh the folders panel by hitting the F5 key or by clicking the black arrow on the top right of the folders panel and choosing Refresh from the fly-out menu.

Digital video

When I open a file from a video source, I get a warning message about pixel aspect ratio. What is this?

Digital video uses non-square (rectangular) pixels and computer screens use square pixels. If you open a video image without using pixel aspect ratio correction, your image will look slightly stretched. Some video formats look more stretched than others do. With pixel aspect ratio correction off, you will have optimal image quality but it may look slightly stretched. With pixel aspect ratio correction on, your image looks normal but loses image quality. To turn the pixel aspect ratio correction on or off, choose View ⇨ Pixel Aspect Ratio Correction.

Photoshop community Web sites with tutorials

There are many fantastic Web sites maintained by avid Photoshop superusers. One of the great things about Photoshop is the community support available on the Web and in user groups. Many Photoshop fanatics post great tutorials on their personal Web sites free of charge. Many more encourage readers to post their own tutorials. I've ferreted out some of what I think are the most useful Photoshop tutorial Web sites and listed them here.

Planet Photoshop

http://Planetphotoshop.com

Tutorials, user forums, seminars, and more. I especially like their filter tutorials.

NAPP

www.photoshopuser.com

The National Association of Photoshop Users official Web site. A membership to NAPP provides you with tutorials, tips, and news about Photoshop plus a subscription to Photoshop User Magazine.

Software Cinema

www.software-cinema.com

A free membership gives you access to some great tutorials in the Workshops On Demand section.

Spoono

www.spoono.com/photoshop

Trendy Design Tips for Photoshop users.

Photoshop Support

www.photoshopsupport.com
A collection of tutorials from various sources.

Team Photoshop

www.teamphotoshop.com
User-supported site with tutorials ranging from beginner to advanced user.

Webmonkey

http://webmonkey.com
The design section has several Photoshop tutorials on Web graphics, scanning, and more.

Russell Brown

www.russellbrown.com
Tips and techniques in the form of QuickTime movies. The tutorials are informative.

Photoshop 911

http://photoshop911.com
User-supported Photoshop blog with easy-to-follow tutorials, tips, and tricks. Links to additional tutorial sites.

Wacom

www.wacom.com
Photoshop tips for beginning-to-advanced Photoshop users with Wacom graphics tablets.

Third-Party Filters, Brushes, and Actions

I scrubbed the Internet looking for the most useful and professional-looking actions, filters, and brushes available through Photoshop user sites. Some are free; some are available at a reasonable price. The sites listed in this appendix are supported by individual Photoshop users or small graphics companies. Always use a virus scanner when downloading content from the Internet.

Adobe has its own dedicated Web site for listing additional resources. Adobe Studio Exchange has thousands of free downloads for actions, filters, brushes, layer styles, and more, created by Photoshop users and collected by Adobe to help users find resources quickly. You can visit Adobe Studio Exchange at `http://share.studio.adobe.com`.

Filters

In order for Photoshop to recognize filter plug-in files, you'll need to place them in a special filters folder. You'll need to restart Photoshop for it to recognize your newly added files.

Where to install filters:

- **Mac:** Applications/Adobe Photoshop CS2/ Plug-Ins/Filters
- **PC:** Program Files/Adobe Photoshop CS2/ Plug-Ins/Filters

Photoshop Filters

www.photoshop-filters.com
Over 300 freeware and commercial filters. Great color examples of the filter effects.

Mister Retro

www.misterretro.com
Maker of Machine Wash II. Fantastic texture filters for adding a worn look to images.

Free Photoshop

www.freephotoshop.com
Free downloads of brushes, shapes, gradients, styles, filters, and more.

Redfield Plug-ins

www.redfieldplugins.com
Free and affordable 3-D special effects filters.

Xaos Tools

www.xaostools.com
Makers of the popular Paint Alchemy, TypeCaster, and Terrazzo plug-ins for Photoshop. Xaos has been making professional-quality filters for nearly as long as Photoshop has been on the market.

Andromeda Software Inc.

www.andromeda.com
Creator of professional plug-ins for Photoshop and InDesign. Filters include photographic tools and lens effects, artistic screening tools, and graphic design resources.

Flaming Pear

www.flamingpear.com
I particularly like the SuperBladePro filter package with natural texture filters like water stain, moss, dust, and grit. If you like the distort filters that come with Photoshop, you'll love Flaming Pear's Flexify set. There are two sets for making stars, space, and planets.

Digital Film Tools

www.digitalfilmtools.com
Free and fantastic photo filters. Filter sets for simulating specialized lenses, film grain, and lighting effects.

Akvis Software

www.akvis.com
Makers of professional Photoshop filters. They offer a free trial download so that you can take them for a test drive. If you are colorizing old photos, they have a great product called Coloriage.

AV Bros.

www.avbros.com
Makers of Page Curl Pro and Puzzle Pro.

Graphic Authority

www.graphicauthority.com
Bundles of filters, brushes, and stock photos available for purchase on DVD.

Brushes

Photoshop brushes have their own file extension of .abr and need to be installed in Photoshop's Brushes folder.

You can install Photoshop brushes by copying ABR files to these locations:

- **Mac:** Applications/Adobe Photoshop CS2/Presets/Brushes
- **PC:** Program Files/Adobe Photoshop CS2/Presets/Brushes

8 Nero

www.8nero.net
This Web site has a large selection of contemporary and artistic brushes for creating texture. There are many great brush options for creating gritty, organic, and industrial-looking images.

Miss M

www.rebel-heart.net/brushes
Curvaceous and creative art nouveau–style brushes.

Photoshop Brushes

www.photoshopbrushes.com
Tons of stamp and icon brushes that can be used as clip art or background images.

VBrush

http://veredgf.fredfarm.com/vbrush/main.html
Great brushes for creating textures like crumpled paper, dashes, old paper, and scratches.

500ml.org

http://brushes.500ml.org
Theme-based brushes including vintage, art nouveau, birds, board games, dragonflies, fossils, fruit labels, street signs, x-rays, and zombies.

Free Photoshop

www.freephotoshop.com
Huge collection of free brushes. Given a high rating in Photoshop User Magazine.

Fragile Decay

www.brushes.fragiledecay.com
Brushes for creating broken glass, bullet holes, and peeling paint.

Actions

Actions have a special file extension of .atn and need to be installed in a Photoshop Actions folder. You must restart Photoshop in order for the newly installed action to appear in the Actions list.

You can install Photoshop actions by copying ATN files to these locations:

- **Mac:** Applications/Adobe Photoshop CS2/Presets/Photoshop Actions
- **PC:** Program Files/Adobe Photoshop CS2/Presets/Photoshop Actions

Action Addiction

www.actionaddiction.com
Actions for creating fun text styles. Some styles include chrome, charmed, liquid bubble gum, concrete decay, snacky cake, snot nose, yee-haw, and frisco writers. Over 300 actions available on a CD for about $11.

Photoshop Action!

www.liknes.no/photoshop
Action sets for borders, special effects, and text. There are seven collections of borders from which to choose.

Action Central

www.atncentral.com

A user community–supported Action-sharing Web site. Nice special effects actions for artistic color manipulation. Some professional-looking framing actions including a great matte board emulation.

Shutter Freaks

www.shutterfreaks.com/Actions/Actions.html

A wide variety of actions for frames and mattes, image enhancement, and special effects.

Photoshop Café

www.photoshopcafe.com/actions_dl.htm

Tons of text effects that take advantage of layer styles.

Elated

www.elated.com

Free Action kits including 47 different text and special effects actions.

Cybia

www.cybia.co.uk/actions.htm

This graphic resources Web site offers an action pack for resizing Photoshop documents. Actions include resizing to standard screen sizes and lines per inch for printing, and reducing image size by percentage.

Scream Design

http://screamdesign.daz3d.com/files/freebies/actions

Text, image, texture, and button effects. The text effects like underexposed, grungy text, and starburst text are nice.

Stock Photos, Clip Art, and Fonts

Stock Photography

I've gathered a list of quality stock photo Web sites that offer high-resolution images for professional design. Most stock photo Web sites also offer illustrations.

iStockPhoto

http://istockphoto.com

A community-driven stock photography and illustrator Web site. Images cost as little as $1. I think this is a fantastic Web site and I've had great luck finding the images I need quickly and painlessly.

Corbis

www.corbis.com

Professional royalty-free and rights-managed stock photography and illustrations. Expect to pay standard stock photography prices of $50 to $500 per image.

Veer

www.veer.com

A collection of professional royalty-free and rights-managed stock photography and illustrations from several sources. Also offers fonts, QuickTime movies, and Flash animations.

FotoSearch

www.fotosearch.com

A collection of stock photography and stock footage. Offers photos, illustrations, clip art, video clips, and audio clips. They sell CD-ROMs of professional high-resolution stock photography and clip art for about $150.

Getty Images

http://gettyimages.com

Professional royalty-free and rights-managed stock photography and illustrations. Image categories for creative, editorial, and film. They offer a commission-based service when you need a specific shot.

Fonts

The following pages offer instructions for installing fonts as well as lists of popular font Web sites. I've broken up the lists into two categories. The first is a list of professional font developers. The second is a list of free and affordable fonts. Your design needs are going to determine which fonts you need and when. The free and affordable font Web sites usually offer a wide variety of fun and creative fonts for use in headlines and logos; they are typically created by single individuals or small design companies. Many of the fonts available are of fantastic quality. Others are not suitable for professional design. If you are planning to do professional print design, you will need to invest in a professional font face. In high-end print design, the difference is quite noticeable and well worth the money.

Pointers for downloading fonts

When downloading fonts, be sure to choose the right font version for your operating system. TrueType and PostScript fonts are not interchangeable between Macintosh and Windows operating systems. OpenType, a relatively new and very versatile new font format, can be used on both Macintosh and Windows operating systems.

Before installing fonts, you'll probably need to unzip or unstuff the downloaded files. Use a program such as WinZip, UnZip for ZIP files, or Stuffit Expander for SIT or SEA files. If you do not have an unzip or unstuff program on your computer, you can find one on the Web site www.download.com. Search for unzip or unstuff in the search box at the top of the homepage.

Once your font is installed, you may need to relaunch Photoshop in order to see the newly installed font in your font family menus. Keep in mind that each font you install takes up a small amount of memory on your computer. The more you install, the more likely you are to encounter performance issues.

Installing fonts on a PC

The installation process for Windows operating systems differs slightly. I've listed instructions for the most commonly used operating systems.

You can install fonts on a computer running Windows XP by following these steps:

1. From the Start menu, choose Start ⇨ Control Panel.

2. Click the Appearance and Themes button.

3. Under the See Also section on the left, click Fonts.

4. Choose File ⇨ Install New Font.

5. Locate the folder where you downloaded the fonts.

6. Click the font you would like to install and click OK. You can choose multiple font files by pressing and holding the Ctrl key and clicking additional font files.

You can install fonts on a computer running Windows 95/98/2000 or NT4 by following these steps:

1. Open the Windows control panel. From the Start menu, choose Start ⇨ Settings ⇨ Control Panel.

2. Double-click the Fonts icon. A new window opens and you will see a list of the installed fonts on your computer.

3. Choose File ⇨ Install New Fonts. The Add Fonts window appears.

4. Locate the folder where you downloaded the fonts.

5. Double-click the font file you would like to install and click OK.

Installing fonts on a Mac

You can install fonts on computers running Mac OS X by following these steps:

1. Double-click the font file you would like to install. The application Font Book launches, displaying a preview of the font.

2. Click the Install Font button. Your font installs and you are taken to the main window of Font Book.

3. Choose Font Book ⇨ Quit Font Book.

Fonts

LinoType

www.linotype.com

LinoType is one of the leading professional font developers. Founded in the late 1800s, LinoType has designed a majority of the typefaces you encounter in your day-to-day life. They boast one of the largest font libraries and have more than 6,000 typefaces to offer.

ITC

www.itcfonts.com

The International Typeface Corporation offers many standard professional-quality typefaces. They have been in business for over 30 years. Many of the fonts that came installed with your operating system were licensed from ITC.

Émigré

www.emigre.com

Émigré has been creating stylish and modern typefaces since 1984. Their collection includes font designs from some of the most prominent typeface designers of our times. They are most known for the Copperplate typefaces created in the late 1980s. Fonts are very affordable and are typically under $100 each.

Fonts.com

www.fonts.com

Fonts.com is owned and operated by Monotype Imaging, Inc. They have been making professional fonts and font software for many years. The Monotype font collection includes commonly used typefaces. Fonts.com offers font volumes for under $100, which typically includes several font weights and an italic version.

Girls Who Wear Glasses

http://girlswhowearglasses.com

Retro fonts available for free download. Most of the specialty fonts I used in this book came from this Web site. There are also fantastic clip art font sets available at a reasonable rate.

Dafont.com

www.dafont.com/en

A wide range of creative fonts for headlines or logos. Some of the font themes include gothic, handwriting, techno, tribal, cartoon, western, graffiti, and holiday.

Chank Fonts

www.chank.com

Wonderfully creative and professional-quality fonts for logos or headlines. Prices range from $19 to $99.

MyFonts.com

www.myfonts.com

A large selection of professional-quality fonts. Font styles range from simple fonts for content text, to stylized fonts for logos and headlines. Some categories include sans-serif, slab-serif, script, traditional, mathematical, glyphic, and modern. Many CDs are available. The prices for CDs range from $20 to $100 and have as many as 40 fonts per CD. They have a fantastic tool on the Web site that will try to guess fonts for you. The tool analyzes an image file that includes text and tries to match it to fonts available on the Web site.

1001 Fonts

www.1001fonts.com
Community font Web site full of member-submitted fonts. All fonts are free.

Clip art and stock art

Clip art is typically low-resolution artwork that can be used on Web sites, for presentations, or in e-mails. Most clip art is 72 dpi and shouldn't be used for professional print design. Many of these sites also offer low-resolution photos and fun font collections. Many clip art Web sites bombard users with pop-up ads. I've tried to supply you with a list of the higher-quality sites with fewer ads.

ArtBitz

www.artbitz.com
Professional-quality stock art for print, presentation, or Web. Image packages are fully editable vector art. There is a small section of free downloads so you can try some out before buying. Prices range from $30 to $100 for 20 to 100 images per set.

Broderbund

www.broderbund.com
Broderbund offers very large clip art DVDs from $5 to $150. I've been using my $20 ClickArt CD set for many years, and I can say it was well worth the money to have such a large, extensive library at hand. The libraries include everything from people to cooking utensils, and each has a vast array of photos, line art, fonts, and color illustrations.

Barry's Clipart Server

www.barrysclipart.com

High-quality free clip art. Most images are available in 640 x 480 pixels at 72 dpi. The artwork is higher quality that most free clip art Web sites.

Clipart.com

www.clicpart.com

Weekly, monthly, or yearly subscriptions for clip art, photos, fonts, and sounds. Prices start at $16.95.

Clip Art Inc.

www.clipartinc.com

Offers both low-resolution and resizable vector art. Membership of about $50 for one year is required. You have unlimited downloads as a member.

Recommended Reading

Digital photography with Photoshop

Ames, Kevin. *Digital SLR Photography with Photoshop CS2 All-In-One Desk Reference For Dummies.* Hoboken: Wiley Publishing, Inc., 2006.

Anon, Ellen and Tim Grey. *Photoshop for Nature Photographers: A Workshop in a Book.* Hoboken: Wiley Publishing, Inc., 2005.

Grey, Tim. *Photoshop CS2 Workflow: The Digital Photographer's Guide.* Hoboken: Wiley Publishing, Inc., 2005.

Milburn, Ken. *Photoshop CS2 for Digital Photographers Only.* Hoboken: Wiley Publishing, Inc., 2006.

Moss, Kevin L. *Photoshop CS2 and Digital Photography For Dummies.* Hoboken: Wiley Publishing, Inc., 2005.

Sheppard, Rob. *Outdoor Photographer's Landscape and Nature Photography with Photoshop CS2.* Hoboken: Wiley Publishing, Inc., 2006

Appendix D

Photoshop Camera Raw

Canfield, Jon. *Raw 101: Better Images with Photoshop Elements and Photoshop.* Hoboken: Wiley Publishing, Inc., 2005.

Moss, Kevin L. *Camera Raw with Photoshop For Dummies.* Hoboken: Wiley Publishing, Inc., 2006.

Sheppard, Rob. *Adobe Camera Raw for Digital Photographers Only.* Hoboken: Wiley Publishing, Inc., 2005.

General digital photography

Burian, Peter K. *Mastering Digital Photography and Imaging.* Hoboken: Wiley Publishing, Inc., 2004.

Canfield, Jon. *Photo Finish: The Digital Photographer's Guide to Printing, Showing, and Selling Images.* Hoboken: Wiley Publishing, Inc., 2004.

Grey, Tim. *Color Confidence: The Digital Photographer's Guide to Color Management,* 2nd ed. Hoboken: Wiley Publishing, Inc., 2006.

Moss, Kevin L. *50 Fast Digital Camera Techniques,* 2nd ed. Hoboken: Wiley Publishing, Inc., 2006.

Youngjin.com. *40 Digital SLR Techniques.* Hoboken: Wiley Publishing, Inc., 2006.

Advanced Photoshop techniques and effects

London, Sherry. *Photoshop CS2 Gone Wild.* Hoboken: Wiley Publishing, Inc., 2006.

Singh, Shangara. *Hacking Photoshop CS2.* Hoboken: Wiley Publishing, Inc., 2006.

Photoshop visual learning books

Kent, Lynette. *Photoshop CS2 Top 100 Simplified Tips & Tricks.* Hoboken: Wiley Publishing, Inc., 2006.

Romaniello, Stephen. *Photoshop CS2 Visual Encyclopedia.* Hoboken: Wiley Publishing, Inc., 2006.

Wooldridge, Mike and Linda. *Teach Yourself VISUALLY Photoshop CS2.* Hoboken: Wiley Publishing, Inc., 2005.

Adobe Creative Suite

Padova, Ted, and Kelly L. Murdock. *Adobe Creative Suite 2 Bible.* Hoboken: Wiley Publishing, Inc., 2006.

Smith, Jennifer and Christopher. *Adobe Creative Suite 2 All-in-One Desk Reference For Dummies.* Hoboken: Wiley Publishing, Inc., 2005.

Smith, Jennifer, and Jen deHaan. *Adobe Creative Suite All-in-One Desk Reference For Dummies.* Hoboken: Wiley Publishing, Inc., 2004.

Glossary

action   An action is a set of recorded commands that can be played back on a single file or a batch of files. Most menu commands and tool operations are recordable as actions. Photoshop and ImageReady come preinstalled with several actions for performing common tasks.

adjustment layer   An adjustment layer is separate from an image layer and applies color and exposure settings to layers that appear underneath it in the Layers palette. It does not affect the other layers and can be changed or removed.

Adobe Bridge   An image file browser and organizer. You can use Adobe Bridge to manage files from any Adobe Creative Suite product. You can sort, search, move, and preview any image file and open files directly into Photoshop or other Adobe Creative Suite applications.

Adobe Creative Suite   Refers to the Adobe software bundle that consists of Photoshop, Illustrator, GoLive, Acrobat, InDesign, Version Cue, and Bridge.

alpha channel   You can save selections as alpha channels and load the selections later. You can edit alpha channels using any of the editing tools.

barrel distortion   A common distortion problem caused by wide-angle lenses. The image appears to be slightly fish-eyed or bowed-out in the center.

batch-process   Refers to the processing of multiple images simultaneously.

bit depth   Determines how much color information is available in each pixel of an image for displaying or printing. Sometimes referred to as *color depth* or *pixel depth*.

bitmap image   Also referred to as *raster images,* these are made up of a grid of pixels or dots. Image quality relies on the resolution or number of pixels per inch.

Bridge center   A dashboard for all of your Adobe Creative Suite activities. You can view your recently modified files and folders and manage projects with multiple files.

calibration   A process for correcting the colors of a monitor or printer.

Camera Raw   Often referred to as *digital negative,* the Camera Raw format captures images just as your camera sees them, without any compression applied. You are able to get more control over detail and color by adjusting image settings in the Camera Raw plug-in as you import them into Photoshop.

canvas size   Separate from *image size,* canvas size refers to the work area of your image. When you add canvas size, you are adding to your image area as opposed to resizing your entire image.

chromatic aberration   The color fringes that can appear around the edges of images. The Camera Raw plug-in has a chromatic aberration adjustment for fixing Camera Raw files.

clip art   A ready-to-use graphics file. Clip art can be a number of formats including GIF or JPEG. Many Web sites and companies offer free or cheap clip art libraries for use on Web sites, documents, or presentations.

CMYK   Refers to the CMYK color mode, mainly used for print design. Stands for cyan (C), magenta (M), yellow (Y), and black (K).

color channel   Stores color information separately for each color in the image. For example, RGB images have three color channels.

color mode   Determines what color method is used for displaying an image's color. Color modes include RGB, CMYK, Grayscale, and Lab color.

color separations   Printers that use multiple plates for each color ink use color separations for creating printing plates. The Channels palette in Photoshop shows you what each color plate would look like.

color trapping   When printing to a 4-color printer, color trapping slightly overlaps the images on different color plates so that no gaps in color appear in the final printed piece.

comp image   Free, low-resolution versions of stock photos or artwork that can be used for design mock-ups. They allow you to try a low-resolution version of an image before buying the high-resolution version.

cross-platform   Refers to the ability to share files across multiple computer operating systems. Cross-platform usually refers to files that can be opened on both Windows and Macintosh operating systems.

digital negative   A lossless archival file format for Camera Raw images.

DNG   A commonly used file extension for Camera Raw files. DNG stands for *digital negative*.

Document window   The panel that displays your image canvas. The title bar of your document window displays the file name. The status bar on the bottom of the document window displays information such as file size, dimensions, and color mode.

droplet   A small application that performs specified tasks or actions when a file is dragged and dropped on top of its icon in the file browser.

duotone   Grayscale images that can be printed using tinted inks to represent shades of gray. Duotone is a color mode used primarily for creating designs that will be printed using spot colors.

EPS   The Encapsulated PostScript file format is commonly used as a format of choice for delivery files to professional print shops. It is a versatile format that can store both vector and raster information. It can be opened in most graphics, illustration, and page layout programs.

filter   Filters let you change the look of your images by processing the image information using special software. Filters can create texture, add lighting effects, or distort images.

flattening layers   Combines several layers into one flattened layer. All the information stored in the many layers is combined into one image.

floating palette   The moveable palette windows such as Layer, Colors, Swatches, and Character are referred to as floating palettes because they float on top of your workspace.

Full Screen mode   Fills the screen with a solid background of white, black, or gray. Full Screen mode hides the menu bar, title bar, and scroll bars. You can toggle through the screen modes by pressing the letter F.

Full Screen mode with menu bar   Fills the screen with a solid background of white, black, or gray. Full Screen mode hides the title bar and scroll bars but keeps the menu bar visible. You can toggle through the screen modes by pressing the letter F.

gamut   A color is said to be "out of gamut" when it cannot be displayed properly on another color space. This commonly happens when converting images from RGB to CMYK or from Camera Raw to JPEG.

GIF   A compressed file format commonly used for Web graphics with mainly text or solid colors. GIF stands for Graphics Interchange Format. GIF files can support multi-framed animations.

GoLive   Adobe's Web publishing application, similar to Dreamweaver. Lets you create HTML, CSS, JavaScript, and other languages without having to write any code.

gradient   The gradual blending of two or more colors. Custom color gradients can be created with the Gradient tool.

graphics tablet   A hardware device that acts as a pen-based mouse with pressure sensitivity.

Grayscale mode   A color mode that can display 256 shades of gray.

grid   Non-printing grids can be displayed in Photoshop files to help you place images and text.

guide   When the Ruler feature is turned on in Photoshop, you can pull horizontal and vertical guides from the ruler into your image to help you place images. The guides are non-printing elements that can be moved and deleted.

halftone screen   A filter that simulates the patterns created from printed newspaper or other low-resolution print media.

histogram   A visual representation of how the colors in your shadows, midtones, and highlights are performing in your image. The Histogram palette is the primary place to view histogram data.

History log   Saves a detailed log of all the changes you've made to a file. Choose Photoshop ➪ Preferences ➪ General to change the History log settings.

HSB mode   Stands for Hue, Saturation, and Brightness. You can choose HSB mode in the Color Picker to choose colors based on hue, saturation, and brightness.

image map   Lets you add Web links to areas of an image. You can create image maps in Adobe ImageReady.

ImageReady A sister application that comes with Photoshop and specializes in Web graphics. You can create Web designs or animations and export them as HTML and graphics files.

InDesign Adobe's page layout program for print design. Create books, brochures, or single page designs by integrating text and images.

index color An 8-bit color mode than creates small files with no more than 256 colors.

JPEG A common, lossy file compression format used for photographic images. JPEG stands for Joint Photographic Experts Group, which represents the committee that first defined the standard.

kerning Controls the spacing between characters. See *tracking* for controlling spacing of entire words or selected text.

Lab A full-spectrum color mode that separates light information from color information. Lab stands for Luminosity, an "a" color channel (red to green), and a "b" color channel (blue to yellow).

layer Photoshop documents can be compositions of several images or elements slacked on top of one another in layers. You can add and edit layers through the Layer palette.

layer comp Create multiple compositions of a design by changing layer visibility, positioning, and styles, and then saving them in the Layer Comps palette.

layer group An organization feature that enables you to group multiple layers together into one folder in the Layers palette.

leading Refers to the spacing between lines of text. The term "leading" comes from the little strips of lead spacers that were inserted in between lines in traditional letter presses to increase line spacing.

linking layers A way of performing edits on multiple layers at once. You can link layers by Shift+clicking multiple layers and then clicking the link icon on the bottom of the Layers palette.

Liquify A Photoshop plug-in tool that lets you warp and twist images. Popular for shrinking noses and waistlines in photos.

mask A method of showing or hiding portions of an image by masking out specific parts.

megapixel   Equals one million pixels.

merging layers   Combines the images from multiple layers into one layer.

metadata   Additional information about your file can be stored in the metadata of a file. The metadata is kept in a "sidecar" file and can be viewed only through an application that can read metadata or XMP information. You can store additional notes about your images or search on metadata using Adobe Bridge.

NEF   Nikon's proprietary file format for Camera Raw. NEF stands for *Nikon Electronic Format.*

OCR scan   Optical character recognition scanning recognizes scanned text and converts it to editable text.

offset printer   A cost-effective color printing technology used for large quantities of prints. The printing process involves multiple printing plates and rubber stamps separated by color. Offset printing is typically printed in CMYK inks but can also use spot colors.

OpenType   A font standard developed jointly by Apple and Microsoft. This format takes advantage of Unicode character encoding. OpenType fonts consist of a single file that can be used on both Macintosh and Windows operating systems.

Options bar   Each tool has options settings that can be controlled through the Options bar on the top of your Photoshop workspace. The options change depending on which tool you have currently selected.

palette   A floating menu with features and controls for organizing your images or settings. Some of Photoshop's palettes include Layers, Swatches, Colors, Paths, Character, and Brushes.

palette group   Floating palettes can be combined into a palette group. For example, the Layer, Channels, and Paths palettes are grouped together by default.

palette well   Located on the top right of the Options bar, the palette well helps you organize your palettes and keep your workspace clutter free. The palette well is visible only when your screen resolution is at least 1024 x 768.

Pantone   The industry standard for color matching on CMYK and spot color printing. Creators of the Pantone Matching System, Pantone offers printed books of color samples to ensure accurate printing results. Most print shops have Pantone books available to help customers choose colors for their designs. Visit Pantone.com for more information.

path   Defines the outline of a vector-based shape. Paths are created with the shape or pen tools. You can change the shape of a path by editing its anchor points.

PDF   The Portable Document Format is a file format that can be viewed with Acrobat Reader as well as many other applications. It can store vector, raster, and text elements.

pincushion distortion   A common lens distortion problem that occurs with some telephoto lenses. The image appears slightly pinched towards the center.

pixel   An individual tiny square that represents a dot in your image. Think of your digital photos as a map of tiny pixels.

pixel rating   The number of megapixels a digital camera has, such as 3.2 megapixels.

plug-in   A miniature program that works inside Photoshop as a filter or import/export tool. Many plug-ins come installed with Photoshop. There are many plug-ins, such as import plug-ins for scanners, available through Photoshop community Web sites or hardware manufacturers.

PNG   Stands for Portable Network Graphic, which was developed as a patent-free replacement for the GIF format.

PostScript font   A multiplatform, scalable, outline font standard developed by Adobe.

printer driver   A file that your computer uses to communicate to your printer. Drivers are often updated to support new versions of system software or to fix software bugs. See your printer manufacturer's Web site for the latest versions of printer drivers.

red eye   Common reflection problem that occurs when using flash photography on human or animal subjects. The new Red Eye tool fixes red eye.

redo   If you undo an operation, you can redo it using this command.

RGB   The color mode used mainly for Web images or artwork to be displayed on a monitor or television. RGB stands for Red, Green, and Blue.

rollover An image or button that changes image states when a user mouses over or clicks it on a Web page.

rollover state (ImageReady) Represents the various button states of an image when a user mouses over or clicks a rollover image on a Web page.

sans-serif Typefaces without embellishments are called sans-serif fonts. Sans means "without" in French. Fonts such as Helvetica, Verdana, and Arial are sans-serif fonts.

scanner A hardware device that uses light sensors to record images into your computer as image files.

scratch disk Adobe proprietary version of virtual memory. When your computer does mot have enough memory (RAM) to perform an operation, Photoshop uses space on your hard drive as temporary or virtual memory.

screen mode The viewing mode for displaying documents, tools, and palettes.

script A piece of software that typically executes multiple actions on a file or group of files. Photoshop comes with a set of preinstalled scripts, or you can write your own.

serif A type of font that has short cross lines at the end of character strokes. Times, Palatino, and Garamond are considered serif fonts.

slice A selection of a document that can be saved as a separate image file when saved as a Web graphic from ImageReady or Photoshop's Save As Web feature.

Smart Objects Converting raster images such as photos or other pixel-based art into Smart Objects allows you to resize them multiple times without image degradation. Smart Objects embeds the original image data so that the maximum image fidelity is retained.

snapshot A record of a particular state in your document. Take snapshots throughout the development of a design to backtrack quickly when you make a mistake.

spot color Premixed inks that are used instead of process colors like CMYK. Each spot color is printed using a dedicated plate. Spot color printing is used often with t-shirt printing or designs with simplified or specialized colors.

Standard Screen mode   The default view in Photoshop where the Toolbox, palettes, and document window are free-floating. You can toggle through the screen modes by pressing the letter F.

status bar   Located on the bottom of every document window. The status bar displays information about the document such as image size, dimension, and color mode. It also displays tips for using the currently selected tool. You can change the information displayed by clicking the arrow icon in the status bar and choosing a new option.

Step backward   Reverts your document to the last operation performed. By default, you can step backward as many as 20 steps.

Step forward   If you have stepped backward though one or more operations or undos, you can step forward one operation at a time.

stock photo   A royalty-free image that can be used for most commercial purposes. The Adobe Stock Photos feature in Adobe Bridge gives you access to several leading stock photo libraries.

Targa   A file format supported by MS-DOS color applications.

TIFF   The tagged images file format is used to exchange files between applications. A flexible format is supported by most graphics applications. Photoshop can save layer information in TIFF files; however, that information will not be accessible in other applications.

tool preset   Enables you to save and reuse tool settings. You can save libraries of tool presets in the Preset Manager.

Toolbox   The long panel that appears on the left side of your work area that displays all of Photoshop's tools. You can move the Toolbox by dragging its title bar. Double-clicking the title bar collapses and expands the Toolbox. Secondary tools are located in the fly-out menus of any tool displaying a small black arrow in the corner.

ToolTip   Appears when you mouse over a Photoshop tool, displaying the name and key command for selecting the tool.

tracking   Refers to the amount of space between text characters. You can adjust tracking of two selected characters or an entire block of selected text.

TrueType font   A multiplatform, scalable, outline font standard developed by Apple.

TWAIN   A cross-platform interface often used by scanners or other hardware devices to import or export data from an input device to a computer.

unit of measure   The type of measurement option used for rulers or other measurement devices. Some options include inches, millimeters, centimeters, points, picas, or pixels.

Vanishing Point tool   A Photoshop plug-in that lets you edit and paint images while staying in perspective. Access the Vanishing Point tool by choosing Filter and then Vanishing Point from the menu.

vector   Refers to line art created using vector-based drawing tools. Vector graphics are created by mathematically defined lines and curves. They can be resized without losing image quality.

workspace   Describes the entire work area in Photoshop including the document window, palettes, and Toolbox.

zero origin   Where the zero point of the ruler starts on your image. You can reset the zero origin by clicking and dragging the cross hairs from the top left of the ruler into your document.

Index

Numbers

8-bit color, 62, 64, 238, 466
16-bit color versus 8-bit, 64, 238
500ml.org Web site, 638
1001 Fonts Web site, 646

A

ABR file format, 144
Accessories and hardware, 583
Action Addiction Web site, 639
Action Central Web site, 640
Action sets
  caution on locked background
    layer, 232
  building in pauses for user
    input, 224
  creating, 222–223, 549
  creating conditional actions,
    556–558
  creating droplet for editing of
    multiple files, 224–226,
    551–553
  described, 222
  interactive actions with dialog
    boxes, 229–231
  nonlinear editing with History
    Palette, 216
  preinstalled, 226–228
  recording for Auto Levels and
    Smart Sharpen, 223–224
  running on photos, 231–232
  saving, 548
  saving as ATN files, 226
  saving as Snapshots, 218
Actions. *See also* History Palette.
  third-party software, 639–640
  undoing or redoing, commands
    for, 143, 214
Actions palette (ImageReady). *See
also* Action sets.
  advantages for repetitive
    functions, 213, 222
  Flaming Text, 555–556

Frozen Text, 555–556
Make Web page action,
  477, 554–555
Metal Slide Gallery Button,
  556, 557
Metal Slide Thumbnail,
  556, 557
Add Adjustment of Fill Layer
  button, 242
Add Anchor Point tool, 108, 111
Add New Adjustment of Fill Layer
  button, 247
Additive color, 58
Adjustment layers
  caution on inapplicability of
    History Brush, 220
  advantages, 238, 562
  Curves, 243–244
  Levels, 242
  for nondestructive color
    correction, 98–100
  photo filter, 245–246
Adobe Bridge
  adding metadata to files,
    18, 265–267
  advantages, 18–20, 257, 265
  categorizing photos with
    keywords, 267–268
  creating contact sheet, 542
  creating panoramas, 411–414
  exploring stock photo library,
    575–578
  finding photos, 268–269
  labeling images with filters, 260
  launch time, 20
  main window, Standard View
    mode, 258
  organizing files, 258–259
  renaming files in batches,
    264–265
  rotating images, 259–260
  Slideshow feature, 20, 262–263
  tracking changes in Version
    Cue, 578–582

Adobe Bridge *(cont.)*
  troubleshooting and tips, 631–632
  uploading images from digital cameras,
    601–603
  various view modes, 261–262
Adobe Bridge Center
  accessing as favorite, 571
  adding RSS feeds, 574–575
  saving file groups, 572–573
Adobe Bridge Preferences dialog box,
  571–572
Adobe Bridge Version Cue
  adding files to project, 579
  adding new project, 578
  administering projects, 580–582
  advantages, 578
Adobe Gamma control panel, 514–515
Adobe help, 574
Adobe Illustrator
  advantages, 101
  and graphics tablets, 586
Adobe RGB working color space setting, 64
Adobe Web site, information downloads, 574
Airbrush effect, with Brush tool, 125,
  126–128
Akvis Software Web site, 637
Alien Skin (third-party plug-in), 606
Alignment options
  Move tool, 89–90
  Snap to Grid, 46
  Snap to Guides, 45
  Snap to Image, 414
  for text, 194
All Channels view, 240
Alpha channels. *See also* Channels.
  for layer mask backup, 174–177
  mask saved as, 180
Anchor point tools, 108
Anchor points
  for images, 361
  for text, 204
Andromeda Software Inc. Web site, 636
Animated GIFs with ImageReady
  caution on file size when tweening, 500
  adding link, 493–494
  adding links to image with image maps,
    495–497
  Animation palette features, 490
  changing replay number, 495
  creating animated button, 502–504
  creating multi-framed animation,
    490–493
  creating with transparent background,
    504–506

exporting to Flash SWF files, 498
fading elements in and out with tween-
  ing, 498–501
fading in reverse order, 501–502
HTML for links to URLs, 493–495
Image Map tools, 495–496
tips for success, 489
Animation palette (ImageReady), 490. *See
  also* ImageReady for animated GIFs.
Annotation tools, 31
Anti-aliasing. *See also* Feathering.
  GIF files, 472
  Hardness of Brush tool, 125
  methods for text, 190, 194, 195
Arc Upper warping effect, 206
Archiving images, documents, and files, 238
Arrowheads, with Line tool, 105
Art History Brush, 220–221
ArtBitz Web site, 646
Artifacts
  avoiding, 243
  reducing noise, 319–321
Artistic filters, 337
ASL file format, 94
ATN file format, 226
Auto Color settings, 240, 521–523
Auto Contrast adjustments, 240
Auto FX plug-ins, 607
Auto Levels
  adjustments, 240
  creating droplet for, 224–226
  recording action set for, 223–224
AutoEye (Auto FX) plug-ins, 607
Automating tools
  creating droplets, 224–226, 551–553
  photomerges, 412–414
  Picture Package, 420–421
Autumn Leaf brush preset, 132
AV Bros. Web site, 637

B

B&W. *See* Black and white images
Background color
  adding layer, 25–26
  with charcoal sketch filters, 339
  choosing, 70–71
  illustrated, 6
Background Contents, choosing from New
  window, 6
Background Eraser tool, 162, 163–166
Background layers, renaming and unlocking,
  83, 143

Backgrounds
blurring out, 366–368
distinguishing from foreground by
channel masking method, 401–402
Backups
in Adobe Bridge, 264
as alpha channel for layer masks,
174–177
CDs for, 238
importance of keeping copies of images,
238
Bandwidth considerations of image size, 290
Barrel distortion, 308, 310–312, 368, 370
Barry's Clipart Server Web site, 647
Batch processing, 213, 264–265, 548–551
Batch Rename dialog box, 263–264
Bevel and Emboss, 93
Bézier curves, 110–111
Bicubic Downsampling, 546–547
Bicubic interpolation method, 292
Bicubic Sharpener interpolation method,
292
Bicubic Smoother interpolation method, 292
Bilinear interpolation method, 292
Bit depth, 63–64
Bitmap color mode
caution on inoperability of filters, 370
described, 23
Black and white color mode
bit depth, 64
converting to, 254
reverting to default, 70
Black and white images
converting to, from color, 432
with sketch filters, 339–342
Black point, 250
Black text, rich versus regular, 459
Blacks, darks, and shadows. See Color adjust-
ments; Exposure adjustments; Shadows
Bleed beyond crop marks, 459
Blending modes
for Brush tool, 125–126
Difference, 341–342
with filters, 355
Blending Options dialog box, 74–76, 116
Bloat tool in Liquify window, 302
Blur effect, 211
Blur tool, 138–139
Blurring
creating with filters, 362–368
Gaussian, 211
as JPEG optimization option, 468
sharpening, 315–319
BMP file format, 568

Boldface, faux bold effect, 195–196
Book cover example of graphics design,
427–432
Border
around cropped image with Rectangular
Marquee tool, 154
with Frames action set, 232–233
Bounding box, for text, 192–193
Bridge
adding metadata to files, 18, 265–267
advantages, 18–20, 257, 265
categorizing photos with keywords,
267–268
creating contact sheet, 542
creating panoramas, 414
exploring stock photo library, 575–578
finding photos, 268–269
labeling images with filters, 260
launch time, 20
main window, Standard View mode, 258
organizing files, 258–259
renaming files in batches, 264–265
rotating images, 259–260
Slideshow feature, 20, 262–263
tracking changes in Version Cue,
578–582
troubleshooting and tips, 631–632
uploading images from digital cameras,
601–603
various view modes, 261–262
Bridge Center
accessing as favorite, 571
adding RSS feeds, 574–575
saving file groups, 572–573
Bridge Version Cue
adding files to project, 579
adding new project, 578
administering projects, 580–582
advantages, 578
Brightness adjustments. See also Color
adjustments.
brightening lights and darkening
shadows, 241–242
with Brightness/Contrast dialog box,
61, 98–99
with Lens Flare filter, 358–359
teeth whitening and brightening,
525–528
Brochure example of graphics design,
421–427
Broderbund Web site, 646
Brown, Russell, Web site, 634
Brush Detail settings, for Artistic filters, 335
Brush fly-out menu, 9

Brush Tip Shape options panel, 129
Brush tool. *See also* Graphics tablets.
   Airbrush setting, 126–128
   appending, 132–133
   blending modes, 125–126
   creating custom, 130, 139–142
   custom brush preset libraries, 144–146
   Custom Brush Tip Shape, 417–418
   custom tips from Web, 417
   diameter and hardness, 49, 125, 126, 419
   erasing, 142–143
   presets, 130–133
   resetting, 132
   selecting, 124
   sizing, 49, 126, 134
   tip shape options, 129–130
   using, 7–9, 67
Brush-type tools, 123
Brushed Aluminum Frame action set,
  232–233
Brushes
   folders for, 638
   third-party software, 637–639
Brushes drop-down list, 124
Brushes palette
   accessing, 128, 418
   adjustment settings, 130
   appending new brush preset, 132–133
   brush presets, 130–132
   Brush Tip options panel, 129, 417
   Brush tool, 129
   expanding for displaying options, 417
   floating, 128–129
   Shape Dynamics panel, 588–590
Business cards
   example of graphics design, 416–421
   printing as Picture Package, 546
Butterfly brush tip, 417–418, 419
Buttons, exercise for creating, 92–94

C

Calibrating monitors, 510–518
Camera Raw
   Adjust panel, 273
   advantages, 62, 257, 269
   applying adjustment settings to photo
     sets, 278–279
   available tools, 271
   Camera Raw Save Settings Subset dialog
     box, 280
   color calibration, 275–276
   color and contrast adjustments, 273–275
   Curves panel, 273–275

   Detail panel, 276, 277
   editing window, 269–270
   exposure, contrast, and saturation
     adjustments, 273
   file and edit function buttons, 273
   halo color fixes, 276–277
   Lens panel, 276–277
   plug-ins for digital cameras, 603–604
   returning images to original settings, 273
   rotating images, 270
   Save Raw Conversion Settings dialog
     box, 279–280
   saving settings for future use, 279–280
   setting digital camera for, 272
   sharing settings with other users, 280
   sharpness, smoothness, and noise
     removal, 276
   Synchronize button, 278–279
   Tone Curve drop-down list, 275
   troubleshooting and tips, 631–632
   updating plug-ins from Web site, 603
   vignette effects, 277
   zooming, 276
Canvas size, 292–295
CCW (counterclockwise), rotating images, 11
CDs for backup copies, 238
Chalk & Charcoal filter, 339
Chank Fonts Web site, 645
Channel drop-down list, 242, 244
Channels
   alpha, 174–177, 180
   available in color modes, 63–64
   creating, 174–177
   creating mask from, 401–404
Channels palette, 59, 60, 174, 175–176
Character palette, 190–192, 195–196
Charcoal filter, 339–340
Chrome Text Effect action set, 229–230
Circles, 102–105, 150
Circular Marquee tool
   for circular mask, 394
   options, 144
   selecting, 140, 149
   selection as vignette, 151–153
Clean Plane tool, 327
Clip art
   in shape libraries, 106–107
   sources, 646–647
   symbol fonts as, 196
Clip Art Inc. Web site, 647
Clipart.com Web site, 647
Clipping mask, 201, 203
Clone Stamp tool, 133–134, 399, 400,
  405–406

Close-up thumbnails, Marquee tools, 154–155
Clouds filter, 379–381
CLUT custom color palette, 62
CMYK color mode
  caution on nonequivalency warning, 69
  avoiding artifacts, 243
  bit depth and color channels, 63–64
  converting to, 452–453
  described, 23
  installing profile for laser printer,
    453–455
  out-of-gamut colors, 518
  when to use, 59–60, 452
CMYK working color space setting, 64
Collages, creating
  adding circular mask around image, 394
  adding outlines with Blending Options,
    395–396
  adding type on curve, 394–395
  choosing document size, color mode,
    and resolution, 390–391
  combining several images, 391–392
  converting images to Smart Objects,
    393–394
  example and process overview, 389–390
Color
  additive, 58
  from Art History Brush, 221–222
  bit depth considerations, 63–64
  changing default Auto Color settings,
    240, 521–523
  changing for text, 192, 193
  choosing with Eyedropper tool, 66–68
  choosing for foreground and back-
    ground, 70–71
  saving custom swatches and styles, 72–74
  selecting and changing areas, 159–162
  subtractive, 59
  Web-safe, 69, 70, 472
Color adjustments. *See also* Brightness
  adjustments; Exposure adjustments.
  caution on monitor warmup prior to
    calibration, 510
  adding spots of color to B&W image,
    254–256
  advanced shadows and highlights
    options, 530–532
  advantages of 16-bit color, 238
  auto adjusting levels, colors, and
    contrast, 240
  color cast, 244–246
  converting to images to black and white,
    432

  with Curves dialog box, 242–244
  with Curves panel in Camera Raw,
    273–275
  eye sparkles, 528–530
  with hue and saturation shifts, 252–254
  removing out-of-gamut colors, 518–521
  with Replace Color tool, 404–405
  sepia tone, 247–248
  skin tones, 523–525
  teeth whitening and brightening,
    525–528
  tips for, 237–238
Color balance, 242
Color blending mode, 125
Color calibration
  Bridge Center, 572
  Camera Raw, 275–276
Color Dynamics adjustment setting for
  brushes tools, 130
Color Intensity setting, 245
Color modes
  choosing from New window, 6, 23
  considerations for choosing, 23
  illustrated, 6
  indexed, 62–63
  interpreting, 57–58
  troubleshooting and tips, 630
Color Overlay feature, 187
Color palette
  CLUT custom, 62
  illustrated, 6, 71
  tips for professional look, 113
Color perception by human eye, 57–58
Color Picker window
  accessing, 65, 68, 83
  avoiding out-of-gamut colors, 520
  Eyedropper tool, 67
  main window, 68–69
  selecting colors, 69, 71
Color profiles, 453–455
Color Range dialog box, 174, 176
Color Replacement dialog box, 160
Color Sampler tool of Camera Raw, 271
Color settings, 64–65, 453, 454
Color spectrum, 6, 9
Color swatches, 70, 71, 72–74
Color tools, 31
Colors. *See also* Color adjustments; Color
  modes.
  reducing in GIF files, 471–472
  sharing among files, 68
ColorVision Spyder2 USB monitor calibrator,
  517

Comic book effect
  file format for, 466
  with Photocopy filter, 341
Commands
  history kept in History Palette, 214
  on menus, 15
  for undoing actions, 143, 214
Compression
  of files, 145, 198, 460, 537, 643
  of PDF presentations, 547
Conditional actions, 556–558
Cones of human eye, 57–58
Constrain Proportions check box, 13, 291
Contact Sheets automation script, 539–542
Conté Crayon filter, 337
Contrast adjustment
  with Auto Contrast, 240
  in Camera Raw, 273–275
Convert Anchor Point tool, 108
Coolscan (Nikon) slide/film scanners, 595
Copyrights to images, 11, 265, 538
  adding in batches, 548–550
Corbis Web site, 641
Costco online print ordering, 461
Countdown clock with Polar Coordinates
  filter, 374–377
CPP (cost per page) for printers, 445
Create Droplet dialog box, 225
Create New Action button, 223
Create New Document from Current State
  button, 214
Create New Fill or Adjustment Layer button,
  83, 86, 98, 246
Create New Layer icon, 85
Create New Layer Mask icon, 168
Create Snapshot button, 218
Create Warp Text button, 206
Crop marks, bleed, and trim, 459
Crop tool (Camera Raw), 271
Crop tool (Photoshop), 11–13, 284–290
Cropping
  compared to copying to new document,
    155
  compared to resizing, 14
  with Crop tool, 11–13, 284–285
  nondestructively, 285–286
  to specific width and height, 286–290
  stopping, 289
  using mask saved as alpha channel, 180
Curves
  drawing, 107–113
  saving on adjustment layers, 243–244,
    251–252
  wrapping text around shapes, 204–205
Curves Adjustment layer, 243–244, 251–252

Curves dialog box, 242–244
Curves panel in Camera Raw, 273–275
Custom Shape libraries, 106–107
Custom Shape tool, 106, 177
Customize Proof Condition dialog box,
  455–456
Cutout dialog box, 336–337
CW (clockwise), rotating images, 11
Cybia Web site, 640

D

Dafont.com Web site, 645
Darks and shadows. See Color adjustments;
  Exposure adjustments; Shadows
Default settings, changing or reverting to
  Auto Color settings, 240, 521–523
  black and white color mode, 70
  customized for Auto Color, 521–523
  for scanners, 601
  styles, 77
  workspace, 16, 41
Delete Anchor Point tool, 108, 111
Density setting, 246
Dents, adding with Spherize filter, 372
Design considerations
  typefaces, 189–190
  value of moderation, 415
  value of observation and analysis,
    415–416
  vector drawing, 114–116
Difference Clouds filter, 380
Diffuse filter, 383
Diffusion dither setting, 63
Digital cameras
  availability of Camera Raw file format,
    443
  Camera Raw plug-ins, 603–604
  correcting red eye and flash problems,
    302–305
  installing third-party plug-in filters,
    604–607
  pixel ratings, 442–443
  popularity and advantages, 283
  problem of distortion by lenses, 308, 310
  setting for Camera Raw Mode, 272
  uploading from, into Bridge, 601–603
Digital Film Lab (Digital Film Tools) plug-in
  filter, 607
Digital Film Tools Web site, 637
Digital video, 632–633
DiMage (Konica Minolta) slide/film
  scanners, 596
Direct Selection tool, 108, 111, 115, 117–119
Displace filter, 378

Display fonts, 196
Distort filters, 334, 344–345, 368–379
Distort tool, 307
Distortion
barrel- and pincushion-style, 308,
310–312, 368–370
with Distort tool, 307
with filters, 334, 344–345, 368–379
spherical, 409
Distressed-look effect, for text, 201–203
Distribution options, Move tool, 89, 90
Dither settings, 63, 472
Document and file management
adding RSS feed to the Bridge Center,
574–575
advantages, 561
creating instant Web Photo Gallery from
layer comps, 568–570
saving groups in Bridge Center, 570–574
saving layer comps, 562–566
saving layer comps to separate files,
566–568
searching in Adobe Stock Photos,
575–578
Document version control with Adobe
Bridge Version Cue
adding files to project, 579
adding new project, 578
administering projects, 580–582
advantages, 578
Document version control with Layer Comps
caution on loss of color changes, 564
advantages, 562
creating instant Web Photo Gallery,
568–570
palette options, 565–566
saving to separate files, 566–568
saving to, 563–564
switching between, 565
Document window, 6, 17–18
Documents and files. See also Adobe Bridge;
Images; Resizing.
creating from History Palette, 214
creating new, 5–6
creating from Snapshots, 218
dimensions display, 17, 18
organizing, 258–259
reverting to last saved version, 214
reverting to pre-edit condition, 296
saving, 10, 28
saving as Snapshots, 215
saving for Web, 289
switching between open, 16
Dodge tool, 138
Dpi (dots per inch), 24

Dragging and dropping
caution on inability to drag and drop
images between programs, 491
history between files, 217
layers between files, 97
Drawing
circles, squares, and lines, 102–105
modified vector designs, 114–116
paths, 117–120
from shape libraries, 106–107
with shape tools, 102
tracing images, 112–113
vector masks, 119–120
vector shapes and curves, 107–113
DreamSuite (Auto FX) plug-ins, 607
Drivers for printers, 446–447
Drop Shadow effect, 75, 96, 115
Droplets
adding frames to several photos at once,
551–553
described, 224
drag and drop editing of multiple files,
224–226
Dual Brush adjustment setting for brushes
tools, 130
Dust & Scratches filter, 321–322
Dust and scratches, removing, 321–322

E

Edge Highlighter tool, 169–170
Edges, accentuating with Trace Contour
filter, 385–386
Edit (Adobe Bridge)⇨Find, 269
Edit (Adobe Bridge)⇨Select All, 264
Edit Layout dialog box, 420
Edit Menu, 15
Edit⇨Adjust Threshold, 140
Edit⇨Color Settings, 64–65, 453, 454
Edit⇨Copy, 392
Edit⇨Define Brush Preset, 140, 142
Edit⇨Fade, 341
Edit⇨Fade Wind, 363
Edit⇨Free Transform, 309–310, 398, 409
Edit⇨Free Transform Path, 105, 120
Edit⇨Paste, 392
Edit⇨Select All, 83
Edit⇨Step Backwards, 9
Edit⇨Stroke, 154–155
Edit⇨Transform, 205, 313
Edit⇨Transform⇨Distort, 312
Edit⇨Transform⇨Flip Horizontal, 398
Edit⇨Transform⇨Flip Vertical, 186, 211, 314
Edit⇨Transform⇨Perspective, 328–330
Edit⇨Transform⇨Rotate 180 degrees, 115

Edit⇨Transform⇨Scale, 555
Edit⇨Transform⇨Skew, 185, 186, 211
Edit⇨Transform⇨Warp, 207, 398
Edit⇨Undo, 9
Editing. *See also* Action sets; Brightness
  adjustments; Color adjustments; Exposure
  adjustments; Filters; *menus by name.*
    with action sets in droplets on multiple
      files, 224–226, 551–553
    adjusting perspective, 323–330
    advantages of Actions palette, 213
    advantages of History palette, 213
    avoiding stretching images, 391, 442–443
    collage example, 389–396
    creating grid design using contact
      sheets, 542
    creating reflections in water, 210–212,
      313–315
    fixing barrel and pincushion distortion,
      308, 310–312, 368–370
    greeting card example, 407–411
    with Healing Brush tool, 298–299
    JPEG photos, 11–14, 269
    with Liquify tool, 300–302
    panorama Photomerge example,
      411–414
    with Patch tool, 299–300
    Pegasus example, 399–406
    photomontages with Clone Stamp tool,
      133–134, 399, 400, 405–406
    removing green glow from pet's eyes,
      304–305
    removing red eye, 302–303
    renaming images, 553
    repetitively in batches, 213, 264–265,
      548–551
    reverting to pre-edit condition, 296
    rotating images by degrees, 312–313
    sharpening blurry images, 315–319
    Smart Objects, 297–298, 393
    straightening tilted images, 309–310
    undoing edits, 143
    vegetables with eyeballs example, 396–399
8 Nero Web site, 638
8-bit color, 62, 64, 238, 466
Elated Web site, 640
Elliptical Marquee tool, 168, 408
Elliptical Shape tool, 395
E-mail. *See also* Sharing with friends and
  other users.
    image size considerations, 13, 290, 466
    linking Web site GIF to e-mail address,
      495
    PDF presentations, 546–548

Emboss effect, 75, 93
Emboss filter, 384
Émigré Web site, 644
Enable Airbrush button, 127
Enlarging images versus scaling down, 184
EPS file format, 27, 28, 459
Eraser tools, 142–143, 162–166
Error and warning messages, 631
Expert Support subscription service of
  Help Center, 610, 615
Exposure adjustments. *See also* Brightness
  adjustments; Color adjustments.
    adding light source, 359–362
    in Camera Raw, 273
    to isolated areas of photo, 250–252
    lightening dark photos, 249–250
Exposure dialog box, 249–250
Exposure setting of brush tool, 138
Extract tool, 168–171
Extrude filter, 384–385
Eye, color perception by humans, 57–58
Eye sparkles, 528–530
Eyeballs on vegetables, 396–399
Eyedropper tool, 65–68, 161, 524

F

Fade dialog box, with filters, 355–356
Fade value, 245
Feathering. *See also* Anti-aliasing.
    caution on setting value prior to
      selecting image, 156
    Brush tool, 125
    choosing thickness, 398, 404
    Lasso tool, 183
    Marquee tool, 152
Fibers filter, 381–383
55mm (Digital Film Tools) plug-in filter, 607
File (Adobe Bridge)⇨New Window, 262, 603
File (Adobe Bridge)⇨Save As Version, 579
File (Adobe Bridge)⇨Save Version As, 579
File extensions. *See* File formats
File formats
    ABR, 144
    ASL, 94
    ATN, 226
    BMP, 568
    caution on use of Rename feature, 28
    EPS, 27, 28, 459
    GIF. *See* GIF file format
    JPEG. *See* JPEG file format
    options for saving, 26–28
    PDF, 10, 28, 546–548, 566, 568
    PNG, 466, 475–476
    PSB, 22

PSD, 10, 27, 566, 568
saving for Web, 289, 486
SEA, 643
SIT, 643
SWF, 498
Targa, 568
TIFF, 27, 28, 459, 460, 566, 568
troubleshooting and tips, 631
ZIP, 145, 198, 460, 643
File (ImageReady)⇨Export⇨Macromedia
Flash SWF, 498, 499
File (ImageReady)⇨Output Settings⇨Saving
HTML, 484–485
File (ImageReady)⇨Preview In, 494, 497
File (ImageReady)⇨Preview In⇨Edit
Browser List, 494
File (ImageReady)⇨Save Optimized As,
467, 494, 501
File Menu, 15
File types. See File formats
File⇨Add to Favorites, 259
File⇨Automate⇨Batch, 551
File⇨Automate⇨Contact Sheet II, 540–542
File⇨Automate⇨Create Droplet,
225, 552–553
File⇨Automate⇨Crop and Straighten
Photos, 600–601
File⇨Automate⇨PDF Presentation, 546–548
File⇨Automate⇨Photomerge, 412–414
File⇨Automate⇨Picture Package, 420–421,
543–546
File⇨Automate⇨Web Photo Gallery,
536–538, 570
File⇨Browse, 28, 573
File⇨Import, 599–600
File⇨Install New Font, 198
File⇨New, 5–6, 470
File⇨Page Setup, 448
File⇨Print, 448
File⇨Print One Copy, 448
File⇨Print Online, 448, 460–462
File⇨Print⇨Print with Preview, 448, 449,
450–452
File⇨Revert, 296
File⇨Save, 298
File⇨Save As, 10, 453
File⇨Save for Web, 289, 486
File⇨Scripts⇨Layer Comps to PDF, 567
File⇨Scripts⇨Layer Comps To Files, 566–568
File⇨Scripts⇨Layer Comps to WPG, 569–570
Files. See Adobe Bridge; Documents and files
Fill control, 96
Fill effect, 117, 119
Fill Path button, 119

Fill Pixels Drawing Option, 102
Film or slide scanning, 595–596
Filter Gallery, 334, 345–346
Filter menu, 15
Filter⇨Artistic⇨Cutout, 336–337
Filter⇨Artistic⇨Watercolor, 334–336
Filter⇨Blur⇨Gaussian Blur, 211
Filter⇨Blur⇨Lens Blur, 366–368
Filter⇨Blur⇨Surface Blur, 364–366
Filter⇨Distort⇨Lens Correction, 368–371
Filter⇨Distort⇨Ocean Ripple, 344–345
Filter⇨Distort⇨Polar Coordinates, 374–377
Filter⇨Distort⇨Shear, 373–374
Filter⇨Distort⇨Spherize, 371–373, 409
Filter⇨Extract, 169–170
Filter⇨Liquify, 300–302
Filter⇨Noise⇨Dust & Scratches, 321–322
Filter⇨Noise⇨Reduce Noise, 319–321
Filter⇨Other⇨Offset, 350
Filter⇨Pattern Maker, 346–349
Filter⇨Render⇨Clouds, 379–381
Filter⇨Render⇨Fibers, 381–383
Filter⇨Render⇨Lens Flare, 358–359
Filter⇨Render⇨Lighting Effects, 360–361
Filter⇨Sharpen⇨Smart Sharpen, 223,
317–319
Filter⇨Sketch⇨Chalk and Charcoal, 339
Filter⇨Sketch⇨Charcoal, 339–340
Filter⇨Sketch⇨Halftone Pattern, 429
Filter⇨Sketch⇨Photocopy, 340–342, 423
Filter⇨Stylize⇨Solarize, 431
Filter⇨Stylize⇨Trace Contour, 385–386
Filter⇨Stylize⇨Wind, 334, 362–363, 383–386
Filter⇨Texture⇨Patchwork, 353–355
Filter⇨Texture⇨Stained Glass, 352
Filter⇨Vanishing Point, 326–327
Filters
advantages, 33
applying multiple, 345–346
Artistic category, 337
blending modes with, 355
Brush Strokes category, 334
Chalk & Charcoal filter, 339
Charcoal filter, 339–340
choosing from Photo Filter dialog
box, 99
Clouds, 379–381
comic book effect, 341
Conté Crayon, 337
copying and pasting in perspective,
326–327
Difference Clouds, 380
Diffuse, 383
Displace, 378

Filters *(cont.)*
  Distort category, 334, 344–345, 368–379
  Dust & Scratches, 321–322
  Emboss, 384
  Extract, 169–170
  Extrude, 384–385
  Fade effect, 355–356
  fading and blending, 355–356
  Fibers, 381–383
  folders for, 635
  Glass, 343
  Lens Blur, 366–368
  Lens Correction, 368–371
  Lens Flare, 358–359
  Lighting Effects filter, 359–362
  Liquify, 300–302
  Mosaic, 351
  Motion Blur, 362–363
  Ocean Ripple, 343–345
  Offset, 349–351
  Patchwork, 352–354
  Pattern Maker, 346–349
  photo filter adjustment layer, 245–246
  Photocopy, 340–342
  Pinch, 378
  Polar Coordinates, 374–377
  previews of effects, 335, 348
  Reduce Noise, 320–321
  reducing noise, 319–321
  removing dust and scratches, 321–322
  Render category, 358–362, 379–383
  screen print effects, 336–337
  Sepia, 431
  sharpening blurry images, 315–319
  Shear, 373–374
  Sketch category, 334, 339–343, 423
  Solarize, 431
  Spherize, 371–373
  Stained Glass, 351–352
  Stylize category, 334, 383–386
  Surface Blur, 364–366
  Texture category, 334, 351–355
  third-party software, 333, 635–637
  third-party software for digital cameras,
    604–607
  tips for choosing images, 344
  Trace Contour, 385–386
  Twirl, 378
  Water Paper, 342–343
  Watercolor filter, 334–336
  Wave, 378
  Web sources of plug-ins, 333
  Wind, 362–363
  ZigZag, 379
Find dialog box (Adobe Bridge), 268–269
Finding photos (Adobe Bridge), 268–269
500ml.org Web site, 638
Flaming Pear Web site, 637
Flaming Text effect, 555–556
Flash plug-in, 498
Flash SWF files, exporting GIF animations to,
  498
Flatbed scanners, 592
Flattening layers, 449
Floating palettes, 129
Flowers, 109
Fluid Color plug-in, 607
Fluid Mask plug-in, 607
Fluorescent Chalk action set, 231–232
Fly-out menus for tools, 28, 31–33
Focal point, emphasizing with Sharpen and
  Blur tools, 137–139
Folders
  for action sets, 226–227, 549
  adding to favorites list, 259
  for brush preset libraries, 144
  for brushes, 638
  for Camera Raw settings, 280
  for custom swatch sets, 73–74
  for filters, 635
  for "How To" files, 617
  for Install Profile file, 455
  "master" for unedited originals, 238
  for Photoshop plug-ins, 606
  renaming in Adobe Bridge, 264–265
  running actions in batches, 548–551
  for scanner plug-in software, 596
  for Web Photo Gallery, 536, 537, 570
Font Book font installation program
  (Mac users), 198–199
Fonts/typefaces
  categories and families, 195–196
  changing, 192, 193
  design considerations, 189–190, 642
  installing on Macs, 644
  installing on PCs, 643
  pointers for downloading, 642–643
  preview size adjustment, 198
  serif and sans serif, 196
  symbol fonts, 196
  third-party, 197–199, 642–646
  troubleshooting and tips, 629–630
  TrueType versus PostScript, 198–199
Foreground color
  with charcoal sketch filters, 339
  choosing, 9, 70–71
  filling layer, 50
  illustrated, 6

Foregrounds, distinguishing from background by channel masking method, 401–402
45-degree angles, constraining for, 102, 155
FotoSearch Web site, 642
Four-color offset printers, 457
Fragile Decay Web site, 639
Frames action set, 232–233
Frames, adding to multiple files, 551–553
Free Photoshop Web site, 636
Free Transform feature, 309–310
Freeform Pen tool, 108, 112–113
Freeze Mask tool in Liquify window, 302
Frozen Text effect, 555–556
Full Screen Mode, 46–47, 51
Funhouse mirror effect, with Shear filter, 373–374
Fuzzy effects, with Airbrush setting, 126–127

G

Gamma control panel for Windows-based machines, 514–515
Gamma option (Exposure dialog box), 250
Gamma settings on Macs, 511, 512, 513
Gaussian blur, 211
Genuine Fractals (OnOne Software) third-party plug-in, 607
Geometric shape selection, 148–155
Getty Images Web site, 642
Ghost text effect, 96
GIF animations
    caution on file size when tweening, 500
    adding link, 493–494
    adding links to image with image maps, 495–497
    Animation palette features, 490
    changing replay number, 495
    creating animated button, 502–504
    creating multi-framed animation, 490–493
    creating with transparent background, 504–506
    exporting to Flash SWF files, 498
    fading elements in and out with tweening, 498–501
    fading in reverse order, 501–502
    HTML for links to URLs, 493–495
    Image Map tools, 495–496
    tips for success, 489
GIF file format
    advantages, 469
    dithering, 472
    interlacing, 473
resizing and optimization, 469, 471–473
saving, 469–471
selecting, 483
Transparency and Matte options, 473–474
Girls Who Wear Glasses Web site, 645
Glass Buttons, 77
Glass filter, 343
Globe (spherical) effects, 371–373
Gradient Editor, 211–212
Gradient effect, 182, 211, 314–315, 409
Gradient Overlay effect, 75
Gradient tool, 181–183, 315
Graphic Authority Web site, 637
Graphics design
    book cover example, 427–432
    brochure example, 421–427
    business card example, 416–421
    rescalable vector art example, 432–438
    tips for professional look, 415–416
Graphics tablets
    adjusting settings, 586–587
    advantages, 583–584
    for Airbrush setting, 126
    controlling brush flow, 588–590
    downloadable brushes, 587
    with Lasso tool, 155
    size considerations, 586
    tracing from paper sources, 590–591
    varying brush pressure, 131
    Wacom Graphire tablet example, 584, 585
Gray point, 250
Grayscale color mode, 23, 64
Grayscale image, converting to, 254
Green glow, removing from pet's eyes, 304–305
Greeting card example, 407–411
Greeting cards, online printing services, 463–464
Grid texture, with Patchwork filter, 353, 354, 355
Grids, 45–46, 369
Group Properties window, 87
Groups of layers. See Layer groups
Guides, 43–45, 421

H

Halftone dot effect, 429
Halo color fixes with Camera Raw, 276–277
Hand tool
    in Liquify window, 302
    selecting or switching to, 52, 54

Handwriting-recognition for Wacom graphics tablet (Mac users), 586

Hardness of Brush tool, 125

Hardware accessories, 583. *See also* Graphics tablets; Scanners.

HDR (High Dynamic Range) color mode, bit depth and color channels, 63–64

Healing Brush tool, 298–299

Help and resources
Adobe-authorized training centers, 619–620
Adobe user forums, 622, 623
Adobe Web site, 618–619
classes at local colleges, 622
fly-out menus for tools, 28, 31–33
Help menu, 16
tips and tutorials on Adobe Studio Web site, 620–622
tool tips, 9, 34–35

Help and resources, troubleshooting and tips
Adobe Bridge and Camera Raw, 631–632
color modes, 630
digital video, 632–633
error and warning messages, 631
file format, 631
type, 629–630
workspaces, tools, and palettes, 625–629

Help Center
advantages, 32–33, 610
bookmarking favorite topics, 610–612
checking for software updates from Adobe, 617
Contents tab, 610
Expert Support subscription service, 610, 615
How To Tips of Contents Navigator, 617–618
Index tab, 610
More Resources button, 610, 616
printing topic content, 614–615
resizing panels, 610
searching for specific topics, 612–614
toggling between Full and Compact View, 612
tutorials, 16, 609, 617–618
welcome screen, 611

Help Menu, 16

Help⇨How to Create How Tos⇨Create your own How To Tip, 617

Help⇨Photoshop Help, 33

Hiding
guides, 45
layers, 95–96

Highlight brush, 169

Highlights
adding with Lens Flare filter, 358–359
adjusting with Auto Color Correction dialog box, 522
adjusting with Levels dialog box, 240, 241–242
adjusting wiht Exposure dialog box, 250
advanced adjustment options, 530–532
clipping warnings in Camera Raw, 271

Histogram palette, 239–240

Histograms, 239, 241

History Brush, 219–220

History Options dialog box, 216

History Palette
advantages, 214
caution on loss of history upon file closure, 214
caution on loss of Snapshots upon file closure, 214
caution on loss of states, 215
dragging and dropping history between files, 217
increasing number of states saved, 215
nonlinear undoing, 216
opening, 214
saving Snapshots, 217–218
undoing actions, 215
undoing actions of action sets, 228

Horizontal guides, 43–45

Horizontal Type Mask tool, 199, 200

Horizontal Type tool, 83, 190, 192, 203, 204

Horizontally Scale (option in Character palette), 194

How To Tips of Help Center, 617–618

HTML for Web pages, 476. *See also* ImageReady; ImageReady for animated GIFs.

Hue, 69, 252

Hue/Saturation controls
correcting out-of-gamut colors, 520–521
creating layer mask, 255
creating old sepia tone, 247–248
improving skin tones, 524–526
improving whiteness of teeth, 526–528
shifting color in color spectrum, 253–254

Human eye, color perception by, 57–58

I

Illustrations, 113
Image Effects action set, 231–232
Image Map palette (ImageReady), 497
Image Map Select tool (ImageReady), 496
Image size, considerations for e-mailing or posting to Web sites, 13, 290, 466
Image Size dialog box, 13, 290–291
Image Menu, 15
Image⇨Adjustments, 240
Image⇨Adjustments⇨Auto Levels, 223
Image⇨Adjustments⇨Brightness/Contrast, 61
Image⇨Adjustments⇨Desaturate, 256, 432
Image⇨Adjustments⇨Exposure, 249–250
Image⇨Adjustments⇨Hue/Saturation, 187
Image⇨Adjustments⇨Invert, 203, 403
Image⇨Adjustments⇨Levels, 521–522
Image⇨Adjustments⇨Match Color, 245
Image⇨Adjustments⇨Posterize, 434
Image⇨Adjustments⇨Replace Color, 161, 404–405
Image⇨Adjustments⇨Shadow/Highlight, 248, 531–532
Image⇨Adjustments⇨Threshold, 178, 179, 202–203, 401–402, 430
Image⇨Canvas Size, 286, 424
Image⇨Crop, 151, 154, 155
Image⇨Free Transform, 180
Image⇨Image Size, 13, 289, 295, 436, 466–467
Image⇨Indexed Color, 62–63
Image⇨Mode⇨CMYK, 453
Image⇨Mode⇨Grayscale, 254
Image⇨Mode⇨Lab Color, 61–62, 243
Image⇨Mode⇨RGB Color, 289
Image⇨Rotate Canvas⇨Arbitrary, 11
Image⇨Rotate Canvas⇨Rotate 90 degrees CW, 11
Image⇨Vector Mask⇨Current Path, 120
ImageReady
    adding flaming or frozen text, 555–556
    adding images and text, 479–481
    adding links to buttons, 482
    advantages, 31, 54, 465, 535
    advantages for size-limited sites, 475
    caution on inability to drag and drop images between programs, 491
    creating instant Web page templates, 554–555
    creating simple page, 47–48
    customizing Make Web page template, 478–479
    generating HTML and image slices, 484–485
    GIF file resizing and optimization, 469, 471–473
    illustration of palettes, 55
    JPEG file resizing and optimization, 466–468
    naming images, 480
    optimizing and file size considerations, 466, 474–475, 484
    page size considerations, 465
    resizing multiple slices, 479
    setting up image slices for optimization, 483–484
ImageReady for animated GIFs
    caution on file size when tweening, 500
    adding link, 493–494
    adding links to image with image maps, 495–497
    Animation palette features, 490
    changing replay number, 495
    creating animated button, 502–504
    creating multi-framed animation, 490–493
    creating with transparent background, 504–506
    exporting to Flash SWF files, 498
    fading elements in and out with tweening, 498–501
    fading in reverse order, 501–502
    HTML for links to URLs, 493–495
    Image Map tools, 495–496
    tips for success, 489
Images. See also Documents and files; Editing; ImageReady; Resizing.
    copyrights to, 11
    e-mail image size considerations, 13, 290, 466
    handling with Adobe Bridge, 18–20, 260
    renaming, 553
    saving for Web, 289, 486
    sharing with friends, 460, 462
    stock photos, 400, 575–578, 641–642, 646–647
Index of help topics, 610
Indexed Color dialog box, 62–63
Indexed Color mode
    caution on inoperability of filters, 370
    described, 62–63
Ink (handwriting-recognition software for Wacom graphics tablet) (Mac users), 586
Ink cartridges for printers, 444
Ink wash effects, with Wet Media brushes, 133

Inkjet printers, 58, 443–444, 445
Inner Bevel effect, 75
Inner Glow effect, 75, 185
Inner Shadow effect, 75, 115
Installing downloaded fonts, 198–199
Intellihance Pro (OnOne Software)
  third-party plug-in, 607
Interlacing of GIF files, 473
Interpolation, 292
IPhoto, 257
IStockPhoto Web site, 641
ITC (International Typeface Corporation)
  Web site, 644

J

Jitter adjustment setting for brushes tools,
  418
JPEG compression quality, 537
JPEG file format
  description, 27
  editing, 11–14, 269
  resizing and optimizing, 466–468
  saving layer comps as, 566–568
  saving for online printing, 460
  saving for Web, 289
  saving in PSD format first, 10
JPEG Options dialog box, 14
JPEG photos. See JPEG file format
Justifying text (option of Character palette),
  194

K

Kerning (option in Character palette), 194
Key commands associated with menu
  items, 15
Keywords
  for categorizing images (Adobe Bridge),
    267–268
  caution on manageable list size, 267
Kodak Easy Share system, 460
Konica Minolta DiMage slide/film scanners,
  596

L

Lab Channels, 61
Lab color mode, 23, 60–62, 238, 243
Laser printers, 444, 453–455
Lasso tools
  options, 155
  switching to, 160, 161

Layer Comp To Files dialog box, 567
Layer Comps
  caution on loss of color changes, 564
  advantages, 562
  creating instant Web Photo Gallery,
    568–570
  palette options, 565–566
  saving to, 563–564
  saving to separate files, 566–568
  switching between, 565
Layer Comps To WPG dialog box, 569, 570
Layer groups
  creating, 85–87
  duplicating, 87
  linking and aligning, 87–90
  renaming, hiding, and changing
    opacity, 87
Layer masks
  backing up as alpha channels, 174–177
  creating, 156
  creating circular, 168
  creating from channel, 401–404
  creating in Quick Mask Mode, 171–173
  creating with combination of skills,
    183–187
  creating with Create New Layer Mask,
    168
  creating with Extract tool, 169–171
  creating with Gradient tool, 181–183
  described, 167
  disabling or deleting, 168, 178, 410
  moving together or separately, 168
  with Threshold adjustment, 178–180
  for type, 199–203
  using custom shapes, 177–178
Layer Menu, 15
Layer Style dialog box, 74, 91, 92–93
Layer Style window, 92
Layer Styles
  appending, 104
  copying and pasting, 97, 115
  creating, 92–93
  dragging and dropping between files, 97
  loading saved, 94
  saving, 94
  temporarily disabling, 396
Layer Visibility icon, illustrated, 6
Layer⇨Create Clipping Mask, 201, 203
Layer⇨Duplicate Layer, 84
Layer⇨Flatten Image, 449
Layer⇨Layer Style⇨Color Overlay, 187
Layer⇨Layer Style⇨Gradient Overlay, 211

Layer⇨Layer Style⇨Stroke, 394
Layer⇨Merge Visible, 406
Layer⇨New Adjustment Layer⇨Photo Filter, 431
Layer⇨New Fill Layer⇨Solid Color, 158, 165
Layer⇨New⇨Background From Layer, 25
Layer⇨New⇨Layer, 50, 66
Layer⇨Rasterize⇨Shape, 350
Layer⇨Rasterize⇨Type, 207
Layer⇨Release Clipping Mask, 201
Layer⇨Smart Objects⇨Group Into New Smart Object, 296–297, 393, 436
Layers
    adding adjustment layers, 98–100
    adding bevels, overlays, and shadows, 90–92
    advantages, 81, 100
    caution on overlaying, 427
    creating custom styles, 92–94
    creating from photo, 83–84
    creating from Snapshots, 218
    dragging and dropping between files, 97
    duplicating, 84–85
    flattening, 449
    hiding or changing visibility, 95–96
    linking and aligning, 87–90
    making groups, 85–87
    merging visible, 406
    naming, 6, 392
    reusing in other files, 97, 406
    selecting from keyboard, 84
    thumbnail, 6
    working with multiple, 82–84
Layers palette, 6
Leading (option in Character palette), 194
Lens Blur filter, 366–368
Lens Correction filter, 368–371
Lens Flare filter, 358–359
Letter spacing for text (kerning and tracking options in Character palette), 194
Levels adjustment layers, 242
Levels dialog box, 240, 241–242
Libraries
    brush presets, 144–146
    shapes, 106–107
Light! (Digital Film Tools) plug-in filter, 607
Light as perceived by human eye, 57–58
Light source
    adding with Lighting Effects filter, 359–362
    considering when combining images, 184

Lighting Effects filter, 359–362
Lightness control (Hue/Saturation dialog box), 253, 255
Line spacing for text (leading option in Character palette), 194
Line tool, 102
Lines, 102–105
Link Layers button, 88
Linking layers, 87–100, 201
LinoType Web site, 644
Liquify tool, 300–302
Logo stamp as a custom brush preset, 141–142
Lossy process
    with Extract tool, 169
    for GIF files, 473
Luminance setting, 245
Luminance smoothing with Camera Raw, 276

M

Mac users
    Adobe user forums, 622
    calibrating monitors, 510–513
    caution on third-party fonts, 197
    Ink handwriting-recognition for Wacom graphics tablet, 586
    installing downloaded fonts, 198–199
    installing fonts, 644
    PhotoStamps, 463
    Text Smoothing Warning Message, 26
    Use Adobe Dialog button, 10
    use of fn key with function keys, 40
Magic Eraser tool, 143, 162, 164–165
Magic Wand tool
    examples of use, 134, 172
    selecting and changing areas of color, 159–162
Magnetic Lasso tool, 155, 156–159
Magnetic option of Freeform Pen tool, 112
Magnetic Select (Lasso) tool, 155, 156–159
Make Work Path from Selection button, 435
Marquee tools
    adding, subtracting, or dissecting selections, 148–150
    circular vignette around selection, 151–153
    close-up thumbnails, 154–155
    selecting and saving presets, 35–36
    selecting single row of pixels, 150–151
Mask Pro (OnOne Software) third-party plug-in, 607

Masking
  adding blending mode to masked layer, 159
  channel method for distinguishing background from foreground, 401–402
  circular, 168, 394
  in Quick Mask Mode, 47–51, 171–173
  third-party plug-in, 607
  type with photos, 199–204
  vector masks, 119–120
Masking with layer masks
  backing up as alpha channels, 174–177
  creating, 156
  creating from channel, 401–404
  creating circular, 168
  creating with combination of skills, 183–187
  creating with Create New Layer Mask, 168
  creating with Extract tool, 169–171
  creating with Gradient tool, 181–183
  creating in Quick Mask Mode, 171–173
  described, 167
  disabling or deleting, 168, 178, 410
  moving together or separately, 168
  with Threshold adjustment, 178–180
  for type, 199–203
  using custom shapes, 177–178
Master Diameter of Brush tool, 125
Match Color dialog box, 244–245
Matte option
  GIF file format, 473–474
  JPEG file format, 468
Measurement by rulers, 42–43
Measurement tools, 31
Measurement units, changing, 22, 36, 43, 44
Megapixels, 442
Menus. See also Menus by name.
  compared to palettes, 14
  hiding, 47
  key commands on, 15
  overview of organization, 14–17
Metadata in Adobe Bridge, 18, 257, 265–267
Metal Slide Gallery Button, 556, 557
Metal Slide Thumbnail, 556, 557
Midtones. See also Color adjustments; Exposure adjustments.
  adjusting from Exposure dialog box, 250
  adjusting with Auto Color Correction dialog box, 522, 523
Minolta DiMage slide/film scanners, 596
Mirror tool in Liquify window, 302

Miss M Web site, 638
Mister Retro Web site, 636
Monaco Optix XR Pro monitor calibrator, 517
Monitors
  calibrating for Macs, 510–513
  calibrating for Windows machines, 514–516
  caution on CRT warmup prior to calibration, 510
  caution on expectations for color Web graphics, 516
  caution on inadequacies of calibration, 510
  hardware monitor calibrators, 516–518
Monotype Imaging, Inc. Web site, 645
More Resources button of Help Center, 610, 616
Mosaic filter, 351
Motion Blur filter, 362–363
Move Grid tool (Lens Correction filter), 369
Move tool
  alignment options, 89–90
  illustrated, 6
  switching to, 52, 89
Movie Prime Lens Type filter, 359
MyFonts.com Web site, 645–646

N

Nagel brushes, 133
National Association of Photoshop Users (NAPP) Web site, 633
Navigator palette, 53–54
Nearest Neighbor interpolation method, 292
Neutralize check box, 245
New Document Preset dialog box, 22
New Layer button, 6
New Layer Comp dialog box, 563
New Layer dialog box, opening, 25
New Layer Group button, 86
New Layer icon, 84
New Set dialog box, 222–223
New Snapshot dialog box, 217–218
New window, 5–6, 21, 22
Nikon Coolscan slide/film scanners, 595
Noise adjustment
  with Camera Raw, 276
  reducing, 319–321
  setting for brushes tools, 130
Note tools, 31

O

Ocean Ripple filter, 343–345
OCR (optical character recognition), 598
Offset filter, 349–351
Offset option (Exposure dialog box), 250
Offset option (Pattern filter), 347
Offset printers, 444, 452, 457
1001 Fonts Web site, 646
Online printing services for digital photos, 283, 448, 460–462
OnOne Software (third-party plug-ins), 607
Opacity adjustments
    in Gradient Editor, 211
    for Gradient tool, 183–184
    from keyboard, 405
    for layer groups, 87
    for previewing cropped area, 285
    in Quick Mask Mode, 51
    for shadow creation, 187
    transparent parts to matte as optimization option, 468, 473
Opacity slider, 84, 95
Optical character recognition (OCR), 598
Optimization options (ImageReady)
    caution on loss of layer data, 493
    GIF file format, 469–473
    JPEG file format, 466–468
Optimization options (Photoshop), 486
Optimize palette (ImageReady), 467, 474–475
Options bar
    illustrated, 6
    saving presets, 35–36
    variable options, 7
    Zoom tool options, 51
Other Dynamics adjustment setting for brushes tools, 130
Out-of-gamut colors, removing, 518–521
Outer Bevel effect, 75
Outer Glow effect, 75, 398
Outlines, adding with Blending Options, 395–396
Ozone (Digital Film Tools) plug-in filter, 607

P

Paint Bucket tool, 170, 171
Paint tools, 6, 31, 133. *See also* Brush tool.
Paintbrush. *See* Brush tool
Palette well, 38–39
Palettes
    advantages, 36
    Brushes palette, 128–130
    collapsing display, 38
    compared to menus, 14
    customizing arrangement, 37–38
    floating, 129
    hiding, 47
    sets, 38
    viewing with function keys, 39–40
Panorama example, 411–414
Paper quality/size considerations for printing, 445–446, 458
Paragraph palette, 190–192
Paragraph type, 190, 192–194
Passwords, on PDF presentations, 547
Patch tool, 299–300
Patchwork filter, 352–354
Path Selection tool, 108
Path tools, 31, 108
Paths button, 120
Paths Drawing Option, 102, 177
Paths palette, 117–120, 177
Paths, modifying with Direct Selection tool, 117–119
Pattern Maker filter, 346–349
Pattern Overlay effect on text, 74–76
Pattern Stamp tool, 133, 134–137
Patterns
    downloading from Web sites, 76, 135
    loading, 137
PCs (Windows-based systems)
    Adobe user forums, 622, 623
    calibrating monitors, 514–516
    installing downloaded fonts, 198, 643
PDF file format, 10, 28, 546–548, 566, 568
PDF presentations of photos, 546–548
Pegasus example of photomontage
    blending images together using Clone Stamp tool, 405–406
    creating consistent colors across multiple layers, 404–406
    creating mask from modified channel, 401–404
    process overview, 399–400
Pen tool, 107–108, 109, 110–111
Pencil tool, hardness setting, 125
Performance considerations
    action sets, 227
    Adobe Bridge launching time, 20
    file size, RAM, and virtual memory, 22
    History Palette, 215
    loading of patterns, 137
    loss of color quality with Indexed color mode, 62
    previews of filters' effects, 335

Performance considerations *(cont.)*
   printing speed for flattened layers, 449
   quality loss with color conversion, 452
   16-bit color mode, 238
   thumbnail size, 259
Perspective adjustments, 323–330
Photo filter adjustment layers, 245–246
Photo Filter dialog box, 99, 246
Photoblog Web sites, 467
Photocopy filter, 340–342
PhotoFrame (OnOne Software) third-party
   plug-in, 607
Photo/Graphics Edges (Auto FX) plug-ins,
   607
Photomerge window, 410–414
Photomontages
   with Clone Stamp tool, 133–134, 399,
     400, 405–406
   panorama example, 411–414
Photos. *See* Documents and files; Images
Photoshop Action! Web site, 639
Photoshop Brushes Web site, 638
Photoshop Café Web site, 640
Photoshop Filters Web site, 636
Photoshop format, importance of saving
   in, 10
Photoshop 911 Web site, 634
Photoshop Support Web site, 634
Photoshop⇨Preferences⇨General, 215
Photoshop⇨Preferences⇨Guides, Grid &
   Slices, 45–46
Photoshop⇨Preferences⇨Plug-ins & Scratch
   Disks, 23
Photoshop⇨Preferences⇨Transparency &
   Gamut, 519, 521
Photoshop⇨Preferences⇨Type, 198
PhotoStamps.com, 462–463
Picasa, 257
Picture Package, 420–421, 542–546
Pinch filter, 378
Pincushion distortion, 310–312, 368
Pixel ratings of digital cameras, 442–443
Pixels
   described, 24
   idiosyncrasies of image selection, 147
   selecting single row, 150
Planet Photoshop Web site, 633
Plug-ins
   digital camera filters, 604–607
   Flash, 498
   Web sources, 333
PNG file format, 466, 475–476
Point type, 190, 204
Polar Coordinates filter, 374–377

Polygon Image Map tool (ImageReady), 496
Polygon Lasso tool, 155, 158, 161, 165
Postage stamps, personalized, 462–463
Postcards
   mailing costs, 458
   online printing services, 463–464
Posterize effect, 337, 434–438
PostScript versus TrueType fonts, 198–199
Preserve Luminosity setting, 99, 246
Presets
   Brush tool, 130–133
   Brushes palette, 130–132
   file size options, 21
   libraries of, 144–146
   Marquee tools, 35–36
   Rectangular Marquee tool, 35–36, 142
   saving, 35–36
Preview button, 170
Previews
   of filters' effects, 335, 348
   increasing area of, 352
Printer drivers, 446–447
Printers
   color laser, 444
   color management options, 450–452
   color modes, 58, 78
   CPP (cost per page), 445
   inkjet, 443–444, 445
   laser, 453–455
   purchasing for home use, 443–447
   SWOP (Specifications for Web Offset
     Publications), 452
Printing
   Help Center topic content, 614–615
   menu options, 447–448
   by online services, 283, 448, 460–462
   paper quality/size considerations,
     445–446, 458
   picture package, 542–546
   previewing for scaling to fit printable
     area, 448–449
   by professional service, 24–25
   by professional services, 456–460
   recommended resolution, 25
   resolution for, 442
   speed considerations for flattened layers,
     449
   spot-proofing colors, 455–456
Printing services for digital photos, 283
Professional printing services, 456–460
Proportions, retaining when resizing images,
   291
PSB file format, 22
PSD file format, 10, 27, 566, 568

Pucker tool in Liquify window, 301
Push Left tool in Liquify window, 302

Q

Quality (image options drop-down list), 14
Quick Mask Mode
    change color and opacity settings, 51
    creating mask, 47–51, 171–173
QuickTime movies, SWF files, 498

R

Radial Gradient tool, 182, 409–410
Radius of rounded rectangles, 103
Rasterizing
    text, 207
    vector objects/shapes/images, 297, 350
Reconstruct tool, 300, 301
Rectangle tool, 92, 93, 424–425
Rectangular Image Map tool (ImageReady),
    496
Rectangular Marquee tool
    options, 144
    selecting, 149
    selecting and saving presets, 35–36, 142
Red eye, removing, 302–303
Redfield Plug-ins Web site, 636
Redoing actions, commands for, 214
Reduce Noise filter, 320–321
Reflections
    of text on shiny surface, 210–212
    in water, 313–315
Remove Distortion tool (Lens Correction
    filter), 369
Renaming files in Adobe Bridge, 264–265
Render filters, 358–362, 379–383
Rentals of slide/film scanners, 596
Replace Color tool, 404–405
Replace Color window, 160, 161, 162
Resample Image option, 291
Rescalable photos as Smart Objects, 295–298
Rescalable vector art example of graphics
    design, 432–438
Resizing
    avoiding stretching, 391, 442–443
    bandwidth considerations of image size,
        290
    canvas size, 292–295
    changing resolution first, 28
    compared to cropping, 14
    with conditional actions in ImageReady,
        556–558
    cropping to specific width and height,
        285, 286–290

GIF files, 469, 471–473
image and canvas size, 290–293
in indexed color mode, 62
JPEG files, 466–468
limitless, with Smart Objects, 393
scaling down versus enlarging, 184
scaling to fit printable area, 448–449
scanned images, 596–597
Resolution
    caution on increasing, 288
    caution when dragging and dropping
        layers, 97
    changing, 13
    choosing from New window, 6
    considerations for choosing, 24–25
    cropping to rescaled, 285, 287
    JPEG images options, 468
    for printing, 442
    rescalable photos as Smart Objects,
        295–298
    on scanners, 592
Retro '50s sign design, 114–116
Returns, for new line of text, 192
RGB color mode
    avoiding artifacts, 243
    bit depth and color channels, 63–64
    converting to Indexed color mode,
        62–63
    described, 23
    out-of-gamut colors, 518
    for Web pages, 289
    when to use, 58–59, 452
Ring-Double Inner Shadow effect, 115–116
Rods of human eye, 57–58
Rotate tools of Camera Raw, 271
Rotating
    by degrees, 312–313
    paragraph text, 193
Rounded Rectangle tool, 102–104
RSS feeds, 574–575
Rubber Band check box, 111
Rulers, 42–43, 421

S

Sans serif and serif typefaces, 196
Saturation
    adjustment in Camera Raw, 273
    controls, 247–248, 253–254, 255
    defined, 252–253
Save As dialog box, 10, 26–28
Save For Web window, 289, 290
Save Styles dialog box, 94
Save Swatches dialog box, 73
Save Workspace dialog box, 41

Saving
    Action sets, 218, 226, 548
    Camera Raw settings, 279–280
    curves on adjustment layers, 243–244, 251–252
    custom swatches and styles, 72–74
    custom workspace settings, 40–41
    file groups, 572–573
    files, 10, 28, 215, 289
    GIF file format, 469–471
    images from Web sites, 11
    JPEG files, 10, 289, 460, 566–568
    layer comps, 562–568
    Layer Styles, 94
    presets, 35–36
    prior to optimization, 493
    Snapshots, 217–218
    for Web, 289, 486
Scanners
    changing scale and resize settings, 596–597
    flatbed, 592
    resolution considerations, 592
    scanning directly into Photoshop, 596
    scanning text into Photoshop, 598
    for slide or film scanning, 595–596
    straightening and cropping crooked scans, 598–601
    tips for choosing, 591–593
Scattering adjustment setting for brushes tools, 130, 418
Scratch disk, 22, 23
Scratches
    adding effect of, 248
    removing, 321–322
Scream Design Web site, 640
Screen print effects with Cutout filter, 336–337
SEA file format, 643
Select Menu, 15
Select⇨All, 392
Select⇨Color Range, 174
Select⇨Feather, 398, 526, 529
Select⇨Inverse, 134, 151
Select⇨Modify, 174
Select⇨Save Selection, 177
Select⇨Similar, 203, 433
Selecting
    all areas of same color, 203
    all text in layer, 191
    closing selection automatically, 158
    from copied layer, 156
    in Full Screen mode, 250
    geometric shapes, 148–155
    with Lasso tools, 155–156
    with Magic Wand, 159–162
    with mouse click and dragging, 52
    previewing selection, 156
Selection tools, 31
Selective Color feature, 174
Sepia tone look, 247–248, 431
Serif and sans serif typefaces, 196
Set Black Point option (Exposure dialog box), 250
Set Gray Point option (Exposure dialog box), 250
Set White Point option (Exposure dialog box), 250
Shadow clipping warnings in Camera Raw, 271
Shadows
    adjusting with Auto Color Correction dialog box, 522
    adjusting from Exposure dialog box, 250
    adjusting with Levels dialog box, 240, 241–242
    advanced adjustment options, 530–532
    creating, 185–186
    intensifying, 246
    washing out for sepia-aged look, 248
Shape Dynamics adjustment setting for brushes tools, 130, 418, 589–590
Shape Layers Drawing Option, 102
Shape libraries, 106–107
Shape tools, 31, 102–103
Shapes drop-down list, 106
Shapes, rasterizing, 297, 350
Sharing with friends and other users
    Camera Raw settings, 280
    colors, 68
    images, 460, 462
    on photoblog Web sites, 467
Sharing, e-mail image size considerations, 13, 290, 466
Sharpen tool, 139, 529
Sharpening blurry images, 315–319
Shear filter, 373–374
Shutter Freaks Web site, 640
SIT file format, 643
16-bit color, 238
Sketch filters, 334, 339–343, 423
Skew feature, 185, 186, 211
Skin tones, color adjustments, 523–525
Slice palette (ImageReady), 480–481, 482, 493–494
Slice Select tool (ImageReady), 482, 483
Slide or film scanning, 595–596
Slideshow window, Adobe Bridge, 20

Smart Highlight options of Extract tool, 169
Smart Objects, 295–298, 393
Smart Sharpen
    creating droplet for, 224–226
    improving blurriness, 315–319
    recording action set for, 223–224
    saving settings for future use, 319
Snapfish.com, 461–462
Snapshots
    advantages for editing, 214
    caution on loss upon file closure, 214
    saving, 217–218
    as source for History Brush edits,
        219–222
Snowflake Custom Shape tool, 119–120
Soft Posterize action set, 231–232
Software Cinema Web site, 633
Sony Artisan Monitor calibrator, 517
Speed. See Performance considerations
Spherical distortion, 409
Spherize filter, 371–373
Sponge tool, 518–519
Spoono Web site, 633
Spot Healing Brush tool, 298
Spotlight effects, with Lighting Effects filter,
    359–362
Spot-proofing colors before printing,
    455–456
Spyder2 USB monitor calibrator
    (ColorVision), 517
Squares, 102–105
SRGB working color space setting, 64
Stained Glass filter, 351–352
Stamp of logo as a custom brush preset,
    141–142
Stamps (personalized postage stamps),
    462–463
Standard Mode, 50
Standard Screen button, 46
Stars
    airbrushing, 127–128
    drawing, 109–110
Status bar, 6
Stock photos, 400, 575–578, 641–642,
    646–647
Straighten tool of Camera Raw, 271
Straighten tool (Lens Correction filter), 369
Straightening
    and cropping crooked scans, 598–601
    tilted images, 309–310
Stretching of images. See Resizing
Stroke effect, 75, 115, 116, 117, 119, 394–396
Stroke Path button, 119
Stroke width, 154–155

Styles, 76
Styles palette, 76–78
Subtractive color, 59
Surface Blur filter, 364–366
Swatches palette, 72–73
SWF files, exporting GIF animations to, 498
SWOP (Specifications for Web Offset
    Publications), 452
Symbol fonts, 196

T

Targa file format, 568
Team Photoshop Web site, 634
Teeth whitening and brightening, 525–528
Text
    adding flaming or freezing effects,
        555–556
    adding to images in batches, 548–550
    aliased and anti-aliased, 195
    appending layer styles, 209
    applying effects using action sets,
        227–228
    black, rich versus regular, 459
    caution on adding to button layer, 104
    caution on colored, 459
    changing attributes, 192
    choosing typeface font families, 195–196
    coloring with Eyedropper tool, 66–68
    curving, 204–205, 394–395
    faux bold, 195–196
    italics for emphasis, 195
    masking with photos, 199–204
    overflow indicator, 192–193
    with paragraph-box type, 190, 192–194
    Pattern Overlay effect, 74–76
    with point type, 190, 192
    rasterizing, 207
    rotating, 193
    scanning with optical character
        recognition, 598
    selecting all in layer, 191
    serif and sans serif typefaces, 196
    special effects with layer styles, 208–212
    symbol fonts, 196
    3-D reflection on shiny surface, 210–212
    typeface design, 189–190
    warping around objects, 205–208
Text anchor, finding under text, 204
Text Effects action set, 229–231
Text Smoothing Warning Message
    (Mac users), 26

Text or type tools
  Character and Paragraph palettes, 191–192
  Horizontal Type tool, 83, 190, 192, 203, 204
  list of, 31
  Options bar, 191
  Vertical Type tool, 190
Texture
  adding with brush presets, 220–221
  adding with filters, 334, 351–355
  adjustment setting for brushes tools, 130
  creating with Background Eraser tool, 165–166
Texture filters, 334, 351–355
Thaw Mask tool in Liquify window, 302
Third-party software
  actions, 639–640
  brushes, 637–639
  custom brush sets, 144–145
  digital camera plug-in filters, 604–607
  filters, 333, 635–637
  fonts, 197–199, 642–646
3-D reflection of text on shiny surface, 210–212
Threshold adjustment, 140, 178–179, 202–203, 401–402
Thumbnails
  advantages, 258
  enlarging, 107, 392
  Marquee tools, 154–155
  performance considerations with bigger size, 259
TIFF file format, 27, 28, 459, 460, 566, 568
Title bar, 6
Tool tips, 9, 34–35
Toolbox, 6–7, 29–31
Tools. *See also* Automating tools; *tools by name.*
  categories, 31
  fly-out menus for, 28, 31–33
  mouseless switching between, 34–35
  saving presets, 35–36
Tools (Adobe Bridge)⇨Batch Rename, 264
Tools (Adobe Bridge)⇨Version Cue⇨New Project⇨, 578
Trace Contour filter, 385–386
Tracing
  images, 112–113
  from paper sources using graphics tablet, 590–591
Tracking (option in Character palette), 194

Training centers, Adobe-authorized, 619–620
Transparency options, 468, 473–474
Trimming printed images, 459
TrueType versus PostScript fonts, 198–199
Turbulence tool in Liquify window, 302
Tutorials
  on Adobe Studio Web site, 620–622
  in Help Center, 16, 609, 617–618
Twirl filter, 378
Twirl tool in Liquify window, 301
Type tools
  Character and Paragraph palettes, 191–192
  Horizontal Type tool, 83, 190, 192, 203, 204
  list of, 31
  Options bar, 191
  Vertical Type tool, 190
Typefaces/fonts
  categories and families, 195–196
  changing, 192, 193
  design, 189–190
  installing on Macs, 644
  installing on PCs, 643
  pointers for downloading, 642–643
  preview size adjustment, 198
  serif and sans serif, 196
  symbol fonts, 196
  third-party, 197–199, 642–646
  troubleshooting and tips, 629–630
  TrueType versus PostScript, 198–199

U

Undoing actions, commands for, 143, 214
Units of measure, changing, 22, 36, 43, 44
Unzipping downloaded files, 145, 198, 460, 643
User forums, 622, 623

V

Vanishing Point Marquee tool, 326–327
Vanishing point, selecting for Photomerge feature, 412
VBrush Web site, 638
Vector art example of graphics design, 432–438
Vector masks, 119–120
Vector objects, rasterizing, 297, 350
Vector tools, 101

Vectors
    curving text onto, 204–205
    drawing modified designs, 114–116
    drawing shapes and curves, 107–113
Veer Web site, 642
Vegetables with eyeballs, 396–399
Version Cue (Adobe Bridge)
    adding files to project, 579
    adding new project, 578
    administering projects, 580–582
    advantages, 578
Vertical guides, 43–45
Vertical Type Mask tool, 199
Vertical Type tool, 190
Vertically Scale (option in Character
    palette), 194
Vertus Fluid Color plug-in, 607
Vertus Fluid Mask plug-in, 607
View (Adobe Bridge)⇨Compact Mode, 603
View (Adobe Bridge)⇨Slideshow, 262–263
View (ImageReady)⇨Show⇨Text Selection,
    491
View (ImageReady)⇨Snap, 491
View Menu, 15
View⇨Clear Guides, 45
View⇨Gamut Warning, 518–519, 520
View⇨New Guide, 44–45
View⇨Proof Colors, 456
View⇨Proof Setup, 456
View⇨Proof Setup⇨Custom, 455
View⇨Rulers, 43, 44, 311, 421
View⇨Show⇨Grid, 45
View⇨Slide Show, 20
View⇨Snap to⇨Grid, 46
View⇨Snap to⇨Guides, 45
View⇨Snap to⇨Image, 414
Virus checking of downloaded files, 146, 198
Visibility icon, 87, 95, 113

W

Wacom Graphire tablet, 584
Wacom Web site, 634
Warning messages, 631
Warp tool in Liquify window, 301
Warping text around objects, 205–208
Water, creating reflections in, 210–212,
    313–315
Water Paper filter, 342–343
Watercolor effects
    with Watercolor filter, 334–336
    with Wet Media brushes, 133

Wave filter, 378
Web Photo Gallery creator
    advantages, 535, 536
    creating, 536–538
    creating grid design using contact
        sheets, 542
    creating from Layer Comps, 568–570
    generating contact sheets of images,
        539–542
    Security panel, 538, 539
Web site design. See also ImageReady;
    ImageReady for animated GIFs; Web Photo
    Gallery creator.
    background patterns for, 349–351
    creating animated buttons, 502–504
    creating instant Web page templates,
        554–555
    caution on use of PNG-24 file format,
        475
    HTML used for, 476
    recommended resolution, 25
    saving files for, 289
Web sites
    caution on viruses in downloaded files,
        146, 198
    copying images from, 11
    online printing services for digital
        photos, 283, 448, 460–462
    photoblogs, 467
    of Photoshop superusers, 633–634
    professional printing services, 456
    third-party filters, 333
    third-party fonts, 197–199
Webmonkey Web site, 634
Web-safe color, 69, 70, 472
Welcome Screen, 4, 16
Wet Media brushes, 133
Wey Edges option, 418
White Balance adjustment tool of Camera
    Raw, 271, 273
White point, 250
Whites, brightness. See Brightness
    adjustments
Width/height units of measurement, 22, 36,
    43, 44
Wind filter, 362–363
Window (Adobe Bridge)⇨Workspace⇨File
    Navigation, 263
Window (ImageReady)⇨Actions, 477–478
Window (ImageReady)⇨Image Map, 497
Window (ImageReady)⇨Slices, 480–481,
    482, 493

Window Menu, 16
Window⇨Brushes, 588
Window⇨Channels, 175, 401
Window⇨Character, 191
Window⇨History, 214, 220
Window⇨Layer Comps, 563
Window⇨Optimize, 467, 471
Window⇨Paths, 111, 177
Window⇨Workspace⇨Default Workspace,
    16, 41
Window⇨Workspace⇨Save Workspace,
    40–41
Windows-based systems
    Adobe user forums, 622, 623
    calibrating monitors, 514–516
    installing downloaded fonts, 198, 643
Wood texture effects, with Fibers filter,
    381–383
Workspace
    choosing color setting, 64–65
    described, 5–12
    preinstalled, 41
    reverting to default settings, 16, 41
    saving custom settings, 40–41

X

Xaos Tools Web site, 636

Z

ZigZag filter, 379
ZIP file format, 145, 198, 460, 643
Zoom ratio, 6
Zoom tool
    Fill Screen button, 51
    illustrated, 6
    percentage increments, 17
    Resize Window to Fit, 51
Zooming
    in Camera Raw, 276
    from Document window, 17
    from keyboard, 52
    in Liquify window, 302
    with mouse scroll wheel, 17
    when highlighting or extracting images,
        169, 170
    when sharpening and blurring, 139

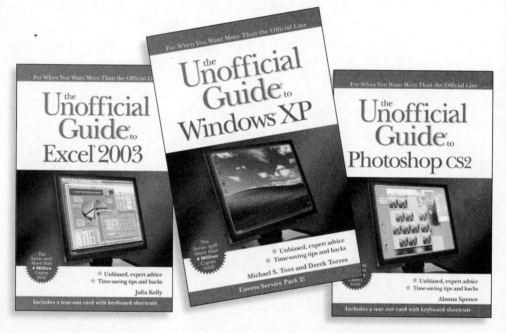
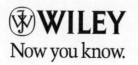